MIND—SOCIETY

OXFORD SERIES ON
COGNITIVE MODELS AND ARCHITECTURES

Mind–Society

FROM BRAINS TO SOCIAL SCIENCES AND PROFESSIONS

Paul Thagard

OXFORD
UNIVERSITY PRESS

OXFORD
UNIVERSITY PRESS

Oxford University Press is a department of the University of Oxford. It furthers
the University's objective of excellence in research, scholarship, and education
by publishing worldwide. Oxford is a registered trade mark of Oxford University
Press in the UK and certain other countries.

Published in the United States of America by Oxford University Press
198 Madison Avenue, New York, NY 10016, United States of America.

Library of Congress Cataloging-in-Publication Data
Names: Thagard, Paul, author.
Title: Mind-society : from brains to social sciences
and professions / Paul Thagard.
Description: New York, NY : Oxford University Press, [2019] |
Includes bibliographical references and index.
Identifiers: LCCN 2018033235 | ISBN 9780190678722
Subjects: LCSH: Social sciences and psychology. | Cognitive neuroscience.
Classification: LCC BF57.T534 2019 | DDC 150—dc23
LC record available at https://lccn.loc.gov/2018033235

9 8 7 6 5 4 3 2 1

Printed by Sheridan Books, Inc., United States of America

To John Holmes and Bob McCauley, good friends and social minds.

Contents

List of Illustrations

Foreword

Frank E. Ritter

THREE DECADES AGO, Newell, Anderson, and Simon shared a desire for a unified theory of psychology, that is, how cognition arises, and what a mechanistic explanation would look like. Today, much still remains to be done to pursue that desire, but much has been accomplished.

Allen Newell talked about narrow and deep theories, and broad and shallow theories, and that theories could differ in these ways. Many psychology theories are deep, explaining a few phenomena in great detail but not explaining many phenomena nor how they interact and mutually constrain each other.

In the trio of books making up his treatise, Paul Thagard creates a much broader and accessible explanation than we have seen before of what a mechanistic explanation of mind and human behavior would look like for psychology and also areas related to psychology. These books explain the cognitive science approach to cognition, learning, thinking, emotion, and social interaction—nearly all of what it means to be human—and what this means for a wide variety of sciences and philosophy. These books provide a good overview of cognitive science and its implications. Different readers will be drawn to the treatise in different ways. It does not matter where they start.

The lessons in these books are based on the semantic pointer architecture (SPA) by Chris Eliasmith, Thagard's colleague at the University of Waterloo. SPA is a very useful dynamic theory that can do multiple tasks in the same model, and it is explained in journal articles and by Eliasmith's (2013) book in the Oxford Series on Cognitive Models and Architectures. Most of the implications based on SPA are also supported by and have lessons for other computational models of cognition, so these books can be useful to users of other cognitive architectures, particularly related architectures. *Mind–Brain,* another book in Thagard's treatise, focuses on what SPA means for brain and mind.

In this book, *Mind–Society,* after explaining the use of SPA, Thagard examines what this approach means for social science and related professional fields. This book provides a very broad, singular framework for explaining the breadth of human behavior.

Is this framework useful? Very much so. This three-book treatise starts to address some problems that I have seen in various fields by using multilevel analyses, with a cognitive architecture at its middle level. These topics include how cognitive limitations can be addressed by legislation and professional practice. This treatise also notes how the SPA provides explanations naturally for many phenomena directly and that many similar cognitive architectures also provide. While this treatise does not note the linkages for other cognitive architectures, many architectures can be seen to provide most (but not all) of the support for this framework to explain how minds work in society.

In his book, *Natural Philosophy,* Thagard examines what this approach means for philosophy, including important topics of philosophy of mind and of beauty. It provides a useful and engaging overview of philosophy, particularly for those interested in cognitive science or working in cognitive science.

These books introduce several useful theories and methods about how to do science as well. Beyond allowing and using explanations via multilevel mechanisms, particularly valuable are Thagard's introduction and use of three-analysis for definitions and coherence. The three-analysis definitions are a way to explain concepts without using simple definitions. They define a concept using *exemplars,* *typical features,* and *explanations.* This approach resolves several problems with simple dictionary definitions.

Coherence is a valuable concept for reasoning and is used in this book as a way to describe the quality of theories. Theories are not just good when they predict a single result but also how they cohere with multiple sources of data and with other theories. Coherence is hard to quantify itself, in some ways, but it is clearly useful. But the use of coherence is not just normative—we should use it—it is also descriptive in that scientists and laypersons appear use it in everyday life and that even scientists use it in their work. Making this often implicit reasoning process explicit will help us to apply, teach, and improve the process.

These books will be useful to cognitive scientists and those interested in cognitive science. They will also be useful to those who simply want to learn more about the world and cognition. They offer one of the best and clearest explanations we have for cognition and how it would apply to the humanities and to the social sciences. Pieces of liberal education are sprinkled throughout because this book draws examples and support from a wide range of material. Thus, humanists and social scientists interested in knowing how cognitive science works will find some answers here.

These books contain powerful ideas by one of the most highly cited living philosophers. They can change the way you think about the world, including brains and mind, and how you might think that the mind works and interacts with the world. Thagard calls these trio of books a treatise, and I found them so compelling that I've decided to use them in a course this next semester.

REFERENCE

Eliasmith, C. (2013). *How to build a brain: A neural architecture for biological cognition*. New York, NY: Oxford University Press.

Preface

THIS BOOK IS part of a trio (Treatise on Mind and Society) that can be read independently:

Brain–Mind: From Neurons to Consciousness and Creativity
Mind–Society: From Brains to Social Sciences and Professions
Natural Philosophy: From Social Brains to Knowledge, Reality, Morality, and
    Beauty.

Brain–Mind shows the relevance of Chris Eliasmith's Semantic Pointer Architecture to explaining a wide range of mental phenomena concerning perception, imagery, concepts, rules, analogies, emotions, consciousness, intention, action, language, creativity, and the self. This book, *Mind–Society*, systematically connects neural and psychological explanations of mind with social phenomena, covering major social sciences (social psychology, sociology, politics, economics, anthropology, and history) and professions (medicine, law, education, engineering, and business). After the chapters 1 to 3, the remaining chapters can be read in any order. Chapters 4 to 9 concern social sciences, and chapters 10 to 14 discuss professions.

My aim is not to reduce the social to the psychological but rather to display their harmony and interdependence. This display is accomplished by describing the interconnections among mental and social mechanisms, which interact to generate social changes ranging from marriage patterns to wars. The major tool for this description is a method I call the *social cognitive-emotional workup*, which connects the mental mechanisms operating in individuals with social mechanisms operating in groups. I call this general approach *social cognitivism*.

Because this book includes in chapter 2 a succinct summary of the relevant ideas about mind and brain, it can be read on its own. But readers who want a deeper discussion of mental mechanisms can read *Brain–Mind* and the more technical journal articles it cites. *Natural Philosophy* extends the integrated mental–social approach to apply to the humanities, primarily philosophy but also the arts, especially painting and music. An integrated account can be given of all branches of philosophy—epistemology, metaphysics, ethics, and aesthetics—by applying the intellectual tools developed in *Brain–Mind* and *Mind–Society*.

The integration of cognitive sciences, social sciences, and professions in this volume requires new methods that have broader application. The method of three-analysis characterizes concepts by identifying examples, features, and explanations rather than definitions. Value maps (cognitive-affective maps) provide a concise depiction of the emotional coherence of concepts. The general method of social cognitive-emotional workups guides the investigation of societies as groups of interacting individuals with complex minds.

These methods can also be applied to understanding the development of the natural sciences, whose cognitive and social processes I have discussed in previous books: Thagard 1992b, 1999, 2012b. Most of my papers can be found via paulthagard.com, which also contains live links for the URLs in this book.

Acknowledgments

MOST OF THIS book was newly written in 2015–2018, but I have incorporated some extracts from other works, as indicated in the notes and in the figure and table captions. I have also used excerpts from my *Psychology Today* blog, *Hot Thought*, for which I hold the copyright.

I am grateful to University of Waterloo students, especially Peter Duggins and Louise Upton, for corrections to earlier versions. I have benefitted greatly from discussions with Tobias Schröder, Thomas Homer-Dixon, John Holmes (comments on chapter 4), and Robert McCauley (comments on chapter 8). For helpful suggestions, I am grateful to Richard Carlson, Shawn Clark, Christopher Dancy, William Kennedy, Laurette Larocque, Jonathan Morgan, Frank Ritter, Jose Soto, and anonymous reviewers. I thank Joan Bossert for editorial advice, Phil Velinov and Shanmuga Priya for organizing production, Alisa Larson for skilled copyediting, and Kevin Broccoli for professional indexing. CBC Radio 2 and Apple Music provided the accompaniment.

MIND–SOCIETY

I

PART I

Mechanisms

1

Explaining Social Change

When I was a child in Saskatchewan in the 1950s, my parents and their friends smoked cigarettes, women were mostly housewives, birth control and homosexuality were illegal, and pornography was scarce. Today, almost no one I know smokes, many women are professionals, Canada and some other countries allow same-sex marriage, and hard-core pornography is available to anyone with Internet access. What causes such enormous social changes?

Contemporary social science is oddly incompetent to explain such transformations. Many economists and political scientists still assume that individuals make rational choices, despite the abundance of evidence that people frequently succumb to thinking errors such as motivated inference, confirmation bias, sunk costs, and framing losses differently from gains. Much of sociology and anthropology is taken over with postmodernist assumptions that everything is constructed on the basis of social relations such as power, with no inkling that these relations are mediated by how people think about each other. Social psychology should serve as the connection between changes in individual minds and social transformations, but the study of social cognition tends to focus on how pairs of individuals make sense of each other, rather than on the group processes that produce the spread of concepts and emotional attitudes across societies.

A better approach to explaining social change needs to be constructed by building on current work on the neural mechanisms responsible for cognition and emotion. *Brain–Mind* shows how all mental representations—images, concepts, beliefs, rules, analogies, emotions, desires—can be built out of patterns of neural firings that Chris Eliasmith calls semantic pointers, which can function like symbols but unpack into sensory-motor representations. His Semantic Pointer Architecture aims to provide a unified, brain-based account of the full range of human thought, from perception to language. What does social change look like from this perspective?

If all thinking in individuals builds representations out of semantic pointers, then communication between individuals produces approximate transfer of such neural processes. It is possible to identify the full range of social interactions that produce transmission, which go beyond verbal means such as conversation and argument. Nonverbal ways of communicating semantic pointers include pictures, gestures, and touches, as well as collective activities like singing, marching, and participating in religious rituals. Technologies such as television and Facebook use words, images, and sounds to communicate emotional attitudes in addition to verbal and pictorial information. Because semantic pointers cover nonverbal information from the senses and emotions in addition to words and sentences, they can provide the basis for a general theory of communication. Social changes result from adjustments in the neural representations in individuals and from the exchanges between people that causally interact with what goes on in their heads.

Social change comes from the combination of communicative interactions among people and their individual cognitive-emotional processes. This approach, which I call *social cognitivism*, does not attempt to reduce the social to the individual as rational choice approaches want, nor does it attempt to reduce the individual to the social as social constructionist approaches want. Rather, it views social change as the result of emergence from interacting social and mental mechanisms, which include the neural and molecular processes that make minds capable of thinking. Validation of hypotheses about social cognitivism and multilevel emergence requires detailed studies of important social changes, from norms about smoking and pornography to economic practices, political institutions, religious customs, and international relations. The study of social change should serve not only to explain past developments but also to suggest how to deal with ongoing problems such as racism, gender discrimination, inequality, global warming, and technological development.

It would be futile to try to give an exact definition of social change, but the new method of three-analysis provides a useful alternative. This method draws on a new theory about concepts to characterize them using exemplars, typical features, and explanations, rather than necessary and sufficient conditions. Exemplars are standard examples, such as Fords and Toyotas for the concept of car. The typical features of cars need not belong to all and only cars, but usually apply to them, including their standard parts such as wheels, engines, and doors. The third aspect of a concept captured by a three-analysis is its explanatory use, including both what the concept explains and what explains the concept. We use cars to explain how people often get around their environments and travel from place to place. The existence and operation of cars is in turn explained by the history of the invention of the automobile, the social processes that led to their adoption, and the physical interactions of their parts.

Similarly, we can characterize social change by identifying exemplars, typical features, and explanations, as summarized in Table 1.1. Important examples of social change are prominent in politics, economics, and numerous collective behaviors. In politics, consider the origins and adoption of influential ideologies, such as free enterprise capitalism, communism, and fascism. In economics, there are dramatic general trends such as industrialization in the nineteenth century and increasing uses of information technology in the twentieth century. Sociology studies dramatic changes in social norms such as patterns of behavior concerning marriage and smoking. In anthropology, there are the origins and spread of cultural innovations, including religions such as Christianity and Islam. History and international relations investigate major events such as the great wars of the twentieth century and ongoing international conflicts, for example, in the Middle East.

Social change also occurs in the professions, for example the rise of science-based medicine in the twentieth century, and the spread of universal healthcare. Remarkable legal changes include the development of common law in medieval England and the adoption of the Napoleonic code in France in the nineteenth century. Education has witnessed many social changes such as the development of universities and the spread of public education. Business changes are partly reflections of economic ones, such as cycles of prosperity, but they can also reflect different ways of managing and marketing, for example using television. Finally,

TABLE 1.1

Three-Analysis of *Social Change*

Exemplars	Cultural shifts, political revolutions, industrial transformations, religious movements, technological replacements
Typical features	Individuals, groups, institutions, communication, old system, new system
Explanations	Explains: changes in individual behavior and institutional practice
	Explained by: mental mechanisms, social mechanisms

engineering as a profession has undergone frequent changes in the past century, for example the increasing use of computers in design projects.

The great variety of social changes makes it hard to say what they have in common, but we can identify typical features. Social changes take place in groups of people, not just isolated individuals. They often affect institutions, which are organizations such as churches governed by goals and rules. In addition to institutional modifications, social changes also take place in individuals through alterations in their beliefs, attitudes, and behaviors.

What does social change explain? The existence of broad social changes helps to explain more particular kinds of events. For example, to understand why a particular household contains a single parent with one or two children rather than a husband, wife, and three children, we can see it as an instance of a general social trend. Much more challenging is to explain how and why social changes take place, for example why economies crash, why wars break out, and why ideologies flourish or fail. What form should such explanations take?

EXPLANATORY STYLES

Explanation in science usually takes one of three forms: narrative, deductive, or mechanistic. A narrative explanation tells a story about how something came to be, for example about how Canada and some other countries came to legalize same-sex marriage. Most current explanations of social change employ such stories. In more mathematical sciences such as physics, deductive explanations of events show how they follow from general laws of nature. I am not aware of any deductive explanations of important social changes, but mathematical-deductive explanations are sometimes used in economics.

The style of explanation most relevant to society describes mechanisms whose parts and interactions produce regular changes. Relevant mechanisms occur both in the minds of individuals and in the interactions of people who communicate with each other. Mechanistic explanations are familiar in biology, where interactions between parts such as cells and organs explain the successful functioning of living things and can also explain breakdowns that lead to diseases.

Narrative explanations are employed in other fields besides the social sciences. For example, in evolutionary biology, we can explain the existence of our species, *Homo sapiens*, by telling how millions of years of mammalian evolution led eventually to the development of more than a dozen species of human-like animals. *Homo sapiens* eventually became the dominant human species and the only surviving one, perhaps because of our greater intelligence and capability of cooperation. Even physics has its share of narrative explanations, for example in the evidence-supported story about the formation of our planet and solar system from the condensation of gases and dust whose origins date back to the Big Bang. For social change, narrative explanations apply to developments such as how the current economic system came about through the rise of capitalism since the Middle Ages. Similarly, the development of democratic government can be seen as the result of historical events such as the elected parliaments in medieval England.

Narrative explanation has two great sources of appeal. First, people love stories, and storytelling plays a major role in human cultures independent of literacy. Second, there can be substantial truth in the stories that are told to explain social changes that resulted from sequences of events naturally told in story form.

On the other hand, narrative explanation has some obvious weaknesses. First, narrative explanations may be short on truth, because stories can be appealing for reasons other than their correspondence to reality. For example, we may like a story because it makes us feel happy or because it fits with various unsubstantiated prejudices that we hold. Mythology is full of fanciful stories that are beguiling but have no basis in correspondence to fact, as in the creation myths that are found in hundreds of different cultures.

Second, narrative explanations rarely consider alternatives, that is, different stories that may yield the same result based on very different assumptions and relevant facts. For example, stories about the evolution of human traits often rely on elements gained from analogy with current societies, which may not correspond to the crucial circumstances under which humans actually evolved their genetic makeup. Social phenomena are always so complex that there are alternative stories that might be told about the developments, and it is hard to choose between alternative stories when the links between the events are quite arbitrary. For example, some sociologists endorse Max Weber's story about the capitalist economic system resulting from the adoption of Protestantism and its associated work ethic. But there are other stories about the origins of capitalism that trace it to other factors such as population shifts.

Third, narrative explanations often string together events while leaving it mysterious how one event led to the next. The story is appealing of how the activities of Martin Luther and other critics of Catholicism generated Protestant religions that encouraged behaviors conducive to capitalist enterprise. But it would be much more compelling to know precisely how protest led to successful churches, how these churches established patterns of behavior, and how these behaviors encouraged the flourishing of capitalism.

Ideally, deductive explanations would avoid these three problems. Deduction would give us a solid mathematical link from one event to the other because transitions would be explained as instances of general laws. Alternative stories could be comparatively evaluated according to how well they predict past and future events. The truth of competing deductive explanations would largely be assessed by this kind of predictive value, with mathematics providing the predictions, supplemented by checks to ensure that the assumptions fed into the deductive explanations correspond to observed events. Physics has made such use of deductive explanations, from the basic mechanics of Galileo and Newton up to the much more complicated mathematics of relativity theory and quantum theory. Sadly, however, the general mathematical laws found in physics are extremely rare in the social sciences, so they cannot help us much to fill in the gaps in narrative explanations of social change.

Fortunately, mechanistic explanations provide a powerful alternative. Such explanations sometimes employ stories but try to show how one event leads to another as a result of the mental and social mechanisms that connect the two events. Sometimes these mechanisms can be described in mathematical form, when equations describe precisely the behaviors and interactions of the parts that make up a mechanism. But the core part of a mechanistic explanation is a description of parts whose interactions lead to regular changes, including the social change to be explained. For example, in Weber's explanation of the rise of capitalism we can ask what was going on in the minds of Luther's followers that made the critique of Catholic practices plausible to them and others who shifted to Protestant religions. Crucial to this account is the consideration of social mechanisms by which people communicate with each other and transfer beliefs, goals, and emotions. To put it succinctly, social change results from the interplay and interdependence of cognitive and social mechanisms.

The mechanistic approach to social explanation should identify connections between events that are stronger than narrative explanation provides but more obtainable than mathematical deduction requires. Mechanism avoids the potential mythology of narrative explanation because of the demand that the relevant parts, structural connections, and interactions fit well with evidence concerning what goes on in the world, both in minds and in social interactions. Rather than being satisfied with one appealing narrative, alternative mechanistic accounts can be comparatively evaluated with respect to how well they (a) explain a wide array of social changes, (b) make empirically verified descriptions of parts and interactions, and (c) employ assumptions about contributing conditions that are consistent with available evidence. Table 1.2 summarizes the concept of mechanism using a three-analysis.

TABLE 1.2

Three-Analysis of *Mechanism*

Exemplars	Machines such as bicycles, physical systems such as the solar system, organisms such as bacteria, organs such as the brain, groups such as political parties and markets
Typical features	Wholes, parts, connections, interactions, regular changes
Explanations	Explains: changes in parts and wholes
	Explained by: underlying mechanisms inside parts

Mechanisms are invaluable for explaining the successful functioning of machines, organisms, and groups, but they can also be useful for explaining failures. Machines sometimes break because of weakness in their parts, connections, and interactions, so that they fail to produce the regular changes that accomplish their function. Later chapters show that mechanism breakdown is important for explaining romantic disasters, economic crashes, mental illness, and wrongful convictions. Some mechanisms lack functions or purposes, for example the solar system. But machines built by humans always have a purpose, and biological mechanisms resulting from natural selection always have a function unless they are vestigial results of earlier adaptations.

Mechanisms always operate in an environment, for example the physical world that people interact with using their sensory-motor systems. To understand how the mechanistic explanatory style operates, we need a more detailed description of socially relevant mechanisms.

MENTAL, NEURAL, AND SOCIAL MECHANISMS

Consider a very simple machine, a pair of scissors like the one shown in Figure 1.1. This machine has two main parts, each consisting of a blade and handle, connected by a screw. The interactions of the three parts take place when someone moves the handles in order to bring the blades together or apart. The regular changes produced by the scissors are primarily the cutting of pieces of paper or cloth that are placed between the blades when the handles are moved. This machine operates in an environment that includes the person whose hand moves the handles and also the paper or cloth placed between the blades for cutting.

Biological, psychological, and social mechanisms are more complicated systems but work like a machine in that they have connected parts whose interactions

FIGURE 1.1 A simple mechanism with only three parts.

produce regular changes. In the brain, the most important parts are neurons, which are cells connected to other cells by synapses. The synapses allow neurons to interact with each other, so that when one neuron fires it can excite another neuron, making it more prone to firing, or inhibit the other neuron, making it less prone to firing. Other parts of the brain include neurotransmitters, which are chemicals that move from one neuron to another across the synapse between them. Biological mechanisms operating in the human brain also include molecular interactions of genes and proteins inside each neuron and the influence of hormones circulating in blood supplies on neurons. The changes resulting from these interactions generate all the thoughts and feelings that occur in human minds, as *Brain–Mind* argues.

Mental occurrences can also be described in terms of higher level mechanisms, where the parts are representations such as perceptions, images, concepts, beliefs, rules, and analogies. For example, anyone reading this volume has the concept of a book, consisting of standard examples such as the Bible, typical features such as having pages with words on them, and explanations such as that books enable you to read. Mental representations are connected to each other in various ways, for example by part–whole relations: the concept *book* is part of your belief that the Bible is a book. The interactions among mental representations are diverse, ranging from simple associations such as the one between the concepts *peanut butter* and *jam* to more elaborate inferential relationships that occur when there are beliefs that correspond to elaborate sentences such as: the Bible is the most frequently printed book in the world. One of the most challenging questions for cognitive science is to figure out how mental mechanisms derive from neural mechanisms; current ideas about how this works are outlined in chapter 2.

Although it is becoming more common in the social sciences for writers to describe social change in terms of mechanisms, theorists are usually vague about what a mechanism is. I want to be more precise following the scheme of parts, structural connections, interactions, and regular changes. Here "regular" does not have to mean universality but merely causal correlation: some events make it more probable that other events will occur. Social mechanisms can operate in very small systems, such as a family, or in much larger ones, such as a whole country. In all such mechanisms, the main parts are people who are connected to each other physically and/or psychologically. Through connections, people can interact with each other by different forms of verbal and nonverbal communication but also by purely physical acts such as violence. These interactions can lead to regular changes, for example in the reciprocal behaviors of a romantic couple becoming attached to each other or in the political activities of a whole country whose people communicate with each other by talking, writing, marching, or voting.

The central question to be answered for the explanation of social change is: What are the relations among neural mechanisms, mental mechanisms, and social mechanisms? A full answer must wait for the end of chapter 3, following a more detailed description of specific social and mental mechanisms. This answer requires an understanding of emergence.

EMERGENCE

Mechanistic explanations relate the whole to its parts but do not assume the reductionist view that the whole is nothing but the sum of the parts. A reductionist approach to social change would require that all changes at the group level be derived from changes in individual people. In contrast, the mechanistic explanations that I advocate frequently identify emergent properties that belong to wholes but that cannot be reduced to the properties of parts, because they result from the interactions of parts. A university, for example, has properties such as being able to grant degrees not possessed by any individual administrators or professors or by any aggregate of these people.

The concept of emergence is often attributed to Aristotle, in the form of the saying that the whole is greater than the sum of its parts. What he actually said is that the totality is not a mere heap, and the whole is something besides the parts. The slogan that the whole is greater than the sum of its parts is confusing because it does not indicate the respects in which wholes are supposed to be greater. Many discussions of emergence in philosophy and in complexity theory are equally mysterious, making it seem that emergence is some magical property rather than a frequent part of scientific explanation.

Fortunately, a comprehensible and scientifically respectable characterization of emergence has been given by the philosophers of science William Wimsatt and Mario Bunge. In their view, emergence occurs when (a) the whole has a property not found in any of its parts, (b) the property of the whole is not simply the sum or aggregate of the properties of the parts, and (c) the property results from the interactions of the parts. Even machines can have emergent properties, for example when a whole bicycle has the property of carrying a rider along a street when none of the parts such as wheels and pedals could do so alone.

Examples of such emergence abound in science, from physics to psychology. Molecules of water have the property of being liquid at room temperature, unlike their constituent hydrogen and oxygen, which are gases at room temperature. Cells have properties such as the ability to divide and send signals, which are not just the aggregate of the properties of their parts—proteins and other molecules. Organs such as the heart have properties such as the ability to pump blood, which are not merely the sum of the properties of the cells that compose them. The whole body has properties such as the ability to move around and have sex, which are not properties of individual organs, because they require the interactions of numerous organs such as the heart, the brain, and the limbs. Brain processes such as perception have emergent properties, for example the recognition of ambiguous figures in different ways, as in the duck-rabbit shown in Figure 1.2. In contrast, body weight is a not an emergent property, because it is just the sum of the weights of the body parts.

Attempts to explain social change need to watch for emergent properties of whole groups that include couples, families, governments, ethnicities, and countries. Recognizing a property as emergent does not locate it outside the realm of scientific explanation but rather points to the need for detailed accounts of the

FIGURE 1.2 Duck-rabbit illusion, which can perceptually emerge as either a duck or a rabbit depending on whether you notice ears or a bill.

mechanisms operating at all levels from which social changes emerge. Social cognitivism does not aim to reduce the social to the mental, because it recognizes that there are emergent social changes that result from the interactions of individual thinkers and also from the interactions of groups. My goal is not to dispense with the social but rather to understand social change as interdependent with mental change in individuals.

Accomplishing this goal requires recognizing that emergence is more complicated than the account so far given. Social mechanisms depend on mental mechanisms, which depend on neural mechanisms, which depend on molecular mechanisms, and so on. Without going down all the way to the level of subatomic particles and quarks, we need to recognize recursive emergence, which is repeated emergence from emergence. For example, the properties of the heart such as pumping blood emerge from the properties of the muscles in it, where the properties of muscles such as contracting and relaxing result from the interactions of the cells in them. Hence the pumping of blood comes from emergence from emergence. We will see in later chapters that recursive emergence is important for understanding the operations of brains, minds, and social groups.

To understand social change, however, we also need an even more complicated kind of emergence. Emergence is usually identified as a relation between two levels, a higher and lower one. Properties of the whole at the higher level emerge from the interactions of the parts at the lower level. The scientific strategy of looking at just two levels at a time is often highly productive, but for social change we need to pay attention to the simultaneous interactions of more than two levels, resulting in what I call multilevel emergence.

Brain–Mind (chapter 12) argues that the human self is a case of multilevel emergence, in that a full understanding of human selves or persons requires looking at interactions among four levels: social, mental, neural, and molecular. Multilevel emergence is more intricate than recursive emergence, which would allow that the social emerges from the mental, which emerges from the neural, which emerges from the molecular. Understanding the self requires appreciating how social changes can lead to molecular changes. For example, social interactions such as compliments and insults translate quickly into molecular changes in individual brains, such as increase in dopamine levels for compliments and increase in cortisol levels for insults. Figure 1.3 portrays the differences among ordinary, recursive (repeated), and multilevel emergence.

Later chapters will show that important instances of social change, ranging from the spread of ideologies to the outbreaks of wars, are cases of multilevel emergence. For example, chapter 7 argues that explaining economic crashes requires noticing interactions among people that influence their molecular states such as

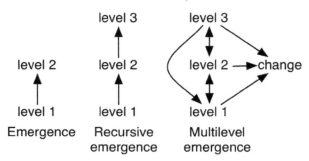

FIGURE 1.3 Three kinds of emergence. Arrows indicate causality and explanation.

the stress hormone cortisol, which feed back to influence social interactions such as buying and selling.

The concept of emergence can be summarized in the three-analysis provided in Table 1.3. The exemplars of emergence include water molecules, cells, organs, bodies, and social groups. The typical features of emergence include a lower level of parts, a higher level of wholes, a property of the whole that is not a property of its parts, and interactions among the parts that generate the property of the whole. Emergence explains why wholes have properties that are not just the sum of the properties of the parts. Explaining emergence is often difficult because of lack of knowledge of the mechanisms operating at both higher and lower levels. Fortunately, in many cases in physics, biology, and neuroscience, advances in scientific knowledge have moved to fill in these gaps. A major aim of this book is similarly to fill in the gaps between social and mental mechanisms while recognizing several kinds of emergence.

If the cognitive and social sciences used deductive explanations, then filling the mental–social gap would amount to the reductionist project of mathematically deriving the higher levels from the lower levels. This project fails for two reasons: the difficulty of finding general laws for biological, psychological, and

TABLE 1.3

Three-Analysis of *Emergence*

Exemplars	Molecules such as water, biological systems such as cells and organs, social systems such as universities
Typical features	Whole, parts, interactions, properties that belong to the whole but not the parts
Explanations	Explains: complex change
	Explained by: interconnections, mechanisms inside parts

neural systems; and the prevalence of causal effects of changes at the higher level on the social level at the lower level, for example the effects on mental states of compliments and insults. Accordingly, explanations of how emergence works in the social sciences need to go beyond simple two-level cases by paying attention to recursive emergence and multilevel emergence. How this works will be shown generally at the end of chapter 3 and in much more detail in later chapters with particular examples across the social sciences and professions.

Systems with emergent properties are often prone to unpredictable changes. In the study of complex systems, the term "chaos" describes systems where small changes can lead to large effects, for example when introduction of a new animal such as zebra mussels to an ecosystem can lead to extinction of other species. In the duck-rabbit example in Figure 1.3, a small change in focus of attention can lead to a large perceptual shift. Because emergent properties result from ongoing interactions, sometimes small changes can take a system past a tipping point that produces a critical transition to new properties of the whole. A tipping point is a threshold that can turn small changes into large ones, and critical transitions occur when crossing a threshold produces major changes. We will see that many social systems from romantic couples to stock markets are chaotic with tipping points that lead to critical transitions, all because of multilevel interacting mechanisms.

THE SOCIAL COGNITIVE-EMOTIONAL WORKUP

The task of identifying multiple mechanisms might seem daunting but becomes tractable through a method for tackling change across all the social sciences and professions. I call this method a social cognitive-emotional workup. In American medicine, a workup is a systematic set of diagnostic procedures designed to diagnose a disease, including a battery of tests that help determine the causes of a patient's symptoms. I use "workup" to describe a battery of questions that help identify the interacting causes of a social change. Obviously, social change requires attention to social mechanisms, but we will also see the advantages of considering mechanisms at the mental, neural, and molecular levels. A workup should attempt to answer all of the following questions:

1. Who are the relevant individuals participating in the social change?
2. What are the groups that constrain the social interactions of the individuals, including institutions with identifiable goals and rules?

3. What are the representations in the minds of individuals and how do they change as the result of mental, neural, and molecular mechanisms?
4. What social mechanisms contribute to the changes in representations across individuals?
5. How do the changes in representations and interactions lead to changes in the behaviors of individuals and groups?
6. What are the emergent properties of groups and how do they result from interdependencies of social, mental, neural, and molecular mechanisms?
7. What are the tipping points that produce critical transitions, turning small mental and social changes into major ones?

The description of the relevant mental and social mechanisms in chapters 2 and 3 will make it much clearer how a social cognitive-emotional workup can proceed.

The seventh question requires attention to dramatic changes that can occur as the result of apparently minor occurrences. For example, in 1914 the assassination of an Austrian archduke set off a cascade of events that led to millions of people dying in World War I, establishing political and economic conditions that contributed to World War II in which even more people died. Many important social changes result from critical transitions at both the mental and social levels, for example revolutions, economic crashes, religious frenzies, and wars. Such critical transitions often produce new emergent properties in individuals and groups, when local interactions produce global changes.

APPLICATIONS

Much work in current social science is dominated by two inadequate methodological approaches: the methodological individualism that prevails in much of economics and political science in the form of rational choice theory, and the postmodernism that prevails in much of anthropology, sociology, and history in the form of vague discussions of discourse and power relations. The cognitive sciences, especially psychology and neuroscience, can provide a powerful third alternative, but not simply by reductively explaining the social in terms of the psychological. Rather, social cognitivism shows how to integrate the social and the cognitive sciences nonreductively, displaying both psychological effects on social processes and social effects on psychological processes. The social sciences and professions need to be mindful, not mind-blind and brain-blind.

Social cognitive-emotional workups are applicable to a wide range of social phenomena, but this book provides only some important cases. I will try to show the method is useful for answering two sorts of descriptive questions and two sorts of normative questions. The descriptive questions, concerning how the world actually is, are (a) Why did a particular social change take place? and (b) Why did various social changes *not* take place? The second question shows that a workup should be able to explain social stability as well as social change by identifying mental and social mechanisms.

Normative questions concern how the world ought to be, not just how it is, including (c) How can the world be made better? and (d) How can the world be prevented from getting worse? A workup can be applied to the third question by considering the mental and social mechanisms that are relevant to bringing about the desired change, such as reducing poverty and malnutrition. Sometimes, as with global warming, social interventions based on people's thinking are needed to keep things from getting worse. The fourth question considers what mental and social mechanisms are relevant to preventing a dangerous change from occurring. My emphasis is primarily on explaining social change, but I occasionally address social stability and allude to the normative questions about promoting good changes and preventing bad ones. The ethical question about what makes changes normatively good or bad is addressed by considering human needs in *Natural Philosophy* (chapters 6 and 7).

After a review of mental and social mechanisms in chapters 2 and 3, the next six chapters show the usefulness of performing social cognitive-emotional workups for the following branches of social science: social psychology, sociology, politics, economics, anthropology, and history. Chapter 4 considers social psychology as operating at the intersection of psychology and sociology but develops a synthesis not found in either of them. The subfields of social cognition and micro-sociology can be enhanced by an account of how romantic human relationships depend on a complex of social, mental, neural, and molecular mechanisms.

Close relationships involve a small number of individuals, as few as two in a romance, but much larger groups are involved in the all too common practice of discrimination on the basis of sex, race, ethnicity, age, and disability. Chapter 5 uses social cognitive-emotional workups of misogyny and antisemitism to show how prejudice tied to social stereotypes can lead to discrimination. Overcoming discrimination requires changes in social norms, which are conscious and unconscious emotional rules rather than rational choices.

Various kinds of political change require explanation, but chapter 6 focuses on changes in ideologies, which are systems of ideas, beliefs, and values that affect a political community. The rise and fall of ideologies—their adoption and rejection in a community—results from the interplay of mental and social mechanisms, as illustrated by the recent rise of the Islamic State.

Many important kinds of social change are economic, concerning the production and trade of goods and services. Chapter 7 investigates a particularly salient kind of economic change, the booms and crashes that have been prominent in capitalist economic systems for hundreds of years. Both the psychology and the molecular neuroscience of individual minds turn out to be relevant to explaining dramatic economic changes, which also result from social interactions constrained by economic institutions and other groups. The 1929 and 2008 economic crashes are good examples of multilevel emergence involving interactions at the social, mental, neural, and molecular levels, leading to critical transitions.

Religion is a ubiquitous social phenomenon studied by anthropologists and other social scientists. The rise, spread, transformation, and sometimes decline of religious movements are important social changes whose explanation needs to knit together the social and the mental, right down to the molecular. In chapter 8, I offer a psychological explanation of why religions in general are so appealing to individuals, and I also consider how their spread is an important kind of social change resulting from social mechanisms interconnected with mental ones. How this works is shown by a social cognitive-emotional workup of a rapidly growing religion, Mormonism.

Chapter 9 treats history as a social science whose aims should include providing explanations, for example of the origins of wars. The pathetic story of the inception of World War I illustrates the interplay of mental and social mechanisms. This chapter requires an excursion into the field of international relations, which also belongs to politics. Wars are a good example of social changes that need explaining, but they also demand normative investigation of how they can be avoided in the future.

The rest of this book describes applications of the method of social cognitive-emotional workups to the professions, including medicine, law, education, engineering, and business. In each chapter, case studies are used to develop new accounts of central concerns, including mental illness, wrongful convictions, teaching, creative design, leadership, and marketing. Taken together, chapters 4 to 14 provide a long argument that the best explanations of social change stem from the interactions of mental and social mechanisms described in chapters 2 and 3.

SUMMARY AND DISCUSSION

I am proposing a new approach to the social sciences and professions that assesses the following hypotheses:

H1. All social change results from mental mechanisms in individuals and from social mechanisms for the interactions of thinking individuals.

H2. The relevant mental mechanisms operate with these representations: images, concepts, rules, analogies, and emotions.

H3. All of these representations derive from neural mechanisms based on an important kind of neural process called semantic pointers.

H4. The interactions of individuals contribute to changes in their mental representations through cognitive and emotional communication that transfers, prompts, and instigates semantic pointers.

H5. Changes in the mental states and behaviors of individuals and groups result from changes in representations and interactions.

H6. Explanation of social changes requires identification of emergent properties of groups that are not simply the sum of change of changes in individuals.

H7. Social change resulting from cognitive and social mechanisms often results from critical transitions, not just gradual accumulations.

H8. Emotional gestalt shifts are important critical transitions that occur when individuals and groups reconfigure their arrays of attitudes and values.

These eight hypotheses are not dogmatic pronouncements but rather conjectures that need to be tested against numerous historical cases. Evidence for their plausibility arrives when they yield novel, plausible, and rich explanations of cases of social change and stability, occurring in romantic relationships, social prejudice, political ideologies, economic cycles, religious practices, and wars. If historically justified, these hypotheses provide the basis for explaining social changes and stability, and they yield a framework for addressing normative questions about how to bring about desirable changes and about how to prevent dangerous ones.

The approach developed here differs markedly from the purely individual explanations offered by rational choice theorists and from the purely social explanations offered by social constructionists and postmodernists. My integration of the individual and the social is accomplished by combining rich accounts of mental, neural, and molecular mechanisms with a full description of social mechanisms that allow the minds of people to influence each other. Understanding the operations of brains turns out to be crucial for understanding how minds and societies make each other work.

NOTES

I use quotation marks to indicate words and italics to indicate concepts. For example, the word "book" can stand for a book that is mentally represented by the concept *book*.

For an overview of social change, see Weinstein 2010. Varnum and Grossman 2017 discuss the psychology of cultural change.

Other attempts to synthesize the cognitive and social sciences can be found in Sun 2012, Turner 2001, and Huebner 2013. Social neuroscience is reviewed by Schutt, Keshavan, and Seidman 2015 and Decety and Cacioppo 2011.

On semantic pointers, see Eliasmith et al. 2012, Eliasmith 2013, *Brain–Mind*, and chapter 2. Published papers can be found at the following websites:

http://compneuro.uwaterloo.ca/publications.html
http://cogsci.uwaterloo.ca/Biographies/pault-new.html

The semantic pointer theory of concepts is presented in Blouw, Solodkin, Thagard, and Eliasmith 2016. The method of three-analysis originates with this *Treatise*. Traditional conceptual analysis in philosophy presumes a theory of concepts that psychological experiments have made obsolete: Murphy 2002. The method of three-analysis is useful for describing current concepts and also for laying out the dynamics of conceptual change, as described in the chapters on prejudice and education.

For an overview of explanation, see Woodward 2014. Velleman 2003 discusses narrative explanation. Work on mechanistic explanation includes Bechtel 2008, Bunge 2003, Craver and Darden 2013, and Findlay and Thagard 2012. *Natural Philosophy* (chapter 5) examines the strengths and weaknesses of additional explanatory styles, along with a more thorough account of reduction and emergence. For present purposes, field A reduces to field B if all phenomena in A can be explained by B. A good review of scientific reduction is van Riel and Van Gulick 2014.

Sometimes deductive, mechanistic, and narrative explanations can be complementary, for example when mathematical models of neurons are used to describe how neural interactions lead to mental changes.

The narrative explanation of the rise of capitalism is in Weber 2009.

My account of emergence adapts Wimsatt 2007 and Bunge 2003. Aristotle says that the whole is besides the parts in his *Metaphysics*, Book H, 1045a. I do not know who introduced the phrase "the whole is greater than the sum of its parts." It is sometimes attributed to the Gestalt psychologists, who were actually closer to Aristotle.

On complexity, see Mitchell 2011. Scheffer 2009 examines critical transitions, which are sometimes also called tipping points, bifurcations, inflection points, catastrophes, and singularities. Complexity, chaos, and critical transitions explain little without specification of mechanisms that produce them.

PROJECT

Compile a catalog of important social changes and analyze the kinds of explanation that have been given for them.

2

Mental Mechanisms

Why do we do what we do? To understand how people interact with each other, we need to know what is going on in their individual but interdependent minds. Since the 1950s, cognitive science has developed an understanding of how minds work using mental representations and procedures. You are already familiar with representations in the world, for example verbal ones such as words and sentences and visual ones such as signs and diagrams. Much less familiar is the hypothesis that people have representations operating in their minds that can also stand for things in the world. Just as you can use the word "apple" to stand for apples, so your mind can use the concept *apple* to stand for apples in the world.

Mental representations would be useless if they did not have procedures that operate on them. For example, if you have the concept of an apple as a kind of fruit, then you can move from the belief that something is an apple to the conclusion that it is a fruit. Representations and procedures working together constitute mental mechanisms, where the parts are mental entities such as concepts and images and the interactions are procedures such as inference and image construction.

Brain–Mind shows how human thinking can be explained using basic kinds of mental representation: perceptions, images, concepts, beliefs, rules, analogies, and emotions. This chapter gives a compact summary of how these representations contribute to human thinking, including the intertwining of cognition and emotion. All mental representations are formed out of the same underlying neural mechanisms, including representation by groups of neurons, binding of these representations into more complex ones called semantic pointers, and competition among semantic pointers. Hence the mental mechanisms needed to explain human thinking emerge from neural mechanisms, which in turn emerge from molecular mechanisms such as the interactions of proteins inside neurons and the movement of neurotransmitters between them.

The point of this chapter is not to review all of *Brain–Mind* but merely to provide the condensed highlights needed for explaining social change. Human interactions are not just the transfer of verbal signals from one person to another. The full range of communication requires conveyance of nonverbal mental representations including images and emotions. People's interactions depend on the transmission of semantic pointers from one person to another using speaking and listening but also using physical actions such as pointing, gesturing, smiling, grimacing, singing, and marching. The method of social cognitive-emotional workups requires identifying both individual semantic pointers and the means by which they are transmitted.

BRAINS AND SEMANTIC POINTERS

A cognitive architecture is a general proposal about the representations and processes that produce intelligent thought. Dozens of competing architectures have been used to explain important aspects of human thinking such as problem solving, memory, and learning, but a complete architecture would also apply to the full range of human thinking, including imagery, emotions, and consciousness. Chris Eliasmith's Semantic Pointer Architecture provides a synthesis of the two main current approaches to cognitive theorizing: rules built out of word-like symbols and neural networks that avoid symbols through processes that use large numbers of simple neurons. Eliasmith's approach employs brain-like neural networks to accomplish sensory-motor tasks, but it also can generate symbol-like representations capable of high-level thinking such as deductive inference.

Human brains consists of around 86 billion cells called neurons and around the same number of supporting cells called glia. Each neuron by itself contributes little to thought, even though it can be connected with thousands of other neurons. A neuron receives chemical signals from the neurons that feed into it and builds up an electrical charge that enables the neuron to fire and send signals to thousands of other neurons. Each neuron can respond to features of the world by its ability to fire faster or slower and to fire in particular patterns analogous to the beats of different songs. When thousands or millions of neurons work together, they can constitute representations of perceptual features such as redness and roundness. A group of neurons working together is analogous to a band where the result of musicians playing together is much better than what each musician could do alone. Representing aspects of the world is an emergent property of neural groups.

Perception and recognition of objects such as apples requires more than disconnected representations of redness and roundness. Humans and other animals can combine features into representations of whole objects by neural mechanisms for binding. Binding takes up a pattern of firing in one group of neurons and combines it with another pattern of firing in another possibly overlapping group of neurons. The result is a pattern of firing that combines the simpler perceptual features into an organized whole, for example the perception of an apple that combines red, round, and having a stem on top and bruise on the side.

Further binding is required to move beyond transient perceptions to more permanent and general representations. Your concept of an apple includes not just what it looks like but also its taste, smell, texture, and feel in your hand. Moreover, there are motor movements associated with the apple, such as bringing it up to your mouth, biting it, and maybe even throwing it. Hence thinking of apples requires binding sensory and motor features in addition to visual ones, including both current experiences of apples and your memories of them.

For humans, mental representations of apples also integrate verbal information, such as that apples are fruits and tasty. In addition, the tasty aspect shows an emotional dimension, implying that most people like apples, although there may be a few people who hate them or are indifferent to them. Hence the representation of an apple is not just the result of binding a few visual features but rather of combining a whole complex of multisensory, motor, verbal, and emotional aspects. The concept *apple* is bounded by the information found in a three-analysis: exemplars, typical features, and explanations.

Binding complexes of sensory, motor, verbal, and emotional representations produces brain processes that Chris Eliasmith calls semantic pointers. Semantic pointers are important because they are the first proposed neural representations powerful enough to accommodate all of human thinking, from simple perception up to problem solving, consciousness, and creativity. Figure 2.1 illustrates how semantic pointers are patterns of firing neural groups that result from binding sensory, motor, verbal, and emotional representations. For example, your concept *cat* can operate in your brain as a neural firing pattern that integrate sensory information such what cats look like, motor information such as stroking them, emotional information such as how much you like them, and verbal information such as that cats are mammals.

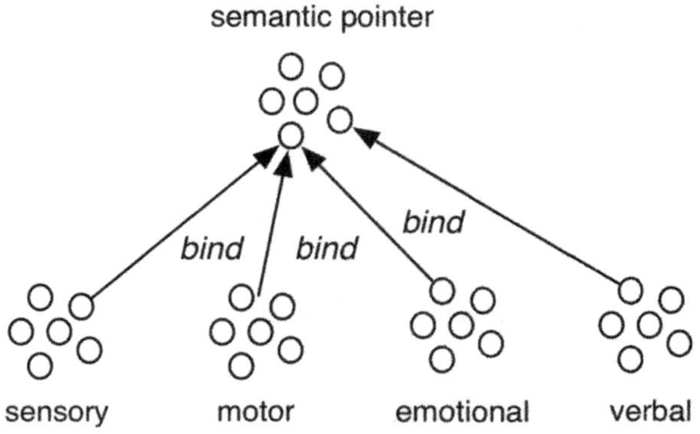

semantic pointer

FIGURE 2.1 Semantic pointer resulting from binding sensory, motor, emotional, and verbal information. The circles represent thousands of neurons. Reprinted by permission of Elsevier from Thagard and Stewart 2014.

Chapter 3 argues that human communication primarily consists in the transfer of semantic pointers from one person's brain to another, encompassing sensory, motor, and emotional information as well as verbal. If human brains worked like digital computers, we could set up a wired or wireless channel to transmit semantic pointers directly between them. Instead human communication requires the full range of verbal and nonverbal interactions described in chapter 3. The result of these interactions is not exact transfer of one person's semantic pointers into another person's brain but rather reproduction of functionally similar neural representations.

Table 2.1 provides a three-analysis of the concept of semantic pointers. *Brain–Mind* describes how concepts, beliefs, images, and other representations can be construed as semantic pointers, so these are the standard examples. The typical features of semantic pointers are that they are patterns of neural firing formed by a mathematical method called convolution that binds neural representations including ones derived from sensory-motor inputs. This binding compresses the information into a neural representation that if needed can be decompressed to regain an approximation of the sensory-motor contribution.

Semantic pointers are semantic in two ways, by their relations to the sensory-motor inputs that connect them to the world and by their relations to other semantic pointers. The term "pointer" indicates that such representations point to their sensory origins by virtue of the how convolution can be undone to approximate to the perceptually derived inputs that went into it. The purpose of the semantic pointer hypothesis is to provide an explanation of how billions of neurons can accomplish complex thought. Computer simulations of different kinds of cognition make it plausible that semantic pointers operate in the brain and suffice to

TABLE 2.1

Three-Analysis of the Concept *Semantic Pointer*

Exemplars	Images (a white cat), concepts (*cat*), beliefs (cats have tails), desires (wanting a cat), and emotions (admiring cats)
Typical features	Pattern of neural firing, produced through binding by convolution
	Connections to other semantic pointers
	Connections to the world by sensory and motor interactions
	Capable of being decompressed into sensory-motor components
	Used in communication
Explanations	Explains: How neural groups can perform cognition, emotion, behavior, communication, social interaction
	Explained by: neural mechanisms that include firing, excitation, and inhibition of neurons; tuning of neurons to environments; and binding by convolution

accomplish its many functions, even though there is currently no way to determine experimentally if brains really operate with semantic pointers.

Semantic pointers can be treated mathematically as vectors, and convolution is a well-defined mathematical operation. But my exposition in this book is nontechnical, so I need to resort to analogies. A semantic pointer is like a musical performance that combines the patterns of various instruments and singers, but combination by convolution is not just synchronization, because it produces a process that can be combined further with other processes. Convolution is something like braiding that combines strands of hair into a braid that can be arranged with other braids. For a more exact description, see *Brain–Mind*, chapter 2.

After simpler patterns of neural firing are bound into semantic pointers, they can be used to perform all the inferential functions of images, concepts, beliefs, rules, analogies, and emotions. Even consciousness can be understood as the result of neural mechanisms that include competition among semantic pointers. At any moment, your billions of neurons may be supporting the formation, activation, and processing of large numbers of semantic pointers, but consciousness is limited to only a small number of experiences carried by representations that outcompete other active ones. Semantic pointers also compete in categorization, for example in trying to determine whether something is an apple or a pear.

In sum, the neural mechanisms that are most important for understanding how brains make minds are the following. A neuron fires as a result of input from other neurons and then sends an output to all of the neurons to which it is connected. A group of thousands or millions of connected neurons can fire in a pattern that represents features of the world. With enough neurons, brains bind features into more complex patterns of firing that represent whole objects such as an apple. Moreover, binding can combine perceptual features from multiple senses, along with verbal and emotional information. The result is a powerful kind of neural representation called a semantic pointer, which integrates sensory, motor, verbal, and emotional components. Semantic pointers retain their ties to sensory inputs but can also support symbolic inferences and all the operations needed for complex thinking with images, concepts, beliefs, rules, analogies, and emotions. Semantic pointers can be combined into more complicated semantic pointers through recursive binding—bindings of bindings of bindings.

IMAGES

Consider the differences between sensations, perceptions, and images. Sensation is stimulation of bodily receptors and can occur in worms with only a few hundred neurons that sense light, tastes, and sounds. With more neurons to process sensory and motor information, animals such as chickens can bind sensations into richer perceptions of entire objects. Perception operates across many modalities, including both the external senses of sight, sound, touch, smell, and taste and the internal senses of pain, fullness, balance, and nausea.

Imagery is still more powerful, enabling the minds of humans to modify perceptions to produce novel experiences. For example, you can imagine a banana that is a particularly bright shade of yellow, that tastes a bit like a strawberry, and that has skin as scratchy as sandpaper. Moreover, you can imagine a complex scene in which a large banana with a working mouth starts to sing your national anthem. Even if you like bananas, you can imagine having an allergic reaction to eating one that replaces your liking with disgust.

Sensations are easy to explain as brain processes. The external world stimulates your receptors, such as the retinal cells in your eyes and the molecule detectors in your nose. These receptors send signals to your brain and activate groups of neurons which identify simple features. Perception is more complicated because it requires additional neural processing to bind features into objects, with many brain areas jointly responsible for vision. Perception requires binding, so that a banana is perceived simultaneously as yellow and long.

How the brain operates with imagery is much more difficult to explain, requiring the representational and procedural power of semantic pointers. Imagery needs the ability to bind and transform perceptions resulting from all external and internal senses, for example when you imagine your injured big toe as swollen, painful, and smelly. All kinds of imagery are susceptible to these transformations: focusing, intensification, combination, juxtaposition, and decomposition.

Focusing occurs when the mind concentrates on one part of a perception, for example when you are looking at a picture of a house and zoom in on the front door. Focusing also works for auditory images, for example when you notice and listen to the sound of a guitar in a piece of music. Intensification happens when you take an aspect of a perception and make it stronger, for example making the color or the smell of banana more vivid in your imagination.

A more creatively powerful transformation of images involves combination of ones not usually observed together, for example when you imagine a purple banana curved into a C shape. Multisensory combination results from imagining the purple banana with a putrid taste and slimy texture. Juxtaposition requires combining multiple objects in time and space, for example when you picture your mother eating a banana while stomping her feet. Finally, decomposition occurs when you take an image apart, for example when you try to separate out the purple from the purple banana or the sound of stomping from the image of your mother's moving feet.

These transformations result from brain mechanisms where the parts are the images that interact with each other and the interactions are carried out by semantic pointers. First, semantic pointers explain how an image such as your mother stomping while eating a smelly banana can be produced by repeated bindings of sensory representations in different modalities. Second, semantic pointers can explain how images are transformed, because they are unified representations that can be modified in the requisite ways. Intensification such as making the yellow brighter is just a matter of changing the firing patterns of the neurons that represent the yellow. Combination results from the same kind of binding that builds semantic pointers in the first place, for example binding purple and banana into purple banana. Juxtaposition is a more complicated kind of combination, taking into account spatial and temporal information that can also be represented by firing patterns in neural groups.

Decomposition is easy with semantic pointers because they have the capacity to unbind and decompress the information that was bound into them. Decomposing a complex semantic pointer can produce other semantic pointers, for example when *banana* breaks down into components such as *peel*. But simpler semantic pointers decompose into sensory-motor aspects such as the color yellow. Focusing results from decomposing an image and allowing one of the semantic pointers that went into it to become dominant as a result of semantic pointer competition.

Later chapters show that several kinds of mental imagery are important for understanding the social interactions that underlie social change. Political ideologies, for example, thrive on images such as flags, salutes, and national anthems. Religious rituals employ visual images such as crosses and crescents, auditory images such as chants and hymns, and olfactory images such as incense. Hence images will be important in social cognitive-emotional workups. All the different kinds of imagery that contribute to social change result from mental transformations that can be understood as neural operations on semantic pointers.

CONCEPTS

Social changes always require conceptual change. For example, gender issues such as same-sex marriage require adjustments in many important concepts such as *husband, wife,* and *marriage* to allow a marriage to have two husbands or two wives. To understand how concepts affect the ways that people interact with each other, we need to see them as more than just words on paper: they need to be processes operating in people's minds and shaping their decisions. Nor can concepts be taken as abstract, supernatural entities remote from human action. So it is best to think of concepts as an important kind of mental representation, but how do they work?

Decades of psychological experiments suggest that we should not expect to define concepts precisely in terms of their necessary and sufficient conditions. Instead, concepts are best characterized in terms of exemplars (standard examples), typical features, and explanatory roles. These can shift over time, as for marriage which in Canada and a few other countries now encompasses unions between people of the same sex. Such changes are accompanied by changes in standard examples, for example adding the singer Elton John and his husband onto the list.

Changes in typical features also occur, away from listing a husband and a wife toward allowing other combinations. The revised concept of marriage allows expanded explanations, for example of why two men or two women are living together. These three aspects of concepts—exemplars, typical features, and explanations—can all be accommodated by a neural theory of concepts that views them as semantic pointers. The same neural representations can function as sets of exemplars, typical features, and explanations.

The resulting concepts can be both embodied and transbodied (going beyond the body), because concepts get their meanings both from sensory-motor bindings and from connections with other concepts. Embodiment results from concepts that bind sensory and motor information retrievable when semantic pointers are decompressed. For example, the concept *man* operating in people's brains may be associated with examples such as Brad Pitt and typical features such as what a man looks, sounds, and possibly smells like.

But there is more to concepts than embodiment, because human concepts can be combined to produce more complicated concepts that go well beyond the senses. For example, marriage is not just a sensory concept but also a social one requiring abstract associations such as legal contracts. If concepts were only formed from sensory experience, it would be a mystery how humans developed concepts like marriage, atom, electron, chemical bond, gene, and virus. Concepts can be transbodied because conceptual combination produces representations far removed from what the body experiences. Contrast the difference between the concept *man*, which is strongly associated with sensory processes, and the concept *husband*, which also depends on abstract social and legal relations.

The semantic pointer theory of concepts easily handles both embodiment and transbodiment of concepts. It accommodates embodiment because the neural representations that get bound into semantic pointers include ones based on sensory and motor inputs. It handles transbodiment because semantic pointers can also be formed by binding together other semantic pointers to produce concepts that do not have direct associations with sensory motor inputs. Transbodied concepts may have indirect associations via the semantic pointers that get bound into them. For example, an atom is an invisible particle, so the concept *atom* has to be formed by conceptual combination of *invisible* and *particle* rather than from observations of atoms. Hence the concept of an atom gets its meaning as much from association with other concepts as from sensory-motor input about tiny objects. Today, quantum microscopes generate images of atoms that are unlike what ordinary senses could provide to early atomic theorists.

The most important procedure associated with concepts is categorization, for example deciding whether a person is a man or woman, or figuring out whether someone's relationship is a marriage or just casual. Categorization is a kind of semantic pointer competition, in which different concepts are applied to a situation depending on how well they fit. For example, an ambiguous person can be categorized by the brain's determining whether your perceptions of the person fit better with your concept of man or with your concept of woman, with all their sensory, verbal, and emotional connections.

A major task in performing a social cognitive-emotional workup is to identify the concepts central to the thinking of the relevant individuals. Because we cannot directly observe the minds of those individuals, the first clue to their concepts is to look for spoken and written words. Prevalent words are an indication of what concepts operate in the minds of humans to determine their inferences and actions. But investigation must go beyond words to grasp what the concepts are doing via exemplars, features, and explanations. That people use the same words does not imply that they are working with the same concepts, because people's mental representations can differ because of their connections with other mental representations. For example, someone working with the old concept of husband would simply deny that Elton John has a husband, which only makes sense in the new conceptual scheme of same-sex marriage.

Values and attitudes result from binding of concepts and emotions, for example when someone likes apples and dislikes grapefruits. Values are not just verbal behaviors, social constructions, or abstract entities, but rather brain processes that combine a representation of something with an emotional assessment. Like images, concepts often have specific emotions associated with them and are bound into the relevant semantic pointer. For example, depending on your history, you may have emotions associated with concepts like *husband, wife, man, woman*, and *marriage*, ranging from excitement to disgust. These emotional bindings can have major effects on decisions that you make, such as whether to pursue relationships and get married. *Natural Philosophy* (chapter 6) provides a more extensive discussion of values.

In sum, concepts are not words defined by necessary and sufficient conditions. Rather, they are multisensory mental representations resulting from brain mechanisms of neural firing and binding into semantic pointers, which can encompass exemplars, typical features, explanations, and emotions. Concepts play indispensable roles in categorization and belief formation.

BELIEFS

The belief that Elton John is married requires a mental representation of Elton John, which could be a combination of images such as what he looks and sounds like plus verbal information such that he is a singer and British. But the belief also requires the concept of marriage, which is not just a matter of imagery because of its abstract social and legal aspects. Beliefs are semantic pointers resulting from binding of other mental representations that can also be semantic pointers, for example when the neural representation that Elton John is married results from binding of the representation of the singer with the concept *married*.

People have thousands of concepts and beliefs, so it is difficult to include all of them in a comprehensible cognitive-emotional workup. Instead, we need to figure out which concepts and which beliefs play the most important role in the inferences, decisions, and actions that people employ in interaction with each other. Importance will often be a matter of emotions, which can bind with concepts or beliefs. Attitudes can apply to a concept, for example *marriage*, or to a belief, for example concerning the fact that same-sex marriage is now legal in the United States. Just as representations of concepts and objects can be bound into beliefs, representations of beliefs and emotions can be bound into attitudes about states of affairs.

RULES

Rules are an important kind of belief with an *if–then* structure, for example *if something is a banana then it has a peel*. Rules have been important in cognitive theory since the 1960s, because they can be used to explain important phenomena such as problem solving and language use. A rule in this sense is much broader than familiar moral and social rules, such as *if you bump into someone then apologize*. Rules can also include broadly descriptive statements such as *if a person is a woman then she has two X chromosomes*. Rules do not have to be universally true to be useful, as long as they capture some typical features, statistical regularity, or causal relation.

Like all beliefs, rules are semantic pointers built out of concepts. Rules can be nonverbal, because the *if* part and the *then* part can be images rather than words. For example, the nonverbal counterpart of the verbal rule about bumping into someone can have an *if* part that includes the perception of bumping and a *then* part of moving your lips and larynx to produce the sound "I'm sorry." Because nonverbal rules need not have an explicit "if" and "then," they are better expressed by the form <*condition*> → <*action*>, where <*condition*> is a semantic pointer to be matched against the current situation and <*action*> is another semantic pointer that can include motor, sensory, and emotional representations. For example, <*bump*> → <*say sorry*> and <*bump*> → <*angry*> are nonverbal rules about what happens when you get bumped. Many activities such as marching, kissing, making music, and playing sports require application of nonverbal rules. Chapter 4 will describe how social interactions in romantic relationships are also strongly influenced by rules that are unconscious because they are multimodal, using sensory and emotional representations as well as verbal ones. Multimodal rules are also important for explaining animal behavior and rituals in politics and religion. *Natural Philosophy* (chapter 3) applies multimodal rules to explaining procedural knowledge of how to do things.

The most important mental procedures for rules are forward and backward inference. Forward inference uses a chain of *if–then* rules to make a series of conclusions. For example, you may start with the recognition that you bumped into someone and make inferences using rules like:

> If you bump into someone, then you apologize.
> If you apologize, then the recipient is not mad at you.

Applying these rules in sequence produces the conclusion that the person you bumped into will not be mad at you. If the rules are nonverbal with no explicit *if–then*, then forward inference is just matching the <condition> and then executing the <action>. Sequences of such executions can be used to simulate behaviors without explicit verbal inference.

The procedure of backward inference works by having a goal to be achieved and using rules to work backwards to produce a whole sequence of actions that will achieve it. For example, if I have the goal to go to Toronto and a whole sequence of rules about the steps required to get from Waterloo to Toronto, then I can work the rules backwards to figure out that I need to start by getting to the bus depot.

Because rules contribute mightily to the inferences that people make and the actions that they take, identifying rules in the minds of individuals is an important part of a social cognitive-emotional workup. Often the rules can be recognized by verbal expressions in speech or writing, for example when people make general utterances such as "Canadians are polite," which translates into the rule *if someone is Canadian then he or she is polite*. It is much more difficult to identify nonverbal rules, of which people may not even be aware. For example, you probably do not think of whether you brush your teeth by applying water to your toothbrush before or after you put on toothpaste. The existence of nonverbal, unconscious rules can be inferred from people's behavior on the grounds that they provide the best explanation of what they do.

Rules can be acquired in several ways. Some rules are plausibly innate, such as nonverbal ones that enable newborn infants to drink milk and attend to faces. Other rules are learned by instruction, for example the rule of etiquette *if you sneeze then cover your face with your arm*. Most rules are learned by generalizing observations, for example that grass is green. Finally, some rules result from explanatory inference as part of scientific investigation, for example Newton's laws of motion. To understand social change by means of a social cognitive-emotional workup, it is important to recognize the format, origin, and alterability of rules.

Explaining social change also requires appreciation of the emotional associations of rules. Some rules are of little emotional importance, for example that coal is black. But other rules acquire substantial emotional significance to people, particularly moral rules such as the ancient one that marriage should be between a man and a woman. In *if–then* form, this amounts to *if two people get married, then one should be a man and the other a woman*. A major part of social cognitive-emotional workups is identifying important rules, including the emotional aspects of the *if* part, the *then* part, and the entire rule.

ANALOGIES

Much of the thinking of individuals can be explained by specifying their images, concepts, beliefs, and rules, all understood as semantic pointers. But another kind of mental representation that is more complicated can also contribute to social interactions. In political and social debates, people often use analogies, which are systematic comparisons between one situation and another. For example, economists often compare the economic crisis of 2008 to the great crash of 1929. Politicians unsure of how to deal with rising political forces such as the Islamic State fall back on analogies to previous problems such as al-Qaeda and Nazi Germany. Arguments about social norms often invoke analogies, for example when opponents of same-sex marriage pronounce that it is tantamount to bestiality.

Analogies are not always explicit, for they may be submerged in metaphorical utterances such as the claim that the economy is a pie that needs to be divided. A social cognitive-emotional workup must be sensitive to metaphorical uses of language, for example the difference between a wife calling her husband a prince rather than a pig, neither of which is literally true.

Analogies are not just verbal, for they can incorporate sensory, motor, and emotional information. For example, diagrams or mental images can underlie the teaching analogy that the atom is like the solar system because electrons going around the atom's nucleus correspond to planets revolving around the sun. Hence analogies can be mappings between sets of images, not just between groups of sentences. Semantic pointer representations have the range to cover all kinds of images and therefore the full range of multimodal analogies. For example, analogies between some troublesome politician and Adolf Hitler can invoke the scary face of Hitler, his manic voice, and all the negative emotions associated with the disasters caused by his actions.

The major procedures associated with analogies are retrieval of relevant analogs from memory, mapping between a potentially useful source analog and a target problem to be solved, and transfer of information from the source to the target. A social cognitive-emotional workup needs to recognize the analogy's purpose, which can include problem solving, decision making, argumentation, and entertainment. The workup should include recognition of explicit analogies marked by verbal comparisons using words such as "like" and "just as." But the workup should also be alert to the use of important metaphors that may not be explicitly flagged as analogies. For example, application of the word "crash" for two economic downturns is a metaphor that assumes an analogy between what happens to the economy and what happens in the crash of vehicles or other objects.

The social cognitive-emotional workup should also notice the emotional role of analogies. Some social analogies are used to transfer positive emotions and others to transfer negative emotions. For example, comparing a situation to Nazi Germany or the American debacle in Vietnam is usually used to transfer negative emotions. In contrast, previous successes such as triumphant wars and fertile economic policies have positive emotions associated with them that can be transferred to encourage the implementation of similar policies.

EMOTIONS

Many people still think that emotions are merely a sideshow to thinking, an impediment to rational cognition. But there is abundant evidence from psychology and neuroscience that emotions make fundamental contributions to all kinds of thought, from perception to creativity. Emotions serve to evaluate current situations, enabling people to constantly appraise the relevance of what is happening to their overall goals. This evaluation enables people to decide how to act in ways that accomplish their goals, for example spending time with people they care about. The emotional evaluations also help people to focus their attention on what matters to them, selecting what aspects of perception and reflection are worth thinking about. The contributions of emotions to evaluation, action, and attention are fundamental to human thought, not peripheral.

These psychological functions are accomplished because the brain has no sharp division between emotion areas and cognitive areas. The old idea that there is a high-level, human, cognitive brain developed on top of a primitive, reptilian, emotional brain has been demolished by neural investigations. These investigations show that allegedly primitive parts of the brain such as the amygdala are intensely interconnected with all of the most high-level areas of the brain such as the prefrontal cortex. The brain is wired to be an emotional engine as well as a cognitive one.

Psychologists, neuroscientists, and philosophers continue to argue about competing theories of emotion. The cognitive appraisal theory says that emotions are judgments about the relevance of the current situation to goals. For example, if you win a lottery, then you are happy because the winnings can help satisfy your goals of having enough money to support yourself and your family. Alternatively, the physiological perception theory says that emotions are reactions to bodily changes such as heart rate, breathing rate, and hormone levels. Then being happy that you won the lottery is the perception of the changes in your body prompted by hearing the good news. A third theory of emotions is that they are just social constructions, a reaction to situations based on social experiences, expectations, and language patterns.

Semantic pointers show how these three theories of emotion can be viewed as complementary rather than competing. Cognitive appraisals, physiological perceptions, and social interpretations are all patterns of neural firing, which semantic pointers can bind into a complex interpretation of the current situation. Emotional semantic pointers are patterns of neural firing that integrate appraisals, based in part on social and linguistic information, with physiological perceptions. For example, your happiness about winning the lottery is a parallel process operating in numerous brain areas that produces patterns of firing representing winning, appraisal, and physiology.

This unified perspective on emotion has large consequences for individual cognition and also for social interactions based on communication. Communication is a matter not only of transmission of verbal signals but also of emotional evaluations encapsulated in attitudes and value judgments. Emotional communication is important for romantic relationships, overcoming prejudice, and many other social processes.

Therefore, a social cognitive-emotional workup has to consider the emotional component of all of the mental representations discussed so far, including images, concepts, beliefs, rules, and analogies. Emotion is not just an add-on to cognition but central to it. All cognitions are emotional, and all emotion has a cognitive aspect reflected in the appraisal that gets bound into the overall result. Whenever a workup identifies the mental representations that are relevant to understanding the minds of individuals in a social interaction, it should indicate their emotional significance.

The physiological component of emotion indicates another way in which cognition is embodied besides the sensory-motor aspects that get bound into concepts and images. People's emotional states depend in part on what is going on in their hearts, lungs, skin, and stomachs, and also on levels of hormones such as cortisol and neurotransmitters such as dopamine. However, emotion is also transbodied because of the role of abstract representations, for example when someone is happy that the United States legalized same-sex marriage. Appraisal can similarly take into account abstract goals such as equality, as well as linguistic associations that encapsulate social history. As they did for imagery and concepts, semantic pointers show how emotions are both embodied and transbodied.

In sum, emotion is crucial to cognition in individuals and also to interactions among individuals in social mechanisms such as communication. All of the social examples to come, from close relationships to religious rituals, have a large emotional component operating both at the level of individual minds and also in their interactions and social practices. Emotions combine with concepts and beliefs to constitute values, which form systems that can be depicted in maps.

MAPPING VALUES

Minimally, emotional significance is captured by two dimensions: valence and intensity. The valence of an emotion is whether it is positive or negative, with good or bad feelings. Positive emotions include happiness, pride, and gratitude, in contrast to negative emotions that include sadness, fear, anger, and shame. Positive and negative emotions come in varying intensities, from the mild happiness of contentment to the extreme joy of elation. Intensity goes with arousal, which spurs people to act. The emotions attached to mental representations do not occur in isolation from each other but depend on emotionally coherent systems of concepts.

Systems of emotional values can be conveniently displayed using a diagramming technique that produces a value map, also called a cognitive-affective map. This technique employs the following conventions:

1. Ovals represent emotionally positive (pleasurable) elements.
2. Hexagons represent emotionally negative (painful) elements.
3. Rectangles represent elements that are neutral or carry both positive and negative aspects.

4. The thickness of the lines in the shape represents the relative intensity of the positive or negative value associated with it.

5. Solid lines represent the relations between elements that are mutually supportive.

6. Dashed lines represent the relations between elements that are incompatible with each other.

7. The thickness of the lines in the connection represents the strength of the positive or negative relation.

When color is available, value maps conventionally represent positive elements by green ovals (go), negative ones by red hexagons (stop), and neutral ones by yellow or black rectangles. Figure 2.2 schematizes this kind of representation.

A value map can be drawn by following these steps:

1. Identify the main concepts, beliefs, goals, and emotions of the person being modeled.

2. Identify these elements as emotionally positive or negative and accordingly represent them by ovals or hexagons.

3. Identify relations between elements that are either complementary (solid lines) or conflicting (dashed lines).

4. Show the resulting map to other people to see if it captures their understandings of the person and situation.

Figures 2.3 and 2.4 are value maps of opposing views concerning whether people should be vegetarians. Figure 2.3 is my reconstruction of the system of values that lead some people to avoid eating meat, and Figure 2.4 shows the more conventional view that eating meat is fine. These examples illustrate how value maps can serve to (a) display sets of values, (b) show the interconnections within sets of

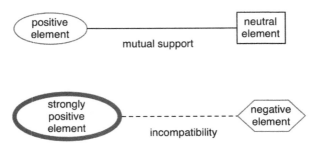

FIGURE 2.2 Schema for a value map. Ovals are positive values, hexagons are negative values, rectangles are neutral, solid lines are support links, and dotted lines are incompatibility links. Reprinted from Thagard 2015b by permission of the Philosophy Documentation Center.

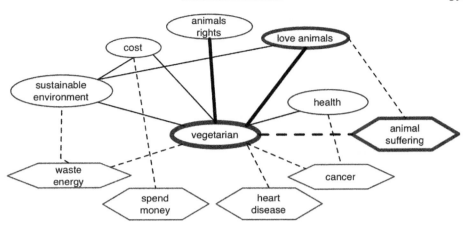

FIGURE 2.3 Value map of some vegetarians. Adapted from Thagard 2015b by permission of the Philosophy Documentation Center.

values, and (c) display the similarities and differences between different systems of values. The positive values (ovals) that support being a vegetarian include sustainable environment, cost, health, and animal welfare. In contrast, the positive values opposing being a vegetarian include taste, time, freedom, and nutrients.

Value mapping is a useful tool in social cognitive-emotional workups because it shows interconnected concepts with their associated emotional valence and intensity. But it is far from a full account of emotional cognition, because it does not address the cognitive complexities of concepts, images, beliefs, rules, and analogies. Moreover, it oversimplifies the nature of emotions, because it deals only with intensity and valence. A full workup needs to attend to specific emotions, for example the differences between happiness and pride and between fear and anger. Value maps are used in all of the workups in later chapters but as part of

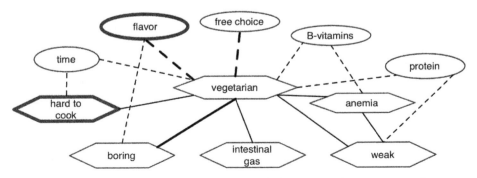

FIGURE 2.4 Value map of some nonvegetarians, in which vegetarian has a negative value. Adapted from Thagard 2015b by permission of the Philosophy Documentation Center.

a much richer discussion of particular mental representations and specific emotions. Equally important are the many inferences that people make based on cognitive and emotional coherence.

INFERENCE AND COHERENCE

Intelligent thinking requires inferences, where people draw new conclusions from old representations. The standard view of inference derives from mathematics and logic, in which theorems are derived from axioms step by step. On this view, inference is the same as reasoning, in which people give verbal arguments to figure out what to believe and what to do.

But much psychological and neuroscientific evidence shows that inference is different from reasoning, which is verbal, serial (step by step), and conscious. In contrast, inference in the brain can be nonverbal using sensory and emotional representations, parallel in considering many kinds of information all at once, and unconscious because we have little access to the simultaneous neural operations of the brain. Chapter 12 discusses the relevance of the inference/reasoning distinction for education.

Most people are familiar with deductive inferences like mathematical calculations and inductive inferences such as generalizations from examples to rules. Even more important is *abductive* inference, when people generate and accept hypotheses because they provide explanations of interesting facts. Abduction is used by physicians when they diagnose diseases, by auto mechanics when they figure out what is wrong with a car, by scientists when they construct and evaluate explanatory theories, and by juries when they reconcile conflicting witnesses to decide whether an accused is guilty. Later chapters will show that it is also used in many kinds of social change.

Abductive inference is parallel rather than serial because hypotheses need to be evaluated with respect to all the relevant evidence and alternative hypotheses. Hypotheses are accepted on the basis of their explanatory coherence, on how well they fit with other beliefs including evidence and alternative explanations. The resulting inference is not the step-by-step process found in deductive proofs but rather operates because the brain operates by parallel constraint satisfaction, for example in the processes of perception and consciousness described in *Brain–Mind*.

The parallel process of evaluating hypotheses can yield critical transitions, when the accumulation of evidence for a new hypothesis results in a dramatic shift toward alternative points of view. Such shifts commonly occur in scientific revolutions when new theories replace old ones, for example when Darwin's theory of evolution by natural selection supplanted the prevailing theory that all species were the result of divine creation. Thomas Kuhn called these transitions "paradigm shifts," by analogy to the gestalt shifts perception of figures like the duck-rabbit discussed in chapter 1. Such revolutions occur both in individuals and in groups of scientists, through interactions between cognition and communication described in chapter 3.

An equally important mental shift occurs in emotional changes such as falling in and out of love, overcoming prejudice, adopting a political ideology, moving from an economic bubble to a crash, and undergoing a religious conversion. Emotional gestalt shifts can be explained by a theory of emotional coherence that has been applied to a wide range of phenomena including decision making and trust. On this view, people's decisions and other judgments arise from a process of balancing different elements based on their emotional values, or valences.

The theory of emotional coherence can be summarized in three principles:

1. Mental representations have positive or negative valences.
2. Representations can have positive or negative emotional connections to other elements.
3. The valence of an element is determined by the valences and acceptability of all the elements to which it is connected.

Decisions often result from emotional coherence when people figure out what to do on the basis of what how different actions fit with their various goals. Value maps are a good way to visually display sets of representations and their connections, before and after changes in emotional coherence.

Goals are like beliefs in representing situations by binding concepts and objects, but they also bind emotions that capture the importance of the goal. For example, my goal to finish this book is represented in my brain by a semantic pointer that binds representations of finishing, myself, this book, and the emotion of wanting this to occur. We will see numerous cases, from romantic developments to marketing decisions, that involve emotional gestalt shifts resulting from critical transitions in networks of emotional coherence.

Coherence processes are naturally modeled by neural networks, including ones using semantic pointers. The brain performs inferences by parallel interactions of billions of neurons that can use semantic pointers to represent beliefs, goals, and actions. Decisions about what to believe and what to do emerge from these interactions in ways that interconnect cognitions and emotions so that inference often depends on emotion much more than reasoning.

EMOTION-DRIVEN INFERENCES

Motivated inference, the tendency to reach conclusions unduly influenced by personal goals, is a well-researched phenomenon in social psychology. For example, a coffee drinker will be inclined to be skeptical about claims that caffeine has negative health effects but will tend to be gullible about claims that it has positive health effects. Motivated inference is more complex than mere wishful thinking, in that people do not simply believe whatever makes them happy. Rather, their goals lead them to be selective about how they acquire and evaluate evidence. Similarly, people are prone to motivated ignorance when they avoid acquiring information that may threaten their goals, for example by refusing to learn about how global warming threatens human well-being.

Emotional coherence easily explains motivated inference: people naturally misinterpret the attractiveness of a conclusion arising from its fit with their goals as attractiveness arising from fit with evidence. For instance, entrepreneurs' confidence that new ventures will make them rich may result more from emotional coherence with their financial goals than with explanatory coherence with available evidence.

Emotional coherence can also explain other kinds of inferential distortions that are driven by negative rather than positive emotions. Motivated inference is desire-driven, in that people believe what they want to on the basis of their goals. Another kind of emotional distortion occurs when evaluation of evidence is affected by fears and anxieties. On the face of it, it seems ridiculous that people should adopt beliefs that both lack evidence and make them unhappy, but many instances of this kind of fear-driven inference occur in a wide range of domains, including personal relationships, health, politics, and economics. A famous literary example is Shakespeare's Othello, who becomes convinced on the basis of scant evidence that his wife Desdemona is unfaithful to him.

Fear-driven inference arises from emotional coherence when attempts to rationalize worries away using motivated inference fail: one can swing from irrational exuberance to irrational despair if the negative feelings that arise from considering worrisome outcomes are misinterpreted as evidence supporting the likelihood of those outcomes. In such cases, one's beliefs cohere with fears for which there is little independent evidence. Othello got caught in a vicious emotional circle in which his fear itself becomes mistaken as evidence that he had something to fear, so that his belief arose from an amplifying feedback loop rather than careful assessment of alternative hypotheses.

A third kind of emotional inference is driven by intense anger or rage. Rage-driven inference occurs when people become so angry at what they perceive as wrongs done to them (or to others whom they care about) that they are impelled to take extreme actions that may not be well suited to accomplish their goals. Radical political movements on both the left and right are often driven by anger arising from perceived wrongs, generating zeal to commit extreme acts such as terrorism, attempted revolution, and intense state repression. Rage-driven inference arises from emotional coherence through a chain of connections: intense anger means that someone has done something bad, and the anger is itself evidence that he or she deserves to be punished. It is misleading to characterize the mental process in such verbal terms, making its illogical character all too evident.

In the minds of political radicals, however, there may be no explicit awareness of the connection between anger and action, so the force of the determination to take extreme measures is concealed. Nevertheless, rage-driven inference can be rational when both the anger and the extreme actions that result from it are fully justified, for example in the American civil rights movement of the 1950s and 1960s that included massive civil disobedience.

Chapter 6 provides further discussion of how motivated, fear-driven, and rage-driven inferences contribute to political ideologies. But they are also important for explaining changes and stability in romantic relationships, prejudice, economic booms and busts, and religion. A common pattern in humans takes place in people when events and new information cause a critical transition from motivated inference to fear-driven inference, producing a swing from irrational exuberance to excessive despair. This transition occurs, for example, when romantic infatuation turns to disappointment and when economic bubbles turn into crashes.

Another common pattern goes in the opposite direction, from fear-driven inference to motivated inference. In social prejudice and religion, people get an exaggerated view of a problem by fear-driven inference and then use motivated inference to leap at a possible solution. For example, Hitler worked to make people afraid of Jews and communists so they would want the Nazis to succeed.

SUMMARY AND DISCUSSION

The hypothesis that minds operate by procedures applied to mental representations is supported by its ability to explain hundreds of psychological phenomena. This hypothesis is fleshed out by identifying specific kinds of mental representations and their associated procedures, including images and their transformations such as juxtaposition, concepts and their combinations such as beliefs, rules and their inferences such as forward chains, and analogies with their functions such as persuasion. All of these representations blend with emotional interpretations that integrate appraisal of significance for goals with perception of physiological changes. Combinations of images, analogies, and rules provide people with mental models that enable them to explain and predict events in complex situations.

Psychological explanations based on representations and procedures can be deepened by showing how they emerge from neural mechanisms. Neurons represent aspects of the world by collective patterns of firing. These patterns can be bound into more complicated patterns that can transcend the limitations of sensory inputs. Semantic pointers are a special kind of representation that operates by binding neural patterns encompassing sensory, motor, verbal, and emotional information.

The justification for emphasizing these psychological and neural mechanisms is their use in accounting for all kinds of human thinking. *Brain–Mind* summarizes some of the relevant evidence, and much more evidence is available in textbooks of cognitive psychology and cognitive neuroscience. The semantic pointer theory applies not only to the ordinary operations of mental representations like concepts and rules but also to the most high-level kinds of human thinking, including language, creativity, and consciousness. Semantic pointers also encompass emotions, construed as bindings that combine cognitive appraisal with physiological perception.

This approach to understanding the mind contrasts with approaches assumed by many social scientists. Rational choice theory, which remains dominant in economics and common in political science, has a simplistic view of mind as calculation of expected utilities. There is now a large array of evidence that people deviate from this kind of reasoning, in ways naturally explained by richer theories of cognitive and emotional processes. For example, the large role of emotions in human decision making provides deeper psychological and neural explanations why people succumb to thinking errors such as wishful thinking and sunk costs. Chapter 7 provides more discussion of economic rationality.

Attention to cognitive and emotional representations and procedures, especially learning, also undermines the narrow explanations offered by evolutionary psychology. These try to derive current behaviors from genetic factors installed in human brains more than 100,000 years ago. Although there may be some innate concepts and rules, the vast majority of mental representations are learned from perceptual and social experience. Psychological and anthropological evidence supports the hypothesis that human brains are more adapted for adaptability than for specific behaviors. Learning mechanisms have enabled people to invent and adopt a wide array of cultural practices, such as tool use, literacy, mathematics, and democracy. Evolutionary psychologists assume an obsolete notion of the brain as organized into discrete modules, which has been refuted by repeated findings that everything interesting done by the brain involves interconnections among multiple brain areas. Hence the explanations of social phenomena found in later chapters allow much more flexibility in cultural learning than is assumed by proponents of evolutionary psychology.

The psychological and neural theories sketched in this brief overview provide a basis for building much richer accounts of social interaction than have been available to social scientists who have ignored what happens in individual minds. The construction of practices such as politics and science requires more than social relationships, because all relationships depend on mental processes by which individual minds perceive and influence each other. Social construction and individual cognition should not be viewed as competing hypotheses to explain social phenomena. Rather, a sophisticated account of the individual and the social can be based on the interconnections of mental and social mechanisms. Chapter 3 begins to show how social mechanisms and mental mechanisms depend on each other, with concrete illustrations in ensuing chapters.

Chapter 1 listed general questions to be answered for a social cognitive-emotional workup, and the review just conducted generates a much more specific set of questions about cognitive and emotional processes in individuals:

1. What are the most important visual, auditory, and other images and what is their emotional impact?
2. What are the most important concepts, values, beliefs, and rules and what is their emotional impact?
3. What are the most important analogies and metaphors and what is their emotional impact?
4. What are the most important specific emotions?
5. What patterns of inference lead to new representations based on explanatory and emotional coherence?

Answering these questions will provide understanding of the minds of individuals in social contexts and will set the stage for showing how individuals interact with each other to change each other's minds. Chapters to come answer these questions for romantic couples, bigots, politicians, investors, missionaries, diplomats, depressives, jurors, teachers, designers, leaders, and marketers.

NOTES

I take mental mechanisms to include all the cognitive and emotional mechanisms needed to explain human thought and behavior.

For an introduction to cognitive neuroscience, see Banitch and Compton 2011. On the number of neurons in brains of humans and other animals, see http://www.suzanaherculanohouzel.com/lab. Pessoa 2013 provides abundant evidence for neural integration of cognition and emotion.

On semantic pointers, see the references in the notes for chapter 1. Unlike most neural network models in which representations can only be constructed by learning, semantic pointers can be constructed by combining other semantic pointers. Hence they can explain transbodiment as well as embodiment. *Brain–Mind* (chapter 2) provides comparisons of semantic pointers with other theories of mental representation and more references.

Kosslyn, Thompson, and Ganis 2006 review evidence for mental imagery. On concepts see Barsalou 2008; Blouw, Solodkin, Thagard, and Eliasmith 2016; and Murphy 2002. On conceptual change, see chapter 12 and Thagard 1992b, 2012b, 2014b, and *Natural Philosophy*, chapter 3.

Anderson 2007 has a rule-based view of the mind and brain.

For analogy, consult Gentner, Holyoak, and Kokinov 2001, Holyoak and Thagard 1995, and Holyoak 2012.

On emotions, see Kentner, Oatley, and Jenkins 2013 and Barrett and Russell 2015. The semantic pointer theory of emotions is sketched in Thagard and Schröder 2014 and developed in Kajić, Schröder, Stewart, and Thagard (forthcoming). Osgood, May, and Miron 1975 describe social dimensions of emotion that operate across cultures.

For numerous publications on value maps (cognitive-affective maps), see http://cogsci.uwaterloo.ca/empathica.html.

Abductive inference is discussed by Magnani 2009 and Thagard 2012b. Explanatory coherence is fully analyzed in Thagard 1989, 1992b, 2000. Kuhn 1970 discusses paradigm shifts, but Thagard 1992b provides a more historically and psychologically accurate account of scientific revolutions.

On emotional coherence, see Thagard 2000, 2003, 2006. Experimental evidence for it is in Simon, Stenstrom, and Read 2015. Cognitive dissonance is also explained by parallel constraint satisfaction: Shultz and Lepper 1996.

Evidence for motivated inference is provided by Kunda 1990, 1999; Bastardi, Uhlmann, and Ross 2011; and Redlawsk, Civettini, and Emmerson 2010. Motivated inference can lead to other psychological phenomena such as positive illusions and optimism bias. Fear-driven inference is analyzed by Thagard and Nussbaum

2014; Elster 2015 calls it "countermotivated" inference. The phenomenon has been recognized by various thinkers back to Jean de la Fontaine. On motivated ignorance, see https://www.psychologytoday.com/blog/hot-thought/201301/motivated-ignorance.

For limitations of evolutionary psychology and the importance of adaptability, cognitive flexibility, and cultural learning, see Quartz and Sejnowski 2002, Richardson 2007, and Henrich 2016. For arguments that memes are weak explanations of cultural development, see chapter 7 and *Natural Philosophy*, chapter 3.

PROJECT

Do value maps for yourself and another person with whom you are having a disagreement. Do psychological experiments to determine if fear-driven inference operates in human minds.

3

Social Mechanisms

The social sciences—economics, politics, sociology, anthropology, and history—should aim to explain both social stability and social change. For example, why have most countries in western Europe and North America maintained parliamentary governments and capitalist economies over the past century? But why have they also undergone dramatic changes in gender roles such as women working outside the home? Social mechanisms that describe the interactions of individuals should be able to explain why societies sometimes change and why they sometimes remain the same.

Understanding individuals is a crucial part of such explanations, but there is much more to explaining social change and stability than just summing up their thoughts and behaviors. How people think and act is dependent on their interactions with other people and on how the other people think and act. We therefore cannot derive explanations of social stability and change simply from the cognitive and emotional mechanisms summarized in the last chapter. Rather we need to construct an integrated account that merges those neural mechanisms with ones that are intensely social in that they take into account the interactions of people and the operations of groups and institutions. Group change and individual change work together.

This chapter develops a comprehensive account of social mechanisms, incorporating into interpersonal interactions the mental mechanisms based on semantic pointers. Chapter 2 summarized how semantic pointers can explain mental processes ranging from perception to consciousness, a claim defended at much greater length in *Brain–Mind*. To put it in a slogan: mind equals brain with semantic pointers. We can then ask the question: society equals minds plus what? The answer I propose is novel: society equals minds with semantic pointer communication.

Communication is often described as a process in which a sender sends a message to a receiver, with the message assumed to consist of words. But many communications are nonverbal, carried by facial expressions, gestures, body language, and group activities such as singing and marching. We therefore need a much broader view of messaging that goes beyond language. Semantic pointers are rich patterns of neural firing that can capture all of the different kinds of nonverbal and verbal communication, from visual representations such as pictures and diagrams to emotional representations such as enthusiasm and disgust.

I am not suggesting that semantic pointers are the messages communicated. Rather, the sender has neural representations in the form of semantic pointers such as beliefs and attitudes, and sends a message to establish in the receiver's brain a complex of similar semantic pointers. The net result is approximate transfer of one or more semantic pointers from one brain to another by means of verbal or nonverbal messages. The main function of this chapter is to show how communication builds on neural mechanisms in individuals.

This account of communication as the elicitation of semantic pointers provides a new theory of social mechanisms, in which the fundamental change that results from interaction of individuals is the establishment of mental representations in the recipients. The standard terms "transmit" and "transfer" are misleading here, because the neural representation does not actually move from one brain to another in the way that a sentence can go by email from one computer to another. Semantic pointers are communicated in the sense that there is a causal process that approximately reproduces them through the sending of messages that are not themselves semantic pointers. Rather, verbal and nonverbal communication send messages using words, pictures, and other modes that have the effect of generating in the receiver's brain semantic pointers similar to ones in the sender. This generation often requires instillation of whole systems of concepts, images, beliefs, and actions that depend on and help build a common culture.

However, this view of communication as transmission is still too simple, because communication sometimes has broader functions than semantic pointer transmission. Sometimes people use communication to influence the minds of people to acquire representations different from ones that the sender has, for example with lies, deception, and propaganda. Then communication instills in the brains of receivers semantic pointers that the sender merely wants them to have.

The two main ways of doing this are prompting, where the deceptive message activates representations that the receiver already has, such as dormant prejudices, and instigation, where the receiver obtains a novel belief or attitude. For example, a powerful sender may use threats to instill fear in a receiver. Hence communication may elicit semantic pointers rather than transmitting them.

Many social scientists have invoked the idea of social mechanisms in their explanations of social change and stability, but they have been vague about what mechanisms are. For example, Jon Elster has used mechanisms to discuss important social phenomena, but he characterizes them broadly as "frequently occurring and easily recognizable causal patterns that are triggered under generally unknown conditions or with indeterminate consequences". What are such causal patterns and how do they have consequences?

Chapter 1 presented a much more specific analysis of mechanisms in terms of parts, wholes, connections, interactions, regular changes, and emergence. Chapter 2 applied this schema to mental mechanisms, describing how the causal patterns of thinking are produced by interactions among neural representations and processes. Similarly, a rigorous theory of social mechanisms needs to spell out the constituents and causal patterns of social interaction.

This chapter develops an account of social mechanisms that works across the social sciences, including sociology, politics, economics, anthropology, and history. It also applies to the professions (medicine, law, education, engineering, business), all of which are inherently social. For example, medical doctors interact with patients and work with other doctors and nurses in clinics or hospitals. A country's legal system depends on interactions of lawyers and juries in courts and trials. I provide a three-analysis of social mechanisms broad enough to apply to all the social sciences and professions.

Social mechanisms are interdependent with molecular, neural, and mental ones. Many social scientists such as economists ignore psychology altogether, preferring abstract logical ideas such as utility maximization and game theory. Other fields such as sociology rely on folk psychological theories based on beliefs, desires, and intentions. My aim is to show that a much richer account of social interaction results from understanding how mental representations operate as semantic pointers.

A multilevel account of social mechanisms should explain change and stability by showing how they result from communication but should also provide guidance about how to transform society in ways that meet the needs of its members. The main normative questions, about how society ought to be rather than how it is, are pursued in *Natural Philosophy* (chapter 7). But this book provides glimpses of how to use knowledge about cognitive, emotional, and social mechanisms to suggest how society can and should be changed. For example, chapter 5 has advice about overcoming social prejudice and discrimination.

WHAT ARE SOCIAL MECHANISMS?

Little is gained by defining a social mechanism as a system of interconnected people whose communicative interactions produce emergent changes. It is much more informative to present a three-analysis (Table 3.1) that identifies standard examples, typical features, and explanatory roles, including what social mechanisms causally explain and what explains them.

The social sciences and professions provide many rich examples of social mechanisms. Social psychology studies couples, families, and friendships. Sociology investigates nations and ethnicities. Politics concerns countries, governments, parties, and international organizations such as the United Nations. Economics and business consider companies and markets. Anthropologists learn about clans and tribes. It may not be customary to describe these groups as mechanisms, but all have parts, interactions, and somewhat predictable changes.

These examples exhibit the typical features of social mechanisms, not to be confused with sufficient and necessary conditions that apply to all and only the examples. For each social mechanism, we can attempt to identify its parts, wholes, structural connections, communicative interactions, and regular changes. The most prominent parts of social mechanisms are people, but there are sometimes other kinds of part as well. Nonhuman animals can also be parts of social interactions, for example the pets that are important to many families and the animals that are

TABLE 3.1

Three-Analysis of *Social Mechanism*

Exemplars	Families, clubs, political parties, markets, schools, international organizations, religions, hospitals, courts, schools, companies, clans, tribes
Typical features	People as parts, groups as wholes, groups as parts of larger groups, connections among people and groups, interactions through verbal and nonverbal communication, purpose or function, changes in individuals and groups
Explanations	Explains: changes in people and groups
	Explained by: human needs such as food and relationships

central to the operation of some farms. Moreover, technology has played an increasingly important role in human interactions over the past century, with inventions such as the telephone, television, computer, and Internet making possible kinds of interactions among people that previously were much more slow and sparse.

A disorganized set of people such as a crowd at a park is not a mechanism unless there is a group that constitutes a whole. In the simplest social mechanism, groups are formed out of people, but groups can also be formed out of other groups. For example, the United Nations organization is a group of countries, many of which are groups of provinces or states. An institution is a group subject to rules about how its members should behave; chapter 5 discusses the cognitive-emotional operation of rules construed both as social norms and mental representations.

Organizing parts into a whole is accomplished by structural connections. In the simplest case, these are paired emotional bonds, for example the love between romantic partners and the affection among friends. Some connections between people result from conceptual representations. You may think of yourself as a member of an ethnic group, nation, country, profession, or club. These thoughts are usually emotional but merely ascribing the collective concept to yourself is a big part of being a member of that group. Thinking of yourself positively as a Canadian will provide a bond with other Canadians.

Additional mental representations can also help to establish the structural interconnections between individuals. For example, you might have a mental picture of your family that reinforces your idea of being a part of it. Rules can also be part of the connection that a person has with others, for example if you subscribe to the rule that good spouses are sexually faithful. Some structural connections can be spatial rather than just emotional, for example when people live in the same building.

If people in a building never talk to each other, then they do not form much of a group, because social mechanisms depend on another typical feature: communicative interactions. People can have some interactions with little communication, for example when bumping up against each other in a crowded subway car. But the operation of social mechanisms requires more systematic forms of both verbal and nonverbal communication. Usually communication is approximate transmission of semantic pointers, for example when the sender has a belief and uses a sentence to try to establish that belief in the mind of the receiver in the form of a pattern of neural activity analogous to the pattern in the brain of the sender. For example, if the sender believes that a group such as a marriage, political party, or company is valuable, the point of communication can be to strengthen the group by convincing the receiver to agree that the group serves the needs of its members.

The typical features of a social mechanism also include the social changes that it brings about, including small changes that preserve overall stability. The interactions of people include the formation of groups and their maintenance, actions, and dissolution of groups. Their actions can affect individuals within a group, individuals outside the group, and other groups.

Some actions serve identifiable purposes and functions. For example, good close relationships in couples and families serve to enrich the lives of their members. Economic mechanisms such as markets and companies serve to facilitate financial dealings. Political parties function to further their interests of their members, and governments ideally serve to accomplish the needs of the people whose lives they administer. Some organizations have well-defined purposes, for example the educational role of universities. Institutions have rules meant to ensure that they serve the purposes for which they were formed.

Sometimes, however, the functions of a mechanism can be hard to identify because the organization has ceased to serve its original purpose, like a marriage that has degenerated to the point that it makes both its members miserable. The police force, army, or intelligence service that a government establishes to protect its people may become devices to enchain them. Like a car with a flat tire, mechanisms sometimes break down and fail to accomplish their purposes.

The last crucial aspect of social mechanisms are their explanatory roles—what they explain and what explains them. Identifying mechanisms serves to provide the causes of stability and change. In the social sciences and professions, there is never enough information to be able to specify universal laws that can enable deductions of observed results. But little understanding is provided by merely noticing statistical associations or effects: we want to know why there are statistical associations that are more important than mere correlations.

Mechanisms provide rich causal accounts by describing the interactions of parts that produce changes. A social mechanism is a causal pattern based on the communicative interactions of people with individual mechanisms of cognition and emotion. Without providing a deductive derivation, fitting a mechanistic pattern can be illuminating with respect to relevant changes. For example, a marriage breakdown can be explained by the mental states of the spouses such as their beliefs and emotions, as well as by the communications that the spouses engage in, such as arguing, fighting, insults, and stonewalling.

A complete three-analysis of a concept should not only indicate what the concept helps to explain but also what explains the phenomena described by the concept. What explains the operation of social mechanisms? Why do they exist at all? Some species of animals such as orangutans are largely solitary, only getting

together at infrequent intervals to mate. Mating obviously has a biological explanation, with sex drives genetically inherited to ensure the survival of the species.
Humans are much more social than orangutans, for example, and have formed
groups of at least 50 people for the entire history of the species going back at least
100,000 years. There is abundant psychological evidence that people have social
needs for relating and belonging that encourage them to form groups for purposes
other than sex and procreation. Hence the best explanation available for the existence of social mechanisms is the operation in human beings of sexual, emotional,
and more broadly social needs. As *Brain–Mind* (chapter 12) argues, you cannot be
a self by yourself.

In sum, social mechanisms are not just causal patterns but rather systems of
parts, wholes, connections, interactions, and changes, including emergence of
properties of wholes from interactions of parts. They are not just sets of mathematical equations, although they may use math for efficient descriptions of interactions and changes. The aptness of the three-analysis in Table 3.1 can only be
shown by applying it to many important cases, as is done in chapters 4 through 14.
Before diving into applications, however, we need to explore the nature of social
bonds, communication, and emergence.

STRUCTURAL CONNECTIONS

The structure of a mechanism concerns how the parts are organized and attached,
that is, how they are brought together and held together. For example, in a bicycle,
the wheels, handlebars, and pedals are all connected to the frame. Each of these
parts is itself a whole built out of other parts, for example with the wheel consisting of a rim, tire, and spokes.

The connections of people with each other may originate with physical locations such as buildings and organizations such as companies. But the connections
that hold groups together result from the mental representations that provide
psychological bonds among people, especially emotional ones such as affection in
families and respect in companies. Emotions construed as semantic pointers help
to explain what brings people together into groups, what holds them together in
groups, and what generates various kinds of change and stability. Chapter 4 analyzes love and trust as complex emotions.

Besides emotional bonds, social connections can also be established by institutional arrangements. For example, an employee in a company will usually have a
boss, with a connection established by the rules of the institution that prescribe

who is in charge of whom. Many other social groups are hierarchical, for example the traditional patriarchal family with a husband dominating the wife and children.

New groups can be organized into hierarchies, with some subordinate to others. For example, subsidiary companies are controlled by their corporate owners, and branch campuses are subordinate to their controlling universities. The structure of groups is usually aligned with the hierarchy of individuals, for example when the president of a university dominates the vice president in charge of a branch campus.

Structure in groups is not merely a matter of authority. Because changes in groups depend on communication, what matters most is the network structure of who communicates with whom. Communication networks depend on several factors including contiguity and similarity. People are more likely to communicate with each other if they are physically and geographically close to each other. They are also more likely to communicate if they are similar to and respect each other. A perfectly connected community would be one in which everyone communicates with everyone else, but sparser networks are much more common.

One person can influence the mental state of another only if there is some connection between them. This connection can come by direct contact such as face-to-face speech, writing, or telephoning. The interaction network increases dramatically if one person can communicate with large numbers of people through various media: public speeches; printed word in newspapers, magazines, or books; and electronic vehicles such as blogs, Facebook, YouTube, and Twitter. Hence people can be connected in more complicated ways than machines such as bicycles with simple physical connections between the parts. Sociologists have investigated how human interactions are affected by homophily (the tendency of people to associate with others similar to them) and relational cohesion (the tendency of joint activity to unleash positive emotions that lead to commitments).

SOCIAL INTERACTIONS

The mental operations that form people into groups also provide the basis for the communicative interactions that produce stability and change. Most human interactions involve some kind of communication, the transmission of verbal or non-verbal signals. But there are various kinds of interactions that sometimes occur without communication. To take an extreme example, soldiers shooting at each other in a war are interacting, but there may be no transmission of signals between them. Fighting can involve communication when combatants shout threats at each other, but sometimes the interaction is just physical in the form of blows or other attacks.

Similarly, sex usually involves much communication, but it is also possible to have automatic or forced sex with minimal signaling. Other kinds of human interaction that occasionally occur with little communication include playing, as when two children engage in a physical game without actually talking to or gesturing to each other. Normally, feeding occurs with communication between the caretaker and the person fed, but it can also be a purely physical activity as when a cafeteria worker throws slop on a customer's plate. Pushing, holding, or constraining someone is usually filled with communication but sometimes can be a merely physical act that is not intended to convey information.

Another interaction that can contribute to communication but need not is interagent inference, where one individual thinks about what is going on in the mind of another and uses this information to predict behavior. Such inference occurs in humans and in other advanced species such as apes and crows, for example when people reach conclusions about the emotional states of others. As chapter 2 cautioned, inference is broader than the verbal process of reasoning using arguments, so that inference about other agents can be multimodal, parallel, and unconscious. All inferences concerning other agents by nonhuman animals, and some inferences by humans, operate nonlinguistically.

Figure 3.1 shows a classification of human interactions, including ones that sometimes proceed without communication. Verbal communication requires the utterances of words and sentences, along with their approximate comprehension by others who hear or see them. Nonverbal communication proceeds without words, thanks to additional forms of perception including touch and smell. The results of nonverbal communication can be cognitive representations such as sentences and pictures, but they can also be emotions including attitudes and values.

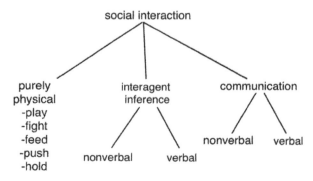

FIGURE 3.1 Kinds of social interaction.

All of these kinds of communication can be understood as the transmission or elicitation of semantic pointers, neural representations that cover sensory modalities as well as verbal ones.

VERBAL COMMUNICATION

Figure 3.2 offers a deeper taxonomy of many kinds of verbal and nonverbal communication. Verbal communication divides naturally into speaking and writing, each of which can be enhanced by using technologies. For example, speaking is enhanced by telephones and by recordings used in televisions and movies. Writing used to be done merely using pen and paper but now can be transmitted electronically by email, text messaging, and social media sites such as Facebook and Twitter. Sign language combines verbal and nonverbal communication through hand gestures, body movements, and facial expressions.

Verbal communication is much more complicated than simply the transfer of a verbal signal into the mind of a hearer or reader. For humans, receiving a message

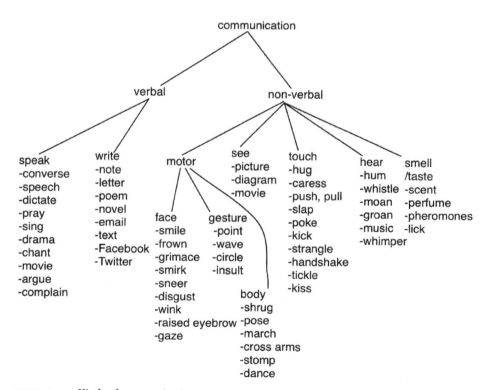

FIGURE 3.2 Kinds of communication.

is not like the automatic storage that occurs with a computer but requires the human to process and understand the message. As *Brain–Mind* (chapter 10) argues, language comprehension requires an integrated grasp of syntax, semantics, and pragmatics to capture the structure, meaning, and purpose of the other's utterance. The typical occasion of an utterance is that the speaker or writer has some mental representation to be conveyed to the recipient. Hence the speaker must translate mental representations into words and sentences, produce them by sounds or writing, and hope that the receiver will then translate the words and sentences into mental representations analogous to the ones that the sender wanted to convey. The mental representations to be conveyed include images, beliefs, and analogies, encoded in both minds by semantic pointers. Hence speaking and writing serve to transfer semantic pointers from one brain to another.

Often, the sender hopes to convey not only factual information but also why the information matters. Words are chosen because of their emotional associations as well as their meanings. For example, compare the different emotional associations in the utterances that Bertrand Russell called irregular verbs: I am firm, you are obstinate, he is a pigheaded fool. Because the semantic pointers in the mind of the sender include bindings with emotions, the sender can choose words so that emotional attitudes are transmitted to the receiver as part of the comprehension process.

Emotional transmission can also occur through more complicated kinds of verbal constructions such as analogies. A recommendation to see a movie because it is as good as *Casablanca* aims for emotional transfer from *Casablanca* to the new movie. The mention of *Casablanca* activates a mental representation of it whose positive emotional associations then get transferred to the mental representation of the new movie. New technologies have introduced additional ways to convey emotions pictorially, for example through emoticons ;) and emojis ☺.

Tone of voice is another way to convey emotions. The same words with a rising or wavering inflection will convey different information than ones uttered with a deep, authoritative tone. The New York philosopher Sidney Morgenbesser responded to the utterance by J. L. Austin that there is no such thing as a double positive by saying with a sneer, "yeah, yeah." Of course, sneers are usually captured not only by tone of voice but also by facial expressions, part of nonverbal communication. Speed and rhythm of speech can also carry emotional significance, for example when a parent says slowly to a child "Go . . . to . . . your . . . room!"

The simplest form of verbal communication from one person to another is given by this schema:

person1's brain → *words* → *perception* → *comprehension* → *person2's brain.*

Additional mental work has to be a done by the recipient if the message is cognitively or emotionally incompatible with what the receiver already believes or feels. In such cases, adoption of the belief or attitude by the recipient will require accommodation or revision to make it fit with existing mental representations. *Natural Philosophy* (chapter 3) explains such revisions by parallel mental mechanisms of explanatory and emotional coherence. Before absorbing the transmitted message, the recipient needs to figure out how to make it coherent with prior beliefs and emotions. Only then has communication been fully successful.

Chapter 1 described how semantic pointers capture the two main dimensions of the meaning of concepts: sensory-motor relations to the world and relations to other concepts. Consideration of communication shows an important third, social dimension to communication. People learn how concepts relate to other concepts primarily by communicating with them, and they sometimes understand how concepts relate to the world by social gestures such as people pointing to interesting parts of the world.

NONVERBAL COMMUNICATION

People readily communicate with more than words. Instead of just using sentences, we can communicate with each other visually, by exchanging pictures such as drawings, photographs, diagrams, maps, graphs, and videos. This exchange is the natural way of approximately transferring a visual image from one mind to another and is much more efficient than trying to recreate a scene using words. Visual images can convey emotional significance as well as pictorial content, for example in inspiration gained from a waving flag.

Verbal and nonverbal communication often work together. Human bodies can be used to convey both cognitive and emotional information, via gestures, facial expressions, and body language. Gestures can supplement verbal information with pictorial information, for example when a sender uses arm or finger movements to produce a circle. Gestures can also indicate emotional judgments that are positive such as a thumbs up or negative such as holding one's nose.

In face-to-face communication, facial expressions are powerful for conveying emotional attitudes. An utterance accompanied by a smile or raised eyebrows conveys different emotions than the same utterance with a frown or a scowl. Facial expressions can serve to attract, repel, or terrify the recipients. They can also be used to convey more complex emotions, such as interest, surprise, disgust, or moral disapproval. An intense gaze implies rapt attention, while looking away suggests boredom. Eye rolling can indicate disbelief and even contempt.

Similarly, body language can express emotional attitudes with or without verbal accompaniment. Compare the differences between a shrug and a raised fist or between crossed arms and leaning forward. The power pose of an upright person with legs apart and hands on hips is very different from the air of submission of someone bent over with a hanging head, which may be sign of despair or shame. Body language needs to be supplemented with verbal utterances, visual diagrams, or gestures to convey factual information, but by itself it can suggest complex emotions.

Vision is the most important medium for nonverbal communication, but hearing, touch, and even smell can also transmit signals. Hearing is primarily a mode of verbal transmission, but there are also many nonverbal sounds that carry information, such as moans, groans, whimpers, chortles, laughter, and whistles. Songs with words are verbal, but the music can also communicate emotions such as sadness, happiness, anger, and even gloating, as in Bob Dylan's masterpiece "Like a Rolling Stone." Music without words can be arousing, calming, soothing, elevating, or depressing. Songs do not have to be happy to be pleasurable as long as they evoke other intense emotions.

One person touching another can communicate cognitive information such as whether to go in a particular direction or to stop. Touch can also transfer emotional information such as affection, consolation, hostility, or solidarity. Smell can also transfer emotional information, as people can unconsciously detect whether another person is afraid or happy.

Like verbal communication, nonverbal communication is not simply a matter of sending a signal and having it received. All forms of nonverbal communication, from gestures to facial expressions to touches, need to be interpreted and comprehended by brains that can take into account the context of utterance. Both verbal and nonverbal communications are modulated by expectations concerning status, sex, age, and even race. For example, a touch will have a different meaning if you are expecting a caress rather than a slap. Depending on the social situation, a wink can indicate a joke, complicity, solidarity, or a sexual invitation.

Nonverbal communication from one person or animal to another is captured by this schema:

person1's brain → nonverbal action → perception → interpretation →
person2's brain

The semantic pointers in the brain of person1 produce actions such as gestures and facial expressions that are perceived through various senses by person2, who interprets them by coherence with existing mental representations, leading to new cognitive and emotional representations in the form of semantic pointers.

I have been discussing communication as a paired activity, with one person sending a signal to another, but communication can also take place among groups of people through simultaneous interactions, in activities such as chanting, singing, marching, and saluting. Such activities include political rallies, sports matches, and church hymns. Group activities are particularly effective for communicating emotions because they synchronize and coordinate bodily actions. Perception of bodily changes is a major component in the semantic pointer theory of emotions, along with cognitive appraisals, which can be heavily influenced by verbal communication about the consequences of actions and the significance of goals. Hence verbal and nonverbal communication can combine to change the beliefs, emotions, and behavior of individuals.

Rule communication can also result from verbal and nonverbal means. Explicit, conscious rule transfer works best by words, but unconscious rules are better communicated by sensory images such as diagrams and physical expressions of emotions such as disapproval. For example, children can learn as much from the scowl of a parent in response to a particular behavior as from a verbal rule against the behavior. Other examples are unconscious rules that are important for romantic relationships and social norms that arise from nonverbal communication.

INTERAGENT INFERENCE

Communication is often enhanced by making inferences about what is going on in the minds of others. I can do a better job of informing you if I understand your beliefs, concepts, and interests. But interagent inferences can be performed for other purposes. I may make inferences about what you are thinking in order to hide something from you, or just out of curiosity.

What I am calling "interagent inference" sometimes goes by the names "theory of mind," "mindreading," and "mental state attribution," but these are misleading. One agent, human or animal, can make inferences about the mental states of another without anything like a verbal theory, for example by simulating the other agent. The metaphor of reading minds is also too verbal, and mindreading is usually a kind of extrasensory perception. Mental state attribution is a better description but still is too narrow, because it does not apply well to nonverbal animals like apes and birds capable of inferring what other members of their species will do without the ability to apply explicit concepts such as *belief* and *intention*.

Semantic pointers help to make sense of both verbal and nonverbal interagent inference. Humans can use verbal rules to make explicit deductive and abductive inferences about the mental states of others. For example, the approximate rule *if people cry, then they are sad* enables you to infer that a crying friend is sad. Such rules can be built out of semantic pointers by binding verbally expressed concepts. In addition, semantic pointers can be used to form multimodal rules such as *<visual/tactile/kinesthetic representation of crying>* → *<emotional experience of sadness>*, where the brackets indicate nonverbal semantic pointers. Animals without verbal representations, and sometimes people too, can use such rules to infer the mental states and behavior of others by a process more like simulation than like theory application. The simulation requires running sequences of nonverbal rules consisting of semantic pointers, as described in chapter 4.

SOCIAL MECHANISMS FOR SPREADING EMOTIONS

For belief change, verbal communication is paramount, but there are kinds of nonverbal communication that are important for spreading emotions and hence for instilling attitudes and values. The following is a provisional list of social mechanisms for spreading emotions, including specific emotions like happiness and fear as well as the more general emotional characteristics of intensity and valence.

1. Mirror neurons. Some neural populations in both monkeys and humans are activated in similar ways by both actions and perceptions of actions. Similar mirroring occurs in the perception and experience of pain and may occur in the perception and experience of some emotions. If I see you displaying an emotion, I can have some of the same neural activity that I would have if I were experiencing the same emotion myself, leading me to actually have that emotion. This process provides a neural mechanism by which emotions can spread from one person to another, leading to the acquisition of desires, fears, and angry reactions.

2. Emotional contagion by mimicry. A more indirect kind of emotional spread occurs via facial and bodily mimicry. People naturally mimic the facial expressions of those with whom they interact, inclining them to acquire similar emotional reactions because emotions are in part responses to bodily changes. Emotional contagion can also encourage the spread of patterns

of thinking through a group such as motivated, fear-driven, or rage-driven inference.

3. Nonverbal emotion spread. People can influence the emotions of others by smiling, gazing, making eye contact, raising or lowering eyebrows, changing facial expressions, nodding, touching, gesturing, and changing posture. Besides mimicry, these actions can influence the emotions of others by shifting attention and generating new interpretations of the situation: if someone is smiling, things are probably okay. Emotions such as happiness and fear can even be transferred among individuals by smell, through chemical signals carried by body odor.

4. Verbal emotion spread. Words help to spread emotions when people say things that change the appraisals and physiology of others. For example, complimenting people tends to make them happy, insulting them makes them angry, warning them makes them afraid, and telling jokes generates mirth. Verbal and nonverbal emotion spread can lead to conceptual change in values, for example with respect to discrimination as described in chapter 5.

5. Attachment-based learning. Emotional attitudes can be easily acquired from people such as parents to whom a person is emotionally attached. People commonly acquire ideologies from their parents and other close associates. Mirror neurons and emotional contagion by mimicry may account for part of this kind of transmission, but verbal communication also contributes.

6. Empathy. In empathic learning, people acquire an emotional response from others by imagining themselves in the others' situations and experiencing emotions similar to theirs. The underlying mechanisms for empathy include basic physiological responses such as mirror neurons, higher level cognitive operations such as analogy, and multimodal rule simulation described in chapter 4. Empathy can result from perception, verbal analogical inference, or nonverbal interagent inference using unconscious rules. A fuller account of these three modes of empathy appears in chapter 4 and in *Brain–Mind*, chapter 7.

7. Altruism and sympathy. Except for psychopaths, humans are generally capable of caring for other people and acting toward them altruistically, taking into account the needs of others rather than mere self-interest. A key part of altruism is sympathy, or feeling sorry for the misfortunes of others. Through altruism and sympathy, people can acquire emotional responses directed toward the well-being of others. Empathy can lead to

sympathy but differs from it in requiring that the empathizer replicates
more or less the feelings of the other person.

8. Social cuing. In the social context of a group, people's facial expressions
can cue negative emotions in their targets. For example, expressions of
anger cue guilt, and expressions of disgust cue shame. Thus negative social emotions can be induced in others. This kind of social cuing is unlike
mirror neurons, mimicry, and empathy, which produce in the observer
approximately the same emotion as in the person observed: here different emotions are produced in the observer.

9. Power manipulations. Many social scientists have discussed the importance of power in interpersonal relations. From the perspective of emotions, there are two main ways in which one person can gain power over
others: by offering them something they desire or by offering to protect
them from something that they fear. The first kind of power manipulation provokes motivated inference, while the second instigates a combination of fear-driven inference (making people even more afraid than
they might be otherwise) and motivated inference (encouraging them
to think that the manipulator can protect them). Either way, a person
or group achieves power by enhancing peoples' desires, fears, and beliefs about how to manage those desires and fears. Other ways of gaining
power, by achieving respect and trust, are discussed in chapter 6 on politics and chapter 14 on leadership.

10. Persuasion and advertising. Media can be effective for emotional management. For example, propaganda can be used to generate rage-driven
inference when it displays the enemy as evil and disgusting and therefore
deserving of extreme retribution. One subtle way to make propaganda
work is to use text and images to prime associated ideas and behaviors,
for example when odious stories containing images of reviled ethnic
groups are used to prime a full negative stereotype. Priming results from
mechanisms that operate at neural, psychological, and sociological levels.
Social media such as Facebook and Twitter can facilitate the spread of
propaganda. Chapter 14 describes how advertising and other forms of
marketing sway emotions.

11. Teaching. There is much more to teaching than the transmission of
verbal information. Someone said that education is not the filling of a
pail but the lighting of a fire. The fire metaphor indicates that teaching
requires the eliciting of such emotions as interest, enthusiasm, and pride
in learning. Teaching works better if the teacher has the students' trust,
which is a complex emotion also important for romantic relationships,

politics, and economics. Hence good teachers work to get students to trust them by various kinds of verbal and nonverbal communication. See chapter 11 for further discussion of emotions in teaching.

12. Interaction rituals. According to sociologist Randall Collins, an interaction ritual is "a mechanism of mutually focused emotion and attention producing a momentarily shared reality, which thereby generates solidarity and symbols of group membership". Such rituals occur in everyday life, for example greeting by shaking hands, and abound in organizations such as religions and corporations. Collins says that interaction rituals transfer emotional energy among participants, although he is vague about what emotional energy is. In physics, energy is the ability of a system to perform work, and the psychological analog would be that emotional energy enables people to act. The semantic pointer theory of emotion can turn emotional energy from a metaphor into a mechanism by noticing that strong emotions combine physiological changes and cognitive appraisals to produce actions through a combination of neural and molecular processes. For example, positive emotions come with increased firing in neurons using the neurotransmitters dopamine and norepinephrine, leading to increased firing in brain areas responsible for motor control and action.

These 12 social mechanisms can contribute to the spread of emotions from one individual to another, sometimes working together, as when a good teacher uses a combination of smiles, empathy, attachment-based learning, and contagion to convey enthusiasm to students. The social mechanisms complement the mental mechanism of emotional coherence and the kinds of inference generated by it, showing how emotional information can be transmitted from one person to another, leading to emotional change in groups of individuals. Emotional communication is usually aimed at building consensus, but sometimes it produces polarization. Later chapters describe emotional changes in groups ranging from romantic relationships to international alliances.

MULTILEVEL EXPLANATIONS

Sociologist James Coleman provided a useful type of diagram for understanding the psychological roots of social causation, shown in Figure 3.3. Weber explained the development of capitalism as the result of the rise of Calvinist religion, but Coleman argues that this depends on the psychological values and behaviors of

FIGURE 3.3 Coleman diagram for deepening social explanations by psychological ones. Arrows indicate causality.

individuals. Unfortunately, his account of psychology assumes that people are making rational choices rather than emotional judgments. Figure 3.4 shows how to deepen Coleman's explanation by incorporating neural and molecular mechanisms. In addition to adding two more levels, the neural and the molecular, Figure 3.4 makes the causal arrows bidirectional in keeping with the arguments about multilevel interactions in chapter 2.

Knowledge is not yet sufficient to fill in the details of all the arrows shown in Figure 3.4, but findings about molecular–social interactions show the need to operate at both these levels as well as at intermediate neural and mental ones. The influence of social events on molecular changes is shown by observations such as the following:

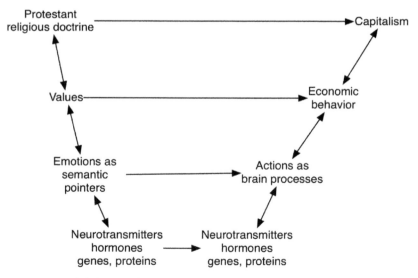

FIGURE 3.4 Expanded diagram for recognizing relevance of neural and molecular causes as well as social and mental ones. Bidirectional arrows indicate that causality runs in both directions.

- Wars and resulting famines change the epigenetics (chemical attachments) of genes with effects across several generations.
- Early nurturing in rats regulates the expression of a gene important for regulating the stress response.
- Low social status in monkeys and humans stresses the immune system, leading to more disease.
- Social rejection increases inflammatory gene expression and releases natural painkillers in the brain.
- When a doctor or other caretaker says that a pill will reduce pain, people have increased brain levels of natural opioids.

Such findings justify rejecting the ruthlessly reductionist view that explanation always goes up from the molecular to the social, from the parts to the whole, rather than in both directions.

Similarly, there are many reasons for noticing how social processes have psychological effects, even without knowledge of the resulting neural and molecular changes. Psychologists have noticed numerous effects of social class and status, including on physical health, aesthetic preferences, language, subjective well-being, and cognitive performance.

Nevertheless, the attempt to reduce the psychological to the social is futile because of bountiful evidence for effects of mental, neural, and molecular mechanisms on social processes. People's interactive communications depend on the neural processes operating in the minds of individuals, including the concepts and rules that people use to represent themselves, others, and social situations. Evidence is also mounting for causal connections between molecular processes and social interactions; for example, increases in trust results from administration of the hormone oxytocin, and the dopamine receptor gene moderates cultural differences.

In sum, social explanations should not try to explain everything bottom up or top down but rather should look for multilevel interacting mechanisms. These mechanisms can produce many kinds of change and emergence.

CHANGE AND EMERGENCE

Table 3.2 displays four kinds of changes to look for in a social cognitive-emotional workup that considers both groups and the minds of people in them. Some changes in individuals are minor additions or deletions of beliefs or emotional attitudes,

TABLE 3.2

Kinds of Change Resulting from Social Interactions

	Aggregative Example	Emergent Example
Individual	Adding a new belief.	Adopting a new worldview
Groups	Adding a new member	Adopting new goals and strategies

for example when you learn that Beijing has more than 20 million people. Other changes can be much more dramatic because they require large-scale additions and deletions of interconnected beliefs and emotions based on explanatory and emotional coherence. Then change is emergent, not just the aggregate of changes in the representations, because it results from interactions among a whole system of representations. Examples of emergent mental changes in individuals include religious conversions, political switches, falling in or out of love, and rejecting a scientific theory in favor of an alternative.

In the simplest case, one person's mind can change as a result of an interaction with another person. Through a combination of noncommunicative actions, verbal communication, and nonverbal exchanges, the state of one person's mind influences the state of another person's mind. The influence can induce change in the recipient's mind by adding, deleting, or modifying mental representations such as images, concepts, beliefs, and emotions. These influences can be enhanced when the interactions are repeated and reciprocal, with A's communication to B followed by B's communication to A. Moreover, the changes in a person's mind are influenced by interactions with other people, so that the total change in an individual is affected by all the interactions with connected people. For example, when my department is making hiring decisions, I sometimes change my belief about who is the best candidate by speaking with the candidates and various colleagues, acquiring some of their beliefs and emotional attitudes.

Changes in groups can also be aggregative or emergent. If communication leads a single person to join or leave a group, or if the group adopts a new practice consistent with previous ones, then the change is merely aggregative. But groups sometimes take dramatic new directions, for example when Sunni Muslim insurgents in Syria decided in 2014 to become much more ambitious, invade Iraq, and declare themselves the Islamic State (chapter 6). This direction allowed them to attract more members, including foreigners as well as locals. Other cases of emergence in groups include the risky behaviors of gangs, the blinkered decisions of leaders who succumb to groupthink, and the exuberant successes of theatrical productions where the interactions of actors lead to an overall superb performance.

I have coined the word "demergence" to describe cases where the whole is worse than the sum of the parts, for example when a group fails even though it has talented individuals. Examples of demergent groups include dysfunctional families, underperforming sports teams, discordant political organizations, and bungling companies. Demergence results from social structures and interactions that make people interfere with each other's performances rather than cooperate to produce results better than they could do alone. For example, most medical errors result from communication failures among personnel. As chapter 1 noted, emergence only requires that the whole be different from the sum of the parts, not greater, but fortunately there are important cases in biology and society where interaction of parts does produce results that are better than the parts could do alone with respect to proper functioning of bodies and groups. We might call this outcome "promergence," which then joins demergence as a variety of emergence.

New groups begin when people decide to form them or come together informally. Existing groups can dissolve because of lack of interest or self-destruction. For example, political parties wax and wane with varying support and activity and in some cases simply cease to exist. Even within groups, the communication structure can change over time, as changes in friendships and conflicts lead people to interact with each other more or less than previously. Groups can become increasingly or decreasingly effective at pursuing their functions depending on the motivations and effectiveness of the individuals.

In both human bodies and social groups, small local changes can be the key to overall stability, thanks to ongoing adjustments and replacements. Skin cells are replaced every few weeks and blood cells every few months, but the overall structure and function of the body is maintained. Similarly, the social mechanisms of capitalism allow large changes while maintaining overall function. Of the 30 major companies in the Dow Jones Industrial Average in 1956, only 4 were still important enough to be included in the average in 2015 (du Pont, General Electric, Procter & Gamble, and Exxon Mobil—originally Standard Oil of New Jersey). In a close personal relationship such as a marriage, the overall stability also depends on manageable changes in the people and their interactions.

Emergence of new groups and group behaviors is clearly an important feature of social change, but is it simple (two levels), recursive (three or more levels), or multilevel (interactions of three or more levels)? It is clearly recursive, with the molecular affecting the neural, which affects the mental, which affects the social. For example, individuals addicted to heroin or alcohol have molecular changes to neurotransmitter receptors that change neural firings, alter psychological representations such as beliefs, and lead to new interactions with other people such as sharing needles.

The more complicated question is whether social change involves multi-level emergence with feedback loops that include downward causation from the social to lower levels. Examples of such causation abound, such as when insults generate cortisol in a stress response and compliments generate dopamine in a reward response. Later chapters document important cases of multilevel emergence where the properties of the whole have causal effects on the properties of the individuals. For example, a good marriage makes the spouses happier, a successful political movement increases the activity of its members, and a rising economy makes investors more optimistic. Chapter 13 describes how creativity in engineering design and other fields results from group interactions.

Besides emergence, social groups exhibit other characteristics of complex systems such as chaos, tipping points, and critical transitions. For example, a group can tip from collective euphoria to despair as the result of a single failure. Motivated, fear-driven, and rage-driven inference operate in the minds of individuals, but they can be strongly influenced by groups when communication spreads emotions. As emotions change within the members of a group, patterns of inference will also change. A group can therefore undergo a critical transition from having most of its members engaging in one kind of inference to another. For example, chapter 7 describes how a stock market can transition from a bubble to a crash when its interacting members tip from motivated to fear-driven inference. A sports team that gains some valuable new players can tip from fear-driven inference resulting from frustration and annoyance to motivated inference resulting from exuberance.

SUMMARY AND DISCUSSION

Why did the species *Homo sapiens* develop from a few thousand individuals in Africa around 100,000 years ago into a worldwide force of 7 billion? Large brains and language contributed to human ascendancy but so did social capacities that are markedly different from those found in other species. Biologists and anthropologists have noticed the much greater ability of humans to form large groups, to cooperate in finding food, to collaborate in raising young, and to teach new generations the knowledge and methods acquired by previous ones. Cooperation and teaching require the social mechanisms of interagent inference and multimodal communication. These mechanisms generate emergent properties in groups that enable them to perform much better in complex environments than individuals could do separately.

This chapter has provided a general and detailed account of social mechanisms as systems of parts whose connections enable them to interact in ways that produce regular changes. In the social world, the main parts are individual people, but parts can also be groups formed out of those individuals. The interactions between individuals and groups are primarily verbal and nonverbal communication but can also include purely physical acts such as fighting and the inferences that people make about each other. There are many kinds of verbal communication using speaking and writing, and even more kinds of nonverbal communication by seeing, hearing, touching, smelling, and moving. Interactions between people can occur in pairs or in larger groups where communication links multiple people.

The study of social mechanisms depends on but does not reduce to the study of how individual people think and how they communicate with each other. Hence the mental mechanisms described in chapter 2 are a crucial part of the theory of social mechanisms. The semantic pointer theory of brain/mind provides a unified explanation of mental representations, including images, concepts, beliefs, rules, analogies, and emotions. But groups are not just the aggregate of individual thinkers, because group properties and behaviors result from the interactions of individuals. Beliefs and emotions spread from person to person by transfer and elicitation of semantic pointers. The same features that determine whether semantic pointers break through into the consciousness of individuals also determine the extent of contagion from one thinker to another: goal relevance and physiological arousal integrated by emotions.

Semantic pointers suggest a novel way of understanding communication that accommodates both verbal and nonverbal processes. Communication is not just the transmission of verbal messages in speech acts. Just as important is the conveyance of sensory images and emotional reactions, which are often effectively passed on by visual displays, gestures, body language, facial expressions, and other nonverbal means. Communication is therefore a complicated brain-to-brain process in which the semantic pointers in one person lead to changes in the semantic pointers in another person. Hence Eliasmith's semantic pointer hypothesis provides unified accounts of cognition and emotion in individuals and of verbal and nonverbal communication among individuals.

Appreciating these interactions and the resulting emergent changes provides a solution to the deep problem in the social sciences of understanding the relationship between individuals and groups. Individuals form groups, but the behavior of the groups is not reduced to the behavior of individuals for two reasons. First, the groups can have emergent properties such as legal powers. Second, the behaviors of individuals depend in part on what they think of groups, which provide the individuals with social identities and structures of communication. Being a citizen of a country makes it more likely that you will think of yourself as belonging to it and more likely that you will interact with fellow citizens.

This issue is variously called the "agent-structure," "person-group," or "mind-society" problem. Its solution requires a rich account of the interdependence of mental mechanisms in individuals with social mechanisms in groups. Semantic pointer theories of cognition and communication provide this account, with answers to the person-group problem in specific cases from romantic couples to businesses. The general explanation is reviewed at the end of chapter 9 in connection with international relations.

We need to be cautious with slogans about collective emotions, intentions, and beliefs that are claimed to constitute social facts. These ideas should not be taken to indicate that there are mental states that belong to groups or that there are social facts independent of any mental facts. The interactions between cognitive and social mechanisms are complex, as later chapters show in detail.

The analysis of social mechanisms in terms of parts, connections, interactions, and changes makes it clear what questions to ask in a social cognitive-emotional workup for particular cases of social change. In addition to those posed at the end of chapter 2 concerning mental mechanisms in individuals, we need to ask the following questions:

1. What are the most important groups that affect the behavior of individuals?
2. How are individuals connected into groups by emotional bonds?
3. How do individuals and groups interact with each other verbally, nonverbally, and noncommunicatively?
4. What changes in individuals and groups results from these interactions, both in the short and long term?
5. Are the changes in individuals and groups aggregate or emergent and are emergent changes recursive or multilevel?

Table 3.3 shows a template for performing a workup that is applied to six social sciences in chapters 4 to 9 and to five professions in chapters 10 to 14.

The test of social cognitivism is how well it explains the vast array of changes occurring across the social sciences and professions. A culture is a system of mental representations and customary behaviors shared by a group of people, which social cognitivism aims to explain using interacting mental and social mechanisms. The rest of this book is a long argument for multilevel emergence as the key to understanding and instigating social change, beginning in the next chapter with close personal relationships.

TABLE 3.3

Template for Performing a Social Cognitive-Emotional Workup

A. Mental	Concepts and Values	Images	Beliefs and Rules	Analogies and Metaphors	Emotions	Inferences
Individual 1						
Individual 2, 3, …						

B. Social	People	Connections	Interactions	Changes	Emergence
Group 1					
Group 2, 3, …					

C. Interactions	Verbal Communications	Nonverbal Communications	Interagent Inferences	Purely Physical Interactions
Group 1				
Group 2, 3, …				

Note. A: mental mechanisms in individuals. B: social mechanisms in groups. C: interactions among individuals and groups.

The mechanism quote is from Elster 2015, p. 26.

Ravenscroft 2016 reviews folk psychology, which is also assumed by the BDI (belief-desire-intention) approach to artificial inelligence (e.g., Wooldridge, 2000).

For reviews of social mechanisms, see Demeulenaere 2011, Hedström and Swedberg 1998, and Hedström and Ylikoski 2010. For more on levels and emergence, see *Natural Philosophy*, chapter 5.

Mead 1967 and some other sociologists in approaches such as symbolic interactionism have recognized the importance of communication among minds but have weak theories of mind. McPherson, Smith-Lovin, and Cook 2001 discuss homophily. Thye, Yoon, and Lawler 2002 review relational cohesion.

Baumeister, Ainsworth, and Vohs 2016 discuss how groups can be more or less than the sum of their members.

On needs for relatedness and belonging, see Deci and Ryan 2002, Ryan and Deci 2017, and Baumeister and Leary 1995.

Concerning nonverbal communication, see Leathers and Evans 2017, Goldin-Meadow 2003 on gesture, and Tversky 2011 on visualization. Kraus and Slater 2016 analyze how human sound communication goes beyond words.

The following are some sources on social mechanisms for transferring emotions: mirror neurons: Rizzolatti and Craighero 2004; emotional contagion by mimicry: Hatfield, Cacioppo, and Rapson 1994; nonverbal spread: Darioly and Mast 2014; smell: de Groot et al. 2015; attachment-based learning: Minsky 2006; empathy: Thagard 2010b, Zaki and Ochsner 2012; altruism and sympathy: Batson 1991, Hoffman 2000; social cuing: Giner-Sorolla and Espinosa 2011; power manipulations: Mann 1986, 2013; priming: Schröder and Thagard 2013; interaction rituals: Collins 2004, quote from p. 7. An earlier list of mechanisms for transferring emotions was in Thagard 2015a, reused by permission of Springer Nature, © 2015.

For the source of the quote on education as the lighting of a fire, see https://quoteinvestigator.com/2013/03/28/mind-fire/.

Coleman 1990 diagrams social change, and Weber 2009 explains the rise of capitalism.

Social class affects thinking: Kraus et al. 2012.
Social changes have molecular consequences: Cole 2009.
Molecular changes have social consequences: Carter 2014.
Social mechanisms explain the success of *Homo sapiens*: Hrdy 2009, Sterelny 2012, Henrich 2016.

PROJECT

Build an agent-based model for human interactions where the individual agents have semantic pointers and they communicate both verbally and nonverbally. Current agent-based models have simplistic mechanisms of cognition, and they ignore emotion, except for extended HOTCO (hot coherence): Thagard and Kroon 2005, reprinted in Thagard 2006; Thagard 2012a; Wolf, Schröder, Neumann, and de Haan 2015.

PART II

Social Sciences

4

Social Psychology

ROMANTIC RELATIONSHIPS

RELATIONSHIPS MATTER

What is love? Why did Angelina Jolie and Brad Pitt fall for each other, get married, and eventually divorce? Romantic attachments are a central part of most adult lives.

A full account of social mechanisms has to scale up to deal with large groups, such as the thousands of people at a football game. But it is clearer to begin with the smallest groups, the pairs of people who participate in friendships, feuds, and romantic relationships. Human behavior depends not only on what happens in an individual's head but also on the relationships that are fundamental to human flourishing. Successful close relationships such as marriages are key predictors of happiness, well-being, and health. Looking at the dynamics of romantic relationships should help to spell out the parts, interactions, and changes that are important for all social mechanisms.

Understanding how cognition and emotion operate in individual minds and how communication connects multiple minds should provide new insights into the nature of close relationships. Topics crucial to human attachments include love, trust, responsiveness, commitment, connection, rejection, compatibility, conflict, support, hurt feelings, personality, stability, and breakups. An account of the cognitive and social mechanisms that produce and maintain close relationships should help to answer questions such as: Why do people eagerly pursue close relationships? Why do romantic relationship such as marriages often succeed? Why do they frequently fail?

Close relationships are only one of the phenomena studied by the field of social psychology, which also concerns attitudes, persuasion, influence, and group dynamics. It would be impossible in a single chapter to present a full theory of social psychology; instead, I use romantic relationships as a case study to show the applicability of cognitive, emotional, and social mechanisms.

Social psychology ought to operate at the intersection of psychology and sociology, but these two fields have approached similar phenomena in different ways. Psychologists usually study social interactions by laboratory experiments, whereas sociologists often employ qualitative methods similar to the ethnography practiced by anthropologists. I think there are advantages to both methodologies, and a general theory of social relationships should be able to explain the results of both sorts of studies.

SOCIAL COGNITION AND MICROSOCIOLOGY

The current divide between psychology and sociology is illustrated by the differences between two prominent approaches in each field: social cognition and microsociology. Social cognition is the branch of psychology concerned with understanding how people think about each other and make sense of each other's actions. The standard approach to social cognition is experimental, using controlled laboratory conditions to identify how people make inferences about others. In recent years, the study of social cognition has broadened to include neuroscientific studies, particularly concerning the brain areas that are active when people are engaged in various cognitive tasks that involve thinking about other people. Social cognition has also broadened to consider social cognition across various cultures.

Behavioral, neuroscientific, and cross-cultural studies are usually just juxtaposed in the study of social cognition, with no overarching theory concerning how minds and brains work in social situations. The currently most popular account of how the mind works relies on the distinction between two kinds of processes: those that are slow, controlled, and conscious and those that are fast, automatic, and mostly unconscious. Unfortunately, little detail is provided about the underlying cognitive or neural mechanisms that support these allegedly dual systems and cause people to switch between them. *Brain–Mind* (chapters 8 and 9) describes the limitations of dual-system accounts.

Microsociology is concerned with face-to-face interactions in small groups of people but uses different methods than social cognition. Instead of laboratory experiments, it uses qualitative observations to reach conclusions about how people influence each other's behavior and emotions. Microsociologists have made interesting observations about work, violence, interaction rituals, and self-presentation but lack an overarching theory of the mechanisms operating in individual minds and the social mechanisms by which people interact. The approach I call social cognitivism should provide a theoretical basis for both social cognition and microsociology, thereby unifying their respective insights.

MECHANISMS IN RELATIONSHIPS

The scheme of cognitive and social mechanisms in chapters 2 and 3 generates a clear set of questions to ask about the operations of personal relationships. The first questions concern the representations and processes in the minds of the relevant individuals such as romantic companions. We need to determine their respective concepts, values, images, beliefs, rules, analogies, and emotions. All of these representations can be considered as neural processes built out of semantic pointers. For both psychological and neural reasons, cognition and emotion are entwined in the minds of people who are thinking about themselves and others with whom they are in close relationships.

The second set of questions concern the social mechanisms by which members of a couple interact with each other. Verbal communication is obviously one important social mechanism when people speak or write to each other. But in romantic situations, nonverbal communication is also crucial, through gestures, facial expressions, gazes, touches, and so on. An enticing smile, caress, raised eyebrow, or sneer can have a more powerful impact than words. In addition to verbal and nonverbal communication, social interactions can include purely physical actions such as providing food, straightening a collar, or slapping. These interactions establish bonds of affection, dependency, trust, and love, all of which require changes in the brains of the participants.

Cognitive and social mechanisms should explain both short-term events such as particular interactions and long-term developments such as marital success and failure. Such events and developments in relationships have been described by social psychologists, so I proceed by applying multilevel mechanisms to their fascinating findings.

MURRAY AND HOLMES ON INTERDEPENDENT MINDS

The book *Interdependent Minds* by Sandra Murray and John Holmes provides a comprehensive account of romantic relationships based on extensive data rather than popular psychology (e.g., *Men Are from Mars, Women Are from Venus*). Murray and Holmes discuss the cognitions and emotions that operate inside the minds of members of a couple, but they also attend to relationship dynamics that concern how partners develop and respond to their interdependence. I explain their results in terms of operation and communication of semantic pointers.

Murray and Holmes recognize that relationships are hard but maintain that satisfying and stable relationships can be achieved through mutually responsive behavior. Partners are interdependent in that they influence and constrain each other's actions in ways that affect their happiness. In situations involving social coordination, one partner has goals that can only be met through the behavior of the other partner. Couples are interdependent because of their need to coordinate their actions concerning life tasks, personal preferences, and relationship goals. Murray and Holmes set out to explain how mutually responsive behaviors emerge or fail to emerge in close relationships. People's working mental models of relationships contain the unconscious know-how to motivate mutually responsive behavior in each other.

Murray and Holmes understand the interdependent mind as a system of interconnected *if–then* rules for adult romantic relationships. These rules are often unconscious but serve to coordinate partner interaction by linking specific features of situations to appropriate ways of feeling, thinking, and behaving. The rules function to coordinate mutually responsive interactions by matching specific features of a situation to congruent behavior. For example, if one person is rejecting, then the other may respond by self-protecting.

Murray and Holmes use their model of interdependence to explain how patterns of mutual responsiveness and nonresponsiveness develop in relationships. They contend that an unconscious *if–then* rule can explain why some relationships succeed while others fail. Rules constrain responsiveness and thereby limit partner compatibility and rewarding interactions.

Responsiveness to a partner is difficult in situations where the interests of the partners are different because of conflicting preferences and needs. Conflicts can arise because of preferences for different activities or from disparate domestic responsibilities such as laundry, cooking, cleaning, and shopping. Problems of coordination can also result from conflicts concerning money and family. The likelihood of conflicts depends on the compatibility between partners' personal attitudes, preferences, goals, and personality. Two partners will inevitably encounter situations where they want different things, for example with respect to sex. All relationships involve the risk of not having basic physical, emotional, and psychological needs met. Individuals are self-interested in that they have motivations to be selfish and to protect themselves from the pain of rejection.

People need to know how to deal with situations where there is a conflict between connection goals and self-interest. According to Murray and Holmes, there are five elements that are basic to this relationship know-how: trust, goal direction, commitment reciprocity, efficient but flexible goal implementation, and suitability for the relationship circumstance. Trust involves rules about when it is safe for one partner to approach the other, when the partner is likely to be responsive, when to be vigilant, the strengths of one partner's commitment to the other, and the corresponding strength of motivation to respond to needs. Rules about goals provide ways of answering the basic question: Should I stay or should I go? Commitment reciprocity concerns the willingness of partners to set aside self-interested concerns and to coordinate the partners' commitments to each other.

Murray and Holmes state that coordinating mutual responsiveness to needs requires mechanisms for trumping self-interested concerns on each partner's part. They also say that managing the motivations of partners is a mechanism for keeping goal conflicts from thwarting action. But they do not say what they think mechanisms are, or how unconscious *if–then* rules operate in minds and brains. This gap can be filled by a social cognitive-emotional workup of interdependent minds. The aim of such a workup is to spell out in detail the mechanisms that govern the operations and interactions of minds.

ROMANTIC RELATIONSHIPS: SOCIAL COGNITIVE-EMOTIONAL WORKUP

The powerful account of relationships proposed by Murray and Holmes raises important theoretical questions. What mental and social processes make people interdependent? What is the mental structure of the unconscious rules that affect how people interact with each other? Why are these rules unconscious? What is the neural nature of trust and commitment? Why are interactions based on rules and trust so important for determining whether a relationship will survive? All of these questions have plausible answers provided by semantic pointer theories of cognition, emotion, and communication. For illustration, I use the hypothetical, gender-neutral example of a relationship consisting of two people, Pat and Sam. Here and in all the ensuing chapters, the social cognitive-emotional workup

examines concepts, values, images, beliefs, rules, analogies, metaphors, inferences, and communications.

Concepts and Values

When Pat and Sam talk to and about each other, they do so with words such as
"friend," "lover," "spouse," "kind," "mean," "better half," "ball and chain," and so on.
These words have corresponding mental representations in the form of concepts
as semantic pointers that combine verbal, sensory, motor, and emotional information. Such concepts yield abundant inferences because of the typical features
and explanatory roles associated with them. For example, if Pat thinks of Sam as
kind, then Pat will expect Sam to behave generously when Pat is stressed and will
use the attributed trait to explain why Sam performs actions such as providing
assistance to people in need. Relationships change over time, so Pat and Sam may
both undergo conceptual change as their relationship develops, perhaps from acquaintances to friends to lovers to exes.

Concepts incorporate emotional values. Generally, *kind* is better than *mean,*
and *better half* is more positive than *ball and chain.* Depending on their social circumstances and previous experience, Pat and Sam may attach different values to
husband, wife, and *partner.* Valuations may also attach to appealing or annoying
images such as what Pat and Sam wear and how they sound. Beliefs are frequently
tied to emotional reactions, for example Pat's pride that Sam is successful and
Sam's contempt that Pat often wears plaid shirts.

A configuration of emotional concepts can be displayed by a value map such
as Figure 4.1, which shows Pat's starry-eyed view of Sam in the early, infatuation
stage of their relationship. The map shows the positive view that Pat has of Sam

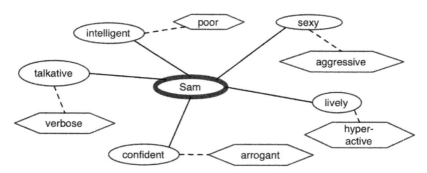

FIGURE 4.1 Value map of Pat's infatuation with Sam. Ovals indicate positive emotions, and
hexagons indicate negative ones. Straight lines indicate mutual support, and dotted lines
indicate incompatibility.

in the early stages of their relationship, which is joyful, passionate, loving, and trusting. When Sam behaves in potentially annoying ways, Pat is inclined to explain them away through motivated inference resulting from overall positive emotions and the goal of maintaining the relationship.

Pat's feelings about Sam form a positive emotional gestalt, a configuration that encourages actions such as spending time together and reinforcing each other's affectionate behaviors. These feelings and actions possess a high degree of emotional coherence that encourages actions such as spending time together and perhaps considering marriage. All these feelings generate emotional energy that Pat uses to pursue the relationship, driven in part by higher levels of neurochemicals such as dopamine.

In contrast, Figure 4.2 shows Pat's disillusionment with Sam in a terminal stage of their relationship, when love, trust, and commitment are evaporating. Pat's inferences about Sam are now more fear-driven than motivated, with worries about the relationship encouraging Pat to think the worst about Sam. The result is an emotional gestalt shift, with the positive configuration shown in Figure 4.1 replaced by the negative one in Figure 4.2.

Unlike the sudden perceptual gifts shifts such as in the duck-rabbit figure, emotional gestalt shifts can occur gradually. Emotional gestalt shifts can also occur in the opposite direction, from negative to positive, for example when two people start off not liking each other much but gradually develop an affection through greater familiarity. The emotional coherence of the negative view of Sam supports actions such as withdrawal and separation, leaving Pat with feelings of sadness and lack of energy.

For real couples who are not getting along, it would be an interesting exercise to draw value maps of how they think of themselves and each other. For

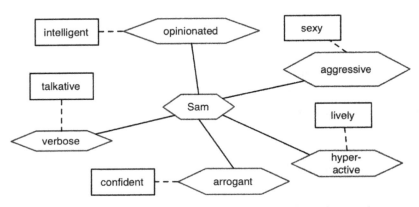

FIGURE 4.2 Value map of Pat's disillusionment with Sam, using rectangles to indicate emotional neutrality.

example, a counselor could ask Pat to map the concepts and values that apply to Sam, as well as the concepts and values that Pat thinks Sam applies to Sam. Moreover, Pat could map Pat's view of Pat as well as Sam's view of Pat and then compare them. Similarly, Sam could also generate four maps of Sam on Pat, Pat on Pat, Pat on Sam, and Sam on Sam. The resulting eight maps should provide insights about the extent of agreement in the participants' conceptions of their relationship.

Images and Embodiment

Pat and Sam can also represent each other using sensory images, including visual ones of each other's faces, auditory ones of each other's voices, tactile ones such as hugs and caresses, and sometimes even smells and tastes. Each may also associate the other with visceral feelings such as the excitement of butterflies in the stomach and the deep pain of rejection. One study found that the qualities that people desire in a mate shift depending on their physical environments such as a shaky chair. Hence mutual representations in romantic relationships are heavily embodied.

But the importance of embodiment is compatible with transbodiment, the ability of concepts used by humans to go beyond the senses. Figure 4.1 shows abstract concepts such as *intelligent* and *confident* that go far beyond sense perception, and there are many others that Pat and Sam might apply to each other. Positively valued concepts include *loyal, honest,* and *caring,* while negative concepts include *obnoxious, disrespectful,* and *mendacious.* All of these traits go beyond observation to suggest underlying, nonobserved dispositions that produce the resulting behaviors.

Beliefs and Rules

The concepts and images that Pat and Sam apply to each other have corresponding beliefs, for example Sam's beliefs that Pat is irascible and wears bright colors. More complicated beliefs such as rules can be built out of sets of concepts.

According to Murray and Holmes, *if–then* rules are the most important mental representations that explain the development of relationships. Box 4.1 shows some of the rules that they have identified as important for managing motivation and maintaining relationships. Rules such as these can lead to the flourishing or dissolution of a relationship depending on how they affect behaviors and perceptions. If a partner accepts you or sacrifices for you, then you naturally have trust

---

BOX 4.1

RELATIONSHIP RULES IDENTIFIED BY HOLMES AND MURRAY

Rules for Managing Motivation
    IF partner sacrifices, THEN trust.
    IF partner values traits, THEN trust.
    IF partner accepting, THEN connect.
    IF partner rejecting, THEN self-protect.
    IF connect goal, THEN escalate dependence.
    IF self-protect goal, THEN withhold dependence.

Rules for Maintaining Relationships
    IF reduce threat, THEN maintain relationship.
    IF increase mutual dependence, THEN reduce threat.
    IF partner hurtful, THEN accommodate.
    IF partner impedes goals, THEN do not devalue partner.

---

and the desire to connect, leading to greater dependence and commitment. Of the other hand, if your partner rejects you, then you naturally try to protect yourself and reduce dependence.

To maintain a relationship, you need to reduce threats by maintaining mutual dependence, for example by responding to hurtful remarks by accommodation (putting up with them) rather than spiteful responses. Pat could use such rules to infer that to maintain relationships, the couple needs to reduce threats, which they can do by increasing mutual dependence by performing actions that will show that they fulfill each other's needs.

What is the cognitive and neural form of these rules that operate in the minds of people in close relationships? If the rules were straightforward verbal expressions, as the *if–then* structure suggests, it would be puzzling why people are often not consciously aware of them. But the semantic pointer interpretation of rules shows how they can be broken down into components that go beyond the verbal.

Consider the rule that if your partner values your personal traits, then you tend to trust him or her. According to the semantic pointer interpretation, a value is a positive emotional state bound with representations, in this case of personal traits such as conscientiousness and agreeableness. Your partner valuing your conscientiousness is a neural process that binds a representation of you, this trait, and a combination of cognitive appraisal and physiological perception. Your inference that someone values you and has a positive emotional state toward you is based partly on verbal utterances but also on facial expressions, body language, tone of voice, and your own gut feelings.

Similarly, trust is a complex mental process with a substantial emotional component that can be difficult to put into words. Hence the rule *if partner values traits, then trust* fleshes out into a neural representation with nonverbal aspects to both the *if* part and the *then* part. Using the convention introduced in chapter 2, this rule might be expressed as <*values traits*> → <*trust*> to indicate the substantial multimodal component of valuing and trusting.

The nonverbal nature of these components of the rules explains why the rules can be hard to put into words and to recognize consciously. In this respect, relationship rules are like the motor control patterns needed to play a sport or musical instrument, requiring procedural knowledge-how as much as declarative knowledge-that. We can be consciously aware of particular images, such as a picture of a smiling face, but there is no image corresponding to the rule that smiling people are usually friendly. Procedural rules are often acquired by nonverbalized observations and practice, for example when children acquire unconscious rules for relationships from living with their parents.

All rules are made of concepts, but the semantic pointer theory of concepts makes it clear why we should not expect the concepts in rules to be equivalent to words. Concepts are formed by binding sensory, motor, verbal, and emotional information in ways that support exemplars, typical features, and explanations. Rules formed from multimodal concepts may be relatively inaccessible to consciousness. Nevertheless, these rules may have major impacts on people's actions, without them being aware of why they do what they do. The emotional attitudes built into most concepts constitute values, and it can take many conversations and behavioral observations for people to be able to infer the extent to which they share the emotional values and implicit rules of a prospective partner.

The governance of behavior by unconscious rules can have more general effects on gender relations. Growing up in a culture provides different sets of rules that may harshly limit flexibilities of behavior, for example when there are strict but nonexplicit rules about how men and women do and should behave. These unspoken rules may be particularly limiting for dealing with nonstandard practices such as homosexuality, transgender identification, and the more than 50 gender options now available for Facebook users. Changing attitudes about such practices requires recognizing and altering unconscious rules, which can be even more difficult than revising conscious beliefs. Chapter 5 discusses the importance of unconscious rules for social norms, prejudice, and discrimination.

Analogies and Metaphors

Murray and Holmes do not discuss the use of analogies in close relationships, but role models and metaphors can have an influence. Some individuals use other couples as role models for how to carry on their own relationship. Most commonly, Pat and Sam can take their respective parents as role models for a good relationship, or possibly friends or celebrities. In the 1981 song "Key Largo," the singer takes Bogey and Bacall as a model for a successful relationship. Couples can consider other couples as negative role models, for example when they do not want to end up like their divorced parents or like warring celebrities. Role-model analogies are clearly emotional, transferring attitudes such as admiration, caution, and derision.

There are also analogies used to make jokes about relationships, as in the remark that marriage is like a cage in which the birds inside want to get out and the birds outside want to get in. Marriage is an institution, and who wants to live in an institution? Both these quips transfer negative emotions.

Another use of analogy in romantic relationships employs metaphorical terms of endearment like "baby," "sugar," "honey," and "sweetheart." When not totally deadened by conventional use, these metaphors transfer positive emotions to the person addressed. The concepts *better half* and *ball and chain* already mentioned are also metaphorical. Metaphors with associated values can also be applied to a relationship as a whole, for example calling a marriage a partnership or a journey in contrast to a trap or a prison. Other metaphors that describe relationships *are going steady, settling down,* and *on the rocks.*

Emotions and Actions

Pat and Sam's mental representations of each other include emotions, ranging from positive emotions such as love to negative emotions such as irritation. When the relationship is going well, they will experience such emotions as happiness, mirth, amusement, affection, pride, and gratitude. But a deteriorating relationship will be plagued with such emotions as sadness, anger, fear, resentment, contempt, jealousy, and even disgust.

Emotions are not free-floating like moods but always about something. Hence they incorporate binding with other kinds of representations, which can be images such as a person's face, beliefs such as that the other is having an affair, or rules that summarize what the other tends to do in ways that are sometimes pleasing and sometimes annoying. In accord with the semantic pointer theory of emotion, all of these emotions bind representations of the person and state of affairs with a combination of the results of cognitive appraisal and physiological perception. Having an emotion about a partner, or something a partner does, is both a bodily reaction and an appraisal of the extent to which the partner satisfies your goals. More is said later about emotional processes particularly important for relationships: trust, commitment, and love.

Sometimes romantic relationships involve nested emotions, emotions about emotions, analyzed in chapter 9 in connection with international relations. For couples, nested emotions can include fear of loss and gratitude for love. Like other emotions, love can be unconscious when it is outcompeted by other semantic pointers that prevent people from recognizing how they are starting to feel about someone.

Emotions often lead to actions through the neural mechanisms described in *Brain–Mind* (chapter 9). Positive emotions such as love cause people to spend time together, whereas negative emotions such as contempt cause them to avoid each other.

Inferences

To get along with each other, Pat and Sam need to be able to understand each other's mental states, at least approximately, by making interagent inferences of various kinds. Some inferences can use verbal and nonverbal rules, as in the deductive inference:

> If ranting, then upset.
> Ranting.
> Therefore, upset.

Rules can also be used abductively, running the rules backward to provide a causal explanation:

> If angry, then shouting.
> Shouting.
> Therefore, maybe angry.

These examples are verbal, but deductive and abductive simulations can also be run using nonverbal rules where the *if* and *then* parts are multimodal semantic pointers.

Concepts can be used to make similar kinds of inferences by applying their typical features, for example, when Pat thinks that Sam is a lawyer and therefore probably argumentative. Analogies can also generate inferences, for example when Sam draws conclusions from similarities between Pat and Pat's parents. Deductive, abductive, conceptual, and analogical inference do not occur in isolation by means of discrete arguments. Rather, they require coherence-based inferences that make sense of the current situations using parallel constraint satisfaction.

Empathy can be a large contributor to how Pat and Sam understand each other in all three modes: perception, verbal analogical inference, and nonverbal simulation using unconscious rules. For example, if Pat sees Sam grimacing in pain, Pat's mirror neurons may generate brain firings similar to ones that occur when Pat is in pain, so that Pat really does feel Sam's pain. More complicatedly, if Sam is distressed by a setback at work, Pat may think of a similar disappointment and analogically infer that Sam is feeling what Pat remembers feeling. Finally, Pat can simulate what Sam is going through by running unconscious multimodal rules that generate feelings and other experiences similar to Sam's. For example, a simulation might use the following nonverbal rules made of semantic pointers to explain past behaviors or infer future ones: <shouting> → <angry>, <angry> → <storm out>.

The discussion of values already mentioned the important roles of emotional inferences in relationships. According to Murray and Holmes, motivated inferences contribute to the health and stability of relationships as people prefer to view their partners in a positive light. On the other hand, fear-driven and rage-driven inferences can be part of the spiral of destruction that leads to breakups.

Communication

Interagent inferences are one kind of communication between Pat and Sam, but other kinds are more observable. They talk to each other with words and sentences, but there are also many kinds of nonverbal communication in a romantic relationship. Some of these are visual such as facial expressions, gestures, and body language, while others are auditory such as moans, groans, and tone of voice. Tactile communications can be positive through hugs and caresses but also negative though slaps or pokes. Donning a special scent may signal romantic interest, and sharing delicious food provides a kind of communication based on taste. Let us now look at romantic interactions more generally.

TRUST AND COMMITMENT

Like other relationship experts, Murray and Holmes emphasize trust and commitment but give little indication how these work in the mind. Some possibilities for the nature of trust are:

1. Trust is a set of behaviors such as acting in ways that depend on another.
2. Trust is a belief in a probability that a person will behave in certain ways.
3. Trust is an abstract mental attitude toward a proposition that someone is dependable.
4. Trust is a feeling of confidence and security that a partner cares.
5. Trust is a complex neural process that binds diverse representations into a semantic pointer that includes emotions.

Behaviors and verbal expressions are certainly evidence for trust, for example when someone treats you well and says nice things to you, but these behaviors are merely evidence for the internal mental state of trust that causes them, not the trust itself. Trusting people may involve estimations of probabilities of how they will behave, but people usually trust others without any understanding of probability or any precise predictions about their behaviors. Some philosophers would say that trust is a propositional attitude, an abstract relation between an abstract self and an abstract meaning of the sentence. But the nature of these selves, relations, and meanings is utterly mysterious.

The psychological alternative that trust is a feeling of confidence and security is much more plausible than behavioral, probabilistic, and philosophical views but leaves unspecified the nature of this feeling. I propose that trust is a brain process that binds representations of self, other, situation, and emotion into a semantic pointer, as illustrated in Figure 4.3. Consider the simple case that Pat trusts Sam to buy groceries. For this structure to operate in Pat's brain, Pat needs to have a representation of self, which in turn is built out of a binding of current experiences, memories, and concepts, as described in *Brain–Mind* (chapter 12). Pat's representation of self needs to be bound with a representation of the person trusted, requiring a combination of verbal representations such as gender and sensory representations such as visual appearance. Even with just representations of the self and the person trusted, trust requires recursive binding of bindings. Further bindings are required to incorporate representations of situations and emotions.

Trust is rarely absolute but rather is restricted to particular situations: Pat may trust Sam to pick up the groceries but not to perform surgery. The representation

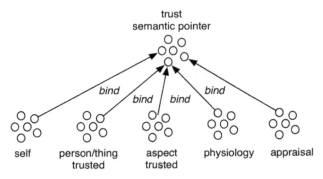

FIGURE 4.3 Trust as a semantic pointer. The full semantic pointer might include additional bindings about the situation.

of the situation such as picking up groceries can again be a combination of verbal, sensory, and motor depictions.

Finally, trust has an inextricable emotional dimension. Pat's trust in Sam is not just an estimate of the probability that Sam will pick up the groceries but also a positive feeling toward Sam in this respect. In accord with the semantic pointer theory of emotions, emotion binds a cognitive appraisal—in this case that Sam will accomplish the required goal—with the neural representation of Pat's physiological state, usually described as a "gut feeling." For example, Pat's doubts about Sam's reliability may manifest as a nervous stomach or sinking feeling. To trust people, you need to feel good about them. Hence the semantic pointer in Pat's brain for trusting Sam is a binding of five representations, each of which binds other representations, all understood as patterns of neural firings operated on by convolution. The feeling of trust arises as an emergent property of all this binding.

How can all this be going on with something as simple as Pat trusting Sam to pick up the groceries? If the brain were a serial computer having to accomplish trust by a series of step-by-step inferences, it would be puzzling how Pat could possess trust in real time. But all these bindings of bindings are accomplished in parallel by billions of interconnected neurons. Parallel processing makes it both efficient and biologically feasible that Pat has all of these representations and bindings that together emerge as trust that Sam will get the groceries.

Similarly, mistrust is an emotional process that goes far beyond estimation of low probabilities about people doing what they are supposed to. It also requires representation of the self, the person mistrusted, and the relevant aspect, but differs from trust in assigning negative emotions akin to dislike and fear. These emotional reactions emerge from the combination of cognitive appraisals about unsatisfied goals and unpleasant physiological reactions to a creepy person. For more on trust and distrust, see chapter 9 on international relations, chapter 13 on technology collaborations, and chapter 14 on leadership.

Commitment is like trust in that it requires recursive binding of self, other, and emotion. The major difference is that commitment is primarily about the intentions of the self, not about the expectations of the other. Pat is committed to Sam if Pat has a semantic pointer that binds a representation of Pat, a representation of Sam, and a set of intentions concerning how to behave in particular situations. All of these are usually bound with positive emotions about Sam and intentions favorably toward Sam. As *Brain–Mind* describes (chapter 9), intentions are multimodal semantic pointers that bind representations of selves, actions, and emotions. Hence, commitments are neural states produced by recursive binding of representations that include a constellation of intentions about what to do in the future. A similar analysis applies to love.

LOVE

We learn little from dictionary definitions of love as an intense and powerful feeling of attachment and devotion. More useful is a three-analysis, as shown in Table 4.1 with exemplars, typical features, and explanations. This three-analysis is not meant to capture ordinary people's concept of love but rather one based on a growing scientific understanding of love and other emotions.

Like other emotions, the process of love requires multilevel emergence from mechanisms operating at social, mental, neural, and molecular levels. At the social level, love results from many kinds of interactions, both verbal and nonverbal: talking, touching, flirting, gazing, and so on. At the mental level, a state of love results from binding various mental representations, including the self, the

TABLE 4.1

Three-Analysis of *Love*

Exemplars	Spouses, parents/children, Romeo and Juliet, Bogart and Bacall
Typical features	Lover, loved one, intense positive feeling about another, caring behavior, chemical changes
Explanations	Explains: people's behavior with each other
	Explained by: biological needs, social learning from interactions, neurotransmitters, hormones

person that the self loves, the cognitive appraisal of the loved one and situation, and physiological changes that occur from interacting with or thinking about the loved one. The appraisal requires conscious or unconscious judgments about the extent to which the other person satisfies the psychological, social, and physical goals of the individual in love. Physiological changes associated with being in love include increased heart rate, increased physical activity, and sometimes a nervous feeling in the stomach.

Semantic pointers show how binding into mental representations can take place through the activities of large populations of spiking neurons. Hence the feeling of being in love at any particular moment can be identified with patterns of neural firing that result from binding by convolution of other patterns of neural firing carrying out representations of self, other, and the integration of appraisal and physiology. Neural firing results from neuron-neuron interactions that depend on molecular mechanisms using neurotransmitters such as dopamine and serotonin, as well as on hormones such as oxytocin, vasopressin, testosterone, and estrogen. Therefore, falling in love is not just chemistry, feeling, or recognizing a soul-mate but the emergent result of the interaction of social, mental, neural, and molecular mechanisms.

Like other mental states, love is both an occurrence and a disposition. The occurrence of love as an active feeling is the complex pattern of neural firing just described. But love is also a disposition to have this feeling at various times, such as when you are asleep or concerned with other matters. You do not have to be thinking about someone to be in love with that person.

A mental disposition is a property of mechanisms where the parts can operate in different ways depending on environmental inputs. At the neural level, the disposition to generate particular kinds of firing patterns results from synaptic connections formed by previous experience through various kinds of learning. Other mechanisms that dispose people toward occurring feelings of love are molecular, ranging from dopamine circuitry to hormonal changes. Also dispositional are stored beliefs, for example that the other person is highly suitable as a mate. Social changes can also dispose people to have more active occurrences of love, such as living with each other so that they spend more time together. All of these mechanisms dispose a person to have the occurrence of love when prompted by the environment.

Hence viewing love as a semantic pointer can explain both its cognitive and physiological aspects and both its occurring and dispositional aspects. Yet another advantage of semantic pointer theories of love, trust, and commitment is that they can explain the conscious experiences that go with these mental states, thanks to the theory of consciousness as semantic pointer competition presented in *Brain–Mind* (chapter 8). You can be unconsciously in love with someone when you have the dispositions described in the last paragraph, but you became aware of love when the semantic pointer representing your attitude toward another out-competes other semantic pointers currently active in your brain. In a later section on whether the heart wants what it wants, I address the question of whether love and other emotions are under conscious control.

ROMANTIC INTERACTIONS

The development of human relationships depends partly on the mental processes of the people in individuals but also on their interactions—how they treat each other. According to Murray and Holmes, high-risk and low-risk relationships differ because the individuals in them have different mental habits of rule use. In low-risk relationships, one partner sacrifices, and shared values lead to anticipations of acceptance. These all encourage connection goals that help people to escalate their dependence and justify their commitments. In high-risk relationships, however, judgments that partners are unresponsive can lead to anticipations of rejection, tendencies to self-protect, and withholding of dependence. Less trusting people protect themselves by differentiating themselves from partners who otherwise might merit greater trust.

Personality traits that incline people to be less trusting include low self-esteem, high neuroticism (tendency to worry a lot), and inclination to provoke conflicts rather than form secure emotional attachments. Ongoing interactions can produce cascades of rule applications, responsiveness or withdrawal, and increases or decreases in trust or commitment. In a positive trajectory, responsiveness, trust, and commitment of each individual feed back on each other to produce strong and satisfying mutual dependency. In a negative trajectory, however, withdrawal resulting from lack of responsiveness, trust, and commitment increasingly leads toward the dissolution of the relationship.

What makes minds interdependent? People depend on each other in two ways: the actions of one person have causal effects on the mental states and behaviors of the other, and one person relies on the other to help satisfy needs. Specifically, Pat depends on Sam if Sam's actions cause changes in Pat and if the satisfaction of Pat's needs requires Sam's actions. So dependence in relationships is not just causality in general but rather special kinds of causal effects determined by needs and emotions. Pat and Sam depend on each other if their needs-based emotions are substantially affected by the actions of the other.

Chapter 3's account of communication as transfer and elicitation of semantic pointers illuminates how dependency arises. When Pat and Sam have enjoyable verbal and nonverbal interactions such as compliments and caresses, they transfer positive emotions to each other and prompt each other to have additional positive emotions such as gratitude. But antagonistic interactions such as insults and scowls transfer and elicit negative emotions such as anger. The appraisal dimension of emotions takes into account the satisfaction of goals and needs. Hence interdependency of minds consists of their ability to influence each other's emotions, for good or bad.

If communication were just transmission of words, it would be much easier than it actually is in personal relationships and in teaching (chapter 12). The semantic pointer theory of communication explains why conveying one's state of mind to another person is so difficult, because it requires instillation or elicitation of multimodal representations that are sensory and emotional as well as verbal.

People's interactions can influence and be influenced by inferences that the people make about each other in accord with explanatory coherence and emotional coherence. Judgments that someone is untrustworthy can be based on the person's actions but also on more subtle cues such as body language: leaning backwards, crossing arms, and face touching. The overall judgment to trust someone is an inference that combines finding the best explanation of behavior with emotional interpretation.

This interaction of cognitive and emotional inferences makes judgments of trust, and other thoughts about relationships, susceptible to motivated inference. Murray and others have documented the valuable role that motivated inference can play in maintaining relationships. Happy couples have a tendency to interpret each other's flaws as actually positive, for example when someone's sloppiness is excused as a sign of being a free spirit. Such positive illusions result from motivated inference where people believe good things about their partners because doing so helps satisfy their relatedness needs. Another contributor might be the mechanism discussed in chapter 7 of mood-congruent imagination. Enjoying being with someone makes it easier both to remember previous enjoyable encounters and to imagine future ones.

The underlying mechanism for motivated inference is emotional coherence, where conclusions such as the desirability of a partner are influenced by emotion-laden goals as well as by causal explanations of behavior. Explanatory and emotional coherence interact as simultaneous forms of parallel constraint satisfaction, balancing aims to explain observations with desires to satisfy personal goals. Love cannot survive on motivated inference alone if the evidence mounts that a partner is abusive. I conjecture that one reason why people with high self-esteem and low neuroticism tend to have better relationships is that they are more inclined to make motivated inferences about their partners, generating positive views like the value map in Figure 4.1 rather than Figure 4.2.

In contrast, people with low self-esteem and high neuroticism may be more prone to fear-driven inference in which anxieties lead them to focus on bad characteristics of their partners. For example, sloppiness could be interpreted as a fundamental personality flaw that indicates untrustworthiness. Because trust includes binding of positive emotion, association of negative emotion with a person will discourage trust.

Interactions between people can be purely physical with no attempts at communication, as with slaps, shoves, and automatic or forced sex. Obviously, such interactions interfere with the development of love, trust, and commitment and therefore are destructive for romantic relationships, which thrive on verbal and nonverbal communication.

The other kind of interaction that is important for relationships is interagent inference, where one person thinks about what is going on in the mind and behavior of the other. Application of the Murray and Holmes relationships rules often requires such inferences, because people need to infer what their partners value and whether they are being accepting or rejecting. Such inferences can be conscious and verbal, or they may be unconscious and multimodal, generating either attributions of mental states or predictions about likely behavior. For example, the nonverbal rule *<fist clenched and raised> and <voice loud>* → *<angry>* may enable unconscious inference that another person is angry and needs to be calmed or avoided. Hence interactions between people in romantic relationships can be explained by semantic pointer theories of communication and inference.

CONTRAST WITH GOTTMAN

The famous relationship expert John Gottman takes a more behavioral approach to relationships than the neural-cognitive one that I have been pursuing as a deepening of Murray and Holmes. Gottman describes trust as a pattern of behavior rather than as a mental state, saying that Pat trusts Sam if Sam acts to look out for Pat's interests by changing behavior to increase payoffs for Pat in their interactions. Such preferential payoffs are undoubtedly an important result of trustworthiness but should not be identified with it. Pat's trusting Sam is not just a matter of judgment about Sam's behavior but also a matter of the feelings that Pat has for Sam.

Gottman is well aware of the importance of emotions in relationships. His famous "four horsemen of the apocalypse" are empirically identified characteristics of failing relationships, and all of them are concerned with emotions. The four are criticism, defensiveness, contempt, and stonewalling.

Criticism occurs when one person suggests that conflicts result from personality flaws in the partner, for example the partner being selfish. Attribution of flaws is always emotionally negative. Defensiveness occurs as insistence on your own innocence in order to ward off a perceived attack or to meet an attack with a counterattack. The various ways of being defensive such as using righteous indignation and whining are all fraught with negative emotions. One of the best predictors of relationship breakdown is when one person shows contempt for the other. Contempt is a negative emotion in which one partner appraises the other as inferior and is often accompanied by insults using negative concepts such as "you're a jerk."

Finally, stonewalling is emotional withdrawal, in which one person ceases to pay attention to the other. Stonewalling can result from emotional flooding in which one person becomes so physiologically aroused in an unpleasant interaction that withdrawal results. Gottman has done extensive research on the physiological correlates of interactions among people in failing relationships such as their heart rates. He also counsels people to improve relationships by increasing awareness, understanding, and tolerance of emotions. But his view of emotions remains oddly behavioral, with no appreciation of the thoughts and feelings that are also part of emotion.

Gottman's proclaimed "new science of love," his *Principia Amoris,* consists of a set of equations for describing the emotional interactions of two people such as a husband and wife. He uses the variable X to represent the emotional expression of the husband at a particular time and the variable Y to represent the emotional expression of the wife at a particular time. X and Y change as the result of their past values and the value of the other variable. Gottman's equations serve to produce some interesting predictions, but their explanatory use is limited because they reveal nothing about the nature of the emotions that two people have for each other and how these emotions change as a result of their interactions. Gottman's behavioral theory of love is as limited as his behavioral theory of trust.

Understanding relationships, including their breakdowns and repairs, requires understanding emotions. The semantic pointer theory of emotions can fill this role because it integrates the brain's perception of physiological states with cognitive appraisals. Gottman is well aware of the importance of physiology but neglects the role that appraisal plays. For example, motivated inference where one person idealizes the other by interpreting possible flaws as actual strengths helps to maintain relationships by encouraging more positive appraisals and emotional reactions.

My account of love as feelings that emerge from multilevel mechanisms is different from Gottman's love equations with only observable variables. How people fall in and out of love is best understood in terms of the combinations of mechanisms for emotions involving neurotransmitters, hormones, binding by convolution, interagent inference, and social communication.

RELATIONSHIP SUCCESS AND FAILURE

Relationships can succeed for various reasons, including common interests, values, personalities, and social networks, all of which depend on cognitive and social mechanisms. Why do relationships so often fail? Why do they sometimes start strong but then end in a bang or a whimper?

Machines break, and so do mechanisms. When your bicycle, car, or toilet stops working, the breakdown can occur in a part or in the interactions among parts. For example, a tire can stop functioning because it has a puncture, which is a breakdown in a particular part. Another way a bicycle can fail to work is if the chain falls off the gear, which is a breakdown of the interactions of parts. Cognitive and social mechanisms are far more complicated than bicycles, but the breakdowns can similarly be identified by locating the parts and interactions that have stopped working. Breakdowns do not have to be all or none but can be a matter of degree, for example when the chain on the gear starts to slip a small amount but gradually becomes looser and looser.

In a close relationship, the parts are the people involved and the interactions are their verbal and nonverbal communications, along with the inferences that they make about each other. So relationships can begin to fail because of problems with the people, their inferences, and/or their communications. Couples are also parts of larger systems such as extended families, and their interactions can change accordingly. If a couple acquires children, then there can be dramatic changes in their goals, interests, and communications.

There are numerous psychological problems that can contribute to the malfunctioning of people in a relationship, for example disorders such as depression, anxiety, and substance abuse. These disorders can interfere with inferences that people make about each other, for example when depression blinds people to how much other people care about them. As chapter 10 relates, mental illnesses have neural and molecular causes, as well as social ones.

Even without individual disorders, communication problems can harm relationships through misunderstandings and hurtful behaviors. Mean utterances and antagonistic gestures generate negative emotions, retaliation, and withdrawal. Miscommunication can arise from differences in unconscious rules about how to interact, for example about what to say and how to say it.

There can be feedback effects from malfunctioning of the parts (mental states of the individuals) and malfunctioning of their interactions (how they talk to each other, treat each other, and make inferences about each other). In a deteriorating relationship, the interactions become as ineffective as the respective parts, with increase in emotionally negative interactions such as insults, scowls, sneers, and even physical blows. These changes in social mechanisms then feed back onto the breakdowns in the individuals, fostering depression and anxiety that in turn lead to more negative interactions. In a good relationship, specific positive emotions such as happiness, pride, and gratitude are encouraged by verbal and nonverbal communication. But in a deteriorating relationship, these are increasingly supplanted by negative ones such as sadness, resentment, contempt, fear, anger, and even disgust.

With this cascade of negative emotions and negative interactions, the crucial processes of love, trust, and commitment deteriorate. Developing these emotions requires emergence from interacting mechanisms at all levels, and their degeneration similarly results from multilevel mechanisms. Relationship failure resulting from multilevel mechanism breakdown will also be important for explaining the outbreak of wars in chapter 9.

A good relationship has emergent properties, enabling a couple to flourish in a way that neither individual could do alone. Love, trust, and commitment are the emotional bonds that form individuals into a novel whole as a couple or family. Couples can become committed to a relationship, not just the other person in it. On the other hand, a bad relationship can be demergent, less valuable than the sum of its parts, if two people are individually fine but have bad interactions that make them worse off than they would be on their own.

In North America, 40% to 50% of marriages eventually fail, but they usually begin in a high state of optimism. The critical transition from infatuation to disillusionment was illustrated in Figures 4.1 and 4.2 using value maps. Such transitions are more than just the shift in emotional gestalts shown in the maps, because there can also be shifts in patterns of inference from motivated to fear-driven and rage-driven and in patterns of communication from encouraging to critical. Relationships fail because of breakdowns in individual and group mechanisms. Similarly, mechanism breakdowns are responsible for illnesses (chapter 10) and wrongful convictions (chapter 11).

DOES THE HEART WANT WHAT IT WANTS?

In an episode of the television show *Girls*, a friend says to the main character Hannah that the heart wants what the heart wants, and Hannah replies: "You do know who you're quoting, right?" I wondered too, and a Web search turned up three sources: a popular song by Selena Gomez, a justification by Woody Allen for his involvement with Mia Farrow's adopted daughter, and a letter by the poet Emily Dickinson, which presumably is the origin. What does it mean to say that the heart wants what it wants? And is it true?

The heart is often used as a figure of speech (metonymy) for emotions, as in Pascal's remark that the heart has its reasons that reason does not know. So I think that the meaning of the saying "the heart wants what it wants" is that emotions such as love are not under conscious, cognitive control. For example, you cannot simply decide to fall in love with someone, no matter how suitable. Similarly, you cannot just decide to stop loving someone, no matter how hopeless. Trust and commitment are analogously not under conscious control.

On the other hand, you can decide to do things that increase the likelihood that you will fall in love with someone, such as having deep, intimate conversations and gazing into each other's eyes. And you might decide to try to fall out of love with someone by avoiding the person, focusing on negative features, and becoming attracted to someone else. These occurrences are hard to explain using the two most common theories of emotions.

On the cognitive appraisal theory of emotions, it should be fairly easy to control your emotions, because you can reappraise the situation and figure out whether falling in love accomplishes your relationship goals. But calculating that someone is good or bad for you is no guarantee of falling in or out of love with him or her. The physiological perception view of emotions fits well with the idea that the heart wants just what the heart wants, putting feelings outside of cognitive control. But mere physiology cannot explain how the brain differentiates among emotions that are physiologically similar, such as fear/anger and shame/guilt, nor how the brain produces socially complex emotions such as pride, gratitude, shame, guilt, envy, and embarrassment.

The problem is resolved by the semantic pointer theory that understand emotions as a parallel brain process that simultaneously performs and integrates cognitive appraisal and physiological perception. This integration explains why emotions are partly, but only partly, controllable by cognition. Reappraisal performed by yourself or with the help of a friend or therapist may be limited in the extent it can modify physiological states. Physiological modification might be helped by other, more physical interventions, such as exercise, meditation, and medication.

On this interpretation, it is only partly true that the heart wants what the heart wants, because there is some limited capacity for cognitive reappraisal that contributes to emotional change. But this capacity can sometimes bring it about that the heart wants what the brain wants.

SUMMARY AND DISCUSSION

This chapter has begun the discussion of social change by considering local changes in the smallest social groups consisting of only two people. A theory of romantic relationships should explain why and how they develop, why they succeed, and why they fail. Mental mechanisms of individual thinking and social mechanisms of verbal and nonverbal communication provide a start to answering these questions.

Central to these mechanisms is the semantic pointer theory of emotions, which views them as neural processes that combine cognitive appraisal and physiological perception. This theory explains central emotions such as love, trust, and commitment. Moreover, it suggests a way of understanding the interactions between people as transfer and eliciting of emotions by verbal and nonverbal communication.

The semantic pointer theories of emotion and communication deepen the rich account of interdependent minds provided by Murray and Holmes. The shaping of interpersonal interactions by unconscious rules fits well with the semantic pointer accommodation of multimodal rules that employ nonverbal perceptions and emotions. Many of the rules that help to generate and maintain relationships concern trust, a neural process that binds representations of self, other, and situation with a positive emotional result of appraisal and physiology. Commitment is also a neural process resulting from binding but differs from trust in that it incorporates intentions, also understood as semantic pointers. Eliasmith's Semantic Pointer Architecture is therefore rich enough to cover the mental representations and processes operating in romantically interdependent minds.

The emotion of love is crucial for romantic relationships but is much more than the pattern of interpersonal behaviors described by Gottman. Rather, love is a neural process that emerges from the interaction of molecular, neural, mental, and social mechanisms. Like trust, love binds representations of self and other but produces more intense feelings, because it also binds stronger physiological responses and appraisals that find the loved one to be enormously relevant to personal goal satisfaction. Because love is both cognitive and embodied, it is not completely under rational control, but neither is it completely independent of cognitive influence. Like other emotions, love can be bizarrely irrational on some occasions, but it can also be profoundly reasonable when it genuinely leads to the satisfaction of fundamental human needs of belongingness.

The philosopher David Hume said that reason is the slave of the passions, a counter to Plato's claim that reason should be the master of emotion, like a charioteer controlling horses. I prefer a different metaphor: reason and emotion should be partners, working together to help people meet their needs. Emotion without reason is blind, but reason without emotion is empty.

Romantic couples are the smallest of groups, but they already display emergent properties that belong to the whole because they result from interaction of two people. Strictly speaking, a couple as a group cannot be happy, because happiness is an emotion generated in brains. But it is useful metaphorically to speak of a happy couple when the communicative interactions of two people make them each happier than they would be without the other, including thinking of themselves as being a couple. This solution to the person–group problem admits the reality of groups as resulting from the interactions of social mechanisms and mental mechanisms in individuals.

I have begun the discussion of social change by looking at the smallest social groups consisting of pairs of people in romantic relationships. This scale is already suitable for showing the interdependence of social mechanisms with cognitive/emotional ones. Later chapters will show the importance of emotional interactions in much larger groups. For example, trust is also relevant to social norms, politics, economics, religion, war, law, and management. These fields are also fertile for application of many ideas used in this chapter for romantic relationships, including multimodal rules, emotional coherence and gestalt shifts, and motivated and fear-driven inference.

Social issues about close relationships go far beyond the individual pairs I have been discussing in this chapter, because of much broader historical changes in the kinds of social relationships that are available to people. Arranged marriages based on social and economic connections have largely given way in many parts of the world to romantic relationships reflecting the choice of the partners. In an increasing number of countries, marriage is no longer a relationship between one man and one woman because of the legality of same-sex unions. Social media such as Facebook and dating sites such as OkCupid recognize an increasing variety of gender identities and possible relationships. These developments require major changes in social norms discussed in the next chapter.

This chapter has focused on romantic relationships, which are largely discussed by psychologists, so I have not yet reconciled social cognition with microsociology. But semantic pointer theories of cognition, emotion, and communication have much to contribute to such important sociological ideas as self-presentation, emotional energy, interaction rituals, and the managed heart. Chapter 5 moves up to larger social groups by considering discrimination and prejudice.

NOTES

Overviews of social cognition include Fiske and Taylor 2013 and Kunda 1999. Lieberman 2010 surveys social cognitive neuroscience. Social psychologists are showing increasing interest in culture (e.g., Heine, 2011). Vallacher, Read, and Nowak 2017 review computational social psychology.

Microsociology is pursued, for example, by Goffman 1959, Collins 2004, and Hochschild 1983. Other approaches that attempt to combine sociology and psychology are cognitive sociology (e.g., Cerulo, 2002, 2010) and affect control theory (e.g., Robinson, Smith-Lovin, & Wisecup, 2006).

On close relationships, see Murray and Holmes 2011, 2017 and Murray, Holmes, Griffin, and Derrick 2015. The study on unstable chairs is Kille, Forest, and Wood 2013. Perhaps this effect results from multimodal priming (Schröder & Thagard, 2013) that activates unconscious rules. Such rules based on multimodal semantic pointers explain why people often know more than they can tell (Nisbett & Wilson, 1977). For more on explanatory and emotional coherence, see *Natural Philosophy*.

DeSteno 2014 reviews trust. Fisher 2004 discusses love from a neural perspective. Bartz 2016 describes mechanisms by which oxytocin may modulate human sociability. Nave, Camerer, and McCullough 2015 raise doubts about whether oxytocin increases trust. *Natural Philosophy* (chapter 5) defends the hypothesis that all dispositions such as trust stem from mechanisms. Personal relationships are sometimes based on power, whose connection with emotional mechanisms is shown in chapter 6.

Gottman's views are in his 2011 and 2015 works. Epstein, Robertson, Smith, Vasconcellos, and Lao 2016 identify relationship skills important for long-term romantic success.

Finkel, Cheung, Emery, Carswell, and Larson 2015 show how marital difficulties arise when partners expect each other to satisfy disparate economic, intimacy, and self-expression goals; see also Finkel, Simpson, and Eastwick 2017. Fitzimmons,

Finkel, and vanDellen 2015 describe couples as self-regulating systems. *Brain–Mind* (chapter 12) explains the self as a multilevel system.

PROJECT

Do a three-analysis of the concept of trust. Use semantic pointers' combination of appraisal and physiology to explain the difference between romantic love and related emotions such as parental love, friendship, and infatuation. Construct an agent-based model of a couple escalating into love and later degenerating into loathing.

5

Sociology

DISCRIMINATION AND PREJUDICE

Have you suffered discrimination because of your sex, race, ethnicity, age, sexual orientation, religion, immigration status, or disability? Discrimination occurs when persons are mistreated merely because of the group to which they belong. This chapter describes how discrimination results from prejudice, which is a cognitive-emotional process that biases some people against others. A major component of prejudice is the operation of stereotypes that emotionally disparage a group and its members. Why are there increases and decreases in the amount of discrimination and prejudice that occur in various societies? What are stereotypes and how do they contribute to prejudice and discrimination?

Sociology is the study of the origins, development, and organization of social relationships. It investigates many aspects of social behavior, including class, mobility, institutions, policy, and religion. In contrast to social psychology, sociology focuses more on social structure than on individual thinking and often displays hostility toward the relevance of psychological explanations. Since its origins in the nineteenth century, sociology has aimed to find social causes for social changes, not psychological ones.

Only recently have sociologists begun to talk about social mechanisms, which are rarely tied to mental mechanisms. Sociologists seem to fear that introducing psychological factors will undermine or render redundant sociological explanations. On the contrary, my multilevel mechanisms approach fully agrees with the

importance of social mechanisms while also integrating them with cognitive and
emotional mental processes.

To illustrate social-cognitive integration, I examine discrimination, which is discussed by sociologists both as a phenomenon to be explained by social forces and
as a cause of unequal distribution of status, rights, and material goods. For explaining discrimination, the crucial link between the social and the psychological
is the operation of prejudice in individual minds, which leads to large social effects
that feed back onto individual thinking about groups.

Prejudice can be defined as an unfavorable opinion formed about a group
without a basis in evidence, but it is much more informative to provide a three-
analysis as in Table 5.1. Standard examples of prejudice include attitudes toward
women, racial groups such as Blacks, ethnicities such as Irish, sexual orientations
such as gays, and religious groups such as Muslims. These cases exhibit typical
features including a stereotyped group viewed as inferior in contrast with another group viewed as superior, for example when White racists view Blacks as
inherently inferior. Evidence-free beliefs about inferiority are tied to a network
of other beliefs concerning ways in which the supposedly inferior group is different from the superior group. These beliefs interact with negative emotions
toward the group viewed as inferior, ranging from dislike to hatred, fear, anger,
and disgust.

The concept of prejudice is important because it helps to explain social facts
about discrimination such as the exclusion of some groups from power, wealth,
and respectability, with bad effects on their happiness and health. More problematic is what social and mental processes explain prejudice, which is complicated
because imbalances in wealth and power are causal factors in producing prejudices
well as results of it. There is no circularity in such explanations, merely recognition that social structures can cause changes in individual thinking at the same
time as thinking affects structures. Feedback in complex systems is not circularity
in explanation or inference.

TABLE 5.1

Three-Analysis of *Prejudice*

Exemplars	Against Blacks, women, homosexuals, Muslims, old people
Typical features	Stereotype, group viewed as inferior contrasted with group viewed as superior, negative emotions, false beliefs
Explanations	Explains: discriminatory behavior
	Explained by: mental mechanisms, communication

Prejudice and discrimination result from both the cognitive-emotional mechanisms that operate in individual minds and the social mechanisms of communication that spread and maintain prejudices in social groups. This chapter provides social cognitive-emotional workups of two groups that have been victims of discrimination and prejudice: women and Jews. In both cases, prejudice operates in individual minds because of interconnected concepts, images, beliefs, rules, analogies, metaphors, and emotions.

These case studies show the need for reinterpretation of important ideas in social science that are usually treated without sufficient attention to mental operations. Social norms and institutions can be understood not as logical abstractions or purely social entities but as complexes built out of integrated cognitive and social mechanisms including communication among individuals. Social change can be explained as both social and psychological, dependent on the interactions of both. These interactions are crucial not only for understanding why and how changes in prejudice and discrimination have occurred in the past but also for bringing about reductions in ongoing kinds of discrimination. Both explaining and overcoming prejudice require a rich account of how prejudices operate in people's minds, in large part through the effects of stereotypes.

STEREOTYPES

As mental representations of social categories, stereotypes have been extensively studied by social psychologists because of their importance for explaining how people think about and act toward each other. People often have strong expectations about genders, races, ethnic groups, age groups, and professions. These expectations result from the concepts, beliefs, and emotions that operate in their minds. Thanks to the semantic pointer theories of concepts, beliefs, and emotions, we can gain an understanding of how stereotypes operate in people's brains.

From the perspective of social cognitivism, stereotypes are neural processes that combine concepts, beliefs, and emotions. All stereotypes have associated concepts such as *African American, lesbian,* and *Mormon*. According to the semantic pointer theory of concepts, these concepts bind exemplars, typical features, and explanations into a pattern of neural firing. The typical features employ images, beliefs, and rules that serve to explain why members of the stereotyped group do what they are alleged to do. Specific examples of the operation of stereotypes are provided for women and Jews.

Not all social stereotypes are emotionally negative: most people seem to consider Canadians as polite, friendly, and benign. Tragically, however, many social stereotypes are emotionally negative and depict social groups in ways that encourage discrimination. Being prejudiced against a group requires having learned a negative stereotype in the form of concepts, beliefs, and emotions. Such prejudice leads to mistreatment of the group in everyday interactions and more systematically through institutional practices. Stereotypes can affect the behavior not only of prejudiced people but even of people who are members of the disfavored groups if they apply the negative views to themselves. Experimental studies show that activating negative stereotypes can impede performance, an effect called stereotype threat. For example, reminding women of the common view that women are not good at mathematics can cause reductions in their results on math exams.

Where do stereotypes come from? Some may result from ordinary cognitive processes of concept learning, when people meet members of a group. More commonly, people learn stereotypes through social communication, picking up concepts, beliefs, and emotional attitudes from their parents, friends, and media. Moreover, people may be motivated to acquire negative stereotypes because of their own needs to feel superior to others and to justify the social order in their society.

Group stereotypes are often resistant to change, even when people encounter members of the groups whose behavior contradicts the stereotype about them. Nevertheless, stereotypes sometimes do change as a result of revisions of concepts, beliefs, and emotions to undermine prejudice and alleviate discrimination. First, we need to look in more detail at stereotypes that have contributed to harmful prejudice.

WOMEN: SOCIAL COGNITIVE-EMOTIONAL WORKUP

In 1949, Simone de Beauvoir published *The Second Sex*, an extraordinarily original and insightful treatise on Western ideas about women and sexuality. A French novelist and philosophy teacher, de Beauvoir brought together biology, history, philosophy, anthropology, and literature to dissect the history and structure of attitudes toward women. Her sources ranged from prejudiced philosophers such as Aristotle and Schopenhauer to images of women in ancient myths and modern novels.

Her profound investigation provides the basis of a social cognitive-emotional workup of prejudice against women. My goal is to understand how the prejudicial views of women described so richly by de Beauvoir operate in misogynistic minds and how they are acquired by communication. Examination of the relevant concepts, images, beliefs, analogies, and emotions reveals the negative stereotype of women as the result of cognitive and social mechanisms, not biological or religious inevitability. The result deepens de Beauvoir's famous conclusion that one is not born a woman but becomes one.

Concepts and Values

Figure 5.1 is a value map that captures most of the central concepts and connections identified by de Beauvoir. She repeatedly stresses the "otherness" of women, how women are historically conceptualized as different from men. The strength and superiority of man is contrasted with the weakness and inferiority of women. Women are the property of men and therefore ought to be submissive servants. Their weakness is manifested in their being frivolous, fickle, unstable, and complaining. Inferiority is not merely a matter of mental incapacity but also of being cursed by God, unclean as a result of menstruation, and mutilated in lacking a penis (a view held by Aristotle as well as Freud). Whereas the concept *woman* is disparaged because of all these associations, the concept *man* is appreciated because of its association with strength and superiority and its opposition to *woman*.

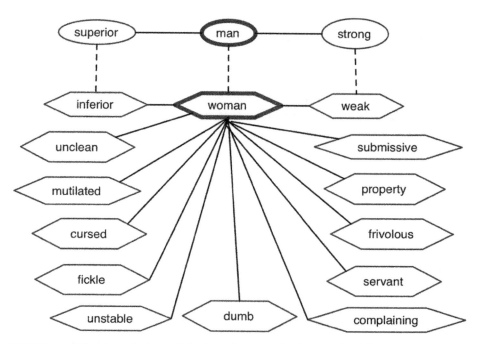

FIGURE 5.1 Value map of misogynistic view of women. Ovals are positive, hexagons are negative, solid lines show mutual support, and dotted lines show incompatibility.

For clarity, many links among concepts are not shown in the figure, for example between *weak* and *submissive*.

No single writer or speaker ever asserted the whole complex of negative concepts associated with women in Figure 5.1. But many misogynistic men and even some women have shared this stereotype, most explicitly today in extreme views such as the Islamic State discussed in chapter 6. Putting all these concepts together in a value map shows the emotional coherence of the sexist worldview. Men are inherently superior to women in a large range of interconnected respects, and the emotionally negative aspects of women are interconnected, such as their inferiority and physical impurity. The otherness of women derives from many ways in which men are better. The result is a stereotype that has much emotional coherence both internally and with the goals of men. People are often not aware that they hold a negative stereotype, because the whole configuration of concepts and the particular emotional bindings are not accessible to consciousness.

Images and Embodiment

The concepts shown in Figure 7.1 are not just words. De Beauvoir presents the dance of visual images that go along with the word "female":

> An enormous round egg snatching and castrating the agile sperm; monstrous and stuffed, the Queen termite careening over the servile males; the praying mantis and the spider, gorged on love, crushing their partners and gobbling them up; the dog in heat running through black alleys, leaving perverse smells in her wake; the monkey showing herself off brazenly, sneaking away with flirtatious hypocrisy. And the most splendid wildcats, the tigress, lioness, and panther, lie down slavishly under the male's imperial embrace, inert, impatient, shrewd, stupid, insensitive, lewd, fierce, and humiliated.

Historically, many other images have been associated with the concept of woman, such as shrew, nymph, and mermaid.

The negative concepts in the value map in Figure 5.1 are associated with familiar sensory images. The visual redness of blood goes with the monthly uncleanness of women. If you think that such views no longer exist, recall the 2015 dismissal by Donald Trump of a critical female journalist as having "blood coming out of her wherever." The shrewish, complaining woman is marked by auditory imagery. There is even kinesthetic imagery in the submissiveness and fragility of women, on the misogynistic stereotype.

These sensory, imagistic aspects of the concept of woman display one kind of embodiment, but there is another kind manifested in the emotional reactions described later. Negative emotions such as contempt and disgust have a large visceral component, combining perception of physiological change with cognitive appraisal. De Beauvoir wrote before modern understanding of testosterone, now known to be associated with dominance in males, and other hormones relevant to behavior such as oxytocin, now known to be associated with trust and maternal behavior. Hence molecular mechanisms are another kind of embodiment relevant to understanding the mental operations of misogyny. Neuroscientists are now investigating the role of brain areas such as the amygdala and insula in prejudicial thinking.

However, many of the concepts shown in Figure 5.1 go beyond the senses and embodiment to incorporate more abstract information concerning intelligence, property, and servitude. Hence misogyny is transbodied as well as embodied.

Beliefs and Rules

The misogynistic stereotype is more than just concepts and images, for it also includes a host of beliefs and rules. For every negative concept in Figure 5.1 there is an associated belief, such as that women are weak and inferior. More elaborate beliefs provide explanations of women's inferiority, for example the Judeo-Christian view that Eve was a secondary creation from Adam's rib. Pseudoscientific explanations rest on beliefs about inferiority resulting from genes, hormones, menstrual cycles, and smaller brains. Freudian psychoanalysis promulgated dubious beliefs about women such as that they suffer from penis envy and distract men from their work.

Many of these beliefs can be expressed as rules in the cognitive sense of representations with an *if–then* structure. Rules can have more structure than the simple associations showing in Figure 5.1, as in the rule *if a woman is menstruating, then she is unclean.* These descriptive rules give rise to normative rules that tell people what to do, as in the rule of Orthodox Judaism that if a woman is menstruating then she must not be touched by men. Some extreme rules are still part of Islamic Sharia law, such as *if a woman is outside her home, then she must be veiled and accompanied by a male relative.* Other social rules that severely limit women's activities prevailed in the West into the twentieth century, such as that women lack the intellectual capacity to succeed in higher education.

Prejudicial rules can also be multimodal, with conditions and actions represented by nonverbal semantic pointers. The prescription for men to avoid unrelated women could be represented as the rule <woman> → <avoid>, where the condition includes visual representation of women and the action includes motor representations of keeping away.

Beliefs and rules about women are interconnected by causal relations. Women's biological or theological history makes them inherently weak, which makes them in need of protection, which justifies rules that restrict their activities. The causal and normative interconnections of beliefs and rules makes them difficult to challenge one at a time. Hence dislodging them requires replacement of a whole system of beliefs by an alternative system of beliefs that have greater explanatory coherence with available evidence. So stereotype change that reduces the contribution of prejudice to discrimination requires replacement of whole systems of concepts and beliefs, through mechanisms described later.

Some discriminatory rules are explicit and verbal, but others may be unconscious and multimodal. Conversational rules may license interrupting and ignoring women with little awareness of prejudice.

Analogies and Metaphors

According to the semantic pointer theory of concepts, an important part of any concept is a set of exemplars. These standard examples can also serve as analogies to which new instances can be compared. De Beauvoir describes historical examples of women that serve as cautionary tales. In the Hebrew Bible, Eve's succumbing to temptation produced the fall of man, and in ancient Greek mythology, Pandora's curiosity led to the releasing of all of the evils of humanity. Not all exemplars of womanhood are evil or incompetent, but positive role models such as the Blessed Virgin Mary are less common.

Stories such as fairy tales can serve as source analogs that can be applied to contemporary targets. For example, the fables of Sleeping Beauty, Cinderella, and Snow White all suggest that women must passively wait until a male savior comes along. Medieval monks were warned about the succubus, a female demon who attempts to seduce men. King James I said that to make women learned has the same effect as making foxes tame: to make them more cunning. Sometimes, however, women can function as source analogs, as in the worst analogy in the history of philosophy. Aristotle claimed that slavery was justified, because non-Greek slaves were naturally inferior, just like women.

Metaphorical terms for women often highlight their weakness, inferiority, and irascibility. A woman can be labeled a bitch, battle ax, harpy, dragon lady, or shrew, using metaphors with underlying critical analogies such as the assumed meanness of a female dog. Although some metaphors applied to particular women are positive, such as angel and rose, many metaphorical utterances about women function as emotional analogies that transfer negative feelings to them. Stories, analogies, and metaphors mesh with concepts and beliefs to paint a derogatory picture of women. Changing prejudicial stereotypes requires new sets of comparisons using different analogies, metaphors, and images.

Emotions and Actions

Given the negativity of the concepts, beliefs, and analogies about women, it is not surprising that the emotions that men direct toward women are frequently damning. Because of their weakness and inferiority, women can be viewed with disdain, contempt, and scorn. Because they are unclean, women can be viewed with disgust, loathing, and revulsion. Because some women such as witches are evil, it is appropriate to view them with fear and anger. However, the purity of some women can make them objects of admiration and pride. There are also emotions deemed appropriate for women to feel toward men because of their strength and superiority, for example admiration and gratitude.

Different emotions justify different actions. Men should avoid the evil woman feared as a witch, castrating bitch, femme fatale, or feminazi but pursue the desired angelic Virgin. Actions are also governed by rules that incorporate negative emotional attitudes. For example, a woman should not be allowed to own property because she is too weak and frivolous. Intense emotions of pride, contempt, and fear provide men with emotional energy to work to maintain their superior status. Negative emotions and properties such as frivolousness render women unworthy of trust.

Inferences

The negative stereotype of women that encompasses concepts, beliefs, analogies, and emotions generates many inferences about what to expect of women and how they ought to be treated. But inferences also contribute to the stereotype, for example inductive generalization from small and biased samples of women who conform to it. More importantly, biases can be introduced and maintained by emotional thinking based on motivated inference and fear-driven inference.

Men are motivated to adopt, retain, and propagate negative views of women because of various goals. Men want to see themselves as strong and superior, and the contrast with women promotes that view. Men want to control property and cultural practices, so they are motivated to view women as incapable of handling these roles. Because men desire sex and domestic comfort, they are motivated to view women as submissive and servile. Motivated inference is not just wishful thinking, because men can selectively draw on observations and stories to provide unexamined reasons for maintaining the beliefs that they want to have.

Men may not be motivated to view women as evil or unclean, but fear-driven inference serves to justify such beliefs. Focusing on individual stories such as Eve, Pandora, and the spy Mata Hari can generate intense anxiety that makes men obsessed with the dangers that women pose. In domestic lives, looming threats of infidelity and false paternity may terrorize men into focusing on their insecurities. This excessive, emotionally intense concentration makes worries about female behavior seem credible, as fear-driven inference turns possibility into plausibility.

Fear-driven inference and motivated inference can sometimes work together. Anxiety may suggest that women are dangerous, then motivated inference can alleviate anxiety by encouraging the belief that women are weak enough to be controlled. Particular beliefs about the inferiority of women are supported not just by specific claims that might be challenged but by a whole network of congruent beliefs and patterns of inference that range from inductive generalization to emotional leaps. The holistic nature of inference and its interconnection with emotion inhibit isolation of the causes or reasons for particular beliefs. Instead, overcoming prejudice needs to identify the network of concepts and beliefs and the interconnected forces of motivated and fear-driven inference that support the whole system.

To understand each other, men and women need to make interagent inferences that can be seriously impeded by inaccurate stereotypes, motivated domination, and fear. Better information and emotions such as respect can stimulate improved interpretations of each other's actions and mental states, based on fully executed explanatory coherence.

Communication

How does misogyny spread? How do people acquire the concepts, beliefs, analogies, and emotions that constitute the negative stereotype of women? Few people develop this pattern of thinking just through their own observations and inferences. Rather, most people acquire negative stereotypes through communication from others, picking up beliefs and attitudes through verbal and nonverbal communication.

In verbal communication, people hear or read assertions and stories that associate women with negative features such as weakness and inferiority. Repeated exposure to utterances that connect women to concepts such as *bitch, whore, slut,* and *dumb* produce inductive generalization by learning of neural connections. The more often people hear an utterance, the more likely they are to believe it. So being in a social group that includes frequent misogynistic utterances makes one tend to acquire the concepts and beliefs that add up to the negative stereotype.

The communication of stereotypes requires much more than the use of words. Stereotypes incorporate emotional attitudes as much as beliefs, and nonverbal communication is more powerful for the transmission of emotions than speech alone. Negative emotions can be conveyed by facial expressions such as frowns, sneers, and eye rolling. Hence utterances accompanied by such expressions will tend to lead listeners to acquire emotionally negative associations that fit with what is said. Sounds can also help to convey negative emotions by means of tone of voice, groans, whistling, or blowing a raspberry. Body language can also convey negative emotions through gestures such as crossed arms, shrugs, raised middle finger, or winding your index finger around your head to convey craziness.

Simone de Beauvoir made a path-breaking contribution to understanding how words, beliefs, and stories have contributed over centuries to a view of women as other than men and markedly inferior. But she neglected the large emotional component of the stereotype of women and the nonverbal communications that tend to propagate harmful feelings. She was clearly hopeful that her diagnosis of the damaging conception of woman would help to lead to the development of views more conducive to the human needs of women.

I hope that understanding the mental structure of negative stereotypes and the cognitive and emotional mechanisms that produce and sustain them can suggest means of achieving social change that eliminates discrimination. Improvements in stereotypes held by members of groups require changes in verbal communication but also changes in the nonverbal exchanges that play a large role in conveying emotions. I will outline a theory of stereotype change based on cognitive and social mechanisms. First we must consider the even more extreme example of negative stereotyping found in anti-Semitism.

JEWS: SOCIAL COGNITIVE-EMOTIONAL WORKUP

De Beauvoir's account of prejudice against women drew on many sources, but probably no one misogynist has ever held the full stereotype I described. In contrast, prejudice against Jews can be captured by a single work by a single writer, the most notorious and tragically effective anti-Semite of all time, Adolf Hitler. In 1923 he was imprisoned for political activities and dictated a book that was published in 1925 as *Mein Kampf* (My Struggle). Hitler described how he came to hate

Jews as a young man in Vienna and goes into great length about their negative characteristics.

Hitler's anti-Semitism was not original, for similar views were frequently expressed in Vienna and had been common in Europe for hundreds of years. But *Mein Kampf* provides a compact source for characterizing anti-Semitism using a social cognitive-emotional workup. Hitler's brutal candor displays the worst form of Jewish stereotype, which he was later able to use to justify discrimination and the execution of millions of people.

Concepts and Values

Hitler's system of concepts and values is shown in Figure 5.2. Just as de Beauvoir emphasized the otherness of woman as opposed to man, Hitler repeatedly contrasted the Jew with its German opposite. Germans are pure and associated with the abstract ideal of a mythical race of Aryans, whereas Jews are unclean and foreign. Hitler describes Jews as filthy and defiled, yet shameless in their lack of intellectual culture. The foreignness of Jews marks them as traitors, not only to the German state but to all humanity. This inhumanity is even more negative than the misogynistic view of women, who still rank as human even though they may

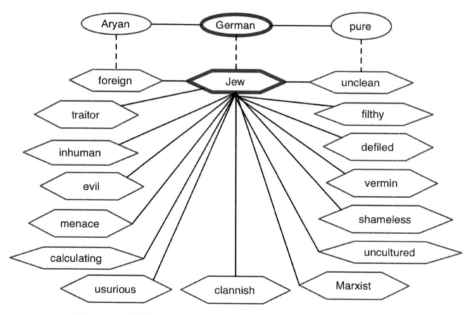

FIGURE 5.2 Value map of Hitler's view of Jews. Ovals are positive, hexagons are negative, solid lines show mutual support, and dotted lines show incompatibility.

not legally be persons. A full value map would show more concepts and links, for example the concept *human* that fits with *Aryan* but is incompatible with *inhuman*.

According to Hitler, the evil of Jews is manifested in their calculating abilities to exploit Aryans by usurious interest, fostered by their clannish ability to stick together. Hitler attacks Jews both for being rapacious bankers and radical Marxists, not worrying about how the same group can be both capitalists and Communists. As with the misogynistic depiction of women as being both weak and dangerous, a negative stereotype can be emotionally coherent without being logically consistent. Figure 5.2 shows how the concept of Jew can be made resoundingly negative through emotional coherence with many malicious concepts.

Images and Embodiment

Some of the concepts in Nazi depiction of Jews are abstract, such as *usurious* and *Marxist*. But the concepts that contrast with German purity such as *unclean* and *vermin* have associations tied to visual and olfactory images. Hitler describes Jews as maggots, slime, and bloodsuckers, all of which are connected to images that may be visual, tactile, and emotional. Later Nazi propaganda used visual images of rat-like Jews to spread prejudice among the German population. Hence Hitler's anti-Semitism is partly embodied through its use of sensory imagery. Another aspect of embodiment is tied to emotions such as hatred and contempt.

Beliefs and Rules

For every concept in Figure 5.2, there is a corresponding belief, such as that Jews are evil and uncultured. Hitler also states other odious beliefs about Jews such as that they are responsible for literary filth, White slavery, and social democratic politics. He blames them for contaminating art, tricking workers into joining trade unions, lowering the racial level of society, and contributing to the defeat of Germany in World War I. He does not, however, repeat some of the beliefs long expressed in European anti-Semitism, such as that Jews killed Christ and are practitioners of rituals using Christian blood.

In the anti-Semitic mind, these beliefs are interconnected by causal relations. It is because Jews are defiled and uncultured that they wreck literature and art. It is because they are traitorous that they helped to defeat Germany. Is because they are evil and clannish that they are able to be financially successful. These contributors to explanatory coherence make the Nazi worldview hard to challenge on a belief-by-belief basis, requiring it to be confronted and supplanted with a systematic alternative set of beliefs and explanations.

Many of Hitler's beliefs about Jews can stated as *if–then* rules, such as: *If someone is a Jew, then he is plotting with other Jews to bring about world domination.* Only after Hitler gained power in 1933 was he able to establish normative rules about how to deal with Jews, initially restricting their ability to own property and intermarry and eventually enforcing imprisonment and mass termination. Some anti-Semitic rules are multimodal, for example *<Jew>→<disgusting>*, where *<Jew>* is a semantic pointer derived partly from the visual stereotype and *<disgusting>* is a semantic pointer that is partly visceral.

Analogies and Metaphors

The images described earlier of Jews as maggots and bloodsuckers also serve as metaphors with implicit underlying analogies. The characteristics of maggots as vile, diseased, and appalling are meant to be transferred over to Jews. Hitler warns metaphorically about other effects of Jewish influence, such as pestilence, parasites, bastardization, and blood poisoning. He compares the Jewish world conspiracy to a hydra and describes Jewish Bolsheviks as devils. All of these comparisons are intended to transfer negative emotions from the repulsive source to the Jewish target. Such transfer is not just verbal reasoning but requires multimodal inference that generates new semantic pointers that include sensory and emotional information.

Emotions and Actions

The concepts, beliefs, and analogies that are part of Hitler's anti-Semitic stereotype feed into cognitive appraisals of the relevance of Jews to his social and political goals. At the same time, the sensory aspects of embodied assumptions about Jews feed into overall reactions. The semantic pointer for the concept *Jew* binds these together with representations of particular situations to generate specific emotional reactions that are strongly negative.

The most visceral emotions that Hitler expressed toward Jews were revulsion and disgust deriving from his perception of them as unclean and inhuman. In addition, Hitler hated the Jews for their economic success and alleged deterioration of art and literature. He was also angry at them for what he perceived as their role in Germany's military defeat, economic decline, and increasing racial impurity. Blame is an action more than an emotion, but Hitler also employed feelings of anger and superiority when he blamed the Jews for all of these wrongs. Because of the complexity of cognitive appraisal, Hitler's contempt for the Jews as inferior could coexist with his envy and resentment at their successes in finance and journalism. Viewing the Jews as menacing because of their international conspiracy generated fear because they constituted a threat to the German people.

Emotions such as these and more general political ambitions spurred Hitler and his followers into vigorous action that rapidly expanded their popular support, leading to the election of the Nazis as the dominant party in 1933. Initially, actions against the Jews were primarily intended to intimidate them, expropriate their property and encourage them to emigrate. But after war started in 1939, victory over Poland put an additional 3 million Jews under Nazi control. Efforts then began to kill as many as possible, eventually eliminating around 6 million—two-thirds of European Jews. It is hard to comprehend how the hatred, anger, and fear that the Nazis felt toward the Jews could be sufficiently intense to motivate this level of extermination. But the configuration of intensely emotional concepts and beliefs described earlier led to genocidal actions. Chapter 6 contains a broader discussion of Nazi ideology.

Inferences

Hitler acquired his beliefs about Jews more from reading the large anti-Semitic literature in Vienna than from any personal encounters. So his negative views were based less on observations and inductive generalizations than on emotional inferences tied to motivation and fear.

Hitler was motivated to adopt anti-Semitism because the Jews served as useful scapegoats for both his personal failings and the decline of Germany. He could explain his poverty and lack of professional success by the dominance of Jews in Vienna, and Jews could also be blamed for Germany's military defeat and cultural downfall. Hitler did not simply wish to believe that the Jews were evil, for he could draw on the anti-Semitic press to find abundant reasons for this hypothesis. Motivated inference supported a large and internally coherent story about Jews as responsible for German suffering. Believing that Jews were both inferior and evil supported Hitler's motivations to see himself and his country as victimized.

Hitler's anti-Semitism was also supported by fear. He did not want to believe that the Jews would manage to dominate the world and force Germany into irrelevance, but he feared such developments. Focusing on such scary consequences provided emotional fuel for the inference that Jews really were evil and conspiring. Hitler drew on the forged *Protocols of the Elders of Zion* to claim that the existence of the Jewish people was based on a continuous lie and that the Jewish menace needed to be broken.

The fear-driven inference that Jews are dangerous can be transformed into the motivated inference that Hitler and the Nazis are the best way to overcome this threat. This pattern of combined fear-driven and motivated inference occurs in other kinds of prejudice that lead to discriminatory actions. The extent to which women, Blacks, homosexuals, and indigenous people are regarded as menacing can be exaggerated by fear-driven inference. Then motivated inference can operate in terrified people to make them decide to support groups that promise to eliminate the danger. Then the groups become a solution to a problem that they themselves have created or exaggerated. As chapter 8 describes, religious groups can also manufacture threats by fear-driven inferences that encourage people to make the motivated inference that religion is the best response to the threats.

Communication

Hitler stressed the need for propaganda to spread his views throughout Germany and Austria. *Mein Kampf* was part of this propaganda, using aggressive, emotionally evocative prose to appeal to people disaffected by the miserable state of Germany in the 1920s. Hitler aimed to transfer his beliefs to other people but also to spread his emotional attitudes about Jews, Bolsheviks, and the prospects of Germany for renewed greatness. Pamphlets and newspapers provided additional written means of communicating both beliefs and emotions.

At least as important were live events such as speeches, rallies, and marches. Available on YouTube, the Nazi propaganda film *Triumph of the Will* shows Hitler as a dynamic and entrancing speaker who uses dramatic cadences and emotional intensity to enthrall a crowd. Rallies and marches transfer emotions not only from the speaker to the listeners but also among the members of the crowd. People mimic the voices, gestures, and body language of leaders and marchers, acquiring similar emotions through the mechanism of emotional contagion. Negative attitudes about Jews could also be spread by group activities in which Jews were criticized and humiliated. Such activities generate strong emotions that increase emotional energy for future hostile actions. Hitler was also able to use radio for propaganda purposes, where his voice alone was sufficiently compelling to draw increasing support from the German people.

I have provided social cognitive-emotional workups to show the extent and mental operation of prejudice against women and Jews. Similar workups could easily be done for other groups that have also been the subjects of discrimination on the basis of race, sexual orientation, religion, age, or disabilities. The point of these workups is to display and identify the emotional thinking that goes into stereotypes and prejudice. This identification aids appreciation of the large interconnected structure of concepts, beliefs, and emotions that needs to be supplanted if prejudice and discrimination are to be overcome. Social change also depends on alterations of social norms and institutions.

SOCIAL NORMS AND INSTITUTIONS

Social norms are customary rules that govern behavior in groups and societies. The following are some norms that directed the behavior of women in Western societies when de Beauvoir wrote *The Second Sex*.

- Women should get married and have children.
- When a woman gets married, she should take her husband's name.
- Women rarely go to college.
- Women rarely work outside the home after marriage.
- Women are subordinate to their husbands in making important decisions.

What are such norms? How are they acquired and maintained? How are they changed?

According to the sociologist Talcott Parsons, a norm is "a verbal description of a concrete course of action . . . combined with an injunction to make certain future actions conform to this course". Norms are not just patterns of behavior but rather rules that produce behaviors. To generate actions, a rule must be more than just a string of words: it must be a brain–mind process than can cause the body to do something. The rules described in chapter 2 as semantic pointers have the required efficacy. Their *if–then* structure uses recognition of situations to produce inferences and actions that are to be carried out in the situation. For example, the first norm in the last paragraph becomes:

- If someone is a woman, then she gets married and has children.

This rule is not just a verbal description because it operates in a processing system that matches the *if* part to a particular person and then generates the inference that she gets married and has children. When a woman applies the rule to herself, then actions of marrying and becoming pregnant are mandated.

Under the semantic pointer interpretation of rules, the matching and inference procedures can be multimodal, incorporating sensory and emotional representations. The sensory component of matching can involve, for instance, the visual recognition that someone looks like a woman. The inference made can involve images such as the woman being pregnant. Rules that constitute norms are not merely predictions about what will happen but indications of what *ought* to happen, which is tied in with a complex of emotions. Someone holding the norm that a woman should get married to a man feels good when she does but disappointed, annoyed, frustrated, and maybe even outraged and disgusted if she does not. Compliance with the rule comes about because the woman has absorbed the rule and its emotional implications, not because she is making a rational calculation that following the rule is the best choice for her to make.

Different cultures employ different social norms, some of which are multimodal rules, for example concerning what to do when you meet someone. A common Western norm is <*meet*> → <*shake hands*>, but other norms require different practices, such as bowing, fist bumping, cheek kissing, and air kissing. Cultures also vary in unexpressed social norms such as how close to each other people should stand when conversing. For more on culture, see chapter 8 on the anthropology of religion.

Social norms construed as multimodal rules can incorporate emotions in two ways. First, the condition and action (*if* part and *then* part) can include emotions bound into the semantic pointers, as in the Nazi social norm <*Jew*> → <*avoid*>. Implicit prejudices—ones that people are not aware of—can operate by means of nonverbal rules such as <*Black*> → <*scary*>, which combines a visual condition with an emotional action. Second, the whole rule, itself a semantic pointer, can have an emotion bound with it such as approval and admiration that encourage people to follow it. Violation of a social norm can therefore generate negative emotions such as guilt, shame, and embarrassment. Opponents can bind other emotions such as repugnance to social norms that should be violated and overturned.

Chapter 4 described the role of unconscious, multimodal rules in close relationships: rules that people are not aware they are following can have large effects on their behaviors. Some social norms such as women deferring to men in conversation may never be expressed verbally but nevertheless strongly affect human interactions. If rules were just verbal statements, it would be puzzling how they can operate unconsciously. But the semantic pointer account of multimodal rules as procedures that can include sensory and emotional components makes unconscious operation natural and comprehensible.

This cognitive-emotional view of social norms is strongly at odds with the prevailing view in sociology and philosophy that social norms are rational choices. According to Cristina Bicchieri, norm compliance is based on people's expectations that most members of a group will conform to a rule and will expect others to conform to the rule, with sanctions if there are violations. People acquire social norms when they rationally recognize these expectations and choose to adopt the rule.

Changing norms is a matter of rationally changing expectations about conformity and sanctions.

From the perspective of social cognitivism, there need be little that is rational about the acquisition of social norms. People acquire norms not by reasoning but by emotional communication that is both verbal and nonverbal. People can acquire verbal rules by hearing them uttered, but even then the emotional force of the rules will be conveyed nonverbally by tone of voice, facial expressions, gestures, and body language. Unconscious rules with nonverbal components such as sensory representations and emotional associations are even more likely to be acquired nonverbally. These kinds of communication and transfer of rules occur in all social settings, independent of rational choices.

Acquisition of social norms is part of the socialization that occurs when people communicate with others who belong to the same groups. Personal and group identity are largely individual mental representations. Thinking of oneself as an Elbonian (the Dilbert cartoon's mythical ethnicity) requires the full array of self-representations discussed in *Brain—Mind* (chapter 12): concepts, images, beliefs, metaphors, and emotions. Acquiring the Elbonian identity requires applying the Elbonian stereotype to oneself, including the associated conscious and unconscious rules that constitute social norms in that group. When you identify as Elbonian, then you acquire the associated social norms, such as that Elbonians wear high hats, live in mud, and exclaim "walla-walla." Identity, however, is also a social process, because these representations are introduced, spread, and maintained by ongoing communication among group members.

Once a person has acquired a social norm through cognitive and emotional communication, the rule is maintained by ongoing social interaction. In the 1940s and 1950s, women and men continued to see, hear, and feel traditional norms about women and therefore continued to accept and to conform to them. Like rule acquisition, maintenance of social norms has nothing to do with rational choices about the costs and benefits of behaving in certain ways but rather with operation of conscious and unconscious rules that direct behavior. Only in the 1960s and 1970s with the rebirth of feminism and the formation of women's liberation groups were social norms about women's behavior challenged. These challenges came about in part because of analogies with movements that challenged social norms about the treatment of Black people. The revision of social norms cannot occur in isolation, because it requires revision of interconnected concepts, beliefs, and emotional attitudes, all part of the process of overcoming prejudice described in the next section.

Social norms are important in the functioning of institutions, which are groups with standardized patterns of rule-governed behavior, such as the family, education, religion, and economic and political organizations. Sociologists often examine the functions of social institutions such as promoting social solidarity or maintaining inequalities, but they rarely discuss the nature and operation of the rules that enable institutions to carry out these functions. The account of social norms as conscious and unconscious cognitive-emotional rules fills this gap, especially when the rules have a neural interpretation as multimodal semantic pointers and a social interpretation as communicated by verbal and nonverbal means.

For example, the institution of marriage is a set of rules about who can be married and what obligations result, along with rules about how to dissolve marriages. In many countries, written, legal rules about marriage have changed dramatically since the 1960s, allowing easier divorce and marriage between people of the same sex. In addition, there are new, less official social norms about the appropriateness of premarital sex, cohabitation, and single parenthood, some of which may operate as unconscious rules.

All of these rules and institutions incorporate values, both as emotions associated with particular actions and as emotions attached to entire rules and representations of institutions. The institution of a university can be represented by the concept *university*, rules such as *if university then teach,* and values attached to *teach* and to the rule that assigns the teaching role to universities.

This social cognitivist view of social institutions does not attempt to reduce them to individuals making rational choices but rather emphasizes the role of emotional interactions in maintaining the rules that allow institutions to function. Institutions such as the family and religion are established through the communications of people that instill sets of social norms in the form of conscious and unconscious rules that can incorporate sensory and emotional components. The emotional components are what govern people's behavior, not comprehensive calculations and expectations about costs and benefits.

A well-functioning institution is one that people view with approval, affection, and even pride; an incompetent institution is one that people view with dislike, anger, hatred, and even contempt. Following the rules that constitute institutions requires feeling, not just beliefs and expectations. The sense of duty to follow institutional rules is also an emotion that may or may not be a rational choice.

Social norms and institutions are major cognitive and social mechanisms for maintaining social stability. A society with accepted institutions, established rules, and interactions that maintain emotional approval can readily resist change. Changing institutions calls for replacing old groups and rules with new ones. Whether such changes are rational or not depends on the extent to which the institutions help to satisfy the basic human needs of those individuals. Chapter 7 on economics and chapter 9 on history display the frequent absence of rationality in individual and group behavior. A full, normative treatment of rationality is in *Natural Philosophy*.

Thus sociological ideas about social norms and institutions can be tied to processes of cognition and emotion. It is natural to connect other influential sociological explanations to mental mechanisms, for example Pierre Bourdieu's idea of habitus. Habitus is a system of lasting dispositions that integrate past experiences to function in perceptions, appreciations, and actions. Such dispositions result from the underlying representations of concepts, beliefs, rules, and emotions, all construed as semantic pointers. For example, people who work together in an industry such as retailing can have a complex of unconscious, multimodal rules such as <*customer approaches*> → <*smile*>. Similarly, cultural capital (nonfinancial assets such as intellect, education, and style of speech) derives from neural representations and processes that support intelligence, learning, and language production.

OVERCOMING PREJUDICE

Feeling negative emotions toward some groups is not irrational or moral if the groups really are observably evil, for example Nazis, pedophiles, and rapists. But prejudices are neither evidence-based, rational, nor moral, and they lead to mistreatment of people merely because they belong to some stereotyped group. Therefore, social progress requires reduction and elimination of prejudice to remove the blight of discrimination.

Figuring out how to overcome prejudice requires good theories about the cognitive and social mechanisms that produce and sustain it. A purely social plan for mitigating prejudice would say that we just need to change institutional practices in order to reduce discrimination, but institutions depend on rules that operate in people's minds. Force alone will not change people's behavior, as the American military discovered during the Vietnam War with the failure of their slogan: If you get people by the balls then their hearts and minds will follow. Reasoning to promote rational choice is a limited route to overcoming prejudice, because people's ignorance of emotions makes it difficult for them to adjust their expectations about their own behavior and the expectations of others.

Overcoming prejudice requires a much more complicated program that depends on the mental and social mechanisms that establish it. Concepts and negative stereotypes need to be replaced by ones that are both more accurate and more emotionally favorable to disadvantaged groups. Replacement of concepts has to harmonize with replacement of beliefs and rules that employ erroneous concepts. At the same time, the images, metaphors, and analogies that feed prejudice need to be supplanted by alternatives. Negative emotions directed toward groups suffering discrimination need to be attenuated or ideally replaced by positive emotions, held both by people who view themselves as superior and also by people who are members of disadvantaged groups who previously thought of themselves as inferior. Finally, because all of these mental processes result from social communication, there must be new interactions that provide verbal and nonverbal ways of introducing and maintaining a new system of ideas and values.

How do concepts get modified and replaced? Lessons about how to change stereotypes come from the semantic pointer theory of concepts, which understands them as combining exemplars, typical features, and explanations. A first step to changing the negative stereotype of women in Figure 5.1 is to abandon a set of traditional examples such as Eve, Pandora, and the 1950s' television housewife. Instead, we can look to a set of more powerful role models ranging from Joan of Arc to Marie Curie and Simone de Beauvoir herself. Media such as television and movies can be a major source of socially prominent exemplars, for example when women are portrayed as doctors, lawyers, and detectives rather than as helpless wives.

Replacement of exemplars encourages substitution of typical features with ones emphasizing equality rather than subordination. On the revised stereotype of woman that Simone de Beauvoir could only hope for in 1949, but which became more prevalent in the 1970s, women are strong, competent, caring, and equal to men in all important respects. The shift is signaled by increasing use of the word "woman" in place of the honorific "lady," the diminutive "girl," and the derogatory "broad" and "chick." The view of woman as inherently other than man and therefore inferior is replaced by concepts that carry the associations of men and women as just different sorts of humans. I recommend constructing an alternative value map of *woman* to supplant the Figure 5.1 stereotype. It would also be interesting to use value maps to contrast the conceptual system of the second-wave feminism that developed in the 1970s with the third-wave feminism concerned with race and class that developed in the 1980s.

The revised concept of woman could not work without major revision in beliefs, replacing the assumptions that women are weak and inferior with principles that they are strong and equal. Especially important is replacement of social norms that sharply curtail the range of behaviors available to women. For example, the norm that women rarely go to higher education has been altered in the West so that now most universities have more women students than men. Beliefs and rules do not get revised one at a time, because they are parts of coherent systems of observations and explanations. So replacing beliefs requires people to recognize alternative systems that have more explanatory coherence with respect to the evidence. For example, limitations in women's past performance in fields such as medicine and mathematics can be explained by the lack of opportunities granted to them rather than by any inherent incapacities.

Systems of rules that constitute social norms and institutions also do not get changed one at a time. Establishing a new set of social behaviors requires changes in individuals and groups through replacement of old sets of rules by new ones. This replacement can occur partly by organizational changes such as new laws, but their success depends on people actually incorporating the new rules into their mental systems. For example, rules granting women equal access to education have limited impact without changes in unconscious rules about how women should be treated in educational contexts.

Stereotype change is not just a matter of changing words, because it can also require new sensory images, metaphors, and analogies. Being able to picture women as physicians or astronauts fits well with verbal descriptions of them as successful and powerful. Such pictures are enhanced by metaphorical descriptions of women as roaring rather than whimpering. Analogies can reinforce the independence and competence of women, as in this 1970s' comparison: a woman without a man is like a fish without a bicycle.

Along with these cognitive changes come dramatic emotional changes. The concept *woman* shifts, from intensely negative through the associations shown in Figure 5.1, to strongly positive through associations with concepts such as *strong*, *competent*, and *equal*. Specific emotions also shift dramatically, relinquishing the feelings generated by the old stereotype of women such as contempt resulting from weakness and shame resulting from mutilation. Instead, women can acquire new emotions such as confidence resulting from strength and pride resulting from identification as equal and competent. To overcome prejudices, the new systems of concepts and beliefs must be cognitively coherent with respect to observations and explanations. New ways of thinking must also be emotionally coherent with respect to values and goals, some of them newly introduced.

The attitude changes required to overcome prejudice are brain processes of emotional rebinding, like falling in or out of love with someone. The negative emotions attached to concepts like *woman, Jew,* or *Elbonian* need to be replaced by ones that are at least neutral. Such emotional change can occur gradually by positive examples gained from meetings, imagined meetings, or media such as television. I conjecture that a major reason for the dramatic shift in public attitudes toward same-sex marriage in the last 15 years is the rapid increase in the number of gay and lesbian characters in television and movies. Shifts also seem to be occurring in attitudes toward transgender and intersex people, adding new differentiated concepts beyond the traditional *male* and *female*.

Empathy can also encourage emotional rebinding when it encourages reimagining a member of a group as similar to the imaginer. In Shakespeare's *Merchant of Venice*, Shylock tries to evoke empathy in Christians:

> I am a Jew. Hath not a Jew eyes? Hath not a Jew hands, organs, dimensions, senses, affections, passions? Fed with the same food, hurt with the same weapons, subject to the same diseases, healed by the same means, warmed and cooled by the same winter and summer, as a Christian is? If you prick us, do we not bleed? If you tickle us, do we not laugh? If you poison us, do we not die? And if you wrong us, shall we not revenge?

Emotional rebinding produces revalencing, changing the values attached to concepts and rules.

The alterations in values, goals, and beliefs should change emotional inferences based on motivation and fear. If males abandon the goal of sustaining their self-esteem by downward comparison to women, then motivated inferences about women's inferiority no longer work. Fear-driven inferences about women's dangerous nature can be blocked by evidence about the capacities of men and women. Changes in goals and beliefs stop the insidious loop by which fear drives inferences about menaces that can be mollified by motivated inferences about what women can actually accomplish.

The elimination of prejudice by the adoption of new systems of concepts, beliefs, and emotions exemplifies emergence rather than incremental change, because the replacement system has properties of explanatory and emotional coherence not found in the individual mental representations. In individuals and groups, there may occur critical transitions in which slow appreciation of the flaws in prejudicial thinking builds up to general recognition of the superiority of alternatives. In some individuals, the critical transition may be an instantaneous epiphany, an emotional gestalt shift, but may be more gradual in others. Because concepts and other cognitive representations depend on neural processes using semantic pointers, and because emotional and other representations depend on neurotransmitters such as dopamine, overcoming prejudice is a case of multilevel emergence from mechanisms that are mental, neural, molecular, and social.

Major changes in concepts, beliefs, rules, and emotions cannot occur or be maintained without social changes in communicative interactions. People need to change not only what they say to each other but also the way in which they communicate values nonverbally by facial expressions, gestures, body language, and tones of voice. For example, new social norms about men's behavior can eliminate such nonverbal behaviors as leers, whistles, winks, and obscene gestures, as well as verbal behaviors such as catcalls, demeaning jokes, and putdowns.

Hence overcoming prejudice requires changes in social practices as well as changes in mental representations that are largely derived from the social practices. It can also require physical and organizational changes, such as ensuring that women have equal access to resources and are not subjected to stereotype threat. These kinds of mental/social change are difficult to bring about, like the relationship communication discussed in chapter 4 and the teaching of values examined in chapter 12. But overcoming prejudice is crucial for a flourishing society, to be encouraged with better understanding of the mechanisms required.

CONCEPTUAL CHANGE

Conceptual and belief change to remove prejudicial stereotypes is even more dramatic than what occurs in scientific revolutions. Adoption of new scientific theories often requires abandonment of old competing ones, along with replacement of obsolete concepts like *ether, phlogiston,* and *humor* with ones like *gravity, oxygen,* and *germ.* Similarly, stereotype change can encourage replacement of socially defective concepts such as *bitch* by more positive ones such as *womyn.* Reduction of prejudices against homosexuals is accompanied by rejection of derogatory terms such as "faggot" in favor of repurposed terms such as "gay" and "queer." The word "queer" used to be a derogatory term for homosexuals, then became a supportive term for them, and is now becoming a positive term for a wide variety of sexual minorities. Revalencing is an important kind of conceptual change that alters the emotional value of a concept.

The process of conceptual change to overcome prejudice is evocatively captured by the native Canadian writer Richard Wagamese in an article ironically subtitled "What it means to be an Indian." He describes the negative terms applied by the dominant White culture to natives: savage, redman, slow, awkward, lazy, shiftless, stupid, drunken, welfare bum, and so on. He eloquently writes: "You learned that labels have weight—incredible, hard, and inescapable. You learned to drink so that you wouldn't have to hear them." But Wagamese then describes a transformation deriving from more positive self-identification: "But when you found your people you became Ojibway. You became Anishinabe. You became Sturgeon Clan. You became Wagamese again and in that name a recognition of being that felt like a balm on the rawness where they'd scraped the Indian away". When Wagamese reconceptualized himself as a Anishinabe rather than a generic, downtrodden Indian, the change was behavioral and social as well as mental: he adopted different interactions such as native cultural rituals. The concept *Indian* needs to be revalenced or abandoned in favor of concepts with less emotional baggage such as *native American* and *First Nations*, increasingly used in Canada.

One of the most radical kinds of conceptual change in science is reclassification, such as when Earth was reclassified as a planet because it revolves around the sun rather than being the center of the universe. Conceptual change with stereotypes can require reclassification, for example viewing woman as a kind of person rather than as just a defective man. Canada only recognized women as persons and therefore eligible to vote in 1929. An even more radical kind of conceptual change is metaclassification, in which the whole basis for putting things into categories changes. Darwin produced this kind of conceptual change when he introduced evolutionary history as a principle of classification in addition to physical appearance. Similarly, scientific advances such as genetic testing can lead to new ways of classifying people into genders, races, and ethnicities.

Stereotype change in overcoming prejudice is more radical than conceptual change in scientific revolutions in two respects. First, it requires more emotional conceptual change, because concepts like *woman* need to shift from connection with negative emotions such as fear and shame to positive emotions such as respect and pride. Some concepts like *queer* can be revalenced, but others like *faggot* and *nigger* are so irremediably toxic that they are best deleted.

Second, sustainable stereotype change requires new social norms concerning modes of communication in the form of behavioral rules about speaking and acting. People need to conduct themselves differently as well as to think differently, which often requires adopting multimodal rules built out of semantic pointers. Deletion is the only solution for noxious nonverbal rules like <*see woman*> → <*catcall*>. Stereotype change and scientific theory change are similar in that they both require development and replacement of whole systems of concepts and beliefs.

In sum, overcoming prejudice is not simply a matter of changing institutions or making rational choices. It requires systematic replacement of defamatory concepts, values, beliefs, rules, images, analogies, metaphors, emotions, and styles of communication. Even when new mental representations have been acquired, the old ones reside in memory and may be revived under stressful circumstances, for example when a female superior criticizes a male employee. Hence overcoming prejudice may require mental acts of control to help keep undesirable old ideas from outcompeting superior new ones. The same problem arises in science education as discussed in chapter 12.

I have sketched how replacement can work in changing stereotypes about women but hope that others will undertake social cognitive-emotional workups of prejudices based on race, ethnicity, sexual orientation, religion, age, and other sources of discrimination.

SUMMARY AND DISCUSSION

Sociology cannot be reduced to or replaced by cognitive science, but it can be enhanced by incorporating understanding of the operations of minds in people who form groups and societies. Social mechanisms of communicative interaction both influence and are influenced by mental mechanisms of representation, inference, and emotion. In place of vague notions of social facts and collective minds we can look for specific ways of thinking and communicating that produce social change. Chapter 6 discusses how social change can be blocked by the use of power to prevent minds from changing.

Groups do not reduce to individuals, nor individuals to groups. Rather, the actions of groups result from the actions of individuals who think of themselves as members of groups. (This principle of social recursion also applies to economics in chapter 7.) What makes a group a group is not the sort of physical attachment that makes a collection of cells into an organ. Rather, social bonds arise from the individuals in the group having mental representations such as concepts that mark them as members of the group. The bonding process is not purely psychological, however, as it can also include various kinds of physical interactions that are social and/or linguistic, such as participating in rituals and legal contracts. These interactions tie people together into groups when they result in mental representations (emotional as well as cognitive) through which individuals come to envision and feel themselves as part of the group.

Discrimination is an important problem that results from social causes such as institutions but also from psychological causes such as prejudice. Prejudice operates in individual minds through representations and processes that include concepts, images, beliefs, rules, and emotions. Particularly important are stereotypes whose emotionally negative concepts include exemplars, typical features, and explanations.

Prejudice and associated stereotypes can be investigated using social cognitive-emotional workups. Discrimination against women and Jews depends on the mental representations and processes of misogynists and anti-Semites. We can understand the mental structure of these use views by noticing the opposition assumed between women and men and between Jews and Aryans. The prejudicial stereotypes of woman and Jew acquire their negativity by association with many other concepts that assume inferiority and by connections with other representations such as rules and analogies. Emotions are a key part of the force of prejudicial concepts, not just because of their general negativity but also because of specific emotions such as fear, anger, hatred, resentment, contempt, and disgust.

Important sociological ideas such as identity, social norms, and institutions can be deepened by understanding how concepts and rules operate in human minds. Social norms are not just rational expectations but rather depend on the acquisition and maintenance of rules that contribute to inference and action. Rules are *if–then* representations that can be nonverbal and unconscious because they can have sensory and emotional components as well as verbal ones. Institutions are groups that depend on collections of rules that are not just verbal documents but mental structures that lead individuals to support and comply with institutional policies.

Understanding social norms requires appreciating how they operate in individual minds as well as how they are communicated across among minds. The semantic pointer theory of communication provides the social mechanism that complements the cognitive mechanism of conscious and unconscious rule operation.

Reducing or eliminating discrimination requires institutional changes and also overcoming prejudices that operate in the minds of individuals. Removing prejudice calls for systematic changes in networks of interconnected concepts, beliefs, rules, images, and emotions. New concepts and beliefs need to be developed that can holistically supplant prejudicial ones through processes of explanatory and emotional coherence. The introduction and alteration of images, metaphors, and analogies are also part of the massive conceptual change required to overcome entrenched prejudice.

Modes of inference and communication also need to change to prevent reversion to prejudicial ways of thinking through verbal and nonverbal interactions. Cognition, emotion, and communication are mechanistically explained by neural and social processes involving semantic pointers. Mental representations are not just a grab bag of unconnected mental processes, because they all operate by the same neural mechanisms. The cognitive and social mechanisms described in this chapter apply equally well to politics, economics, anthropology, and history.

Some sociologists and historians think that their fields require a different kind of explanation different from the natural sciences, based on a kind of interpretive understanding called "verstehen." Verstehen uses empathy to attach meaning to the actions of people, but social cognitivism shows how empathy works by neural mirroring, analogizing, and multimodal rule simulation. A social cognitive-emotional workup investigates the meanings in the minds of social actors using mental and neural mechanisms, not just subjective guesses. Hence the goals of verstehen approaches to capture the rich meanings of human lives and societies can be accomplished in a more rigorous manner. Similarly, sociologists' frequent use of the concept *lived experience* to describe the first-hand experience of people in different culture can be fleshed out using theories about different kinds of mental representation including emotion, sensory-motor processes, and the neural mechanisms for consciousness described in *Mind–Brain* (chapter 8).

The kinds of conceptual change described in this chapter with respect to overcoming prejudice are also important for issues in the professions. Education is rich with conceptual change, as teachers strive to inform students about scientific ways of thinking about the world that need to displace common sense. In medicine, mental illness needs to be reconceived in terms of mental and social mechanisms. Ideas about legal responsibility require new systems of concepts and beliefs that supplant prescientific notions of will and action. Engineering design at its most progressive requires developments of new concepts and methods. In business, management and marketing require leaders and other persuaders to change the ways in which workers and buyers think about the world. In all of these fields, as in the sociology of discrimination, social change requires conceptual change.

NOTES

For a review of contemporary sociological theory, see Calhoun et al. 2012. Goodwin, Jasper, and Polletta 2001 discuss emotions and social movements. Franks 2010 and Cerulo 2010 explore neurosociology.

On discrimination and prejudice, see Allport 1958 and Back and Solomos 2000.

For social mechanisms, see Demeulenaere 2011, Hedström and Swedberg 1998, and Hedström and Ylikoski 2010. Ridgeway 2014 discusses social mechanisms for inequality.

Stereotypes are reviewed by Fiske and Taylor 2013, Kunda 1999, and Stangor and Crandall 2013. Sinclair and Kunda 2000 discuss motivated stereotypes of women. Kunda and Thagard 1996 explain stereotype application as parallel constraint satisfaction.

Amodio 2014 discusses findings about the neuroscience of prejudice and stereotyping.

Steele, Spencer, and Aronson 2002 review stereotype threat. Perhaps reduced performance results from fear-driven inference in which anxiety leads people to believe that they are inferior because the thought scares them.

My analysis of misogyny is based on de Beauvoir 2010 (the quote is from p. 21), supplemented by Holland 2006.

Aristotle's horrible analogy is in his *Politics*, 1254b.

The "truth effect" is that people tend to believe what they hear repeated: Dechêne, Stahl, Hansen, and Wänke 2010.

My analysis of anti-Semitism is based on Hitler 1943 and Perry and Schweitzer 2002.

The definition of norms is from Parsons 1968, vol. 1, p. 75. Rational choice expositions of social norms are in Bicchieri 2006; Coleman 1990; and Conte, Andrighetoo, and Campenni 2013. Schmidt, Butler, Heinz, and Tomasello 2016 show that children as young as three quickly infer social norms.

Bourdieu 1977 discusses habitus.

On conceptual change, see Thagard 1992b, 2012b, 2014b.

The paragraph about Wagamese is from Thagard 2012a (p. 48). The quote about Indians is from Wagamese 2010, p. 9.

For a readable survey of results about unconscious prejudices, see https://aeon.co/essays/unconscious-racism-is-pervasive-starts-early-and-can-be-deadly. Implicit biases may be hard to identify if they consist of nonverbal rules.

Places can be prejudiced as well as people: Murphy and Walton 2013.

Imagined contact reduces prejudice: Miles and Crisp 2014. Paluck and Chwe 2017 describe techniques for reducing hate.

The principle of social recursion is from Thagard 2012a. Related ideas are reflexivity (chapter 7), Hacking's 1999 looping effect of human kinds, and Giddens'1984 structuration, all of which can be fleshed out in terms of mental representations and processes.

PROJECT

Develop an agent-based model of how prejudice and recovery from it can spread through groups. Construct a more detailed account of the multimodal rules responsible for implicit prejudice, habitus and stereotype threat. Show how intersectionality—the overlapping of identities such as gender and race—can yield emergent oppression even worse than the sum of single identity prejudices, for example with indigenous women.

6

Politics

IDEOLOGY

POLITICAL CHANGE

What kind of government do you want? Politics (political science) is the study of government and the state. Changes in governments and countries are important kinds of social change, raising challenging questions. Why do forms of government change dramatically, for example from feudalism to democracy or dictatorship? Why are new countries sometimes created and sometimes demolished through conquering or amalgamation? Within a country, why do different political parties rise and fall, taking control over government or ceasing to exist? Why do states change their policies, for example becoming more authoritarian or more egalitarian?

This chapter does not attempt the overwhelming task of answering these questions in full generality but instead focuses on a more particular question: How do ideologies affect changes in governments and states? An ideology is a system of ideas and values that strongly influences the actions of individuals and organizations. The operations of ideologies are a major part of the explanation of changes in governments and countries, as evident from the impact of ideologies such as liberalism, communism, colonialism, and feminism.

I use social cognitivism to explain how ideologies contribute to social change. After a general discussion of political mechanisms, I provide a three-analysis of ideology that is far more informative than any contentious definition. Understanding ideologies in terms of their exemplars, typical features,

137

and explanatory roles illuminates how ideologies contribute to political and social change. How this works is shown by a case study of the rise of the Islamic
State in 2014, along with briefer accounts of other ideologies such as fascism and
anarchism.

POLITICAL MECHANISMS

Political mechanisms operate on various scales, from small parties to provinces
to countries to international organizations. In accord with the account of social mechanisms in chapter 3, all of these groups have parts consisting of people
and sometimes other groups. The people in these groups should not be viewed
abstractly as operating according to the canons of rational choice but rather as
employing the full range of cognitive and emotional mechanisms described in
chapter 2. Accordingly, for the most important individuals in a political group, we
need to identify their concepts, values, images, beliefs, rules, goals, analogies, and
emotions.

   Political individuals influence each other and the overall behaviors of their
groups through the social mechanisms described in chapter 3: verbal and nonverbal communication, interagent inferences, and noncommunicative (purely
physical) interactions. For example, a political party consists of individuals with
varying beliefs and values, which can be changed through interactions among the
individuals. Through institutions such as conventions and voting, the actions of
the individuals can lead to group behaviors, for example the choice of a leader
or the adoption of policies. Political institutions are rule-governed organizations
that create and apply laws, establish policies, and represent individuals. All institutions, including political parties, courts, trade unions, and legislative bodies can
be understood in terms of social and cognitive mechanisms.

   Institutions and other political mechanisms usually have both purposes and
functions. Their purposes are designed into them by the creators of the political
system, either rapidly as in the writing of the American Constitution or gradually
as in the evolution of the British Parliament. For example, a purpose of courts is
to punish criminals and maintain social order. Through the interactions of the individuals, political mechanisms can perform functions that accomplish such purposes, for example when the operations of courts serve to keep dangerous people
apart from victims. Purposes constitute general goals and generate subgoals, for
example when the defensive purpose of a state generates a goal to institute an
army that may lead to a subgoal to establish a draft.

Political institutions have principles and rules, but how do they exist? A political principle or institutional rule might be taken to be some kind of abstract entity existing apart from human activity, as marks on paper enshrined in a concrete document such as a constitution or as sets of behaviors such as the expression of preferences. The cognitive alternative is much more plausible: principles and rules are mental and neural processes operating in the minds of individuals that explain their behaviors. Such processes always have a strong emotional aspect that motivates the actions of people who hold them. In political communication, individuals influence each other through the verbal and nonverbal transfer of cognitions and emotions that are integral to ideologies.

IDEOLOGY: THREE-ANALYSIS

Michael Freeden describes an ideology as "a set of ideas, beliefs, opinions and values that (1) exhibit a recurring pattern; (2) are held by significant groups; (3) compete over providing and controlling plans for public policy; (4) do so with the aim of justifying, contesting, or changing the social and political arrangements and processes of a political community." This definition is richer than those available in dictionaries but needs to be spelled out further by a three-analysis such as the one in Table 6.1. The purpose of this analysis is not to report the meaning of an everyday concept of ideology but rather to help build a richer concept that can be part of the theory of political change.

TABLE 6.1

Three-Analysis of *Ideology*

Exemplars	Liberalism, conservatism, communism, fascism, anarchism, environmentalism, feminism
Typical features	Concepts, images, beliefs, rules, analogies, goals
	Values and emotions
	Adherents—people or groups
	Competing ideologies
	Justification function
	Change function
Explanations	Explains: individual motivations, group successes and failures, political changes
	Explained by: cognitive and social mechanisms

Rather than vague ideas and opinions, this analysis looks for mental represen-tations that can be precisely characterized as neural processes, including concepts, beliefs, and goals. Emotions are also a typical feature of ideologies, for example national pride and hatred of enemies. Values and goals are mental processes that bind concepts and beliefs with emotions, as when the concept *democracy* is viewed as wonderful or contemptible.

Ideologies are also marked by the people and groups that adhere to them, for example the individuals that belong to a political party and the party itself that officially proclaims the ideology. The actions of individuals result from brain processes of representation and inference, and the actions of groups emerge from the interactions of individuals. Political ideologies always have competi-tors to be fought against, as in the struggles among liberalism, socialism, and fascism.

Ideologies can have numerous individual and social functions, including holding people together in groups and motivating them to take actions that are sometimes radical and violent. Ideologies can be conservative when they justify the status quo but revolutionary when they militate for substantial change.

Ideology is an important component of political theory because it contributes to a wide range of explanations. It helps to explain the motivations of individ-uals, for example why they choose to join groups whose ideas they find appealing and why they work intensely to advance those groups. This appeal contributes to the success of the group, but loss of appeal contributes to failure if circumstances render the ideology less applicable to the current situation. Ideologies can be an important part of the explanation of large-scale political changes, for example the establishment of socialist states in the Soviet Union and China. They can also be an important part of the explanation of stability, for example when a dominant ideology such as liberalism helps to maintain a society and preserve its democratic institutions.

Much more controversial is the question of what explains the operations of ideologies. Political theorists who completely ignore psychology, or assume that it is just rational choice, are incapable of explaining why people adopt ideologies and why these ideologies spread among individuals and groups. In contrast, a so-cial cognitive-emotional workup can spell out how ideologies operate in the minds of individuals and how they spread through communication among individuals. Validation of this interpretation of ideologies requires specific case studies such as the Islamic State.

IDEOLOGY: VALUE MAPS

Ideologies consist of systems of interconnected mental representations, not isolated pieces. The easiest way to convey these emotional connections is the method of value maps. Figure 6.1 shows a highly simplified account of a kind of right-wing ideology that is currently popular in many countries, for example in the Republican Party in the United States and in the Conservative parties of the United Kingdom and Canada. The most important positive concept is *freedom,* which is accordingly shown with a thick oval. Freedom shows favorable associations (indicated by solid lines) with other positively valued concepts such as capitalism and private property. These positive values conflict with negative ones such as government regulation, taxation, and nontraditional lifestyles, whose emotional disfavor is shown by hexagons. I have portrayed the concept *government* using a neutral rectangle, indicating the ambivalence of conservatives: they dislike government for taxation and regulation but appreciate it for its contribution to economic growth and military defense (not shown).

In contrast, Figure 6.2 provides a simplified account of left-wing ideology that is espoused by progressive parties such as the Labor Party in the United Kingdom, the New Democratic Party in Canada, and many European social democratic parties. In the United States, related views occur among the more liberal members of the Democratic Party. In Figure 6.2, the central and most positive concept is *equality,*

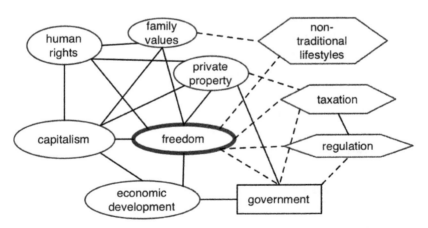

FIGURE 6.1 Fragment of the conceptual structure of right-wing (conservative) ideology. Ovals represent emotionally positive concepts, hexagons represent emotionally negative concepts, and rectangles represent emotionally neutral concepts. Solid lines indicate mutual support, while dotted lines indicate incompatibility.

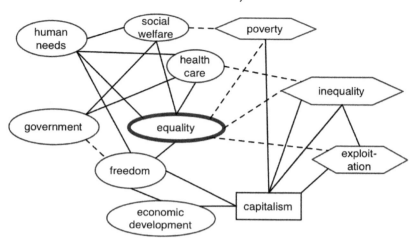

FIGURE 6.2 Fragment of the conceptual structure of left-wing (progressive) ideology. Ovals represent emotionally positive concepts, hexagons represent emotionally negative concepts, and rectangles represent emotionally neutral concepts. Solid lines indicate mutual support, while dotted lines indicate incompatibility.

with links to other emotionally valued concepts such as social welfare and health care. In contrast to the conservative picture in Figure 6.1, *government* is viewed favorably, whereas *capitalism* is shown as neutral reflecting ambivalence about its positive contributions to economic growth and negative effects on equality.

The three-analysis in Table 6.1 makes it clear that there is much more to ideologies than the emotional concepts shown in the value maps in Figures 6.1 and 6.2. A full account of them needs to indicate other mental representations such as beliefs, goals, and full emotions such as hatred. Moreover, there needs to be specification of adherents, functions, and explanatory roles. Nevertheless, value maps are helpful in visualizing the emotional structure of key concepts in ideologies, as well as in identifying changes in them.

The rather loose right and left ideologies shown in Figures 6.1 and 6.2 are too general to have nonverbal symbols associated with them, but all more specific ideologies such as variants of fascism and communism have nonverbal representations that are emotionally important. For example, communism has visual images such as the hammer and sickle and the portrait of Stalin that was ubiquitous in the Soviet Union under his rule. Communism has also had associated songs such as "The Internationale" and radical folk songs and the associated gesture of the raised fist.

IDEOLOGICAL CHANGE

Three kinds of ideological change can be identified in specific cases. First, there is the initial formation of an ideology and its eventual demise if it loses all its adherents. Second, an existing ideology can be transformed by changes in its concepts, beliefs, and other representations. Third, social change for an ideology consists of its spread among individuals, sometimes from an initially small but enthusiastic group to a dominant party.

Ideologies are formed when concepts, beliefs, and goals are packaged together into a coherent whole. Some of these representations may be new, generated by the cognitive mechanisms describe in *Brain–Mind,* for example when the concept *socialism* was formed in the early nineteenth century and the concept *fascism* was formed in the early twentieth. It can be hard to identify the exact beginnings of an ideology, because the conglomeration of concepts and beliefs can take place over time as a result of the interactions of numerous individuals. For example, communism does not have a precise beginning but emerged as the result of the writings and activities among numerous individuals, from Saint-Simon and Robert Owen to Marx and Engels.

Ideologies shift over time when some concepts and beliefs become more or less central, or when values alter because of emotional changes. The Italian fascism of Mussolini was not as racist as the German version developed by Hitler. Ideological changes in individuals can require major shifts in the understanding of fundamental concepts like *freedom, equality, justice,* and *democracy.*

The most striking kind of ideological change occurs when ideas go from having only a small number of advocates to taking over an entire state. The result can be dramatic political revolutions, as occurred in France, the United States, the Soviet Union, and China. These examples show the explanatory power of ideology, because a major part of what motivated and organized the revolutionaries was commitment to ideas that were radically opposed to the ones held by people in power. People are sometimes willing to die for a political ideology in ways that contravene any rational calculation of self-interest.

Once an ideology helps its adherents gain power, its function can change dramatically, into maintaining stability rather than promoting change. New and established rulers can use an ideology to continue their control by insisting on beliefs and values that support the continuation of the current regime. An ideology can shift from motivating revolution to justifying the current state if it exemplifies the proclaimed values. For example, the approximately democratic ideals of the writers of the American Constitution are still used hundreds of years later to justify American government. China still uses communist ideas that originated with Marx and Engels to maintain a society that has adopted many of the practices of capitalism.

Ideological change can be gradual, with small amendments to beliefs and values and slow growth of acceptance of political beliefs. But they can also be dramatic, when critical transitions occur in individuals who form an ideology or who are converted to it, or when many people quickly shift to support an ideology. Particular ideologies are marked by specific mental representations and modes of communication. These can be illustrated by looking at the rise of the ideology of the Islamic State.

THE ISLAMIC STATE: SOCIAL COGNITIVE-EMOTIONAL WORKUP

On June 28, 2014, in the newly captured Iraqi city of Mosul, Caliph Abu Bakr al-Baghdadi declared the birth of the Islamic State, superseding the previous Islamic State in Iraq and Syria (ISIS, ISIL, Daesh). The new state claimed to supersede all borders, providing a basis for the struggle between the Muslim camp of holy warriors (*mujahideen*) and the opposing camp of Jews, Crusaders, and their allies. In 2015, despite American bombing raids, the Islamic State expanded its territory to include the Iraqi city of Ramadi and the Syrian city of Palmyra, moving within 100 kilometers of Baghdad. Thousands of foreign fighters, including men and women from Europe and North America, have gone to Syria and Iraq to support the Islamic State. By 2017, however, the Islamic State was in rapid retreat because of the military power of the United States, Russia, and their local allies. By 2018, the Islamic State in Iraq and Syria had been defeated, but its ideology continued to inspire dispersed fighters and international terrorists, particularly in sub-Saharan Africa.

The rapid ascent of the Islamic State generates many questions. Why was the Islamic State initially so successful in expanding its territory? Why were locals and foreigners so strongly attracted to the Islamic State? What role did ideology play in the spread and military success of the Islamic State? A social cognitive-emotional workup can begin to provide answers to such questions.

The cognition part of the workup requires identifying central concepts, images, beliefs, rules, goals, and analogies of the main adherents of the Islamic State. The emotion part of the workup requires identifying the values attached to concepts, beliefs, and goals and also identifying specific emotions such as devotion and hatred. The social part of the workup requires recognizing verbal and nonverbal communications that contribute to the effectiveness and growth of the Islamic State.

Concepts and Values

To understand the cognitive structure of an ideology, the best place to start is spotting the most important concepts. For a typical adherent of the Islamic State, these include *Islam, Sunni, Quran* (Koran), *Jihad, sharia law, purity, monotheism,* and *caliphate*. In accord with the semantic pointer theory of concepts, these are brain processes that are not purely verbal because they can also bind sensory images and emotions. The binding of concepts with emotions produces values such as the highly positive value of Islam. The concepts in an ideology can also have negative values, which for the Islamic State include *Shia, idolatry, apostasy, the West,* and *infidel*.

Figure 6.3 is a value map that shows some of the conceptual and emotional structure of the Islamic State ideology. Ovals indicate the connected concepts that contribute to the emotional appeal of the Islamic State, and hexagons indicate the negative emotional values that represent enemies. Figure 6.3 is not a complete representation of Islamic State ideology but provides a simplified diagram of some of its most important concepts. Positive and negative values are only one aspect of the emotional mental states of Islamic State adherents, and more specific emotions such as anger and devotion are described later.

Fundamental to the ideology of the Islamic State is the concept of Islam, the religion founded by Muhammad in Mecca in the seventh century. Defenders of the Islamic State attach an intensely positive emotional value to it because of their upbringings, studies, or conversion experiences. This attachment makes it a sacred value, not just in having religious meaning but also in being a value that cannot simply be traded off against other values. Rather, the emotional value attached to Islam is so fundamental to the self-identities and emotional structure of the proponents of the Islamic State that it cannot be challenged. Anyone who does challenge it deserves to die.

The new concept *Islamic State* is formed by conceptual combination from *Islam* and *state,* with each of these concepts transformed in the process. The concept of state incorporated into *Islamic State* is very different from the concept of state

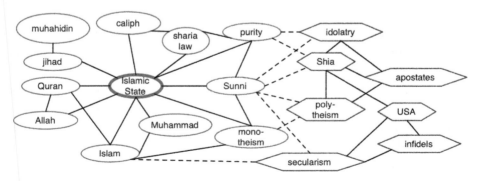

FIGURE 6.3 Value map of the Islamic State, depicting central concepts and associated values of its adherents. For clarity, not all lines are shown.

used in the United Nations, which has more than 200 countries viewed as separate and independent. The Islamic State is not meant to be one country among others but the only legitimate country, just as Islam is taken to be the only legitimate religion. There is no separation of church and state, because the main purpose of the government is to support the religion. The leader of the Islamic State is called the caliph, harkening back to the caliphate that spread through the Middle East and Africa in the centuries after Muhammad, reaching all the way to Spain. The caliph is a powerful symbol of the unification of church and state, with the leader obliged to ensure that all forms of apostasy and infidelity are stamped out. All Muslims must declare allegiance or fealty to the caliph or else be subject to excommunication.

The concept *Islam* incorporated into *Islamic State* is also much narrower than the broad concept of Islam, which accommodates different variants such as Shia, Sufi, and Ahmadiyya. The Islamic State proclaims that the only legitimate version of Islam is a traditional Sunni doctrine that traces its origins directly to Muhammad and the Quran. Whereas modern versions of Sunni Islam have accommodated themselves to the modern state with its own system of laws, for example in Egypt, the Islamic State insists that such legal arrangements are illegitimate. The only legitimate laws are the religious system of sharia law, as proclaimed by Muhammad in the Quran. The name for the extreme version of Sunni Islam maintained by the Islamic State is Salafism, which insists on literal interpretations of the Quran and sharia law.

Because of the assumptions that religious law is paramount and that only the Islamic State is legitimate, jihad is justified. The concept *jihad* signifies militant struggle against the opponents of the correct form of Islam. Holy warriors in support of jihad, the mujahideen, are revered as potential martyrs in accord with the Quran. Hence the concepts *jihad* and *mujahideen* are strongly positive values. Adoption of the ideology shown in Figure 6.3 by people raised in a more secular culture requires conceptual change: adding new concepts such as *sharia* and revalencing (changing the values associated with) concepts such as *democracy*.

The emotional coherence of the ideology of the Islamic State comes from its connected group of emotionally positive concepts but also from its opposition to a set of strongly negative concepts. Islam is opposed not only to other religions such as Christianity and Judaism but also to all illegitimate varieties of Islam. The Islamic State is particularly opposed to Shia, the version that originated with Muhammad's son-in-law Ali. The Islamic State castigates Shia for abandoning the purity of the Quran and for practicing nontraditional rituals such as self-flagellation. Shia leaders now rule Syria, Iran, and Iraq, where the American invasion overthrew the Sunni leader Saddam Hussein. Because Shiites revere their

religious leaders, the Imams, extreme Sunnis view them as abandoning the monotheism of traditional Islam. Shia Muslims, as well as Sunni Muslims who have
shown allegiance to secular states, are accused of apostasy which is punishable
by death.

Apostates are as bad as infidels, who are nonbelievers in the Islamic religion.
Infidels include Christians, Jews, and atheists, associated with secular Western
countries such as United States. The Islamic State pursues jihad against a perceived alliance of Shia Muslims and secular countries, evident in how the current
government of Iraq is supported by both the United States and Iran. Leaders of
the Islamic State are particularly contemptuous of the Yazidis, whose religion is
outside the Abrahamic tradition of Judaism, Christianity, and Islam. When Yazidi
lands are conquered, the men are killed and the women are abused as sex slaves.

This discussion of key positive and negative concepts in the ideology of the
Islamic State indicates its emotional coherence. For someone who shares some of
the values shown in Figure 6.3 such as Islam and the Quran, it may be appealing to
adopt the larger system of associated concepts including the caliph responsible for
promulgating them. But the full attraction of the Islamic State cannot be appreciated without also looking at images, beliefs, rules, analogies, goals, and specific
emotions.

Images and Embodiment

Ideologies are not just sets of words, for they can incorporate images derived
from the senses, especially vision and hearing. The main visual symbol of the
Islamic State is its flag, which adds Arabic writing to the traditional jihadist black
background, proclaiming that there is only one God. Pictures of men holding it
sometimes show them raising an arm with a single finger extended to signify the
monotheism of the Islamic State. This gesture can provide a kinesthetic image as
well as a visual one.

Since 2012, the Islamic State has produced increasingly sophisticated videos
that present powerful images such as men with guns and rocket launchers, along
with bombings, burnings, and sometimes even beheadings. These images provide
concrete instantiations of jihad, showing warriors on trucks and tanks. Maps of
Syria and Iraq displaying the growing territory dominated by the Islamic State furnish an exciting visual image of its success. Extreme sharia law is also associated
with powerful visual images including amputations and beheadings.

Auditory images associated with the Islamic State include the maxim "Allah
Akbar" (God is great). Jihadists also listen to numerous songs, including an un-
official anthem that uses a hypnotic chant to declare that dawn has appeared.

Recruiters of the Islamic State often use religious chants taken from the Quran. Such chants can be used to reinforce the ideology of the Islamic State and also to transmit it to others. The Islamic State builds on the auditory rituals of Islam, including prayers and the standard call to prayer.

The visual images, auditory images, and gestures of the Islamic State demonstrate embodied aspects of its ideology. But the transbodiment of this ideology is evident in more abstract concepts such as *sharia law* and *Allah*: visual images of God and Mohammed are prohibited.

Beliefs and Rules

The leaders and followers of the Islamic State have a set of core beliefs built out of concepts by neural binding into semantic pointers. Some beliefs are doctrines of traditional Islam, such that there is no God but Allah and Muhammad is his messenger. Other beliefs are specific to the Islamic State, for example that the caliph will lead Islam to the final triumph over its enemies. In accord with Quranic prophecy, the leaders of the Islamic State believe that there will eventually be an apocalyptic battle in the Iranian city of Dabiq. They also believe that current rulers of Muslim lands are traitors and sinners and that the United States is trying to give Iraq to Iran. Each of these beliefs is not merely cognitive but also has a strong emotional component, for example joy that the caliph will triumph and anger that the United States colludes with Iran.

These beliefs may be short on empirical evidence, but they fit well together as part of a whole system of beliefs with the central assumption that the utterances and prophecies of the Quran are literally true. The beliefs also cohere emotionally with the central values attached to the core concepts such as *Islam*. Because the Quran is so highly valued, anything that it says must be true. Hence the belief system that is part of the ideology of the Islamic State possesses cognitive and emotional coherence, discussed further in the section on inference.

Rules are an important kind of belief with an *if–then* structure, as in the generalization: *If something is stated in the Quran, then it is true.* Some of the most important rules in an ideology are ones that prescribe behavior. Many of the rules enforced by the Islamic State are derived from sharia law, requiring prayer five times a day and the eating of only Halal meat. Other rules enforced in Islamic State territory include: *If you are a man, then wear a beard; if you are a woman, then wear a veil.* Sharia law has rules that are used to justify practices such as the amputation of hands of criminals, the beheading of apostates, and the sexual enslavement of conquered women. But some sharia rules are much more benevolent, requiring that all believers receive housing, food, health care, and clothing.

The most general rule of the Islamic ideology is procedural, commanding that everyone follow the prophecy and methodology of Muhammad, as laid out in the Quran. More specific military rules have developed over time, for example pursuing jihad by means of suicide bombings. There are many rules about the caliphate, including requirements that Muslims migrate to the Islamic State and declare allegiance to the caliph.

Analogies and Metaphors

Analogies play a small but nontrivial role in the ideology of the Islamic State. The greatest analogical role model is the prophet Muhammad. Just as some Christians ask themselves the question "what would Jesus do?," devout Muslims are supposed to ask themselves the question "what would Muhammad do?" Less personally, the new caliphate in the Islamic State is compared to the early caliphates in the several centuries following the writing of the Quran. Just as jihad enabled the small early group of Muslims to expand their influence across the Middle East and into Africa, Europe, and India, so the new caliphs are supposed to expand the Islamic State across the rest of the world. Previous triumphs provide analogical guidance about what to do, but historical defeats provide analogies for what to avoid. Accordingly, Islamic State ideologues sometimes mention losses such as the conversion of Iran to Shiism.

Metaphors that rely on underlying analogies also contribute to the Islamic State, particularly in the scathing denunciation of Shiite Islam, which is sometimes described as an obstacle, snake, scorpion, or venom. These metaphors employ emotional analogies, which serve to transfer negative feelings from the source such as odious snakes to the Shia target. Poetry is an important part of Arabic culture and is used to contribute to the development and spread of Islamic State ideology, as in the metaphors and similes used in the following:

> I will fasten my explosive belt,
> I will shudder like a lightning bolt
> and rush by like a torrential stream
> and resound like stormy thunder.
> In my heart is the heart of a volcano.
> I will sweep through the land like a flood.
> For I live by the Quran.

This series of metaphors uses underlying analogies to motivate conviction and action.

Emotions and Action

People's goals help to explain their actions, because goals in combination with intentions and emotions produce actions, as described in *Brain–Mind* (chapter 9). Goals, intentions, and emotions are all brain processes that bind neural representations into semantic pointers. Just as a concept can be emotionally positive or negative to produce a value, a goal combines a description of a situation with positive or negative emotional judgments about its desirability. A concept by itself is not a goal because it does not describe the state of affairs to be attained or avoided. For example, *Islamic State* is a concept but only becomes a goal when it is expanded into a description of a situation such as *establishment of the Islamic State as the world's only country*. This goal is intensely positive for the leaders of the Islamic State but emotionally negative for the rest of the world.

The most general goal of the Islamic State is to establish traditional Sunni Islam as the world's only religion. This overarching goal generates subgoals that are instrumental to accomplishing it. Waging offensive jihad to fight enemies becomes a crucial long-term subgoal. More immediately, the Islamic State is fighting to expand and defend its territory in Iraq and Syria. It also hopes to expand its influence in other Arab states such as Saudi Arabia, Yemen, Egypt, and Algeria, in order to overthrow states that are not sufficiently rigorous in their Islamic practices. In order to accomplish its military goals, the Islamic State needs to recruit fighters, both local and foreign, by attracting people who already have strong religious goals of Islamic observance and purification.

To say that the Islamic State has the goal of conquering the world is metaphorical, because states and other groups do not actually have goals, which are brain processes occurring only in individual people. Attributing a goal to the Islamic State is short for saying that each of the individual leaders and supporters of the Islamic State has brain processes that represent the desirability of bringing about particular states of affairs. Group goals are aggregates of individual goals, although communication among the individuals is important for explaining why they each hold the goal.

Having clear and strong goals contributes greatly to the coherence of the choices and actions of the members of the Islamic State. When people make decisions, they rarely can use detailed knowledge about the consequences of potential actions to calculate maximum utilities based on knowledge of probabilities. Rather, decision-making is an emotional process where people try to figure out how to make their choice of actions fit with their goals, a process that can lead to the revision of goals as well as to the choice of actions.

For the leaders and followers of the Islamic State, there is little ambivalence or indecisiveness, because the shared religious and political goals are so sharp and intense. Passion and coherence provide strong motivation for extreme acts such as waging war and participating in suicidal truck bombs. Because the neural representations of concepts such as *Islam* and goals such as *make Islam dominant* are intertwined, the emotional coherence of concepts and values and the deliberative coherence of goals and actions are mutually reinforcing.

The positive attitude toward Islam felt also by less extreme Muslims is approximated in Figure 6.4, which shows a semantic pointer for Islam. The emotional reaction results from binding representations of self and Islam with cognitive appraisals that Islam accomplishes religious and other goals, physiological reactions such as increased heart rate and smiling faces, and motor inclinations such as praying or fighting.

The description so far has highlighted the important role of emotions with respect to concepts and goals but has considered only two basic dimensions of emotions: their positive/negative valence and their intensity. But in Arabic as an English there are hundreds of emotion words that make much finer discriminations among the experiences and causes of different emotions. For example, anger and fear are both negative and intense, but they reflect different cognitive appraisals. Anger is directed at people who thwart your goals, whereas fear is prompted by threats to your survival goals.

Activists in the Islamic State are energized and motivated by a network of positive and negative emotions. For Islam and associated ideals such as sharia law, adherents express positive emotions such as hope, enthusiasm, zeal, rejoicing,

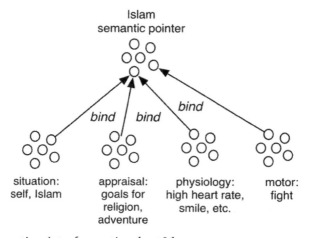

FIGURE 6.4 Semantic pointer for emotion about Islam.

pride, and devotion. On the other hand, against their Shiite and Western enemies, adherents direct negative emotions such as anger, hatred, indignation, and resentment. The Islamic State works to inspire fear in its enemies, by executing captives including the use of videotaped beheadings. The combination of hope and resentment is captured in the following exclamation from a leader: "O Muslims in all places, rejoice, take heart, and hold your heads high! For today you have, by God's bounty, a state and caliphate that will renew your dignity and strength, that will recover your rights and your sovereignty".

John Elster has described how beliefs lead to specific emotions that lead to actions. For example, the belief that someone has harmed you can make you angry and possibly encourage actions aimed at revenge. The belief that some people are evil can inspire hatred that leads to the desire to remove or even kill them. The belief that something is dangerous can lead you to fear it and therefore flee or stop and fight. More positively, the belief that someone is wonderful can inspire you to love him or her, motivating actions that bring you together.

The anger, hatred, and fear that the members of the Islamic State feel toward Shiites and the West all motivate violent actions against their enemies. At the same time, the zeal for Islamic ideals supports these militant actions and other efforts to promote the Islamic State. Hence the mujahideen are driven by emotional energy to extreme actions from frantic fighting to suicide bombing.

Inferences

The psychological mechanism of motivated inference provides justification for evidence-free beliefs that the new caliphate will eventually triumph. People believe in the caliph and the Islamic State because these beliefs fit with their religious and personal goals. Chapter 8 discusses additional psychological supports for religious beliefs. Hope that problems can be solved by governmental actions is a typical aspect of political ideologies, contributing to motivated inferences that the government will be successful.

What is the psychological process behind the decisions of thousands of Muslims in Western countries who have chosen to go fight with the Islamic State? It is implausible that these decisions result from calculations of expected utility, because even approximate probabilities and utilities are unknown. No simple heuristics are available that could direct such momentous decisions. Rather, the most plausible explanation of why people move to Iraq or Syria to fight with the Islamic State is emotional coherence, where the action of fighting coheres with goals and emotions.

As with the prejudices described in chapter 5, motivated inference can interact with fear-driven inferences about the dangers of secularism and domination by Americans and Shiites. Obsession with worries about male–female relations, Western military action in Iraq, and the Shiite threat makes the current situation feel ever more perilous to Sunni Muslims. This feeling is intensified by the fear-driven inference that the threats must be real because they are so scary. Then motivated inference takes over to guarantee solutions to the perils through the triumph of the Islamic State. The conclusion that this solution is the only feasible one generates more worries that it might be blocked by the actions of the West and Iran. Chapter 8 describes how the same insidious loop operates in other religions such as Mormonism. Rage-driven inference may also be a factor in support for the Islamic State in people who are angry about Western culture.

As in all adversarial situations, interagent inference contributes to the thinking of the leaders of the Islamic State. Part of their ideology is based on inferences that Westerners aim to destroy Islam, providing additional motivation for jihad.

Communication

The cognitive and emotional processes so far described operate in the minds of individual proponents of the Islamic State. But the success of the Islamic State depends also on the interactions of its members in pursuit of such goals as fighting effectively, administering conquered territory, and attracting new members. What kinds of communication encourage the maintenance, performance, and spread of the Islamic State?

The major social mechanism supporting the Islamic State is verbal communication, but it is always accompanied by nonverbal signals that enhance the emotional messages. Some of its leaders are gifted orators who use audio addresses to convey information and also influence emotions through what is said and the tone in which it is said. Charismatic leaders whose speech and body language generate interest and excitement are particularly effective at transferring emotions and inspiring actions. Leaders can incite violence by expressing anger, contempt, and disgust.

Recruitment takes place in various venues that support face-to-face verbal communication, such as mosques and prisons. As chapter 3 described, verbal communication is rarely purely verbal, because it is accompanied by gestures and facial expressions that are important for conveying emotions and instilling motivations.

After crude propaganda beginnings in 2012, the Islamic State became effective at using media to spread its messages. The Internet has enabled the Islamic State to use high-quality videos and cartoons that proclaim their verbal messages, often accompanied by vivid images of violent actions such as bombings. The Islamic State also became adept at using social media like Twitter and Facebook to communicate its doctrines to current and prospective members. These media have also served to warn cities that the Islamic State intends to attack, encouraging enemy soldiers to flee. Hence Internet technologies such as videos and social media serve both to instill solidarity and enthusiasm in their own side and to generate fear in people they are about to attack.

Communication with potential recruits is able to appeal to their various personal goals. Some local individuals in Iraq and Syria are motivated by offers of food and money to help alleviate poverty and by provision of relative safety in a secure territory. The conversion experiences of particular recruits may result from religious motivations designed to overcome personal shortcomings, but also from personal ambition, adventurism, and even the perceived desirability of suicide. Like all soldiers, Islamic State fighters can also be motivated by the personal relationships and emotional bonds that they form with fellow recruits.

It is puzzling why women are attracted to a movement that severely restricts them, but the propaganda from Islamic leaders can play up the emotional advantages of sisterhood, motherhood, romantic marriages, martyred husbands, religious duty, adventure, escape from ordinary life, and the sacred transcendence of self. For some women who already value Islam highly, the Islamic State can be attractive enough to join as a matter of emotional coherence.

Hence social mechanisms of verbal and nonverbal communication mesh with cognitive and emotional mechanisms in the minds of individuals to make the Islamic State an effective organization. There are also noncommunicative forms of interaction, such as the fighting that occurs when enemies are attacked, although this can also have an effect of nonverbal communication of terror and hopelessness. Following strict Muslim rules such as praying five times a day brings people together for verbal and nonverbal interactions that help to establish solidarity in pursuit of the common purpose of practicing and spreading Islam.

This discussion of communication completes the social cognitive-emotional workup of the Islamic State. I have hypothesized the existence of important concepts, values, beliefs, rules, analogies, and emotions that operate in the minds of individual proponents. The social component of the workup notices that verbal and nonverbal communications serve to organize and motivate current supporters and to recruit new ones. These cognitive and social mechanisms help to answer the questions raised earlier about the ideological appeal and success of the Islamic State.

Explanations of Success

A major component of the initial political and military success of the Islamic State is the strong commitment of its leaders and members to a common set of religious and political goals. Such commitment is a matter of emotion, not just belief and behavior, using hope, pride, and zeal for Islam to balance fear, contempt, and anger against infidels. Proponents of the Islamic State intensely value Islam, the Quran, sharia law, jihad, and the narrow Sunni interpretation. These emotional attachments cohere in opposition to strongly negative emotional assessments of Shia Islam and Western secularism.

Intense emotional evaluations provide motivation for extreme actions, including suicide bombings and beheadings. The intensity of motivation shared by ordinary soldiers as well as leaders contributed strongly to military success of the Islamic State in 2014 and 2015. Their opponents in battles in Mosul, Tikrit, Ramadi, and Palmyra were ordinary soldiers without the same kind of intense emotional commitment. Even though the Islamic State fighters were hugely outnumbered, sometimes by 10 to 1, their motivation to fight brought them victory over foes who were more concerned with self-preservation.

Because of unquestioning religious faith, the caliphate embraces slavery and executions without apologies: "we will conquer your Rome, break your crosses, and enslave your women." There are other factors in the political and military success of the Islamic State such as efficient organizations, sophisticated use of electronic communications, and the military experience of veterans of the Iraqi army.

The adherents of the Islamic State possess and proclaim an ideology understood as a system of mental representations performed by neural processes based on semantic pointers. The ideas that make up ideologies are not abstract entities, sets of words, or behavioral patterns. Rather, they are structures in the brains of members of a group whose verbal and nonverbal interactions reinforce and spread the ideology. It would be a mystery how abstract ideas and words could lead to bodily actions, whereas it is increasingly well understood how brain mechanisms can move from intentions and goals to concrete actions and behaviors. Ideology, construed in the psychological and neural terms presented here, provides a major part of the explanation of the actions and successes of the Islamic State.

The emotional intensity and coherence of the mental representations of the Islamic State also explains its appeal to new recruits, both locally in the Middle East and in foreign countries. Thousands of foreigners were drawn to fight with the Islamic State because many of its values resonate with their own. An ideology appeals to people when its values and goals match well the values and goals that people already have, but also when the ideology provides solutions to the individuals' problems, both social and personal. The new identity furnished by adoption of an ideology can help people to revalence their lives, analogously to how rejection of a prejudicial culture served to revalence the life of indigenous writer Richard Wagamese as described in chapter 5.

When young people in England, Canada, or Yemen feel discontented with their current situations, the Islamic State can provide a set of religious and political answers that seem to resolve their major problems. Adopting the explicit and intense values of the Islamic State enables people to view their lives as successful, significant, and connected with other like-minded people. The loop of fear-driven and motivated inference operates in individual minds but can be fueled by communicative interactions with other people who have similar worries and hopes. The critical transition from more Western views to strong commitment to the Islamic State is an emotional gestalt shift that produces actions as extreme as joining the fight in Syria and Iran.

Hence an ideology, construed as a psychological process operating in brains in ways that are both cognitive and emotional, provides a major part of the explanation of political activities. By virtue of their emotional components and their strong links to action, ideologies serve to motivate actions that lead to change. Motivated and fear-driven inference have also contributed to other ideologies such as Nazism and anarchism.

Nazi Ideology

Understanding an ideology requires a full social cognitive-emotional workup, but more limited analysis can be useful to display some important additional aspects of ideologies. Value maps of Nazis, anarchists, right-wing extremists, and Hutus clarify the use of multimodal representations and the intermixture of emotion-driven inferences. Notice that ideologies are not inherently extreme or aggressive; there are others that are moderate, benevolent, and pacifist. Everyone has an ideology, not just bad people, as you can see by doing a value map of your own political and social values.

All of the value maps in Figures 6.1 to 6.3 employ verbal concepts such as *equality, freedom*, and *Islam*. But the discussion of images in the Islamic State showed that ideologies include nonverbal representations such as pictures, sounds, and gestures. Like verbal concepts, these representations have emotional associations that can be indicated using the same conventions (ovals, hexagons, links) as the value maps already portrayed, but they add to the understanding of ideologies important but neglected cognitive and emotional aspects.

It would be easy to draw a map of Nazi ideology using verbal concepts such as *Deutschland, national socialism, Führer,* and so on. Figure 6.5, however, shows how such a map could be supplemented by powerful nonverbal representations that contribute to the emotional coherence of an ideology. The visual images in Figure 6.5 include Hitler's portrait, which displays strength and determination in contrast to the old and weak Hindenburg who led Germany before Hitler came to power. Hitler is positively associated with the ancient swastika that was adopted by the Nazi party in 1920 and with the Heil Hitler (*sieg heil*) gesture, which is also a visual image that has an associated sound. Incompatible with Nazi symbols is a depiction of an ugly Jew as a gold-loving communist; this image comes from the cover of a 1937 Nazi pamphlet. Finally, the musical note is a placeholder for a collection of songs that were important to the Nazi movement, such as the German anthem proclaiming "Deutschland Uber Alles," the Horst Wessel song, military marches, and Hitler's beloved Wagnerian operas. Some of the main nonverbal

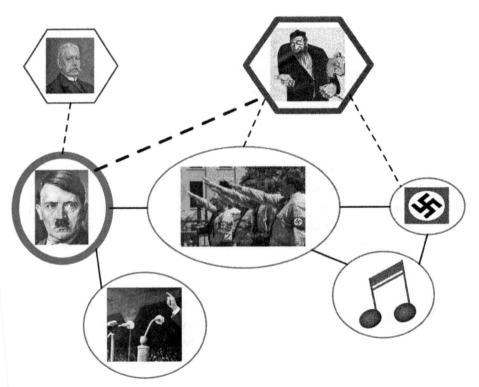

FIGURE 6.5 Multimodal value map of Nazi ideology. Ovals represent emotionally positive concepts, hexagons represent emotionally negative concepts, and rectangles represent emotionally neutral concepts. Solid lines indicate mutual support, while dotted lines indicate incompatibility. Elements include visual images, gestures, and sounds.

elements of Nazi ideology—the swastika, the Heil Hitler gesture, and the Horst Wessel song—are still illegal in Germany.

In 1920, Hitler's party had fewer than 100 members, but in 1933 the National Socialists received more than 17 million votes (43.9%) in the German federal election. How can we explain the rapid spread of Nazi ideology? Explanation should operate both at the individual level, accounting for why a person such as the philosopher Heidegger became a Nazi, and at the social level, accounting for the spread of ideas in groups of people. The primary mental mechanism by which individuals come to adopt an ideology is emotional coherence, outlined in chapter 2.

According to the theory of emotional coherence, people make decisions and other inferences based on how well competing alternatives fit overall with their beliefs and goals, including the emotional values (valences) that they attach to these representations. Decision-making is not a mathematically careful calculation of probabilities and utilities but rather an emotional assessment of how well opposing actions might accomplish valued goals. What matters for understanding ideology is that emotional coherence affects not only decisions but also beliefs by motivated, fear-driven, and rage-driven inference.

Consider, for example, the rapid rise during the 1920s and 1930s of support in Germany for Hitler and the Nazi Party. Obviously, there were different factors operating in the millions of Germans who became Hitler supporters, but for many people they included

- desire and hope that Hitler could lead Germany out of economic depression and international weakness;
- fear that, without Hitler, Germany would succumb to communism, which had considerable popular support, and to Jewish influence;
- anger that Germany had been defeated and humiliated in the Great War.

These emotional components respectively contributed to motivated, fear-driven, and rage-driven inference, all of which combined to make Nazism emotionally coherent for many people, including philosophers such as Heidegger. Chapter 5 described how anti-Semitism contributed to these fears and hopes.

The multimodal value map of Nazism presented in Figure 6.5 captures only part of the multifaceted inference processes that produced adoption of that ideology. Figure 6.6 provides a richer, causal model of the appeal of Hitler and Nazism to many Germans, showing three of the main sources of emotional reasons to support him. People naturally wanted improvement to the dismal economic situation of Germany in the 1920s and early 1930s, and they made the motivated inference

FIGURE 6.6 The emotional coherence of the decision to support Hitler and the Nazis, deriving from motivated, fear-driven, and rage-driven inference.

that Hitler's peculiar "national socialism" could provide a solution, as it did when military expansion produced a dramatic drop in unemployment. Hitler also gained support by fanning the flames of anti-Semitism and anti-communism. Fear-driven inference served to make people even more afraid of Jews and communists than they already were.

Not shown in Figure 6.6 is an additional step of motivated inference in which people were led to believe that they could best manage their enhanced fears about Jews and communists by putting Hitler in charge. Similarly, the rage-based inference that something extreme must be done about Germany's military humiliation fed into a motivated inference that Hitler was the solution. Other kinds of potential support for Hitler and the Nazis are not shown in Figure 6.5, for example German nationalism based on cultural traditions involving language, literature, and history. Also not shown in Figure 6.6 are interconnections between the different kinds of inference: fear of Jews and communists was also exploited by the Nazis through the motivated inference that Hitler would control them. Nationalisms are often supported by the prejudices described in chapter 5, emphasizing the otherness of members of different nations.

The Nazis, led by Joseph Goebbels, were masters of propaganda, exemplified by Leni Riefenstahl's 1933 film *The Triumph of the Will* and the appalling 1940 pseudo-documentary *The Eternal Jew,* both available on YouTube. Propaganda provokes a reaction in people building on motivated, fear-driven, and rage-driven inference. Most advertising exploits people's motivations using multimodal emotional coherence to convince people that they can be sexier, richer, or healthier merely by purchasing the advertised product.

It would be easy to show that other ideologies, such as various kinds of nationalism, are also based on emotional coherence that generates motivated, fear-driven, and rage-driven inference. For example, American nationalism is sometimes motivated (the United States is the best country in the world), sometimes fear-driven (the threat of communists or, more recently, Arab terrorists), and sometimes rage-driven (the reaction to the 9/11 attacks).

Anarchism

Figure 6.7 maps an ideology that has become remarkably popular among radical young people since the 1999 Seattle protests concerning globalization. The anarchist map depicts a core set of values including equality and solidarity that are used to support several kinds of practical activities, including democratic decision-making by "spokescouncils" that operate by consensus rather than by voting or hierarchical direction. The anarchist values and practices conflict with negative values and institutions such as authority, capitalism, and especially the state, and the conflict is used to justify direct actions that confront governments.

The anarchist ideology shown in Figure 6.7 had a large influence on the Occupy Movement that produced major demonstrations in New York City and hundreds of other cities in 2011. Figure 6.8 displays emotional values of the most important concepts behind the initial Occupy Wall Street action, which incorporated identification with ordinary people (the 99%) as opposed to the wealthy elite (the 1%). The

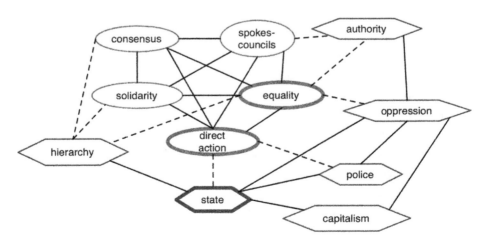

FIGURE 6.7 Fragment of the conceptual structure of contemporary anarchism.

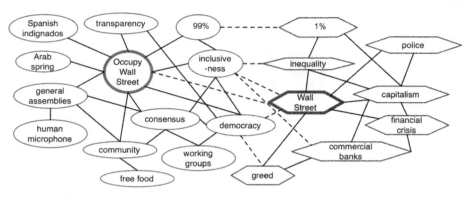

FIGURE 6.8 Value map of the Occupy Wall Street movement of 2011.

analysis in Figure 6.8 was mostly derived from a book produced by participants while the occupation was still in progress.

Figure 6.9 shows some of the visual and auditory images associated with anarchism, including the black (anti-state) flag, the circle-A symbol, the physical activities of the Black Bloc (here shown at the Toronto G20 protests in 2010), and anti-state punk rock music. Contrasting images and values include the police.

Nationalisms are also ideologies, and they usually come with a set of nonverbal symbols. For example, pro-American views are associated with visual images such as the stars-and-stripes flag, songs such as "The Star-Spangled Banner" and "God Bless America," gestures such as the hand-on-chest during the pledge of allegiance, and even foods such as apple pie. Religious ideologies can also be represented by value maps that are multimodal as well as verbal. For instance, the Roman Catholic Church has a wealth of visual and auditory symbols, including cathedrals, crosses, the Pope's hat, prayers, and hymns. In sum, it seems that most ideologies have emotionally important nonverbal representations, and these can be captured in a multimodal expansion of value maps.

Extreme Right-Wing Political Movements

Value maps can also be useful in describing and explaining the rise of right-wing social movements such as the Swedish Democrats, the Danish People's Party, the National Front in France, the neo-Nazi Golden Dawn in Greece, the Tea Party Movement in the United States, and the Alternative for Germany. Figure 6.10 shows mental representations of perceived problems and a nationalist solution. The map applies to European movements but not so well to the Tea Party, which is more libertarian. It displays some of the worries that people have about their current political situation and shows how a right-wing party can provide an

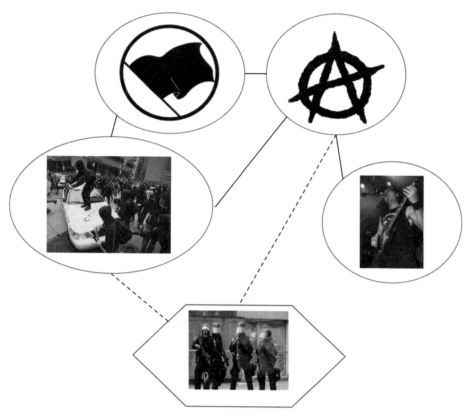

FIGURE 6.9 Multimodal value map of parts of anarchist ideology. Ovals represent emotionally positive concepts, hexagons represent emotionally negative concepts, and rectangles represent emotionally neutral concepts. Solid lines indicate mutual support, while dotted lines indicate incompatibility. Elements include visual images, gestures, and sounds.

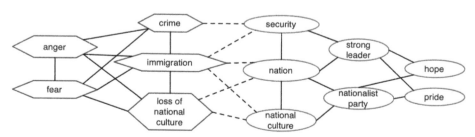

FIGURE 6.10 Value map of fear and anger arising from right-wing concerns about immigration and crime, with hope and pride arising from the right-wing prospects of a nationalist party and leader.

emotionally appealing solution to the negative emotions arising from crime, immigration, and loss of national culture. These figures expand the practice of value maps to include the specific emotions of anger, fear, hope, and pride, all of which are important to the mental functions of ideologies.

Explaining Rwanda Atrocities

In 1994, the Hutu majority in Rwanda slaughtered more than 500,000 members of the Tutsi minority. One of the factors contributing to this action was the explicit development of a Hutu ideology. The role that ideologies play in the causal explanation of atrocities is case-specific, but in general ideologies lead to plans that lead to actions. Figure 6.11 is a sketch of the causes of the Rwanda massacre, showing how a history of Tutsi domination led to the development of a Hutu ideology in the 1950s, which contributed to the massacre of Tutsis in 1994.

The cognitive-emotional structure of the Hutu ideology is depicted in Figure 6.12. It shows the Hutus' positive stereotype of themselves as honest and modest, in contrast to their negative stereotype of Tutus as arrogant invaders, denigrated as cockroaches in the same way that the Nazis denigrated Jews as vermin.

Figure 6.12 could valuably be supplemented by representation of specific emotions, such as the pride associated with the oval concepts, and various negative emotions associated with the hexagon concepts: fear, anger, contempt, disgust. These emotions in turn can be linked to actions, such as killing Tutsis. Ideologies and plans are adopted because they fit with the beliefs and goals of the people exposed to them. The social mechanisms by which ideologies and plans spread

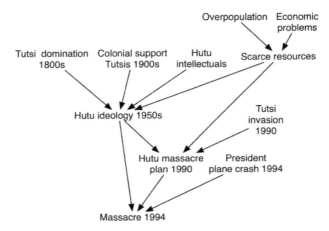

FIGURE 6.11 Hutu ideology as one of the causes of the 1994 massacre. Arrows indicate causality.

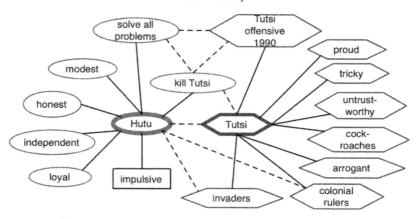

FIGURE 6.12 Value map of Hutu ideology.

through groups of individuals include all forms of verbal and nonverbal communication, including power relations.

POWER

Ideologies are an important part of power relations, as sociologists and political scientists have recognized. But social cognitivism offers a new perspective on power that understands it not only as a social relation but also as a complex of mental processes in both the powerful and the controlled. This section begins with a three-analysis rather than a definition of power and then provides a deeper description of the mental mechanisms that enable people to have power over others. The novelty of this account of power is that it points to the emotional mechanisms crucial to four different kinds of power based on coercion, benefits, respect, and social norms. Moreover, it describes the social mechanisms by which dominators induce emotions in the subjects they control.

Table 6.2 sketches a three-analysis of power. Other standard examples of power could quickly be generated. Power is a relational concept involving multiple individuals or groups, not just a property of single individuals: dominators have control over subjects, typically, although the norm form of power is more diffuse.

The most obvious kind of power is coercive, where one person or group is able to use threats to get another person or group to perform actions that they would not do without external control. For example, a political leader such as Hitler or al-Baghdadi can control people's actions by threats such as imprisonment, torture, and death. The primary emotion in coercive power is fear: people do what

TABLE 6.2

Three-Analysis of *Power*

Exemplars	The Islamic State's power over its adherents and conquered peoples, Hitler's political power over the German people, American economic power, the Catholic Church's religious power, abusive husbands' power over their wives
Typical features	Individuals subjected to power, individuals or groups that control the subjects, actions of the subject that are controlled, emotions of the subjects
Explanations	Explains: why people do things that they would not pursue based on self-interest alone; why some leaders and institutions are able to main control
	Explained by: emotional mechanisms in subjects, communication mechanisms

others want because they fear that the consequences of noncompliance will be physically or emotionally painful. Coercive power also involves the cognitive process of means-ends reasoning, where people imagine the future using rules and conclude that they are better off complying rather than disobeying. The main social mechanism in coercive power is explicit or implicit threats that use verbal and nonverbal means to communicate to controlled people the consequences of noncompliance. Coercive power can also be used to block ideological change by preventing communication of beliefs and emotions, for example when powerful governments restrict freedoms of speech and assembly.

The second main type of power relies on potential benefits that one person or group can provide to another rather than on threats. Some of the power of a political leader, for example, comes not from threats but from the capability of the leader to provide others with financial and other rewards. As in the discussion of interdependent minds in chapter 4, two people depend on each other when the actions of one changes the behavior of others. Couples can provide many benefits to each other, ranging from emotional support to financial contributions to sex. A good relationship is symmetrical, with both individuals having benefit power over the other, but a bad one can have one person wield benefit power as well as coercive power over the other.

The main emotion in benefit power is desire: the subjects of power have desires that the controller can satisfy by providing security, prosperity, or even power over others. For example, a president has benefit power over people who want cabinet appointments that will give the appointees benefit and coercive power over others. The main cognitive mechanism in benefit power is the same one as for coercive power: the ability of people to run mental simulations and imagine the consequences—in this case pleasurable—of the outcomes of complying with or ignoring what the potential controller wants. The main social mechanism of benefit control is communication of the potential benefits, usually verbally but possibly also by nonverbal suggestions of the possibility of desire satisfaction.

Coercive and benefit power both require subjects to infer the consequences of compliance, but there are two other forms of power where behaviors can operate by more implicit mechanisms. Some leaders are so charismatic that they are able to get followers to do what they want without threats or rewards because their followers respect them. Chapter 14 on leadership provides a much deeper analysis of charisma. Here it is enough to note the basic emotional, cognitive, and social mechanisms by which charismatic leaders get people to do what they want.

The main emotions that fuel respect power are liking, admiration, trust, and respect. When people feel deep admiration for a leader, they are inclined to do what he or she wants, independent of consequences based on fear and desire. Of course, respected leaders can also supplement their power by threats and offering benefits. But for respect power to operate there need be no explicit communication of potential of costs and rewards, only the often subtle and non-verbal communications that generate the emotions of liking, admiration, trust, and respect.

The final kind of power is even more subtle, because it can permeate whole so-cieties with little awareness of its operation. I call it "norm power," because social norms make their subjects acquiesce to the plans and goals of an individual or group through agreements that seem to them voluntary rather than based on co-ercion, benefits, or a respected leader. Rather, voluntary compliance operates by social norms that have spread through a society so thoroughly that people may be subject to the control of others while believing that they are choosing the roles assigned to them.

A good example is the position of women in patriarchal societies, where many women feel they are voluntarily choosing roles that subordinate them to men. They have so thoroughly absorbed the social norms governing the appropriate be-haviors of women and men that they go along with them without conscious aware-ness of whether the results are good or bad for them. One of the contributions of the waves of the women's movement, from early suffragettes to women's libera-tion of the 1960s to third-wave feminists of the 1980s, is increasing awareness of the subtlety and alterability of social norms that restrict women's activities.

The emotions associated with norm power are complex. Chapter 4 described how unconscious multimodal rules can affect behavior by operating nonverbally though *if–then* connections where the *if* part and *then* part can be sensory, motor, and emotional. Similarly, the social norms described in chapter 5 with respect to stereotypes of women and Jews were often captured in multimodal rules such as <*Jew*> → <*avoid*>. Hence voluntary compliance in accord with social norms has an emotional dimension because the norms may have emotions built into them.

Moreover, people may have emotions based on the value and consequences of the social norms. Following a social norm can make people feel proud and self-satisfied, whereas violations can lead to negative emotions such as guilt, shame, and self-loathing. At full emotional complexity, social roles can operate via nested emotions such as fear of embarrassment and pride of obedience. People absorb the values that are central to an ideology, for example sharia law in fundamentalist Islam, and comply with it because any other way of doing things is emotionally intolerable.

The main cognitive mechanism of norm power is not imagination of consequences but rather the running of the multimodal rules that constitute social norms. People do not have to think consciously about how to be an appropriate woman, man, mother, father, daughter, or son, because they have already absorbed these rules in a format that is more sensory, motor, and emotional than verbal. Norm power operates by people following the rules built from semantic pointers.

The social mechanisms that implement norm power are the verbal and nonverbal communications that transfer social norms in the form of multimodal rules. Chapters 4 and 5 described how such rules are transmitted by social processes ranging from propaganda to role modeling. When social norms serve the interests and needs of members of society, for example by encouraging civilized behaviors such as kindness and courtesy, then norm power is beneficial. But voluntary compliance based on social norms can also be used to maintain pernicious forms of power such as sexual domination, economic exploitation, and prolonged servitude.

SUMMARY AND DISCUSSION

Explanations of political changes in governments can be developed by means of social cognitive-emotional workups that attend both to the psychological and neural mechanisms in individuals and to the social mechanisms in groups of interacting people. The mental processes of individual leaders and voters use concepts, images, beliefs, rules, goals, and analogies. All of these representations have important emotional aspects, as when concepts are bound with emotions to produce values and when beliefs are bound into specific emotions such as fear, all producing semantic pointers.

Ideologies are coherent systems of concepts, values, and other representations that operate in a group of people to justify the current situation or to motivate change. These sets of values spread among individuals as the result of interactions that typically involve both verbal and nonverbal communication. Ideologies spread through talking and writing but also through nonverbal expressions such as visual and auditory images, gestures, facial expressions, body language, and tone of voice. Additional discussion of religious ideologies can be found in chapter 8 on anthropology and Mormonism.

Ideologies such as the Islamic State worldview can be analyzed by identifying their main cognitive-emotional representations. Not all ideologies are stupid or evil, because some employ values that fit with universal human needs, which include the biological ones of food, water, shelter, and health care and the psychological ones of autonomy, competence, and relatedness to other people. The concentration on wicked ideologies may give the impression that ideologies are always unjustifiable distortions that are best avoided. On the contrary, the idea of an "end of ideology" is itself ideological, and no one can operate politically without an interconnected system of concepts, values, beliefs, goals, and attitudes.

Although inevitably emotional coherence plays a role in the acquisition of an ideology, it is also possible to assemble evidence that can support comparative judgments about the value of differing ideologies. Psychological and biological evidence about the nature of human needs, along with political and historical evidence about the quality of life in the world's countries, supports the conclusion that the best governments are ones that incorporate social-democratic values like those shown in Figure 6.2. Although ideologies often arise from motivated, fear-driven, and rage-driven inferences that ignore relevant evidence, it is possible to build and defend a set of concepts, beliefs, goals, and attitudes based on evidence about the nature of human minds and societies. Not all ideologies are evil, because some are justified by aspects of social and psychological reality. The moral justification of political ideologies and organizations is examined in *Natural Philosophy*, chapter 7.

The same emotional mechanisms that lead people to acquire ideologies can be used to explain why they continue to hold ideologies, spurred by ongoing motivated, fear-driven, and rage-driven inferences. But what causes people to abandon ideologies, for example when people became disillusioned with Nazism or communism? Patterns of movement away from ideologies include

- gradual disinterest that operates in the same way that some people slowly lapse from religious beliefs and practices;
- decisive events that lead people to abandon an ideology, for example when many people abandoned communism in 1956 as the result of the Soviet Union's invasion of Hungary and Khrushchev's revelations about Stalin's atrocities; and
- replacement of one ideology by a competing one, for example when some American Trotskyists of the 1930s became neo-conservatives.

The mechanisms that cause abandonment of ideologies, like those that lead to their adoption, are not merely mental but also depend on social interactions.

Adoption and abandonment of ideologies are emotional gestalt shifts that require replacement of whole systems of concepts and values. These critical transitions are cases of multilevel emergence, because of the interconnections among social, mental, neural, and molecular mechanisms. For example, a thrilling speech by a charismatic leader can produce emotional changes in an individual brain marked by increased dopamine and oxytocin as the person becomes motivated to follow and trust the leader. These chemical changes can then have social effects when the new follower seeks out other people to convert to the cause. These social-mental interactions refute unidirectional explanations such as the Marxist view that economic relations determine ideology and the opposite view that ideas govern the economy.

Ideologies acquired by people provide much of the explanation of their behaviors, including joining political parties, voting, and working for social change or defending the status quo. The ideology of the Islamic State provides strong motivation for military efforts and for recruitment of followers. Similarly, Nazis, anarchists, Hutus, and countless other political activists gain emotional energy from their ideologies. Perhaps there have been psychopathic politicians who reach decisions solely on rational calculations of self-interest, but most people require inspiration through values, goals, social norms, and emotional coherence.

Ideologies contribute to power relations based on coercion, benefits, respect, and social norms, because they tie in with related emotions including fear, desire, admiration, and shame. Ideologies can be part of the communications that subject people to the power of others because of the elicitation of these emotions. Ideology and power both depend on interacting mental and social mechanism that bridge the apparent gap between persons and groups.

The cognitive-emotional structure of ideologies is relevant to the most important social problems facing the world today. Two at the top of the list are climate change and inequality. Concerns about global warming resulting from human production of greenhouse gases are dismissed by motivated inference that values economic growth and government nonintervention higher than scientific evidence and long-term human benefits. The increasing inequality in capitalist countries like the United States and also in professedly socialist societies like China can be dismissed by motivated inference that values personal freedom over social goods. Ideology construed as resulting from cognitive, emotional, and social mechanisms is essential for explaining both social change and resistance to it.

NOTES

This chapter extends Thagard 2015a, reused by permission of Springer Nature, © 2015.

On political ideologies, see Freeden 2003 (quote from p. 32); Freeden, Sargent, and Stears 2013; Haidt 2012; Homer-Dixon et. al. 2013; Jost, Kay, and Thorrisdottir 2009; Jost 2017; Leader Maynard 2013; Morgan and Wisneski 2017.

Other political applications of value maps (cognitive-affective maps) are found in Findlay and Thagard 2014, Homer-Dixon et al. 2014, and Milkoreit 2017.

Decision-making is explained by deliberative and emotional coherence in Thagard 2000, 2006. Tappin, van der Leer, and McKay 2017 document what they call "desirability bias" in political belief revision, a kind of motivated inference.

Details about the ideology of the Islamic State derive mostly from Bunzel 2015 (the "O Muslims" quote is from p. 41), Weiss and Hassan 2015, and Wood 2015. Gesturing is described by https://www.foreignaffairs.com/articles/middle-east/2014-09-03/isis-sends-message. Atran 2016 describes how terrorists are often devoted actors who adhere to sacred values as part of group identities.

Leaders can incite violence by expressing anger, contempt, and disgust: Matsumoto, Frank, and Hwang 2015.

Berns et al. 2012 describe neural studies of sacred values.

TABLE 6.3

Mental and Social Mechanisms for Kinds of Power, with Approximate
Terminological Correspondences for Other Theorists

	Coercive	Benefit	Respect	Norm
emotions	fear	desire, gratitude	admiration, liking	shame, guilt, pride
cognitions	imagining consequences	imagining consequences	analogy	unconscious rule simulation
communication	verbal and physical threats	offers, promises	emotional inspiration	verbal and non-verbal rules
Raven	coercive	reward	expert, referent	legitimate
Lukes	coercion	influence	authority	structural (Foucault)
Galbraith	condign	compensatory		conditioned
Nye	hard	soft	soft	
Mann	military, political	economic, political		ideological

On Islamic emotions, poetry, and metaphors see http://arabic.desert-sky.net/
emotions_pers.html, http://therumpus.net/2015/02/david-biespiels-poetry-
wire-why-jihadists-love-postmodern-poetry/ and http://www.newyorker.com/
magazine/2015/06/08/battle-lines-jihad-creswell-and-haykel.

Elster 2011 discusses emotions and action. Achen and Bartels 2016 argue that
voting is based more on social identities than rational choice.

Anarchism is examined by Graeber 2009 and Marshall 2010. The Occupy
Movement is described by Writers for the 99% 2011.

The causes of the Rwanda massacre are outlined by Melvern 2004.

The section on power goes beyond standard accounts of power by linking it to
mental and social mechanisms. It synthesizes influential accounts of power by
Galbraith 1983, Lukes 2005, Mann 1986, Nye 1990, and Raven 2008, as shown by
Table 6.3, which connects my terminology with theirs.

The needs-based argument for social democracy is in Thagard 2010b and is developed further in *Natural Philosophy*, chapter 7.

PROJECT

Use the techniques of this chapter such as value maps and emotional coherence to explain other ideological changes, for example the rapid rise of Donald Trump in 2016 (see *Natural Philosophy*, chapter 6). Use the same techniques to highlight conceptual differences, for example between competing concepts of freedom and democracy. Develop the discussion of power in this chapter by performing social cognitive-emotional workups of examples of all four kinds.

7

Economics

BUBBLES AND CRASHES

BEYOND ANIMAL SPIRITS

In October 2008, stock markets crashed around the world, precipitating a recession that was the most severe economic downturn since the Great Depression of the 1930s. Such events are puzzling for mainstream economic theory, which assumes that financial markets operate with perfect competition, complete information, and rational individuals who maximize their expected utility. Under such conditions, markets should efficiently reach a stable equilibrium in which prices converge on real values, without the wild swings that characterize bubbles and crashes.

In attempting to explain the 2008 crisis, some economists have fallen back on the archaic idea of animal spirits. John Maynard Keynes used it in his explanation of the 1929 crash and ensuing depression, writing:

> Even apart from the instability due to speculation, there is the instability due to the characteristic of human nature that a large proportion of our positive activities depend on spontaneous optimism rather than mathematical expectations, whether moral or hedonistic or economic. Most, probably, of our decisions to do something positive, the full consequences of which will be drawn out over many days to come, can only be taken as the result of animal

spirits—a spontaneous urge to action rather than inaction, and not as the outcome of a weighted average of quantitative benefits multiplied by quantitative probabilities.

Keynes was pointing out that economic decision-makers are often acting emotionally rather than calculating expected utility.

Alan Greenspan, chair of the Federal Reserve Board in the United States until 2006, was astounded by the crisis of 2008. His postcrisis investigation led to a book that abandons many of his previous assumptions about economic forecasting. Instead, he emphasizes animal spirits and human nature, describing how the financial crisis of 2007–2008 saw investors swinging from euphoria to fear. Like Keynes, he recognized that economic decisions can be emotional and erratic. Investors are capable of going from irrational exuberance in bubble euphoria to panic and paralyzing fear in a crash. Rather than making individually rational decisions, investors succumb to herd behavior, collectively rushing to buy then collectively panicking.

Two Nobel prize-winning economists, George Akerlof and Robert Shiller, similarly use the metaphor of animal spirits to describe how economic crises are caused by changing thought patterns involving confidence, fairness, corruption, illusions about money, and vivid stories. The animal spirits metaphor is useful for highlighting the need to go beyond standard microeconomic assumptions about individual and collective rationality.

More valuable, however, would be a mechanistic explanation of why bubbles and crashes are not only possible but unavoidable. This explanation requires a far more detailed account of cognition, emotion, and social interaction than has been used by economists, who stick at the psychological level of emotional reactions such as confidence, exuberance, and fear. This chapter shows how the cognitive and social mechanisms so far applied to personal relationships, social prejudice, and political ideologies can also be used to explain economic bubbles and crashes.

I begin with an overview of how these mechanisms provide an alternative to traditional economic assumptions about rational markets. Social cognitivism can explain bubbles and crashes as resulting from emotional decisions and communication. The transition from a bubble to a crash is an emotional gestalt shift from primarily motivated inference to fear-driven inference. Just as romantic couples sometimes swing from unjustified enthusiasm about each other to overwrought despair, so markets sometimes swing from irrational exuberance to panic.

ECONOMIC DECISIONS

Mainstream economic theory has been troubled by abundant anomalies in recent decades. Economists have failed to predict economic bubbles and crises, and even to explain them afterwards. Moreover, there have been numerous experimental challenges to the standard assumptions that underlie economic theory. Two new fields—behavioral economics and neuroeconomics—have documented many cases of deviation from rationality.

One might wonder, therefore, why traditional economic theory continues to be taught in leading graduate schools as well as in undergraduate courses. On the popular view of philosophy of science originated by Karl Popper, theories whose empirical predictions fail should be judged as refuted and therefore abandoned. However, historians and philosophers such as Thomas Kuhn and Imre Lakatos have noticed that the development of science is more complicated. Theories are rarely abandoned just in the face of empirical anomalies, because scientists hope that the theory can be adequately patched to deal with problems. Theories manage to survive until a better theory comes along that is able to explain anomalous observations, for example when Copernicus finally superseded geocentric astronomy. Economic theory is afflicted by anomalies in laboratory and real-world studies but survives because no general alternative theory has emerged. Behavioral and neural approaches to economics have largely been experimental rather than explanatory.

Eric Beinhocker reviewed numerous problems faced by mainstream economic theory, but his alternative draws on general ideas about complexity such as attractors (multiple stable states) and transitions, supplemented by biological analogies such as evolution by natural selection. This dynamic view of the economy is more plausible than the assumption that the natural state of markets is equilibrium, but an account of underlying mechanisms is needed to explain why markets undergo transitions among attractors.

The mental and social mechanisms presented in chapters 2 and 3 provide a different way of thinking about economic decisions, challenging the fundamental assumption that individuals make rational decisions by maximizing their expected utility. When the idea of utility was developed by nineteenth-century philosophers such as Jeremy Bentham and John Stuart Mill, it provided a psychological explanation about how people act because they are seeking pleasure and avoiding pain. Economists, however, turned away from psychological considerations toward behavioral ideas such as choices and preferences. Utility became merely a measure of preferences over a set of goods, where preference is not a psychological state but just an observable propensity to pay for something.

Utilities can be mathematically constructed out of preferences that display ideal characteristics such as completeness and transitivity. Hence the concept of utility shifted from a psychological state to a behavioral abstraction to a mathematical construction. Utility was no longer a psychological mechanism for explaining behavior, just a way to describe it. Saying that people maximize utility is just another way of saying that they act in accord with their preferences.

This approach is mathematically elegant but fails for both prediction and for explanation. Economics abandoned any attempt to say why people have the preferences that they have. Preferences are dispositions to behave in regular ways but dispositions always have underlying causes. For example, chemists explain the disposition of salt to dissolve in water by understanding how sodium and chlorine atoms are bound together into sodium chloride molecules and how water molecules displace those bonds. Similarly, we can seek explanations of why choosers prefer one thing over another. Why do most people prefer chocolate to chalk?

Psychology and neuroscience have made much progress since early ideas about utility as pleasure and pain, and we can look to theories of emotion to explain why people make choices. People prefer chocolate to chalk because sensory signals go from their tongues and noses to their brains, where the interactions of areas such as the nucleus accumbens and orbitofrontal cortex generate a positive emotional response to chocolate. More complex decisions such as choosing jobs and making major purchases recruit a wider range of emotions and cognitive processes. There is therefore no scientific reason to take preferences as primitives rather than as resulting from psychological and neural mechanisms for cognition and emotion. Preferences, like all intuitions, result from emotional coherence performed by semantic pointer competition.

Because preferences result from emotional judgments, they do not have the precise logical characteristics required for mathematical generation of utilities. People's preferences can be swayed by minor variations in descriptions of options such as framing outcomes in terms of losses or gains. Daniel Kahneman and Amos Tversky showed that people care more about situations where there is a loss of 10 lives rather than the saving of 10 lives, even though these are logically the same. Depending on context, people may prefer Toyotas to Hondas, Hondas to Fords, but Fords to Toyotas, violating the principle of transitivity.

As a tool to explain behavior, the contemporary view of utility as constructed from preferences is mathematically deficient as well as psychologically superficial. Desirability is not a scalar, a one-dimensional quantity like temperature and weight, but a vector with numerous dimensions, like velocity that requires both magnitude and direction. In the brain, pleasure and pain are not a single dimension but depend on different areas, including the nucleus accumbens for pleasure and the insula for pain. Utility is not a single scale because we toggle between fear and hope when losses are computed differently from gains.

Decisions to satisfy human needs should have at least seven dimensions because of the biological needs of food, water, shelter, and health care, and the psychological needs of relatedness, autonomy, and competence. Emotional coherence is a parallel brain process that serves to integrate these needs and various cultural wants, with no guarantee of optimality.

People's personal and economic choices result from cognitions and emotions rather than mythical utilities or metaphorical animal spirits. Emotions combine cognitive appraisals about the relevance of options to people's goals with physiological changes that occur when people are considering those options. Cognitive-emotional mechanisms make it not at all surprising that people sometimes display inconsistent preferences and act irrationally. As illustrated by romantic relationships, prejudices, and ideologies, cognitive appraisal can go wrong because people's limitations in memory, attention, and processing time can lead them to fail to take into account all the relevant facts and goals. Physiological changes are driven by chemical processes such as activity of dopamine, serotonin, cortisol, and oxytocin. Both lovers and buyers can be flooded by chemicals that interact with appraisals to help generate emotions that sometimes run against interests and needs. Hence we can abandon the dogma of economic rationality and watch for emotional distortions such as motivated inference and fear-driven inference, which encourage people to think that things are better than they actually are or worse than they are.

Irrationality can also arise in social interactions, where economists have tried to use game theory to extend individual rationality to decisions involving multiple people. Although mathematically elegant, game theory has also consistently failed to predict people's actual behavior. In the game of prisoner's dilemma, two people have to decide whether to betray each other or to remain loyal. People's decisions in experiments and in real life depend not just on abstract payoffs but also on psychological states such as trust, which has a substantial emotional component. People who trust each other have good feelings about each other and therefore are much less likely to betray each other.

Similarly, the ultimatum game reveals people acting more on emotional values such as fairness rather than on personal gain. Consider two people who are asked to split $100, with one of them making the division and the other deciding whether to accept it, where saying no results in both people getting nothing. People in most cultures do not behave in accord with game theory, which suggests that the proposer could maximize utility by making an extreme split such as 90–10. This split makes sense because the receiver would rationally take it because $10 is better than nothing. Often, however, people make a 50–50 offer, in accord with mutual

expectations of fairness. People make decisions such as these with substantial resources of cognition and emotion, not just maximization of personal gain.

Social cognitivism provides an alternative to empirically false assumptions
about individual and group rationality. Whether groups such as markets behave
rationally in pursuing the needs of their members is not automatic but rather depends on complex cognitive and social mechanisms. The social mechanisms require transfer, prompting, and instigation of cognitions and emotions through
interpersonal interactions. In contrast to economic models of perfect information, these communications can be severely limited. Not all members of a group
communicate with each other, and even when two people communicate there is no
guarantee of successful transmission. Just like the couples discussed in chapter 4,
communication is never complete. Losses occur in the transfer of both verbal and
nonverbal information that must be assimilated into the mental representations
of the receiver.

Hence the complex of cognitive, emotional, and communication mechanisms
provides a plausible alternative to the empirically problematic assumptions of
mainstream economic theory. We can now look at how social cognitive-emotional
workups can shed light on economic bubbles and crashes.

BOOMS AND BUBBLES: SOCIAL COGNITIVE-EMOTIONAL WORKUP

Mainstream economic theories based on rational expectations fail to explain dramatic economics events such as the crashes of 1929 and 2008, as well as the bubbles that preceded them. In contrast, the semantic pointer theory of emotional
cognition can explain both the exuberance of bubbles and the ensuing despair of
crashes. As in the explanations of relationship change in chapter 4 and of ideological change in chapter 6, the best tool for explaining economic change is the
social cognitive-emotional workup. Identifying the full range of representations
and processes reveals how bubbles and crashes are dramatic cases of multilevel
emergence.

Concepts and Values

The crashes of 1929 and 2008 were preceded by dramatic increases in the prices of
stocks and other properties, such as the Florida land boom of the 1920s and the
upsurge of American house prices in the 2000s. What are the concepts and associated values that provoke exuberant speculation?

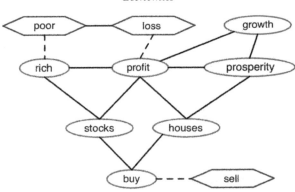

FIGURE 7.1 Value map of bubble mentality. Ovals are emotionally positive, and hexagons are negative. Solid lines indicate mutual support, and dotted lines indicate incompatibility.

Figure 7.1 shows some of the central concepts that became prominent during the boom. Investors focused on appealing ideas such as gains, profit, wealth, prosperity, and becoming rich. This focus suppressed negative values such as loss, poverty, and unemployment. As a bubble develops, people's positive conceptualization of the economic situation increasingly generates the emotional energy that encourages more buying. Economic investment concepts such as stocks, land, and housing derive their strong appeal from their growing association with financial gains.

In accord with the theory of emotional coherence, the goal of wealth supports the positive emotional value of the concept of stocks, but support also feeds back in the other direction. As stocks become more and more exciting, the goals associated with them such as wealth become more prominent, sometimes to the neglect of other personal goals such as family relationships. This reciprocal influence among goals and actions may be less than rational but is psychologically natural given the brain's interconnections between cognition and emotion. Concepts such as those shown in Figure 7.1 constitute an emotional gestalt, a coherent configuration of values that support actions such as buying in a bubble. Figure 7.2 later displays the strikingly different configuration that supports selling in a crash.

Images and Embodiment

Many economic concepts such as *own, buy, sell*, and *wealth* are largely abstract and transbodied, but sensory representations resulting from bodily inputs can also contribute. The concept *boom* associated with rising economic measures such as employment and prosperity retains some association with loud sounds. The concept *bubble* is defensively rejected by people in the throes of irrational exuberance,

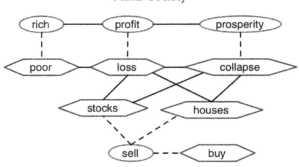

FIGURE 7.2 Value map of crash mentality.

but its application afterwards fits well with the sight and sound of soap bubbles gradually growing and then dramatically popping. Similarly, a crash is not a just an abstract representation of a dramatic drop in prices but carries with it the association of a visual wreck and breaking sound. Buying and selling have to be understood abstractly as transfer of ownership, but they can also be associated with visual and kinesthetic images of money and goods being handed over.

In addition to these sensory accompaniments, concepts such as *boom, bust, bubble,* and *crash* are associated with emotional images. Booms are exciting because of their association with financial gains but also with loud, deep noises. Busts and crashes are emotionally negative because of their associations with broken things and dangerous events. It would be folly to suppose that economic concepts are only embodied, because abstractions such as investments, money, prosperity, and depression go far beyond sensory experience. Rather, they result from transbodied mental operation such as conceptual combination and hypothesis formation. Nevertheless, some economic concepts such as *money* have sensory and emotional connections. When people think of money as an abstract mode of exchange, it is also tied to exemplars such as piles of bills and coins that for many people are emotionally appealing.

This diversity of economic concepts in combining verbal abstractions, sensory associations, and emotional values fits well with the semantic pointer theory of concepts. Binding of neural representations into semantic pointers explains how economic concepts can be both embodied and transbodied. Understanding the roles of economic concepts in decisions requires appreciating both their abstract character and their sensory-emotional associations.

Embodiment in economic thinking is not just a matter of concepts, however. The physiological aspects of emotions cannot ignore the role of molecular mechanisms involving neurotransmitters such as dopamine and hormones such as cortisol. John Coates is a former financial trader turned neuroscientist who investigates the neurochemical basis of financial decisions. He thinks that testosterone is a likely candidate for the molecule of irrational exuberance in bubbles. When prices rise in a bear market, traders who are mostly young males have rising testosterone levels that increase their confidence and appetite for risk, leading to more buying and hence more price increases. Testosterone can increase dopamine levels, making buying successful stocks even more pleasurable, helping to turn a rally into a bubble. The amplifying feedback loop is roughly: more testosterone → more risk → more success → more testosterone.

Coates reports that female traders, whose bodies only have about 10% as much testosterone as males, are less prone to such swings. People's appetite for risk is not constant but fluctuates because of factors such as cortisol levels that rise during the course of a stressful day.

Beliefs and Rules

Continuation of an economic bubble requires a constellation of beliefs to support actions such as speculative buying. The following are some of the beliefs that support continuing economic activity: *Prices have risen. Prices will continue to rise. The economy is strong. Anyone can get rich. I deserve to be rich. This time is different.* The last of these holds that there is something special about the currently rising economic situation that will enable it to persist, unlike previous economic bubbles.

On the standard views of rationality in economics and philosophy, such beliefs are marked by probabilities, which are numerical measures of their credibility. In the brain, however, belief and disbelief correlate with areas of the brain associated with positive and negative emotions. If you are asked whether Toronto is the capital of Canada and you agree, then agreement correlates with activity in your medial prefrontal cortex, a brain area implicated in positive emotions. But if you disagree, there is correlated brain activity in the anterior insula, usually associated with negative emotions. If these experimental findings hold up, then the difference between belief and disbelief is not the abstract numerical difference between high and low probability but more like an emotional reaction. Like desirability and unlike probability, believability is a vector, not a scalar.

Confidence in particular economic assumption and general confidence in the soundness of the economy are therefore emotional as well as cognitive. Akerlof and Shiller emphasize the importance of confidence for maintaining economic growth. They point out that confidence is not just the emotional state of individuals but also how they view other people's confidence, including how confident they are of other people's confidence. They hypothesize a "confidence multiplier," representing changes in income that result from changes in confidence. More confidence can lead to more income which leads to more confidence, an emotional feedback loop crucial to the development of bubbles. This process is both an individual psychological one resulting from motivated inference and a social one resulting from emotional communication.

The understanding of belief and confidence as partly emotional fits well with the semantic pointer theory of belief. Beliefs are brain processes that result from neural bindings of representations that include concepts and emotions that integrate physiology and appraisal. Beliefs can be rational if the appraisal is based on objective goals such as truth (correspondence to reality) and coherence with available evidence. Beliefs can also be held irrationally if the emotional confidence in them is based more on coherence with personal goals, such as the desire to be rich, than on coherence with evidence.

Backers of rational choice will protest that this view of belief confuses probabilities and utilities. This confusion is endemic in the brain, which rather than making a sharp distinction between cognition and emotion integrates them thoroughly. Mathematical theories of probability and utility are recent inventions, produced, respectively, in the seventeenth and nineteenth century. In contrast, the integration of cognition and emotion is found in all mammals, going back more than 300 million years.

How could humans and other animals have survived with such a sloppy mingling of probabilities and utilities? The answer is that you do not need to have an exact calculation of these numbers in order to be able to manage the minimal evolutionary goals of survival and reproduction. Therefore, it is not surprising that people's confidence in booms and bubbles can combine believability and desirability in a messy mix of cognition and emotion.

There is also substantial psychological evidence that people mingle probabilities in utilities in their estimates of confidence. George Loewenstein and his colleagues review evidence that supports the view that people base judgments of risk on their emotional feelings. Norbert Schwartz has described ways in which people use their feelings as information about the world and their place in it. Hence people's judgments about economic developments are more likely to be based on emotions than on cognitive estimates of probabilities. It is small wonder, then, that many beliefs in financial bubbles are erroneous.

Some beliefs are rules, with an *if–then* structure. Investors in a bubble might consciously have the belief that if they invest, then they will make money. But not all rules are conscious beliefs, because some have sensory and emotional components described in chapter 4 in people's unconscious rules about relationships. For example, an investor might acquire the rule *if I buy stocks then I feel good*, where feeling good is an emotional experience rather than something easily put into words. Hence it is better expressed as the multimodal rule <*buy*> → <*feel good*>.

Some investors like to go with their gut feelings, which are emotional reactions based on a combination of physiological perception and unconscious cognitive appraisal. Just as romantic relationships can be based on unconscious rules derived in part from sensory-emotional experience, so investment practices can depend on rules that are hard to verbalize. Traders and lovers may be equally unaware of the unconscious rules they follow and their embodied ties to molecules such as dopamine and testosterone.

Analogies and Metaphors

Capitalist economies have a long history of speculative bubbles, going back to the Dutch tulip mania of the 1630s when single bulbs sold for thousands of guilders. Yet investors in the excitement of bubbles such as the Florida land boom of the 1920s and the American housing market of the 2000s rarely notice these sobering analogies. Why do people fail to retrieve these analogies and apply them to their current situations?

Neglect of the relevant past may result from the psychological process of mood-congruent memory. Retrieval of episodes from memory is affected not only by sensory and semantic similarities between them and the current situation but also by their similar emotional associations. When you are happy, you are more likely to remember happy occasions, and when you are sad, you are more likely to remember sad occasions. Therefore, people exhilarated in a speculative bubble are unlikely to recall the negative lessons of previous disastrous cases that are not seen as emotionally analogous.

I conjecture that thinking about future scenarios is also constrained by emotional similarity. Brain scans show that imagination uses many of the same brain areas as memory, such as the hippocampus. Hence it is plausible that there is mood-congruent imagination that operates like mood-congruent memory. If you are currently happy, then it is easy to imagine a happy future; but if you are currently unhappy, then it is easier to imagine future disasters. Hence speculative investors will find it much easier to remember and make inferences from current cases of success among their fellow speculators than to take sober lessons from past miseries.

So the analogies that govern the continuing speculative behavior of investors and bubbles will be analogies based on recent experiences of themselves and others, rather than on the sobering lessons of history. Investors in a bubble are like newlyweds who cannot imagine how a good situation might turn bad. Abductive inference may also be mood-congruent, with happy people more likely to generate and accept happy explanations, unlike grumpy people with grumpy explanations.

Mood-congruent imagination can also lead economists to seek positive analogies in the face of fears that a bubble might turn into a crash. Greenspan reports that he hoped in 2006 that the growing economic crisis would turn out to be easily managed like the recession of 1987. Akerlof and Shiller describe how people strive to understand their situations by means of stories rather than general principles. In a bubble, stories of success furnished the favorite analogies for guiding thinking and action rather than stories of economic disasters that can be dismissed as not relevant to the current situation, because this time is different.

Metaphors based on underlying analogies can also affect economic activity. The discussion of imagery pointed to metaphorical aspects of concepts such as *boom, bust, bubble,* and *crash.* There are no literal, physical bubbles in markets with a thin sphere of a liquid enclosing a gas. But economic bubbles are analogous in their ability to expand and then burst. Although economics likes to paint itself as an exact and data-driven science, it is rife with metaphors from Adam Smith's invisible hand to the idea of equilibrium, developed by analogy with thermodynamics based on the underlying metaphor of bodily balance. Metaphorical descriptions for rapidly growing economies include concepts like *upswing* and *inflation* in addition to *boom* and *bubble.* For obscure historical reasons, rising prices are called "bull" markets, and falling prices are "bear" markets, although the metaphorical impact of *bull* and *bear* is unclear. Other metaphors used in economic discussions include *green shoots, hit bottom, turn the corner,* and *fall of a cliff.*

Emotion and Action

I have described how concepts, beliefs, images, and analogies are all tinged with emotion, but economic thinking in bubbles also shows the importance of specific emotions. Some of these are relatively mild such as confidence, optimism, hope, and pride in financial success. As chapter 4 showed, trust also has an emotional component that affects people's behavior when they trust their friends or advisors to tell them that the economy is still expanding. Overall optimism results from cognitive appraisal based on coherent concepts and beliefs that assume a burgeoning economy. John Kenneth Galbraith said of the 1920s boom:

> Far more important than rate of interest and the supply of credit is the mood. Speculation on a large scale requires a pervasive sense of confidence and optimism and conviction that ordinary people were meant to be rich.

Greed, like desire, is not strictly an emotion, but it is associated with emotions such as hope and excitement.

More intense emotions can have even more impact on investment decisions. Bubbles are often described in terms of frenzy, mania, and madness, indicating the extent to which peoples' thinking can be dominated by extremely positive emotions. Active buying results from emotions like exuberance and excitement concerning economic prospects. Greed—the inordinate desire to acquire wealth—kicks in as an emotionally powerful motivator for participation in the booming economy.

The negative emotions of anxiety, worry, and fear arise when people start to become aware that the current boom cannot last. But people keep investing as long as this anxiety is less than the fear of being left behind while the economy continues to boom. This balancing of fears is not a calculation of probabilities and utilities but rather an emotional process subject to the whims of fluctuating appraisals and physiology. No one wants to fall behind the other people who are getting rich.

So actions such as buying stocks and encouraging others to buy do not result from carefully maximizing expected utility. Rather, they are driven by neural mechanisms that intertwine cognition and emotion so that the more intense the emotion, the more vigorous the action. Whereas analogies such as historical bubbles should encourage caution, strong emotions provide the certainty to go forward. Uncertainty is the enemy of action, but certainty arising from emotional feedback loops pushes people to act.

Inferences

From a logical point of view, one would expect inferences in economic situations to be based on deductive and inductive reasoning combined with calculations of expected utility. But the mental effects of emotional coherence of concepts and beliefs in economic speculation suggests a different picture. People frequently employ motivated inference in which their goals and emotions can severely distort their judgments.

Investors do make some inductive inferences such as to the conclusion that prices go up. They sometimes also make deductive inferences, such as the calculation that the total of their profits is the sum of profits in individual stocks. But the most important inferences that investors make are practical ones concerning what to do, particularly what to buy or sell. Standard economic theory supposes that people make decisions based on calculations of expected utility, which is implausible because most people lack information about probabilities and utilities.

Instead, decisions to buy or sell result from emotional coherence among actions and goals where people arrive at a feeling about what is the best thing to do.

Decision-making by emotional coherence makes people highly susceptible to motivated inference, in which beliefs are contaminated by their goals. Motivated inference is more than just wishful thinking, because people do not believe something just because they want it to be true. Instead people selectively recruit evidence from memory or outside sources to support the beliefs that they want to be true because they fit with their goals. Motivated inferences can be fueled by mood-congruent imagination, because if you are in a happy mood then you will find it easy to imagine good scenarios that fit well with your goals of being happy and prosperous.

Economic bubbles are cycles of motivated inference. People want to believe that they will be rich, so they tend to believe claims that might help them to become rich. Thinking that a stock will go up or that a house will continue to increase in value fits well with people's emotionally significant goal of being financially successful. In a bubble, people look for reasons to continue believing that their investments will remain lucrative, drawing not only on their own experience but also on the reports of friends, acquaintances, and news media. Motivated inference also helps people to ignore cautionary notes from financial experts who warn about similar bubbles in the past.

Gut reactions can be useful when their emotional judgments derive from cognitive appraisals that accurately estimate the effects of alternative actions on relevant goals. Unfortunately, people have no conscious awareness of the process of emotional coherence, so there is no direct way of assuring that their cognitive appraisals are actually accurate. The contribution of physiological changes to emotions opens up the possibility of gut *over*reactions, in which people take their visceral states to be evidence not just for the desirability of goals but even for the credibility of beliefs. Gut overreaction occurs when people's positive feelings lead them to conclude that the economy is going well and will continue to go well, as physiology feeds into mood-congruent imagination. Individuals then get into an amplifying feedback loop in which buying makes them feel good, which makes them convinced that buying will continue to be a good strategy. Because estimations of risk are based on feeling rather than calculation, feeling good about the economy leads people to overestimate the advantages of buying.

Motivated inference can produce wholesale self-deception, where people have some realization that bubbles are not sustainable but nevertheless continue to believe that prices will keep going up because that belief fits with their goals. Reinhart and Rogoff conclude their history of financial folly with this remark: "Technology has changed, the height of humans has changed, and fashions have changed. Yet the ability of governments and investors to delude themselves, giving rise to periodic bouts of euphoria that usually end in tears, seems to have remained a constant".

So far, my discussion has concerned individuals, but bubbles are obviously group phenomena. We need to look at social mechanisms to understand how concepts, images, beliefs, analogies, emotions, and inferences can spread in groups of people who share an economy.

Communication

Lacking a theory of cognitive and emotional communication, economists have had to fall back on biological metaphors to describe the social dimensions of bubbles and crashes. Greenspan describes the influence of investors on each other as examples of herding behavior, suggesting that people behave like dumb animal groups rather than individually rational decision makers. Akerlof and Shiller describe the spread of animal spirits as a kind of contagion, invoking the medical metaphor of infectious diseases. Beinhocker tries to think of the economy as analogous to evolution by natural selection, with memes spreading through a population like genes in a species.

Metaphors can be useful in suggesting mechanisms in the way that early computers inspired new ways of explaining thinking. But metaphors can also get in the way of developing more sophisticated mechanisms in the way that narrow computational ideas have sometimes hindered recognizing neural complexity. A fully developed theory of integrated cognitive and social mechanisms should be able to provide a much richer account of the spread of ideas than metaphors such as herding, contagion, and natural selection.

According to the theory of communication presented in chapter 3, interactions of people through verbal and nonverbal communication allow them to transfer, prompt, and instigate semantic pointers. These are neural representations that combine the representing functions of concepts and beliefs with sensory-motor aspects and emotional significance. For sensory-motor and emotional communication, nonverbal expression by means of images, gestures, facial expressions, and body language can be more important than the use of words.

In an economic bubble, the transfer of positive emotions such as excitement, exuberance, greed, and trust occurs because of the combination of verbal and nonverbal communication. Verbal communication can contribute to emotional communication by tone of voice and the use of emotion-laden words such as "boom" and "bull market." In the land and stock bubbles of the 1920s, communication was enhanced by new technologies such as telephone and radio. The bubble of the 2000s drew on additional technologies such as television, electronic mail, and the Web, but the function is similar. One person's semantic pointers generate behaviors that have causal effects on the brains of other persons to produce semantic pointers in their brains. Hence one person's enthusiasm carries over to another, which can then feed back into the original person's enthusiasm.

So bubbles operate by feedback loops in both individuals and groups that amplify feelings. An individual's buying, motivated inference, and hormone-fueled emotions lead to more buying, motivated inference, and positive emotions. In a group such as a trading community, actions and emotions in some individuals lead to similar actions and emotions in others, encouraging more actions and emotions among all the members of the groups. This process is causally different from herding, contagion, and natural selection in ways that can only be appreciated if the neural underpinnings of what goes on in individual minds are understood. Animal herds, germs, and most species of plants and animals do not have the cognitive, emotional, and communicative procedures that occur in the brains of humans. With the semantic pointer theory of communication, metaphor can give way to mechanism, through the mental-social processes of collective motivated inference.

PANICS AND CRASHES: SOCIAL COGNITIVE-EMOTIONAL WORKUP

Turning from the exhilaration of bubbles to the panic of economic crashes, a social cognitive-emotional workup follows the same procedure just presented for bubbles. This workup can proceed more succinctly by focusing on the cognitive and emotional differences between bubbles and crashes.

Concepts and Values

The thinking that occurs in crashes uses mostly the same concepts that occur in bubbles, because the same economic concepts apply, such as ones about profit, loss, buying, selling, and goods such as stocks and houses. Many of the values are the same, such as the desire for profits and the dislike of losses. But the overall emotional reaction is very different, as shown in how Figure 7.2 contrasts with Figure 7.1. The shift from an enthusiastic bull market to a skeptical bear market switches the emotional value of buying from positive to negative, with the correlative switch of the emotional value of selling from negative to positive. As before, values are neural representations that bind concepts with emotions.

This switch results from reevaluation of stocks, houses, and other goods as now likely to lead to losses rather than profits. Stocks go from being exciting to scary, so that the semantic pointer for stocks becomes rebound with negative rather than positive emotions. This rebinding has the consequence for action that people will want to avoid stocks rather than pursuing them. The causes of the emotional switch can be various kinds of new information described in the section on inferences.

Images and Embodiment

I have already described how concepts like *crash* and *burst bubble* are associated with visual and auditory images. Other images can vividly stand for economic crashes, such as plummeting graphs, money going up in flames, and bankers jumping out of tall buildings. These images depend on our sensory systems, and other concepts used to describe economic crises such as *downturn* and *collapse* also have an important degree of embodiment. It would be a mistake, however, to try to reduce all negative economic concepts to embodiment, because many concepts such as *own, recession,* and *depression* have an abstract meaning derived by verbal combination. For example, a recession is technically defined as a country's decrease in gross national product for two quarters in a row, which is far too abstract to reduce to embodiment.

Besides sensory aspects of images, another important aspect of embodiment is the physiological changes that occur in crises such as economic collapse. John Coates vividly describes what happens in investors' bodies when they are aware and afraid of impending economic disasters. Instead of the testosterone and dopamine associated with pleasure in economic success, the threat of failure brings steadily rising levels of the stress hormone cortisol, which Coates calls the molecule of irrational pessimism. Traders may experience resulting physiological changes in stomachs and bowels and in appetites for food and sex. All of these physiological changes sensed by the brain contribute to negative emotions such as fear and depression, with lower levels of neurotransmitters such as dopamine and norepinephrine. Emotional energy to act accordingly drops, along with trust in individuals and institutions.

Beliefs and Rules

Economic downturns can introduce new beliefs and the rejection of previous ones. For example, the belief that the economy is fundamentally sound can give way to the suspicion that there are fundamental flaws in the institutions that are relevant to the maintenance of prosperity. Old rules about how to make money that worked well in a bubble have to be abandoned. Belief revision does not occur piecemeal, one belief at a time, but can concern whole systems of belief about the functioning and prospects of the economic system. Whereas adoption and revision of beliefs during bubbles are shaped by motivated inference, in crises people are more influenced by fear-driven inference as described later.

Analogies and Metaphors

In a crisis, positive stories, analogies, and metaphors become replaced by negative ones. At the beginning of the financial breakdown of 2007, political and economic leaders hoped that it would turn out to be as temporary as the downturns of 1987 and 1999. But with the bankruptcy of Lehman Brothers in 2008, the most frequent analogy became the Great Crash of 1929, resulting in strong government measures to try to prevent a similar collapse. The analogy between the 2008 crisis and the 1929 crash made people all the more worried but also motivated leaders to take steps to try to avoid another disaster. Hence analogical thinking played a large role in how people thought about the new crisis.

New economic situations require new metaphors such as the imagery of crashing and bubbles bursting. The concept *depression,* used to describe the severe drop in economic activity after the 1929 crash, has a technical meaning related to gross national product. But it also has a metaphorical meaning that derives from an analogy with low places in the ground and is associated with the emotional state of depression. Political leaders argue whether the economy is in a state of recession or depression, because these concepts have emotional carryover from their metaphorical and imagistic origins.

Attempts to deal with financial crises are influenced by conflicting metaphors. Politicians who prefer to avoid government spending favor the analogy between states and families, who must *tighten their belts* to avoid *living beyond their means.* Alternatively, Keynesians who want governments to spend more to alleviate economic downturns emphasize the need to *prime the pump.* Analogies and metaphors are inescapable when people face novel and difficult problems.

Emotions

In a crisis, the happy emotions previously prevalent in a boom or bubble give way to negative emotions that can be increasingly intense. Instead of joy, exuberance, hope, and optimism, individuals experience more and more sadness, pessimism, despair, anxiety, fear, alarm, shock, and panic. In a boom, people feel gratitude toward the economic and political system that furthers their prosperity, but in the downturn they start to feel resentment and even anger toward a system that is not helping them to accomplish their financial goals. Confidence is replaced by uncertainty and attendant anxiety, which in turn lead to reduced economic activity because people are afraid to take chances that make their financial situations even worse. In a full panic, however, people can be spurred to sell low what they bought high, locking in losses that they will never recover. Like belief revision, this emotional shift does not occur piecemeal but rather requires a large emotional gestalt shift that involves multiple representations, including concepts, beliefs, analogies, and associated feelings.

An individual who feels responsible for increasing losses may experience the negative emotions of guilt and shame. Guilt is a feeling of wrongdoing resulting from violation of a moral code, whereas shame is a social emotion that anticipates critical judgments of others. Guilt, shame, and feelings of hopelessness can feed into depression that may even result in suicide. Emotions can offer opportunities for investors, as in Warren Buffett's recommendation to be greedy when others are fearful and fearful when others are greedy.

Inference

When bubbles turn into crashes, motivated inference is supplanted by fear-driven inference. Motivated inference makes investors think that the economy is better than it is, because they accept beliefs that fit with their goals rather than with the available evidence. Fear-driven inference makes investors think that the economy is worse than it is, because negative emotions such as anxiety make them focus on the worst evidence and worst possibilities. In a financial panic, people have lost the ability to attend to the positive aspects of the economy that made them overoptimistic, and then swing into concentration on negative aspects that make them overly pessimistic.

The amplifying feedback loop that draws individuals into fear-driven inference is both cognitive and emotional, which requires both appraisal and physiology. Just as feeling good provides illusory evidence for the conclusions of motivated inference, so feeling bad provides illusory evidence for the pessimistic conclusions of fear-driven inference. As stocks drop and companies fail, people's negative feelings provide all the more impetus to think that stocks will continue to drop and companies will continue to fail. In 2008, some extreme reactions even held that capitalism is doomed and civilization as we know it is over. Such negative thinking is driven by fear and can then increase fear because of the conclusion that things are only going to get worse.

What makes people tip from motivated inference to fear-driven inference? Similar transitions have already been described in relationship moves from infatuation to disillusionment and in political moves from disgruntlement to ideological fanaticism. All of these transitions can be understood as emotional gestalt shifts resulting from emotional coherence. The drivers of shifts are specific to particular cases in which new evidence, new hypotheses, and new emotional values produce the transition from one set of beliefs and emotions to another. In the crisis of 2008, many events contributed to the transition from optimism to pessimism, especially the collapse of the housing market, drops in the stock market, and the failure of financial institutions like AIG and Lehman Brothers.

Rather than maintain a stable equilibrium, the economy reached a tipping point that led to a critical transition from boom to bust. The ideas of tipping points and critical transitions are merely descriptive and alone provide no causal explanations for dramatic changes. Explanations come from mechanisms that have tips and transitions as causal results. Coherence judgments based on emotions and semantic pointers provide the required causal process for individuals, and communication provides it for groups.

Communication

An economic crash is not just the sum of emotional transitions in individuals, because it also results from interactions of individuals. Complementing the cognitive-emotional feedback loops within each person, there are social feedback loops in which the beliefs and attitudes of multiple individuals reinforce each other. Initially, only a few individuals may detect problems in the economy, but as conditions worsen there will be a spread of information and emotion among communicating individuals.

Spreading of negativity is not just verbal, because people can pick up each other's mounting fears through other indicators of emotions: facial expressions such as frowns, agitation shown by bodily movements, and quavering tones of voice. Panic happens in individuals but also in whole groups because of the non-verbal and verbal ways that they pick up each other's emotions along with changing beliefs.

This transfer of beliefs and emotions could be metaphorically described as herding, contagion, or natural selection, but the semantic pointer theories of emotion and communication provide a deeper explanation. Panic spreads through an economic community because the neural representations of some individuals concerning economic developments are approximately reproduced in the brains of people with whom they interact.

In each investor, the critical transition is from positive to negative emotions with accompanying beliefs about where the economy is headed. In a whole economy, the critical transition in a crash is from negative views held by a few skeptics to widespread worries about the future of the economy. As long as only a few people are pessimistic, there are still more buyers than sellers. The spread of negative emotions through the community generates a preponderance of sellers over buyers.

The occurrence of critical transitions at both individual and social levels shows that economic crashes are prime cases of multilevel emergence, where new properties result from interactions of multiple mechanisms. For each individual, negative emotions emerge from the interaction of numerous beliefs and emotions, each of which emerges from the interactions of billions of neurons whose firing emerges from the interactions of many molecules. For the whole economic community, the overall crash emerges from the interaction of numerous traders, managers, and government officials. The economy as a whole ends up with properties such as recession and depression that are not just the aggregates of the properties of the investors because they result from the interactions of investors. A reductionist account would have social interactions resulting from psychological and neural mechanisms, but causality also runs downward from the social to the molecular: talking with fearful people can increase activity in people's amygdalas and increase production of cortisol.

Attempts to recover from a financial crisis also require emotional communication. Politicians such as Franklin D. Roosevelt and George W. Bush tried to sooth the financial community, where soothing means trying to calm the negative emotions found in a spreading panic. Soothing occurs not only by verbal communication but also by calming behaviors such as a level tone of voice and pleasant facial expressions. However, after the crashes of 1929 and 2008, it took years for investors to regain much confidence in the economy.

MINDFUL ECONOMICS

My explanations of bubbles and crashes using mechanisms of emotional thinking and communication contrast starkly with the methods of most current economists. Some economists have even defended economic theory against psychological challenges by arguing that economics should remain "mindless" by continuing to focus on preferences and choices rather than on mental processes. In contrast, I advocate a theoretical approach to mindful economics that goes beyond the fascinating empirical results of behavioral economics and neuroeconomics by proposing underlying neural and social mechanisms.

Table 7.1 summarizes the differences between current economic theory and a more psychologically and neurologically plausible account. Rather than making behavioral preferences central to economic explanations, mindful economics looks to neural processes of cognition and emotion to provide deeper explanations of preferences and choices.

Mindful economics views preferences as the causal results of emotional cognition, not as behavioral constructions out of observed choices. In place of utility as the mathematical conglomeration of preferences, mindful economics recognizes that people's decisions result from emotional coherence through balancing competing beliefs and feelings. Whereas mainstream economics assumes that individuals maximize utility, mindful economics recognizes that there are cognitive, emotional, and social factors that limit people's coherence calculations to results that are at best approximations to the maximal satisfaction of their needs. In contrast to the economic dogma that people do and should act only in their self-interests, the ultimatum game experiments and other observations show that people are capable of considering the interests of others for reasons such as fairness, altruism, and empathy. A recent study found that only 31 of 446 residents of Tokyo were maximizers of self-interest.

Mindful economics recognizes that people usually lack both the data needed to identify objective probabilities and the cognitive capacity to make valid probability inferences without advanced mathematical training. Instead, buyers and sellers fall back on risk as feeling, with emotional reactions filling in for exact applications of probabilities. Whereas economics imitates some branches of physics in seeing equilibrium as the natural state, mindful economics recognizes that

TABLE 7.1

Differences Between Current Economic Theory and Mindful
Economic Theory Based on Semantic Pointers

Current Economic Theory	Mindful Economic Theory
Preferences	Emotions as semantic pointers
Choices	Actions caused by cognitive-emotional processes
Utility	Emotional coherence
Self-interest	Self-interest and caring based on empathy and altruism
Maximization	Approximation
Probability	Risk as feelings
Rationality	Frequent irrationality such as gut overreactions
Equilibrium	Critical transitions

changes in beliefs and emotions can lead to critical transitions in both individuals and whole economies.

The view that humans are inherently rational has attracted philosophers since Aristotle, but economists' assumption that people are rational in maximizing their expected utility is not empirically plausible. It contradicts both the results of psychological experiments and everyday observations. Many people smoke, overeat, buy lottery tickets, acquire credit card debt at high interest rates, and fail to take prescribed medications. Most stock fund managers underperform the market. Almost half of the population enters into marriages that will eventually end up in divorce. Well over half of the people in the world believe in deities for which there is scant empirical evidence. A scientific approach to mind and economic behavior needs to explain such irrationality, not define it away. Rather than denigrate humanity, recognition of rampant irrationality encourages improvement in education and in social policies that enable citizens to act better in their shared interests, satisfying their needs.

Akerlof and Shiller protest the reliance of mainstream economics on rational expectations: "Conventional economic theories exclude the changing thought patterns and modes of doing business that bring on a crisis". To overcome this exclusion, economists need to embrace rather than ignore experimental results from behavioral economics and neuroeconomics and to use theories about the brain/mind to explain important phenomena such as bubbles and crashes that are otherwise outside their professional range.

This chapter has only begun the development of mindful economics by showing the relevance of emotional cognition to explaining people's behavior in bubbles and crashes. There are many economic phenomena that cry out for similar treatments, for example that losses have a greater impact on people than gains. Loss aversion seems to exemplify a more general psychological phenomenon that bad things are more powerful than good ones. One could speculate that biological evolution selected for survival by making people more attuned to threats than good outcomes, but this speculation is weak without neural explanations of why negative emotions are more intense. The semantic pointer theory of emotions suggests investigating positive/negative differences in both appraisals and physiology that result in differences in neural and molecular activity. But current research provides no basis for choosing among or synthesizing neural explanations of loss aversion based on: different amounts of firing in particular brain areas, differences in which brain areas are involved, and differences in neurotransmitter pathways.

Another well-established psychological effect is that people often make equitable rather than self-maximizing offers in the ultimatum game in everyday life. There are good candidates for social-cognitive-emotional explanation of this effect. People have a socially acquired norm of fairness that is inculcated in two ways. In explicit verbal form it is learned as cultural variants of the golden rule to treat people how you would like to be treated yourself. Fairness is also appreciated by means of unconscious rules such as: *If you treat someone unfairly, then you will feel bad.* Such rules can arise through empathy via emotional analogies in which people suffer to some extent from observing the suffering of others. Fairness is not just a verbal, cognitive ideal but also a pattern of emotions including feeling good about treating people kindly and feeling bad about acting unjustly.

Given empirical failures at both the individual and social levels, one has to wonder at the continuing dominance of mainstream economic theory. I already gave one explanation, the absence of a strong alternative theory, which I hope will be overcome by further developments in mindful economics based on psychological and neural theories that take emotion seriously.

Another reason for the rise and supremacy of mainstream economic theory is its fit with free-market ideology. Nineteenth-century ideas about utility as a psychological process rooted in pleasure and pain raised ethical questions about the appropriate distribution of wealth: more equality could lead to more overall utility if wealth were transferred from rich to poor. In contrast, narrowly behavioral ideas of utilities derived from preferences derived from choices left no room for judgments about whether the preferences themselves are justified or whether the distribution of goods is ethically equitable. Hence mainstream economics provides ideological support for free markets and avoidance of government interventions.

In contrast, a more empirically plausible account of economic decisions as emotional legitimates ethical questions concerning distribution of wealth and democratic control over economic practices. For example, it becomes possible to ask whether it can be justified that in the United States in 2012 the combined salaries of 25 hedge fund managers added up to more than the salaries of all 158,000 kindergarten teachers. These ethical issues are discussed in *Natural Philosophy*, chapter 7.

REFLEXIVITY

George Soros is a billionaire investor who argues for a new way of thinking about the economy that incorporates reflexivity. He says that the role that intentions and future expectations play in social situations sets up a two-way connection between the participants' thinking and the situation in which they participate. When people are optimistic, it feeds back into more buying behavior that can turn into a bubble. Such reflexivity in economic change is hard to explain within the conventional approach that assumes perfect rationality and perfect information.

Reflexivity can be explained more deeply in just the same way that Keynes's animal spirits can be fleshed out in terms of psychological and neural processes. People can mentally represent the world but can also represent themselves in the world. They have various concepts of themselves and the markets in which they participate by buying and selling, and they have beliefs about stocks going up or down. Emotions arise when they are happy that stocks are going up and when they are worried that stocks might lose value. These are all different kinds of mental representations, not just words, with various kinds of images and emotion.

Reflexivity derives from representations that include the representations of yourself and your own social situation and the whole economy. My principle of social recursion (chapter 5) notes that the actions of groups depend on the actions of individuals who think of themselves as members of groups. Understanding the actions of groups requires realization that groups are constituted by individuals but also that the individuals are capable of representing themselves as members of groups, which has a crucial effect on the behavior of the individuals and on the behaviors of the groups. The person–group problem is resolved by appreciating the interactions of mental and social mechanisms.

Soros suggests that reflexivity requires social science to be inherently different from natural science. But if you do social science in a way that integrates neural, mental, and social mechanisms, then you can create a sufficiently complex account that is similar in its methods and results to what happens in natural sciences such as physics and biology. Prediction is difficult because these systems are nonlinear, chaotic in the sense that they are easily perturbed. But mechanistic explanations of what goes on in complex social phenomena like economic booms and busts becomes achievable.

Similarly, chapter 5 argued against the view that sociology requires a special method of verstehen, because empathy and other kinds of understanding make scientific sense as multilevel emergence from mental as well as social mechanisms.

SUMMARY AND DISCUSSION

This chapter has applied social cognitivism to economics by generating new explanations of the occurrences of bubbles and crashes. The mentality of people caught up in booms and busts can be understood by a detailed examination of their cognitive and emotional states, performed by a social cognitive-emotional workup. The irrational exuberance of people in a bubble can be contrasted with the panicked despair of people in a crash by identifying their very different concepts, beliefs, rules, analogies, and emotions. These mental representations depend on neural processes that are embodied in two ways. Patterns of neural firing are influenced by sensory inputs from bodily organs such as the eyes and also by chemical processes using producers and products of emotional states such as dopamine and cortisol.

The different emotional states of people in bubbles and crashes disposes them to two contrasting modes of inference. Motivated inference encourages people to think that good times can only continue, whereas fear-driven inference disposes people to dread that bad times will only get worse. In bubbles, motivated inference and molecules such as testosterone and dopamine provide the feedback loop to encourage individuals to remain optimistic. In crashes, fear driven-inference and molecules such as cortisol promote pessimism.

Bubbles, crashes, and other economic changes are not just matters of individual psychology, because they are also social processes resulting from the communicative interactions of many people. Both verbal and nonverbal communications spread emotions as well as beliefs. Critical transitions occur in social mechanisms where whole economies go from boom to bust and back again. These changes cause and are caused by critical transitions in individual minds and brains, which cause and are caused by molecular changes. Hence bubbles and crashes exemplify multilevel emergence, where the interactions of molecular, neural, mental, and social mechanisms lead to dramatic overall change.

Informal discussions of bubbles and crashes often attribute beliefs and emotions to institutions such as banks and governments. For example, a bank believes that it is at risk of default, and a government fears this default. From my perspective, these descriptions are merely metaphorical, because beliefs and emotions are processes in individual brains, not in groups of people. Nevertheless, this metaphorical usage points to the important fact that the beliefs and emotions operating in each individual are in part the result of the interactions of the individual with other people in relevant institutions.

The claim that an institution such as a bank has a collective mental state therefore just means the following: individuals in the institution have similar mental states that result in part from communications with other individuals in the institution. For actions, institutions may have emergent properties that are not just aggregates of individuals, for example when a bank raises interest rates or a government passes a law, which are actions that no one individual can perform. Therefore, actions can be emergent properties of institutions in a way that beliefs, emotions, and other mental states are not. I return to this question in the next chapter concerning religious institutions such as churches. Chapter 14 discusses related economic issues concerning leadership and marketing.

NOTES

The quote on animal spirits is from Keynes 1936, p. 161.

Natural *Philosophy* discusses how cognitive and emotional coherence can lead to both rationality and irrationality.

On the economic crises of 1929 and 2008, see Akerlof and Shiller 2009, Eichengreen 2015, Greenspan 2013, Krugman 2009, and Stiglitz 2010. Kindleberger and Aliber 2011 and Cassidy 2009 review economic manias and panics more generally. This chapter is about economic panics, not panic attacks and disorders discussed in clinical psychology.

Cartwright 2014 surveys behavioral economics. See also Camerer 2003 on behavioral game theory. Akerlof and Kranton 2010 develop identity economics, which describes how social identities shape work and well-being in psychological ways that need to be elaborated by neural mechanisms. Economics as a science is ripe for conceptual change, with obsolete concepts like *utility* and *perfect competition* replaced by mental and social concepts that are stronger both empirically and theoretically.

Neuroeconomics is reviewed by Glimcher and Fehr 2013.

Philosophical discussions of falsification and theory replacement included Kuhn 1970, Lakatos 1970, and Popper 1959, and Thagard 1992b. For an attempt at a more realistic economics textbook, see http://www.core-econ.org.

Beinhocker 2006 proposes a complexity approach to economics.

On the history of utility, see Driver 2014. On preferences see Hausman 2011. *Natural Philosophy* (chapters 5 and 6) further discusses dispositions and preferences.

Kahneman and Tversky 2000 collects their work on decision making. Lerner, Li, Valdesolo, and Kassam 2015 review recent work on emotion and decision.

Coates 2012 discusses the neuroscience of investing.

Harris, Sheth, and Cohen 2008 examine the neural correlates of belief.

Reinhart and Rogoff 2009 discuss financial folly (quote from p. 292).

On risk as feelings, see Loewenstein, Weber, Hsee, and Welch 2001. On feelings as information, see Schwartz 1990. *Brain–Mind* (chapter 7) presents the semantic pointer theory of emotional feelings.

Mood-congruent memory is reviewed by Mayer, McCormick, and Strong 1995.

Schacter, Addis, and Buckner 2007 link memory and imagination. Mood-congruent imagination is one of the reasons that people are bad at forecasting future emotions.

Galbraith 1972 analyzes the crash of 1929 (quote from pp. 174–175).

Gul and Pesendorfer 2008 defend mindless economics, with effective responses by Camerer and Hausman in the same volume. Bénabou and Tirole 2016 defend mindful economics informed by research on motivated inference.

The Japanese study showing that most people do not fit the standard economic profile is Yamagishi et al. 2014.

The quote about conventional economic theories is from Akerlof and Shiller 2009, p. 167.

Losses (and bad things in general) have more impact than gains (and good things in general): Kahneman and Tversky 1979; Baumeister, Bratslavsky, Finkenauer, and Vohs 2001; Litt, Eliasmith, and Thagard 2008. Zalocusky et al. 2016 find that rats with less loss aversion have different dopamine receptors in the nucleus accumbens.

Hedge fund managers make more than kindergarten teachers: http://www.washingtonpost.com/blogs/the-fix/wp/2015/05/12/the-top-25-hedge-fund-managers-earn-more-than-all-kindergarten-teachers-combined/

Soros 2008 discusses reflexivity in financial markets. My discussion here draws on Thagard 2014a, with permission of Palgrave Macmillan.

For an extended argument against the idea of collective emotions and other mental states, see Thagard 2010a.

PROJECT

Do a three-analysis of important economic concepts such as *property* and *depression*. Use a social cognitive-emotional approach to explain loss aversion and sunk costs. Explain other large-scale economic developments such as trade wars between countries. Perform psychological and neurological experiments to test the hypothesis of mood-congruent imagination. Analyze economic contributions to the four kinds of power mentioned in chapter 6: coercive, benefit, respect, and norm.

8

Anthropology

RELIGION

CULTURES

Why do people practice religion and other cultural pursuits? Anthropology is the study of humans, covering the comparative study of cultures and the physical basis of human evolution and ecology. Historically, anthropology differs from sociology, politics, and economics by greater concern with non-Western societies.

Anthropologists have tried to understand these cultures by the method of participant observation, placing themselves in societies for extended periods of time to understand local beliefs and practices. Cultural anthropologists investigate such topics as language, family, health, work, agriculture, and education. Physical anthropologists consider the relevance of human biology and evolution to understanding the abilities of humans to adapt to their environments.

Since cognitive science became organized in the 1970s, anthropology has been counted as one of the contributing disciplines, along with psychology, neuroscience, philosophy, linguistics, and artificial intelligence. In recent years, psychologists have paid increasing attention to cultural differences in thinking and acting. Psychology has been criticized for only studying people from WEIRD societies, in other words, ones that are Western, Educated, Industrialized, Rich, and Democratic. But social psychology is acquiring interesting findings about how people in different cultures think differently about other people and their environments.

In contrast, cultural anthropology has largely ignored the potential of the study of cognition and emotion for illuminating social patterns and practices across cultures. Like sociologists, anthropologists prefer social descriptions to mechanistic explanations based on cognitive processes. This chapter shows the relevance of cognitive and emotional processes to anthropology by applying them to understand the widespread cultural practices of religion. I propose a social cognitive-emotional workup of one of the fastest rising religions in the world, the Church of Jesus Christ of Latter-day Saints, or Mormons. The social changes that I want to explain include the rise and fall of particular religions and also changes in the general prevalence of religion in society.

RELIGION

Religion is often cited as a cultural universal, but there are some cultures, such as the Pirahã people of the Amazon, who have no religious rituals or beliefs in supreme spirits, although their world is inhabited by a host of forest and other spirits. Among the 7 billion people in the world today, more than 1 billion have no religious association. But that statistic leaves 6 billion people who do, including the big four of Christianity, Islam, Hinduism, and Buddhism. Religion is a major part of human culture, and many social changes are closely tied to the rise and fall of different religions. For example, when Muhammad started Islam in the seventh century, it rose to dominate the Middle East and to become a prominent world religion with over 1.7 billion adherents and strong political influence in dozens of countries.

What is religion? A definition in terms of necessary and sufficient conditions would quickly find itself swamped with counterexamples and circularities, so a three-analysis is more informative. Table 8.1 presents exemplars, typical features, and explanations for the concept of religion.

In Table 8.1, the standard examples of religion include Christianity, Islam, Hinduism, and Buddhism, as well as Judaism, which is historically important even though it has comparatively few members today. Within these religions, there are major subdivisions, such as between Catholic and Protestant Christianity, and between Sunni and Shia Islam. Further subdivisions include many Protestant variants and many Sunni variants. People may disagree about the essential features of religion, but no one denies that these are central cases of it.

The typical features of a religion include stories and beliefs about supernatural agents such as gods and angels, texts about these agents, values that provide

TABLE 8.1

Three-Analysis of *Religion*

Exemplars	Christianity, Islam, Hinduism, Buddhism, Judaism
Typical features	Stories and beliefs about supernatural agents, sacred texts, values and morals tied to supernatural agents, rituals, social norms, institutions like churches with prophets and leaders
Explanations	Explains: individual behavior, social cohesion, powerful organizations
	Explained by: mental and social mechanisms

moral guidance, rituals and prescribed practices, and prophets who are sources of stories and texts. Trying to turn these features into a definition that provides necessary and sufficient conditions would founder on counterexamples such as native religions that are scarcely institutional and lack literary texts, and variants of Buddhism for which gods are of minor importance. Nevertheless, features such as gods are found in many religions and are causally important for explaining their actions and successes. Institutions such as churches are typical of religions in current developed societies but not of religions in the small-scale societies usually studied by anthropologists.

A church is an institution, an organization of people bound together by rules that prescribes the continuation of beliefs and practices. Churches typically have religious leaders such as priests, ministers, rabbis, and imams. Through buildings such as temples and mosques, they provide places where people can meet and interact, under the guidance of the leaders. Often the leaders trace their authorities back to prophets such as Isaiah, Muhammad, or Gautama Buddha.

Religions generally propagate a set of beliefs about supernatural agents and worldly origins. Most religions have creation myths about how gods produced the Earth and the people on it. Most religions are polytheistic, as in the dozens of gods of the ancient Greeks and Romans, but monotheism has become officially predominant through the successes of Christianity (more than 2 billion people) and Islam (more than 1 billion). Unofficially, polytheism survives in the Catholic trinity and devotion to the Blessed Virgin Mary, and Sunni Muslims accuse Shiites of being polytheistic.

Religions concern not only beliefs but also values that guide behavior and establish social norms. The values may be exhibited by specific rules such as the Commandments of Christianity and Judaism but may also be captured by normative concepts such as *piety, fidelity,* and *humility.* The texts of the religion and the spoken and written words of the leaders and prophets provide moral prescriptions and advice. Like political ideologies, religious ideologies are systems of ideas and values, but they differ in their subject matter: concern with supernatural agents rather than forms of government. The ideology of the Islamic State examined in chapter 6 is both political and religious.

Religions typically have rituals, recurring procedures and ceremonies that mark important events such as birth, marriage, death, and worship, but also may be more routine such as Sunday services. Rituals are behaviors that gain their meaning from background beliefs and behaviors, for example when people go to church to pray in standard ways to display and reinforce their beliefs. Religions vary in the relative importance of beliefs and practices. For some religions such as variants of Judaism and Buddhism, practices are more important than adherence to creeds, whereas Christianity and Islam require agreement with doctrines.

The concept of religion has diverse explanatory uses, for both individuals and social groups. Religion can explain numerous aspects of individual psychology and behavior, such as why some people pray every day and go to church every week. Socially, religion explains the existence of groups based on their cohesiveness that derives from common beliefs and ongoing interactions. Religion also accounts for the existence of many moral codes, although philosophers since Socrates have disputed whether religion is actually required for morality.

Much more contentious is the question of what explains religion. A later section considers various answers, ranging from divine intervention to genetics to epidemiology. My own answer is that the development of religions is multilevel emergence from identifiable cognitive, emotional, and social mechanisms.

There is now an established field, the cognitive science of religion, that brings together psychologists, philosophers, anthropologists, and others who want to use the resources of cognitive science to answer questions about religious beliefs and practices. I will show that semantic pointer theories of cognition and communication have much to contribute to the understanding of why religion is so important in many human cultures, beginning with a case study.

THE LATTER-DAY SAINT RELIGION: SOCIAL
COGNITIVE-EMOTIONAL WORKUP

Mormonism, officially called the Church of Jesus Christ of Latter-day Saints, originated in western New York state in the 1820s, when a young farmer named Joseph Smith began to experience visions. He later claimed that he encountered an angel named Moroni, who presented him with gold tablets written by Moroni's father, Mormon. Smith was given a key to translating the tablets and produced the Book of Mormon, which provides a historical account of how North America was settled in 600 BC by Jewish tribes who were later visited by Jesus Christ.

Smith's stories and writings convinced his family and a growing number of neighbors that his book was the basis for the correct form of Christianity. By 1847 the new sect had tens of thousands of members and began the huge trek to settle in Utah under the leadership of Brigham Young, who replaced Smith who had been killed by an angry mob. The Mormons flourished in Utah and have grown worldwide to include more than 15 million members, with the most rapid growth occurring since 1960. The church now has members on all continents, making it the first new world religion since Islam arose in the seventh century.

Proponents, defenders, and scholars of the Mormon church debate whether it is a form of Christianity or a new religion. The question is difficult because Mormons have many beliefs in common with other Christian groups, such as that Jesus Christ is the son of God. But they also have beliefs and practices that are novel to their own institution. Rather than answer this question, my concern is to understand the nature and success of the Latter-day Saints (LDS) by performing a social cognitive-emotional workup.

Concepts and Values

The Mormons have many concepts and values in common with Christianity such as God, the Bible, Jesus Christ, prophets, and saints. But they also add new representations such as the Book of Mormon, the Church of Jesus Christ of Latter-day Saints, and Joseph Smith. Figure 8.1 is a value map of some of the most important Mormon mental representations, showing the important interconnections arising from Joseph Smith's vision and organization.

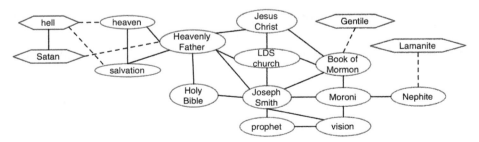

FIGURE 8.1 Value map of Mormons. Ovals are emotionally positive, and hexagons are negative. Solid lines indicate mutual support, and dotted lines indicate incompatibility.

Central to the map is the Church of Jesus Christ of Latter-day Saints. Whereas in Christianity saints are rare and mostly ancient, any member of the church in good standing can be taken as a saint, where "latter-day" means modern in contrast to ancient. The church is positively associated with its founder and prophet Joseph Smith, and with the book of Mormon which he translated from the tablets given to him by Moroni. Being a member of the church and becoming a saint provides salvation which gets you to heaven, enables you to avoid suffering in hell, and allows you to become a god of your own universe. Mormons generally refer to God as "Heavenly Father."

Joseph Smith was the first prophet of the church, but subsequent leaders are also judged to be prophets, from Brigham Young to the current president. Prophets are capable of having revelations that reveal the essence of reality. Revelation is an important concept because it is the basis for the truth and authority of the church and its documents.

Mormons use the term "gentile" to refer to all non-Mormons, including Jews. Whereas critics of the church have considered Joseph Smith to be either a madman or a fraud, Mormons revere him for founding the church. They assign the same moral centrality to the Book of Mormon and other documents he produced that Christians assign to the Bible and Muslims assign to the Quran. Nephites are the ancient tribe of Israel who came to North America centuries before Jesus but who were defeated by another tribe, the Lamanites, whose descendants are the American Indians, according to Smith. Moroni and Mormon were among the last of the Nephites. The positively valued representations shown by ovals in Figure 8.1 provide coherently interconnected set that contrasts with the despised ones shown by hexagons.

A Christian or Muslim who converts to Mormonism must undergo substantial conceptual change. New representations such as *Book of Mormon* and *sealing* (a marriage ritual) must be added to their minds, and old concepts such as *prophet* and *saint* must be modified to include many more kinds of people including the current leaders and members of the LDS church. Most important, representations must be revalenced to acquire new emotional values, so that the church and Joseph Smith become intensively positive. Because Mormons who are exalted to heaven become godlike, the former distinction between gods and humans is undermined, a form of conceptual change called coalescence.

Images and Embodiment

Although concepts such as *church, prophet,* and *salvation* are too abstract to be reduced to sensory inputs, the mental representations of the Mormons are not only verbal. Visual images also contribute to the thinking of leaders and ordinary members, dating back to Joseph Smith's visions of meeting with God and Jesus in 1820, and later with Moroni. Figure 8.2 is a typical depiction of this vision used by Mormons in history books and children's books. This image makes Moroni seem like a real historical figure, not a fictional character. The gold plates that Moroni provided to Joseph Smith for translation similarly operate as visual images shown in pictures, useful since the plates were given back to Moroni after only a few associates of Joseph Smith had seen them. Other visual images that contribute to the stature of the Church of Latter-day Saints are the many imposing and architecturally impressive temples in which the members worship. Temples are often capped by a statue of Moroni blowing a trumpet.

Blowing the trumpet is also an auditory image, with the sound of the trumpet serving as a metaphor for the spreading of the gospel. Singing has played an important role in Mormon practices from the beginning, and the large and famous

FIGURE 8.2 Joseph's Smith vision of meeting Moroni.

Mormon Tabernacle Choir originated in 1847. Mormons sing hymns that melodically are similar to Christian hymns but with unique lyrics reflecting Mormon doctrine such as Joseph Smith's first vision. Hymns are therefore multimodal, combining the sound of music, verbal descriptions, visual images, and mouth movements.

Mormons are told to expect a "burning in the bosom," an intense feeling claimed to result from a visit by the Holy Spirit. This burning is a pleasant feeling that may result from attending rituals, singing hymns, or just thinking about the church. It is partly a bodily image reflecting a good feeling in the chest but also indicates an emotional experience. Another kinesthetic image comes from laying on of hands, which is commonly used in various rituals such as confirmation. Similarly, baptism for Mormons requires total immersion in water with a person being held by a priest, generating kinesthetic experiences. These practices also generate visual images when people observe priests performing the rituals.

Through these sensory images and ritual practices, Mormonism is embodied, although it is also transbodied through components through abstract concepts such as *God* and *prophet*. Another aspect of embodiment arises because of the physiological component of emotions that is important for confidence in the church and its leadership and for religious experiences such as the burning in the bosom.

Beliefs and Rules

Mormons share many beliefs with mainstream Christians, such as that Jesus Christ is the son of God and that the Bible is the word of God. But they also have many beliefs rejected by other churches such as that Joseph Smith is a prophet who translated the book of Mormon originally written by Nephites. Mormons believe that individual humans existed before birth and that our status in this life depends on how righteous we were during the preexistence of life before birth. Similar beliefs are found in Hinduism and ancient Greek philosophy but not in Christianity. For Mormons, salvation depends on knowing Christ, knowledge that can be gained through the LDS priesthood. Exaltation to heaven involves a whole family, not just an individual, and allows exalted humans to become godlike.

Central to Mormonism is a belief about belief: the primary reliable source of knowledge is revelation to prophets as documented in holy books such as the Book of Mormon. Rarely, revelation can lead to changes in official doctrine, such as the 1890 decision to abandon the practice of polygamy and the 1978 decision to allow Blacks to be priests. The belief in polygamy, which is still held by some fundamentalist splinter groups, was instituted in 1852 by Joseph Smith, who had more than 20 wives, some of whom were also married to other men. Brigham Young had more than 50 wives. The abandonment of polygamy was required for Utah's admission to the United States but was justified solely by a revelation to the church president at the time.

Some of the Mormons' general beliefs are in the form of rules such as: *If the president of the church says something, then it must be true; if you follow the principles and practices of the LDS church, then you will be saved and go to heaven.* The practices are codified in rules that tell people what they must do in order to remain Mormons. Some of these are: If you are not married, then do not engage in any sexual activity including masturbation and pornography. If you are a male over 19, then spend two years doing missionary work. If you are Mormon, then do not drink alcohol or coffee. If you are married, then do not divorce. If you have a job, then tithe 10% of your income to the church. If you go to the Temple, then wear special undergarments at all times. These rules constitute social norms with which Mormons feel obliged to comply.

Like all institutions, the LDS church is an organization of people directed by rules that operate in the minds of members to ensure that they act in accord with Mormon principles and sustain the institution. As established by Joseph Smith, the LDS church is tightly hierarchical, with the presidential prophet at the top assisted by two counselors. Below them is the quorum of the 12 apostles, and next is the quorum of the 70 who oversee the church's local leaders including bishops. All of these leaders are priests and therefore male. Detailed rules govern the methods by which people ascend to the ranks of leadership.

Some of the descriptive and normative rules are multimodal in that they involve sensory, motor, and emotional representations. The descriptive rule *if you believe, then you will feel a burning in the bosom* has a nonverbal component because of the positive bodily feeling that it mentions. On the other hand, Mormons are taught that if they violate the principles of the church, then they will feel uncomfortable, guilty, and ashamed, all of which have substantial physiological components. Prescriptive rules about how to perform rituals involve bodily movements such as laying on of hands. Like all religions, Mormonism employs rules that are best understood as cognitive-emotional mental representations.

Analogies and Metaphors

The most important analogy in the Mormon church is between it and the early Jews and Christians. Joseph Smith is taken to be a prophet whose revelations express the will of God, just like prophets in the Bible. The Book of Mormon is analogous to the Bible both in its authoritativeness and its style: Joseph Smith's writing is supposed to be a translation, but it sounds a lot like the King James version of the Bible, with frequent occurrences of "verily" and "it came to pass." Mormons think of their great trek to Utah as analogous to the Jewish exodus from Egypt, with Brigham Young corresponding to Moses.

Like other systems of thought, Mormons rely on metaphors to capture their beliefs and activities. Leaders refer to ordinary people as their flock, like sheep to be tended by a shepherd. LDS history often uses the motif of light breaking into darkness, as in Smith's vision of Moroni. The name "Heavenly Father" commonly used by Mormons for God invokes the Christian metaphor of God as a caring parent.

Emotions and Actions

The Mormon church engages people's emotions in many ways. The 1820s when Joseph Smith started it were times of great uncertainty, but the strong, confident leadership of the church provided comfort and reassurance. With conversion and adherence, anxiety about the future gave way to the happy conviction that salvation can be gained by following the precepts of the church. People could enjoy the pleasant, confident feeling that comes with the burning in the bosom. Because Mormons are not allowed to divorce, people could feel secure in their families and their celestial future.

Sticking with the church alleviates several kinds of fear: of an eternity of torture in hell; of social isolation that would result from abandoning family, friends, and acquaintances; and of catastrophes for which the community stores provisions. People who leave the church are viewed as apostates, a status even more negative than gentile, analogous to how Islamic extremists view apostates as even worse than infidels. Like other forms of Christianity, Mormonism offers the attractive prospect that forgiveness by God can alleviate guilt about past wrongdoings. For Joseph Smith and subsequent Mormon leaders, emotional feelings furnish information about what God wants and what should be done.

Membership in the LDS church provides specific positive emotions. People are happy that their eternal lives, marriages, and social structures are secure. The emotional mechanism of attachment-based learning (described in chapter 3) ensures that children will acquire the values and emotional attitudes of their parents, teachers, and religious leaders. From the age of 12, children are questioned individually by bishops about their sexual practices of masturbation and pornography. Even thinking about breaking the commands of the church can make people unhappy. Men who ascend in the priesthood can feel pride in their accomplishments and their contributions to the church. All members can feel gratitude for what the church provides, which includes financial and social support when people encounter hard times and reassuring preparation for future disasters.

People gain emotional energy from their religious confidence and from the on-going interactions with like-minded people. The Mormon church demands many actions from its members, including the missionary activities of young men, weekly social activities, and participation in unusual rituals. Strong emotions such as attachment to the church, pride, and fear of disapproval cause people to believe in Mormonism and to act in accord with its rules. Mormons are urged to follow their conscience, described metaphorically as the light of Christ, which brings forgiveness and peace in contrast to the negative emotions of remorse and guilt.

Mormons are encouraged to trust in God, their leaders, and each other. Chapter 4 argued that trust is a brain process that binds representations of self, other, situation, and emotion into a semantic pointer. Then trusting in God is a positive emotion that includes representations of the individual and the Heavenly Father. Similarly positive feelings of trust in leaders and members that derive from them all being part of the same church are supported by rituals such as daily prayers. Missionaries are told to try to get prospective converts to trust them by displaying caring and empathy.

Through this rich complex of positive and negative emotions and resulting actions, the LDS church makes its members feel good about themselves and the church, which helps to make it attractive to prospective converts. Hence emotions are a major part of the answer to the question of why the church has grown so rapidly and spread around the world.

Inferences

Like other religions, Mormonism supports and is supported by various deductive, abductive, and emotional inferences. The strict principles of the Mormon church license a variety of deductive inferences such as the following. Whatever the church leader says is true. The church leaders say that Blacks can be priests. Therefore, Blacks can be priests. Apostasy and sex outside marriage are always wrong. Such unambiguous moral rules can make proper behavior a simple matter of making deductive inferences, if you accept the premise that the church is always right.

Mormon beliefs and practices can also be supported by abductive inferences. The Book of Mormon provides a novel explanation of the origins of American Indians as a lost tribe of Jews, the Lamanites. So Mormonism received abductive support in the nineteenth century by its ability to explain something puzzling. People were impressed by Joseph Smith's feat of dictating the Book of Mormon without hesitation and thought that the best explanation was indeed that he was translating from the gold plates provided by Moroni, rather than just making it up. Opposition to the LDS church can be explained by assuming that critics simply have not had a chance to appreciate the power and cogency of the Mormon story. Members of the church are encouraged to make interagent inferences about the intentions of God, leaders, and other members.

Above all, Mormonism is supported by emotional coherence, when people perceive its doctrines and practices as fitting with their desires and fears. In place of the uncertainty and anxiety common in the 1820s and today, the church offers certainty and eternal happiness. People can naturally infer that continuing membership in the church will contribute to their goals of social solidarity and economic security in this life and eternal happiness in the afterlife. Motivated inference is not just wishful thinking where people believe something because they want to but requires recruitment of memories and other evidence to support the desired belief. People are able to incorporate large amounts of information about Joseph Smith, the Book of Mormon, and practices of people they know into a coherent story about how being a Mormon will improve their lives.

Fear-driven inference also encourages belief in the LDS church because worries about personal lives and death make people focus on the strong claims that the church makes about what is required to achieve eternal reward. People may not want to be missionaries, attend frequent church ceremonies and events, or donate 10% of their income to the church. But they are sufficiently worried about their everyday and eternal lives to focus on what the LDS church offers with respect to beliefs and practices. Fear-driven inference makes people intensely concerned about their futures, and motivated inference addresses the concern by offering salvation through the church.

For Joseph Smith's early followers and for modern-day converts, adopting the Mormon faith is an emotional gestalt shift. Conversion replaces the uncertainty and anxiety of a chaotic world with an all-encompassing worldview of facts and values. Like the Islamic State ideology described in chapter 6, Mormonism offers an emotionally coherent solution to problems about what to believe and what to do. Loss of religious faith can also be a gestalt shift resulting from sudden appreciation that emotional coherence is illusory, but sometimes people merely drift away with gradual lessening of belief and attachment.

Communication

The cognitive anthropologist Dan Sperber compares the study of cultural transmission to epidemiology, which looks at the spread of diseases. As with other biological metaphors criticized in chapter 7, this comparison underestimates the complex mental and social processes by which mental representations move from the minds of some people to the minds of others through communicative interactions. The ways that people come to acquire the concepts, values, and beliefs of others are markedly different from the ways in which germs such as viruses invade the human body. The semantic pointer theory of communication allows much closer examination of the spread of religious and other cultural ideas.

Although the Mormon church invests enormous resources in missionary efforts, relatively few new members come from this route. The Mormon church encourages more subtle means of conversion in which established Mormon families watch for new families in their acquaintance who might be open to recruitment. Following a specified pattern provided by the church, Mormon families are encouraged to befriend the new family in an area and only gradually indicate that they are Mormon and how the church improves their lives. Besides these two kinds of conversion, a third method by which the Mormon church grows is through having large families and ensuring that their children maintain Mormon beliefs and values.

How are Mormon beliefs and values transmitted in these three methods of proselytizing and child-rearing? Conversion works partly by telling people about Joseph Smith and the Book of Mormon, with communication that is both verbal and nonverbal through the inclusion of inspiring pictures. Just as important is the transfer of values and emotions, convincing hearers to adopt the attitudes of the proselytizers. The conviction and enthusiasm of Mormons can be conveyed to newcomers through a variety of nonverbal means, including tone of voice, facial expressions, and body language. Once Mormon missionaries are through the door, their sincere excitement can inspire listeners to think about ways in which the Mormon way of life can help to provide solutions to their own personal problems as well as their worries about death.

The major function of communication with nonbelievers is to provide them with the Mormon's emotionally coherent system of beliefs and values. Communication is unavoidably slow and serial, with hearers gradually being exposed to the fundamental doctrines and practices of Mormonism. But emotional contagion via unconscious mimicry of facial expressions and body language can lead prospective members to become interested and eventually adopt the values held by missionaries and parents. For teaching children, the social mechanism of attachment-based learning helps to pass values from parents to the next generation. Conversion by missionaries and friends can be made more effective by empathy in which the Mormons become appealing by identifying with difficulties faced by the potential convert.

Conversion is only superficially like disease transmission, because people's brains are far more complicated than cells that can be invaded by viruses. Rather, mental representations are complex patterns of neural firing that integrate sensory, motor, and emotional information as well as verbal beliefs. Spread of ideas requires transferring, prompting, and instigating semantic pointers, not infection or contagion.

Once people are raised as or converted to be Mormons, many forms of communication serve to ensure their pious continuation. The church encourages intense participation in numerous gatherings that include community activities as well as weekly religious services and regular family prayer. Church officials hold substantial powers over members because of the threats of disapproval, excommunication, eternal damnation, and social abandonment. As chapter 3 described, the social mechanism of power can motivate people to adopt beliefs and emotions both by fear of punishment and by the prospect of personal and social benefits of compliance.

Members of the LDS church are encouraged to make frequent public testimonies about their beliefs in the fundamental doctrines of the church. Engagements in church activities also attest to this commitment. Through both their words and actions, people communicate to other members their commitments to the church. The point of messages from the leaders and among the members is to increase the perceived emotional coherence of the religion. People are told about and perceive the daily and heavenly advantages of the church, fostering their motivated inferences that the church really is a solution to their problems. Threatening communications about what will happen if people abandon the church incite fear-driven inferences that feed into motivated inferences about how the church can provide a solution to anxieties about daily and eternal life. A major form of religious communication is ritual, which requires special attention because of the way in which it combines values, embodiment, and emotion.

Rituals

Anthropologists agree that rituals are important in cultures but debate how to define the concept. As with religion, it is difficult to find the set of necessary and sufficient conditions for rituals because they vary so much across cultures. Table 8.2 provides a three-analysis that captures how most anthropologists discuss religious rituals. Everyone agrees that baptisms, church services, and weddings are good examples of rituals even if not all rituals share exactly the same set of features.

Typically, rituals have agents such as priests performing actions on recipients such as church members, for example when a Mormon leader baptizes a child or convert. Rituals often are designed to have effects on the recipients, which may include supernatural agents as when priests perform sacrifices to appease the gods. Rituals of different kinds have expected frequencies, ranging from daily for prayers to once in a lifetime for baptism.

TABLE 8.2

Three-Analysis of *Religious Ritual*

Exemplars	Church services, baptisms, weddings, funerals, observing holidays, regular prayer
Typical features	Agents performing actions on recipients with anticipated effects, expected frequency, emotional significance, associated values, bodily movements, modes of social communication, instruments
Explanations	Explains: individual behavior, social cohesion, emotional transmission Explained by: mental and social mechanisms

Rituals can have emotional significance for agents and recipients, for example when weddings reinforce commitments and increase trust, in line with values such as that marriage is desirable. Rituals typically require bodily movements such as hand blessings along with verbal communications including chants and songs. Various physical instruments can contribute to rituals, from the water used in baptism to special garments used in the Mormon endowment ritual.

The concept of ritual is anthropologically valuable for explanatory as well as descriptive purposes. It helps to explain why people do unusual activities such as getting together to watch babies get wet. Rituals are also important for explaining the social bonds among people who are connected through a church, by virtue of the sharing and transfer of emotions. The accomplishment of these functions is explained by the combination of mental mechanisms such as emotional inferences operating in individuals with social mechanisms such as the interactions of church members during rituals. Rituals are social mechanisms interdependent with cognitive mechanisms in individuals, who may believe that they are interacting with supernatural agents as well as with people.

Rituals are embodied through physical motions, sensory pageantry, and emotional effects, but they are also transbodied through their invocation of nonobservable deities and mental states. The elicitation and transmission of emotions combines changes in physiological states through actions and cognitive appraisals provided by church doctrines and interpretations. Even regular rituals such as weekly worship can have emotional effects such as commitment and reassurance.

Mormons have many of the rituals practiced by other churches, such as daily prayers, weekly church services, blessings, and recognition of births and weddings. But they also have a set of rituals unique to Mormonism. For example, marriage

is celebrated by a ceremony of sealing, in which couples affirm eternal commitments. Marriage is not only a relationship in this life but a crucial part of salvation
for the next. According to nineteenth-century Mormons and current fundamen-
talists, plural marriage is essential for salvation. Some current sects maintain that
a man requires sealing with at least three wives to be eligible for heaven. But even
for mainstream Mormons, sealing is a private ceremony open only to members of
the church.

The Mormon endowment is a set of rituals that prepares people for being
priests and leaders of the church. It is experienced by men before they undertake
missionary work and by women before they become married. The endowment can
also be repeated on behalf of deceased individuals. The following is a description
of the endowment from an LDS website:

> The Mormon Endowment includes four basic aspects. One is a preparatory or-
> dinance of ceremonial washing and anointing, and dressing in sacred temple
> garments or so-called "Mormon underwear," plus temple robes, always white
> as a symbol of purity and equality between everyone in attendance. Another
> aspect is a course of instruction that features the creation of the world, some
> of the experiences of Adam and Eve, and the plan of salvation or redemption
> available to every human thanks to the sacrifice of Christ. Covenants consti-
> tute yet another aspect of the Endowment: Mormons solemnly promise the
> Lord to be obedient, giving of self, chaste, and loyal to the restored Church
> of Christ and its cause; in return, God is enabled to fulfill promised blessings
> of joy, protection, progress, and eventual return to His glorious presence.
> Finally, temple visitors can actually feel a degree of divine presence even now,
> for Mormon temples are specially dedicated as places of holiness, of light, of
> peace and revelation and understanding.

Thus the endowment ritual integrates beliefs such as salvation, actions such as
anointing, and emotions such as joy.

Another unusual Mormon ritual is baptism for the dead, the practice of bap-
tizing a person on behalf of a deceased person who never had the opportunity
to be baptized. Mormons are baptized just once when they are eight years old
or when they convert, but Mormon temples also perform regular ceremonies in
which people stand in for dead people. Hence the baptism ceremony and all the
beliefs and emotional commitments that go with it can be repeated as a communicative social gathering much more frequently than in mainstream Christianity.

Along with all the more common practices of collective prayer, temple services, and preaching, these rituals provide powerful vehicles for emotional

communication. Sealing, endowment, and baptism of the dead are all occasions that reinforce the beliefs and values of the church in individuals through interactions with others. Verbal and nonverbal interactions help to ensure that individuals will maintain their Mormon convictions and continue to share them with others. With the abandonment of plural marriage, the sealing ceremony is a one-time event for most couples, but other church members can participate when a couple is sealed, reinforcing or anticipating their own sealings. Repeated endowment and baptism ceremonies provide further occasions not found in other religions for strengthening beliefs and attitudes.

Unlike Scientology, the Church of Jesus Christ of Latter-day Saints was not designed by a science fiction writer to draw people in. But it has developed effective ritual practices that help to convince millions of people of its ongoing value. Like missionary work, rituals that are costly in time and money send signals to other people and also to members that Mormons are serious about their religion. Costly signals generate abductive inferences: the best explanation of why Mormons expend so much on their religion is that they really believe in its truth and value. Rituals serve to establish social norms about what to believe as well as what to do.

Performances are based on multimodal rules that can be expressed in words such as *if you baptize people, then immerse them in water*. But a more accurate expression is the semantic pointer rule <baptism> → <immerse> that can capture the motor action and visual appearance of immersion, as well as the positive emotional value of the whole rule and the concept of baptism. Rituals help to establish mutual trust and tighter social bonds by increasing emotional communication that in turn increases people's willingness to participate in rituals. Rituals can work through molecular processes such as the dopamine surges that accompany religious ecstasy and the cortisol reductions that accompany the calming of prayer and meditation. In sum, rituals are social mechanisms that have effects on the minds and behaviors of participants through interactions that draw on cognitive, emotional, neural, and molecular mechanisms to produce multilevel emergence of properties of individuals and groups.

WHY IS THE LDS CHURCH SUCCESSFUL?

The LDS church has grown from a few associates of Joseph Smith in the 1830s to a worldwide organization with more than 15 million members. Its numerical success has depended on three factors: having abundant children and raising them to be Mormons, converting people newly exposed to the religion to become Mormons, and retaining members. What are the neural, mental, and social mechanisms responsible for this growth?

One possibility is that people become Mormons because of rational choices. Once provided with relevant information about the church, people decide that the best way for them to maximize their expected utility is to become members. People realize that, given their preferences, they should join the church. This explanation is both shallow and implausible. It is shallow because it does not say anything about where converts' preferences come from or about what the Mormon church contributes to their utilities. It is implausible because conversion is rarely a matter of deliberate calculation in which people assess the costs and benefits of joining a church compared to the alternatives of joining a different church or remaining unaffiliated. An exception might occur when a prospective spouse converts primarily to make a marriage work.

An alternative explanation, along the lines of the social constructionism popular in some social sciences, is that the rise of Mormonism is the result of power relations, with people coerced to join the church and remain in it. Power is indeed an important factor in people remaining in the church, as the strict rules and hierarchical control make it difficult for people to deviate from the principles of the LDS church or to abandon it altogether. There are also elements of power and coercion in the ways that Mormon parents educate their children to share their doctrines and practices. Religions can wield all four kinds of power discussed in chapter 6: coercive power through threats of punishment, benefit power through daily and eternal rewards, respect power through charismatic leaders, and norm power through social expectations that generate apparently voluntary compliance.

But a large part of the growth of the Mormon church has resulted from missionary work, both the explicit proselytizing carried out by young people and the informal and more effective family-to-family method. In these situations, the proselytizers have no power over the prospective converts, so the growth of the Mormon church cannot be explained just by power relations.

A more plausible explanation of the success of the Mormons views it as a result of a confluence of cognitive, emotional, and social mechanisms. Joseph Smith and his followers put together a compelling package of concepts, beliefs, and images that answers questions for people beset by uncertainty. Even more important, the package includes values and emotions that fit well with the desires and needs of many people. Uncertainty is not merely a cognitive state of being unable to attach high probabilities to future events but an emotional state often attended with anxiety, especially when the events concern matters of great importance to people such as health, relationships, and death. Mormon doctrines also reduce uncertainty about actions through their strict prohibition of extramarital sex and alcohol consumption, along with their precise social norms about frequent activities in the church.

The decision to undergo a religious conversion, like other decisions such as choosing what political party to support, is a matter of emotional coherence. People choose those actions that fit best with their emotional goals and values. There is no need for prolonged calculation of expected utilities based on unknown outcomes, because people only need to feel that there is a good fit between what the church or party offers and what they perceive as their own needs. Needs are not arbitrary wants but derive from fundamental biological requirements such as food, shelter, and health, as well as from psychological requirements for relatedness, competence, and autonomy. Mormon missionaries are told not to instruct people in order to convert them but rather to empathize and share the joy of their beliefs.

The Mormon church helps to satisfy biological needs by guaranteeing distressed members help with food and shelter. Relatedness is satisfied through the strong social networks in LDS churches that go far beyond weekly prayer meetings. In general, researchers have found that participants in churches are happier than nonparticipants, although this effect may have as much to do with the social connections that churches provide as with theological reassurances. Nevertheless, the Mormon church is strong on theological reassurances, providing guarantees about health that go beyond death thanks to the promise of a happy afterlife for people who stick with the religion.

Once people are in the church, there are strong social mechanisms to ensure that they will remain. Regular rituals such as church services, public testimony, repeated endowment, and baptism of the dead bring people together to maintain their commitment to the church and to each other. The appealing emotional coherence of the Mormon church is maintained by frequent re-exposure to the values and benefits of the church and multiple initiations. Rituals and other church activities help to meet people's social and psychological need for relatedness. The need for competence is partly met by people's accomplishments in the activities of the church and their progress through the ranks of being priests, bishops, and other leaders. The price of these benefits is unavoidably a loss of autonomy, as people's choices are highly constrained by the strict rules and social control of the church. But if people think that they are voluntarily choosing to join and continue with the church, then these limitations may not be viewed by them as losses of autonomy.

On the face of it, it seems surprising that a church with such demanding expectations could be so successful. Why would anyone want to acquire all the obligations such as frequent church activities, tithing, and restricting alcohol and extramarital sex? For many people, however, such strictness can be attractive, because it alleviates anxieties about what to believe and what to do. Like other strict and dogmatic religions, Mormonism has all the answers.

These cognitive and emotional benefits explain why Mormonism is successful with particular individuals but are not sufficient to explain the general rise of the church, because other religions from Christianity to Islam to Buddhism can provide similar psychological benefits. Social mechanisms are needed to explain why the Mormons have been proportionately more successful at adding converts.

First, the LDS church does much more proselytizing than most denominations, through the requirement that young men do years of missionary work and the systematic plan for family-to-family conversions. Similarly, the fundamentalist Sunnis described in chapter 6 make vigorous attempts to add adherents, unlike established churches that are much more complacent about their membership.

Second, the Mormon missionaries are generally sincere, enthusiastic, and well trained in methods of communication. Convincing someone to become Mormon is a social process in which people learn from others both the available beliefs and also the emotional gains that conversion can bring. Once people are members of the church, they are constantly reminded both by observation and exhortation that the church provides benefits. People do not just hear reports that they can be saved and redeemed but get them from members who really believe and act on them.

Social mechanisms are similarly significant for raising children to be Mormons, as they are for all kinds of education (chapter 13). Children naturally pick up beliefs from their parents because most of what parents tell children is true. Just as important, children pick up emotional values by the combination of the processes described in chapter 3, including mirror neurons, emotional contagion, and attachment-based learning.

Hence the rise of Mormonism cannot be explained as the result of any single cognitive, emotional, or social factor. Rather, it results from the interaction of numerous mental and social mechanisms, all of which can be understood through the semantic pointers operating in the brains of individuals and the semantic pointer transmission and instigation occurring through communicative interactions. Also relevant are molecular mechanisms such as the role of oxytocin in increasing converts' trust in Mormon leaders and the role of dopamine in the pleasurable expectations of an exalted afterlife. Therefore, Mormon success is a case of multilevel emergence, just like previous chapters' explanations of functioning of romantic couples, spread of prejudice, rise of political ideologies, and occurrence of economic booms and crashes.

WHY IS RELIGION GENERALLY SO SUCCESSFUL?

Multilevel emergence also provides an answer for the challenging question of why religion in general is such a widespread part of human culture. Although not universal, religious beliefs and practices have been common in human groups for thousands of years, and prevail in most countries today. Attempts to eradicate religion in communist countries have frequently failed. Although secular, science-based views have become much more common in western Europe and North America, the majority of people in the world belong to some religion. The success of religion might have a theological explanation derived from the existence of real gods who actually do communicate their existence and wishes to humans, but this hypothesis fails to explain the existence of so many different religions that postulate different gods.

Simple biological explanations for the prevalence of religion are also implausible. Proposals that brain evolution has favored a genetic basis for religious belief have the same problem as proposals that the brain contains a distinct module for religion or an instinct for spirituality. First, no biological evidence has been found for the existence of such genes, modules, or instincts. Second, given the occurrence of a few traditional cultures without apparent religion and the more than 1 billion people currently without religion, it is hard to make the case that the need for religion or spirituality is actually innate.

Third, these biological proposals fall afoul of contemporary understanding of genetics and neuroscience. There may be specific genes for producing a specific protein, but human characteristics are almost always the result of interactions of numerous genes and social environments. Even height is the result of hundreds of genes as well as of nutrition influenced by social processes such as famine and war. The hypothesis that there could be a brain module for religion made sense in the context of 1980s psychology, but decades of brain scanning experiments have replaced the expectation of modularity with emphasis on the intensity of interconnections among different brain areas. As *Brain–Mind* (chapter 2) argues, emotions and other mental processes show that the relation between brain areas and psychological functions is many–to–many rather than one–to–one. For example, emotions such as happiness result from the interactions of numerous brain areas, each of which is involved in other emotions and other psychological functions. Therefore, for the three reasons given, there is little hope of explaining the prevalence of religion as the direct result of evolution by natural selection.

Some anthropologists and sociologists prefer purely social explanations for the prevalence of religion. Religions exist because they serve important social functions, such as organizing people together, supporting the state, and providing a

moral code that can help govern the behavior of people operating in large societies. Hence societies that have religions are more likely to survive and grow than
societies that lack them. That religion can serve all these social functions does not
explain why individuals enthusiastically adopt some religions rather than others.
Social explanations need to be supplemented by and integrated with cognitive explanations and fleshed out to indicate the social mechanisms of transmission of
values and beliefs.

Purely mental explanations understand religion as arising, not from an innate
disposition to religion but from mental mechanisms that are much more plausibly
innate. Humans and other animals are capable of surprise resulting from unexpected occurrences. Thanks to our larger brains and binding capacity, humans are
capable of generating explanations for surprising events such as thunderstorms
by hypothesizing unobserved causes—the actions of gods. People also want to
explain emotional experiences of amazement and awe provoked by nature as well
as religious rituals.

One form of explanation that people habitually use for explaining each other's
behavior is the attribution of mental states, so people naturally explain puzzling
events in the world using hypotheses about unseen agents with beliefs and desires
analogous to those of humans. The most immediate explanation of religious experiences such as awe is that people actually are touched by the gods. Such explanations do not require any innate module for theorizing about minds or detecting
agents, merely cognitive abilities to be surprised, generate explanations, and use
analogies. Therefore, religious beliefs about supernatural agents have a partial
cognitive basis in abductive and analogical inference.

But many theorists such as Freud have noticed that the appeal of religion is not
just cognitive but also emotional. People have numerous anxieties about what will
happen in this world and what will result from their deaths. Religion is successful
in giving reassurances about how to cope with the vicissitudes of life and how to
have positive expectations of an afterlife. Religion is not just wishful thinking, because people are given numerous pieces of information that feed into the beliefs
they want to have that religion, a particular church, and God are the solution to all
their mundane and eternal problems. Conversion builds on motivated inferences
that a particular religion is the right one for them to believe. Religion has documented personal benefits, including longer life, less depression, more prosocial
behavior, better marriages, less crime, and better health behaviors.

Karl Marx's saying that religion is the opium of the people underestimates its
neurochemical capabilities. Religion can also be like amphetamines in generating
excitement, oxytocin in strengthening social bonds, benzodiazepines in alleviating
anxiety, and caffeine in generating energy to perform labor. Religious interaction

rituals provide the emotional energy mentioned in chapter 3, by generating increases in activity of neurotransmitters such as dopamine and norepinephrine.

For religion, as for the personal and political views discussed in previous chapters, motivated inference can operate in a powerful loop with fear-driven inference. Threats of social isolation, material deprivation, and eternal damnation or nothingness can make people ruminate on worries about the present and the future. Fear-driven inference keeps people focused on worries about these intense problems and makes them think that they must be resolved by extreme measures. Then motivated inference encouraged by true believers steps in to resolve the worries through religious solutions to the problems. Religious belief is not just terror management, however, because religion offers positive emotional benefits beyond relief from fear, such as joy, pride, gratitude, and social solidarity. Cross-nation comparisons show that religiosity correlates with fear of death, but it is not clear whether fear of death causes religiosity or vice versa. Religion can also play an ideological role by justifying inequality, for example when elites claim descent from supernatural ancestors.

As my discussion of the success of the LDS church showed, social, cognitive, and emotional mechanisms are not competing explanations but rather complementary and interacting parts of a full explanation. Religion thrives in both individuals and groups because of its ability to satisfy social demands for cohesion and morality, cognitive demands for explanation, and emotional demands for comfort and reassurance. In individuals, cognition and emotion interact intensively. Cognitive processes have a large emotional component because the surprise and uncertainty that drive explanation are inherently emotional, as are the pleasurable and exciting results of finding satisfactory explanations. At the same time, the emotional power of religion is in part cognitive because emotions result from appraisals tied to goals and beliefs as well as from physiological changes.

The apparent gap between the social functions of religion and its operation in individuals can be filled by the semantic pointer theory of communication that shows how cognitions and emotions can spread among individuals. Cognition, emotion, and social communication are all rooted in a common set of neural processes of representation, binding, and competition among semantic pointers. Communication among individuals allows religion to have social functions such as increasing cohesiveness, compliance with authority, and fostering morality. Societies that are too large for everyone to be monitored by everyone else may well benefit from organized religions with Big Gods who encourage moral behavior. But understanding the nature of the benefits and the spread of religions within and across societies requires close attention to mechanisms of individual thinking and group communication.

In sum, religions emerge and survive as common in human societies because of the interactions of mental and social mechanisms, another striking case of multilevel emergence. Religion lacks a direct biological basis in genetics, modularity, or instinct but rather results from cognitive, emotional, and communicative processes carried out by neural mechanisms that are biologically universal. The development of secular societies in the West has shown that peoples' cognitive, emotional, and social demands can be met by alternative intellectual and social operations. Science provide more effective evidence-based solutions than religion to problems about why things happen and how technology works. Other fields such as psychotherapy and philosophy can provide answers to questions about life and death. Families, friends, work, and nonreligious organizations such as clubs provide alternatives to religion as a way of satisfying social needs. Nevertheless, I expect that many people will continue to seek the cognitive, emotional, and social benefits of religion.

SUMMARY AND DISCUSSION

The anthropology of religion is a subfield of social science aimed at describing and explaining religious beliefs and practices across human cultures. However, its narrative explanations need to be developed and interconnected with mechanistic ones based on the minds of religious individuals and the social groups in which they interact. There is no question of replacing anthropology or any other social science by cognitive science, which depends on anthropology for its attention to the diversity of social processes that occur in thousands of different human cultures. Thick descriptions of cultural practices can be enriched by understanding the cognitions and emotions occurring in the minds of the people enacting the practices. Claims about how the mind works cannot be based solely on Western data but must also take into account the cultural variations that occur in humans despite their common neural architecture.

Scant information is available about the origins of most religions, but the Church of Jesus Christ of Latter-day Saints is new enough that its historical developments and ongoing practices are well documented. To explain these developments and practices, I described the images, concepts, values, beliefs, rules, analogies, and emotions that are the most important mental representations operating in Mormon minds. These representations have a neural basis in semantic pointer processes of representation and binding, and they contribute to a variety of deductive, abductive, and emotional inferences. The social process by which

Mormon beliefs and practices spread from one individual to another can best be understood as the results of semantic pointer communication carried out by interactions ranging from church rituals to missionary work.

Explaining the ascent of the LDS church to a world religion in under 200 years requires integration of mental and social mechanisms. The concepts, beliefs, and practices of the church offer to members and prospective converts a high degree of emotional coherence with their fundamental goals and needs. At the same time, the effective Mormon social practices of verbal and nonverbal communication provide ways of ensuring that a growing number of people will be exposed to Mormon beliefs and values, so that they too might be able to appreciate its emotional coherence. As with the development of political movements, a church that wants to grow needs to be effective both psychologically and socially.

Similarly, a plausible answer to the general question of why religion is so prevalent in human societies needs to look beyond simplistic biological explanations to the interaction of cognitive, emotional, and social mechanisms. Mormonism is just one example of how religions can provide appealing solutions to people's cognitive problems about why things happen, emotional problems about dealing with life and death, and social problems about dealing with others. Like many other important features of human culture, religion exemplifies multilevel emergence.

My account has avoided the perils of both methodological individualism, which requires the social to be reduced to the individual, and social holism, which insists on the independence of social facts from psychological processes. Rather, developments within or across religions can be explained by interactions among social, mental, and neural mechanisms. Speaking about shared beliefs and collective goals is legitimate as long as it is recognized that what is common to people is similar mental functioning in individuals. An important part of this functioning is how the individuals mentally represent the group and how their communications and inferences are influenced by the existence of the group. Minds and groups are real, but group minds and group mental states are just metaphors pointing to mental mechanisms in individuals influenced by social communication.

Durkheim insisted that a human institution such as religion cannot rest upon error and falsehood or else it could not endure, so he approached the study of primitive religions with the certainty that they express the real. But what is real about religions need not be the supernatural agents and processes that they propose but rather the human needs and social interactions that can explain the initiation and spread of doctrines, practices, and churches. The next chapter completes the application of social cognitivism to the social sciences by considering how history and international relations explain the occurrence of wars.

NOTES

On the anthropology of religion, see Bowie 2000, Eller 2007, and Winzeler 2008. For information on membership of world religions, see http://www.adherents.com.

On cultural psychology, see Heine 2011; Henrich, Heine, and Norenzayan 2010; Kitayama and Uskal 2011; Nisbett 2003; Wang 2016.

Beller, Bender, and Medin 2012 and Levinson 2012 discuss the place of anthropology in cognitive science. On cognitive anthropology, see Bloch 2012, D'Andrade 1995, Hutchins 1995, and Kronenfeld et al. 2011.

Works in the cognitive science of religion include Atran 2002, Atran and Henrich 2010, Boyer 2001, McCauley 2011, 2017, McCauley and Lawson 2002, Norenzayan 2013, Norenzayan et al. 2014, Whitehouse 2000, and Whitehouse and Laidlaw 2007. Pargament 2013 and Beit-Hallahmi 2015 review the psychology of religion. Haidt 2012 describes how religious rituals help people solve the problem of cooperation without kinship. Maehr and Karabenick 2005 discuss motivational aspects. McNamara 2009 synthesizes research on the neuroscience of religious experience.

Everett 2008 describes the language and culture of the Pirahã.

My account of Mormonism is primarily based on Shipps 1981, Stark 2005, Worthy 2008, and https://www.lds.org/. The quote about the endowment ritual is from http://www.ldschurchtemples.com/mormon/endowment/. McCauley 2012 provides a deep account of Mormon rituals.

On the embodiment of religion, see Soliman, Johnson, and Song 2015. Konvalinka et al. 2011 discuss synchronized arousal in rituals. Schjoedt et al. 2013 show how religious interactions facilitate transmission of ideas by depleting cognitive resources. Purzycki et al. 2016 review the contributions of moralistic gods to human sociality. Bering and Bjorklund 2004 contend that reasoning about the afterlife is a developmental regularity.

Sperber 1996 advocates the epidemiological metaphor.

On human needs, see Ryan and Deci 2017, Thagard 2010b, and Natural Philosophy.

Flannery and Marcus 2012 describe how religion has been used to justify inequality.

Henrich 2009 explains rituals in terms of costly displays. Sosis and Alcorta 2003 assess the costly signaling theory of ritual. Watson-Jones and Legare 2016 review the social functions of group rituals.

VanderWeele 2017 and McCullough and Carter 2013 (p. 123) review the benefits of religion with references to empirical studies. That religiosity correlates with fear of death is shown by Ellis, Wahab, and Ratnasingan 2013.

Durkheim 1995 (p. 2) makes the argument about the reality of religion.

McCauley 2013 shows why the cognitive science of religion need not be reductionist. *Natural Philosophy* discusses the existence of God and other questions in the philosophy of religion.

PROJECT

Provide a three-analysis of the concept of culture. Make the value map of Mormons multimodal. Provide a full list of multimodal rules from Mormon rituals. Analyze other religions, including indigenous ones, using value maps as in Thagard 2012a. Produce a full list of multimodal rules for rituals across all religions.

9

History and International Relations

WAR

EXPLAINING WAR

War is rarely rational. The last two chapters used economics and religion to challenge the common assumption that people are inherently reasonable. If you still think that people are basically rational, consider the origins of the First World War. In 1914, the leading nations in Europe decided to go to war against each other, resulting in four years of carnage, with millions of military casualties and countless suffering civilians. Moreover, this war set up the conditions in Germany for the rise of Hitler and the Second World War, which brought even more casualties and suffering. The 1914 leaders of Germany, Austria-Hungary, France, Great Britain, and Russia did not want to produce enormous misery, but they pursued policies and made decisions that led to a disastrous war.

Why do wars break out? Although leaders' decisions may include some rational choices and power relations are undoubtedly important, social science currently lacks the resources to explain the origins of war and the resulting social changes. The aim of this chapter is to show that social cognitivism provides plausible explanations of the origins of war by identifying the cognitive-emotional mechanisms operating in the minds of leaders and ordinary citizens, and by identifying the social mechanisms by which they interact. I develop a social cognitive-emotional workup of the origins of the First World War, identifying the most important kinds of thinking and communication that contributed to the catastrophic decisions that produced it.

The explanation of war has traditionally been the province of two important fields: history and international relations. I therefore begin by quickly reviewing traditional approaches to them in order to indicate how social cognitivism offers an alternative to historical narratives and current theories about how countries interact. Nationalism was an important contributor to the origins of the First World War and is often discussed more generally in history, international relations, and politics. I provide an account of nationalism using three-analysis, value mapping, and social cognitive-emotional workups.

My workup of the origins of the First World War provides a basis for suggesting a new model of historical explanation and a new theory of international relations. Social cognitivism also shows how to solve the international version of the person–group problem, clarifying the relation between groups such as nations and countries and their individual members. My most general conclusion is that wars and the social changes that go along with them are the result of multilevel emergence from cognitive and social mechanisms.

HISTORY

The field of history is sometimes classified among the humanities rather than the social sciences, but I think that this distinction is artificial. The humanities such as philosophy, literature, and the arts are sometimes said to differ from the social sciences because of their concern with values, but I maintain that values are neural processes so the humanities/sciences division starts to break down. *Natural Philosophy* shows the relevance of semantic pointer theories of cognition and communication for philosophy and the arts. Similarly, history has much to gain by employing the resources of the cognitive sciences to deepen its explanations.

As chapter 1 described, historical explanations are usually narratives, stories about chains of events that led up to the events to be explained. Some historians want to avoid explanations altogether and merely describe what happened, but great historians always want to know *why* things happened. Narrative explanations are a valuable step in this direction but have the problem of spelling out what actually are the connections between the various events that led up to something puzzling and important, such as the occurrence of the First World War. The lack of plausible causal connections between events makes it hard to assess how well one narrative compares in explanatory value with alternative narratives. I try to fill this gap by specifying mental and social mechanisms.

Historians sometimes have drawn on psychology in their explanations but usually use nonscientific psychology of the sort used by ordinary people to explain each other's behavior. For example, we can explain the decisions of leaders by noticing their beliefs and desires that led them to particular actions such as declaring war. Such folk psychology is not altogether wrong, but deeper and more accurate explanations derive from a psychologically rich and neurally instantiated account of how mental representations and processes actually work. Another approach occurs in a field called psychohistory that attempts to use Freudian ideas in its explanations, for example trying to explain the actions of leaders based on their upbringings and neuroses. But little was gained by using theories for which there is little empirical evidence. Cognitive theories that include emotion and link to neural mechanisms should be able to take historical explanation much further.

Another problem that arises in historians' use of folk psychology is that they frequently attribute mental states to whole groups such as countries. Narrative explanations of the origins of war often refer to what Great Britain wanted or what Germany feared. But how can countries have wants, fears, hopes, and other mental states? Are these emergent properties, aggregates, or merely figures of speech for talking about the mental and social mechanisms that go into the events that involve countries?

INTERNATIONAL RELATIONS

Understanding war is also a concern for the field of international relations, which is interested more generally in what sovereign states do and in why and how they do it. There are various competing theories of international relations, going by the misleading names of "liberalism," "realism," "behavioralism," and "social constructivism." In this field, liberalism means an approach to international relations that assumes that states can use reason to set up organizations for the benefit of all. Whereas liberalism is oriented toward explaining peace by concentrating on the harmony of interests between countries, the view called realism assumes that there are profound conflicts between countries, for example between rich ones and poor ones, and that nations and people are wholly self-interested. Realism is therefore more directed at explaining war rather than peace.

The approach to international relations called "behavioralism" is akin to the behaviorism that dominated psychology in the middle of the twentieth century and still reigns in much of economics. Behavioralism attempts to avoid speculations about the reasons and interests of countries in favor of collection of data and formulation of testable hypotheses. Social constructivism (which bears no connection to postmodernist social constructionism in anthropology and sociology) uses discussions of ideas and discourse to explain the making of foreign policies. Marxism assumes that the fundamental conflicts within the world are not between countries but rather between economic classes, particularly between the capitalists who own the means of production such as factories and the members of the working class who have to sell their labor.

All of these theories in international relations ignore the cognitive, emotional, and communicative mechanisms that underlie the actions of leaders in countries. My workup of World War I suggests how social cognitivism can provide a plausible alternative.

NATIONALISM

For background to the First World War and for many current conflicts, it is crucial to understand nations and nationalism. One hopeless approach might try to give strict definitions of the concepts of nation and nationalism, but I instead apply the method of three-analysis.

Table 9.1 presents a three-analysis of the concept *nation* using exemplars, typical features, and explanations. There are hundreds of good examples of nations, such as the French, the Germans, the Serbians, and the Inuit of northern Canada. Such examples show that nations are different from countries, because there are nations that do not have their own countries such as the Inuit, and there are countries such as Canada that include multiple nations including many indigenous nations and the Québecois.

TABLE 9.1

Three-Analysis of *Nation*	
Exemplars	French, Germans, Serbians, Inuit
Typical features	People, leaders, language, culture, dress, symbols, institutions, emotions such as pride
Explanations	Explains: behavior of people and groups
	Explained by: cognitive mechanisms such as concepts and beliefs, emotional mechanisms such as pride, and communication mechanisms such as cultural events

Coming up with defining features that capture all and only these examples would be a daunting task, but it is easy to see that all of them typically have a group of people and their leaders, a language, and a culture including beliefs and practices such as dress and food. Countries always have institutions such as governments and courts, but nations may have more informal institutions such as clubs. Emotions are not usually listed as a key property of nations, but emotions such as patriotism and nostalgia bind people together into thinking of themselves as parts of a group with much in common.

Emotions that connect people into nations can include positive ones like pride and gratitude but also negative ones such as fear of oppressive countries and of the obliteration of the nation. Emotions are often organized by national symbols such as symbols of victory that evoke pride, for example the American Declaration of Independence that separated the United States from Great Britain. Some countries however, also have symbols of defeat that feed into fears of survival, for example the Israeli symbols of the destruction of Solomon's Temple, the group suicide at Masada, and the Holocaust.

Table 9.2 similarly conceptualizes nationalism along the lines of the ideologies discussed in chapter 6. Good examples of nationalism include historical independence movements in many countries in the Balkans, Africa, Latin America, and Asia. Each version of nationalism has an ideology identifiable by a social cognitive-emotional workup like the one for the Islamic State in chapter 6. All nationalisms have ideologies, but not all ideologies are nationalisms. Like other ideologies,

TABLE 9.2

Three-Analysis of *Nationalism*

Exemplars	Independence movements such as those in Serbia, Catalonia, Québec, Scotland
Typical features	Ideology with concepts, beliefs, and values as described in chapter 6
	Proponents including leaders and followers
	Cultural manifestations such as songs and dances
	Opponents such as oppressive countries
Explanations	Explains: behavior of individuals and groups, wars of independence, cultural developments
	Explained by: individual cognitive and emotional mechanisms concerning nations and group membership, along with social mechanisms of communication

nationalisms have identifiable concepts, values, beliefs, goals, and images such as songs and flags.

For each nationalism, one can draw a value map to specify and organize the concepts and goals that constitute the motivating values of a group of people who consider themselves a nation. Nationalisms have groups of people forming a nation (as characterized in Table 9.1), and they typically have opponents that threaten the survival and flourishing of the nation. The workup of the origins of World War I includes value maps of Serbian nationalism as well as of the general patriotism found in European leaders.

The concept of nationalism is useful because it helps to explain the existence and practices of independence movements and of attempts to maintain the nation in the face of other groups that are viewed as hostile. For example, Québec nationalism has sometimes been expressed by referendums to secede from Canada and at other times by efforts to gain more French language rights within the province of Québec.

The social cognitivist explanation of nationalism looks both to the psychological processes operating in the minds and brains of individual members of a nation and to the social processes that keep people together by maintaining and spreading mental states. For each individual, the psychological processes are the brain mechanisms for cognition and emotion described in chapter 2, all explicable using semantic pointers. People are nationalists when they have beliefs, concepts, values, and metaphors about their nation that motivate their actions. But nationalism is not just a matter of individual minds, because it would die out without social mechanisms such as organizing and teaching that ensure that people continue to have similar national identities. Let us now look at some more specific examples.

ORIGINS OF THE FIRST WORLD WAR: SOCIAL COGNITIVE-EMOTIONAL WORKUP

A simple narrative of the beginnings of World War I is as follows. In June 1914, the Austrian Archduke Franz Ferdinand was assassinated by Serbian nationalists. After an ultimatum, Austria-Hungary declared war on Serbia, which was supported by Russia, which mobilized troops toward Austria-Hungary and Germany. Because of previously arranged alliances between Russia and France and between Germany and Austria Hungary, Germany attacked France via Belgium. Great Britain had an alliance with France and a commitment to Belgium's neutrality and so entered the war against Germany and Austria-Hungary. Later participants included the

Ottoman Empire on the side of Germany and the United States on the side of Great Britain.

The war resulted from a long history of negotiations and animosity that went into the alliances and antagonisms that eventually led to war. Margaret MacMillan and Christopher Clark have provided superb histories of the war's origins that eloquently tell the long story, which I do not recount. Rather, my aim is to provide a new perspective by considering the mental and social mechanisms operating in the people and social groups who were responsible for the conflict. A fully detailed account would include social cognitive-emotional workups for each of the countries involved, but I provide a more condensed account by looking more generally at the mental and social processes that occurred in all countries.

Concepts and Values

People in all countries use many concepts to represent themselves and foreigners. Most generally, people have concepts describing their own countries and nations such as French, German, Austrian, Hungarian, British, Russian, Italian, and Serbian. Such social stereotypes may be wildly inaccurate but nevertheless shape inferences about and actions toward other people. For example, the Austrian stereotype of Serbs took them to be violent and deceitful. Some British leaders saw Germany as a bully. Other concepts important to historical developments included such mental representations as *war, peace, Army, Navy, honor,* and *duty.* Leaders contemplating military attacks required more specific concepts such as *soldier, ship, weapon, supply lines,* and *mobilization.* International relations sometimes lead to conceptual change, for example reclassifying regions as nations rather than colonies.

The concepts that have the biggest impact on decisions about war are ones that are bound with emotions to constitute values. You might expect that *peace* would be a higher value than *war,* but the prospect of war was attractive to many military leaders and even to some political leaders. France was unusual in being a republic led by a president, but the other major countries were led by monarchs with substantial power, especially Kaiser Wilhelm in Germany, Emperor Franz Joseph in Austria-Hungary, and Tsar Alexander in Russia. Moreover, the military and political leaders in all these countries where largely drawn from the upper classes of aristocrats and landowners. The values of these monarchs and leaders were often militaristic as part of a package that included patriotism, nationalism, and a personal sense of honor and duty.

Figure 9.1 is a value map of attitudes common in the countries. French values did not include the monarchy but had the same attachments to nation, honor,

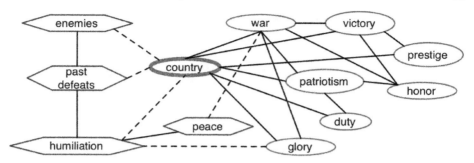

FIGURE 9.1 Value map of many monarchs and leaders in European countries before World War I. Ovals are emotionally positive, and hexagons are negative. Solid lines indicate mutual support, and dotted lines indicate incompatibility.

glory, and the military. In accord with the analysis of nationalism in Table 9.2, the value map of each nation could naturally be expanded to include the language, culture, and history for that nation, all opposed to nations that were viewed as threats. Honor and duty are important for explaining the actions that led to war because they contribute to commitment; they are discussed in more detail in the section on emotions. All the leaders at this time were male, and their sense of honor was linked to a common stereotype of manliness that included eagerness to defend family and country.

To take a more specific example, Figure 9.2 maps the values behind the Serbian nationalism that justified the assassination of the Austrian archduke. Serbian nationalism was threatened both by the power of Austria-Hungry and the record of domination by the Ottoman Empire. Stories of a larger medieval Serbian empire, along with other past glories and defeats captured in epic songs and poetry, supported claims that Serbia needed to expand its borders in conflict with

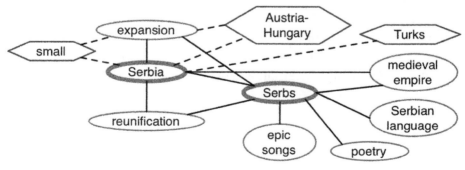

FIGURE 9.2 Value map of Serbian nationalism in 1914. As an exercise, produce a multimodal version.

Austria-Hungary. Figure 9.2 displays part of the ideology of Serbian nationalism as a system of values, not just a set of beliefs.

Images and Embodiment

The use of words in Figures 9.1 and 9.2 may suggest that people in various countries represent themselves and others using only linguistic representations. But sensory representations are also important, as we can see in the operation of a variety of visual and auditory symbols. Countries are often personified by a personal image, such as John Bull in England, Marianne in France, and Uncle Sam in the United States, which is also symbolized by the Statue of Liberty. Flags such as the Union Jack, the French tricolor, and the American stars and stripes can also serve as the visual images and symbols of the country.

Another kind of visual image important for understanding international representations and events such as wars are maps. People in different countries understand their relationships with each other in part by means of maps that indicate which countries are contiguous with them. Germans used the metaphor of encirclement to describe their geographical situation with France on one side and Russia on the other, where encirclement took on the emotional connotation of threat. The plans that each nation prepared before the outbreak of war were largely represented by maps showing movements of troops. For example, the plan that Germany used to invade Belgium and France used maps with arrows to show expected military advances eventually thwarted by trench warfare.

Auditory images can also serve as national symbols, particularly in the form of anthems such as "God Save the Queen" and the French "Marseillaise." These are familiar to both natives and foreigners and are often accompanied by emotions such as pride. Powerful uses of anthems as auditory symbols include the award ceremonies in the Olympic Games and Tchaikovsky's *1812 Overture*, in which musical themes drawn from the Marseillaise and Russian folk songs symbolize the competing armies during Napoleon's invasion of Russia.

Taste and smell can also contribute to national symbolism, for example with American apple pie, French cheese, and German beer. Motor representations are also relevant, for example in the kinesthetic experiences of waving flags, saluting, and marching in a particular organized fashion. Kinesthetic representations operated metaphorically when the president of France and the tsar of Russian met in 1914 and urged each other to hold firm against Austria-Hungary and Germany. The multimodal value maps presented for Nazism and anarchism in chapter 6 illustrate how political thinking can have multisensory dimensions.

Motor imagery can also contribute to nationalism. Like the religious rituals discussed in chapter 8, military rituals such as marching contribute to social coordination by synchronization of emotions. Similarly, public demonstrations can use chanting and arm raising to combine motor, visual, and auditory experiences that encourage solidarity.

These sensory representations show one important respect in which international cognition is embodied, because they depend on the senses that our bodies provide to interact with the world. National identity is also embodied as well as represented verbally through molecular mechanisms that underlie emotional reactions such as patriotism (love of country with dopamine activity) and fear of enemies with cortisol activity. But identity is not just embodied, because abstract concepts such as *duty* are also transbodied through connections to moral codes that invoke general principles linked to deities.

Beliefs and Rules

Concepts and images are important mental representations, but describing the world and acting on it require more complicated representations of whole states of affairs, which are beliefs. People in different countries have beliefs about their own countries, their allies, and their opponents. Such beliefs are a crucial part of international decision-making, which also requires inferences about what other countries are likely to do. In ordinary problem solving, with one person dealing with a situation in the world, the person merely needs to represent the world. But in collective and adversarial problem solving, it is also necessary to have some sense of what is going on in the minds of the other people who are contributors or obstacles for potential solutions. Understanding the outbreak of war therefore requires identifying not only the beliefs that people in each country have about the world but also the beliefs that they have about each other's beliefs.

For example, in the run-up to the First World War, leaders in each country had numerous beliefs about the other countries and about the beliefs and other mental states of their leaders. German leaders believed that the British wanted to limit Germany's colonial and industrial power, and British leaders believed that Germans did not want war with Britain because of their similar cultural values and Britain's superior naval power. MacMillan notes many unwarranted assumptions that leaders in various countries made about the military situation, such as that war would be both short and successful. These assumptions are beliefs that turned out to be false when the war became mostly defensive and went on for four years. The German belief that they could quickly conquer France and then turn their attention to Russia was also erroneous, as was the belief of the leaders of Austria-Hungary that Serbia could be quickly vanquished.

Rules are a kind of belief particularly important for action and inference. German military plans consisted of a large number of rules of the general form: *If we attack here, then France will respond here*. Because of the system of alliances forming countries into two main groups, leaders of the particular countries could operate with plausible rules such as *if Russia attacks Austria-Hungary, then Germany will attack Russia*. However, not all rules are linguistically represented beliefs, because they can also have a multimodal form where the conditions and actions are nonverbal representations. For example, because military plans often have visual representations via maps and associated movements, some strategic rules are better represented as multimodal rules of the form *<our attack here>* → *<enemy response here>*.

Military practices such as attacking and defending using various kinds of weapons may also be better captured by nonlinguistic multimodal rules than by verbal beliefs. Multimodal rules are also important for anticipating the emotional reactions of opponents, as in the visual-emotional rule *<enemy invaded>* → *<enemy humiliated>* where the semantic pointer in the condition is a visual representation of an invasion and the results is an emotional state attributed to the enemy. I later discuss the role of multimodal rules in nonverbal historical understanding.

Like beliefs, goals are mental representations of states of affairs but concern how the world is desired to be rather than how it is. Every country has national goals, represented in the minds of individuals including both leaders and the general public. For example, British goals included maintaining naval superiority, German goals included expanding its small colonial empire, and French goals included regaining the provinces of Alsace and Lorraine which had been taken by Prussia in 1871. A major part of adversarial problem solving in international relations is inferring the goals of the leaders of opposing countries. This inference is abductive, aimed at attributing a goal to an opponent on the grounds that the attribution provides the best explanation of what the opposing country says and does.

The semantic pointer theory of mental representation is powerful enough to capture the full complexity of beliefs and goals. Semantic pointers can explain beliefs about beliefs and beliefs about goals because of the capacity for recursive binding. Because every belief is a semantic pointer (*Brain–Mind*, chapter 4), and semantic pointers can be bindings of bindings, one person's beliefs about another's beliefs can be understood as semantic pointers that bind other semantic pointers. For example, Tsar Alexander's belief that Kaiser Wilhelm believed that Russia threatened Germany can be captured by neural processes that result from convolutions of this sort: *bind (believe Wilhelm [bind (threaten Russia*

Germany)]). Goals operate in individual minds through bindings of representations of states of affairs with emotional states such as desire. Wilhelm's having the goal of expanding Germany's navy was just having the neural representation of Germany with a stronger navy bound to a neural pattern corresponding to desirability.

Analogies and Metaphors

Analogies were not a major contributor to the thinking that produced the First World War but had subtle influences. Analogies, and metaphors based on analogies, contributed to how leaders thought about the current situation, the historical roles of their countries, the nature of war, and the other countries that were their enemies or allies.

In retrospect, there were no good analogies to the situation in 1914, because the First World War was unprecedented in its internationally disastrous effects. But from the perspective of leaders in 1914, there were reassuring analogies of two different kinds. First, Europe had managed to survive a series of international crises in Morocco and in the Balkans. In these cases, diplomats and leaders had reached compromises that prevented the breakout of large-scale war. Second, the wars most alive in people's memories, such as the Franco-Prussian war of 1871, were relatively short and limited in both geography and casualties. Therefore, analogical thinking helped leaders in 1914 to think that war was both unlikely and not disastrous.

Other analogies suggested that war actually could be good. War was compared to a tonic used to treat illness or a life-saving operation to cut out diseased flesh, a kind of hygiene. Social Darwinism was a popular view that saw an analogy between natural selection among species and conflicts among nations: struggle and survival of the fittest made war the best means of determining which nations were actually superior. Warring nations were compared to dueling individuals, with countries having the same obligation as insulted people to demand satisfaction.

Leaders also used analogies with previous historical events to suggest how to increase the glory of their nations while avoiding humiliation. Previous heroic victories such as the Battle of Waterloo for the British and the exploits of Joan of Arc for the French provided analogical directions for future triumphs. But every country also had a history of military disappointments, which served as analogical suggestions about how to avoid future humiliation. Some of these analogies were so prominent in people's minds that they functioned as national symbols of victory or defeat, for example the Serbian loss to the Ottomans in the Kosovo battle of 1389.

People from different countries often use metaphors to refer to each other, usually with derogatory intent. For example, some British refer to the French as frogs
because of their eating habits, and the French refer to the Germans as les Boches
by analogy to cabbage. I already described the embodied metaphor used by the
French and Russians in encouraging each other to hold firm.

Although analogies can impel nations toward war, they sometimes can produce appropriate caution. In the Cuban Missile Crisis of 1962, President John
F. Kennedy resisted the urgings of his military advisors for strong action against
the Soviet Union because he had just read Barbara Tuchman's book about the First
World War, *The Guns of August*. Kennedy did not want to repeat the stumbles into
disastrous war that occurred in 1914.

Emotions and Actions

The analogies just described all had substantial emotional components, ranging
from the arousing to the fear-avoiding. More generally, emotions played a huge
role in the prehistory and occurrence of the First World War, through their impact
on national attitudes and momentous decisions.

The value map in Figure 9.1 already suggested how emotions loom large in
thinking about nations and countries. Patriotism is love of country, where love
is the same combination of cognitive appraisal and physiological perception
that chapter 4 discussed with respect to romance. Patriotism is also connected
with other complex emotions such as pride, prestige, glory, and sense of duty.
As part of the aristocratic culture that most of them shared, monarchs and
leaders were much concerned with the honor of themselves and their countries. Honor is respect given to someone of good reputation in accord with
moral standards of behavior. Emotions are clearly a big part of it, including
the pride that comes from being an honorable person and deserving the respect of others, and the contrasting emotions of shame and guilt that would
attend violations of honor. Gentlemen of the era would fight duels to defend
the honor of themselves and their families, and patriotic honor demanded
analogous sacrifices.

Honor goes with a sense of duty, another complex emotional state akin to conscience, which can be understood as a kind of emotional intuition. Duties are obligations that people have to each other because of moral codes, but a sense of duty
is not just a judgment that it would be advantageous to behave in a certain way.
Rather, it is a feeling, a conscious experience based on the prospect of feeling good
if the duty is matched and on the prospect of feeling bad if duty is violated. Honor
and a sense of duty work together to cause people to act in ways that they view as

enforced by their moral codes. Loyalty is another mental attitude that leads to action because it incorporates intentions to behave in morally expected ways.

The prospect of war can stimulate positive emotions such as the desire for adventure and the accumulation of prestige, including glory for one's country as well as for oneself as a successful soldier. Military strategists in Germany and other countries had come to view offensive war as much more attractive than defensive war, attaching a much stronger emotional value to attack rather than defense.

Patriotism, national pride, honor, prestige, and sense of duty are all positive emotions that people have with respect to their own countries. In international relations, people also think about other countries, with the introduction of strong negative emotions such as fear, regret, and humiliation. Fear dominated much of the thinking in the events leading up to the outbreak of war in 1914. People in each country feared that the other countries would become more powerful and rich, leading to the decline of their own country.

Specifically, the British feared that the German Navy would become as powerful as their own, while Germans feared that their lack of colonies would limit economic growth and world prestige. The French feared that Germany would invade as it had done successfully in 1870. Austrians feared that the rise of Balkan states would lead to loss of empire. Fears mingled with ethnic prejudices, with Slavs and Germanics each fearing the dominance of the other. One of German leaders' greatest fears was that it was being encircled by France and Russia. Leaders of each country feared that a first attack by other countries would provide an advantage. Hence leaders had to make complex inferences about intentions and emotional states in the minds of other leaders, a difficult kind of adversarial problem solving.

Leaders' fears were intermixed with other negative emotions such as suspicion and mistrust. The Moroccan and Balkan crises that led up to the First World War had the unfortunate effect of increasing these negative emotions. Even when a solution was found, the countries involved became increasingly suspicious of each other through realizing that the other leaders were capable of deception and betrayal, with the capacity to produce harm to their own countries. Suspicion is a kind of fear that another agent will do something harmful. As war drew close, some leaders in Germany came close to panic, a version of fear that is extreme, sudden, and overwhelming.

A decade before the outbreak of World War I, there was a modicum of trust among European leaders, based partly on the personal relationships of monarchs who were often cousins and partly on the common aristocratic backgrounds of the political and military leaders. But a series of conflicts in Africa and the Balkans resulted not only in the absence of trust but in the more distinctly negative emotion of mistrust. Chapter 4 gave an account of trust in romantic relationships that applies equally well in international relations and extends naturally to mistrust. Trust is not just a cognitive expectation about the behavior of others but also a good feeling about them. Similarly, mistrust is not just a probability attached to people behaving badly but a negative feeling about them that they are bad persons capable of doing bad things. Like all emotions, trust and mistrust have strong connections with action, leading you to depend on people you trust and be suspicious of people you mistrust. Mistrust integrates physiological gut feelings with judgments about what the other person is capable of doing.

Commitment is important to the romantic relationships described in chapter 4 and also to international relations that involve alliances. The cascade of actions that produced World War I resulted in part from commitments among the two major alliances: Germany with Austria-Hungary and France with Russia and Great Britain. Like trust, commitment is a cognitive-emotional process but differs in including a forward-looking element of intentions concerning how to behave in particular situations.

Even more than positive emotions, negative emotions such as fear, anxiety, suspicion, tension, and mistrust can generate emotional spirals, with one person's behavior increasing mistrust in the other which then results in behaviors that reciprocally increase mistrust. In both romantic relationships and international negotiations, such amplifying feedback loops can lead to situations where possibilities of trust and mutually advantageous cooperation evaporate. Chapter 4 described the theory of Murray and Holmes that there are unconscious rules operating in people's minds for generating trust, and the same is true for suspicion and mistrust. Possibilities include the following: *If betrayal, then mistrust; if deception, then mistrust; if avoidance, then mistrust.* These rules are not simply verbal statements that could easily become accessible to consciousness because of their strong emotional component. The last rule is better represented using the notation <avoidance> → <mistrust> to indicate that avoidance is partly physical movement associated with negative emotion and that mistrust is not just a neutral cognitive state but also a negative emotional state associated with physiological responses such as gut feelings.

Other negative emotions that come into play in international as well as romantic relations are anger, hostility, and resentment. All of these are physiological responses in individuals tied to cognitive appraisals that another agent is blocking accomplishment of goals.

The most complicated emotions that operate in all kinds of human relations are emotions about emotions. Fear of humiliation was a common experience among political leaders who thought that they and their countries might be humiliated as a result of military and diplomatic defeats. Humiliation is already a complex emotion, a loss of pride, self-respect, and dignity, each of which are positive emotions. So fear of humiliation is fear of losing a combination of other emotions. Because the term "meta-emotion" has already been used in a different sense, I call emotions about emotions *nested* emotions.

Some additional examples of nested emotions are: hope for forgiveness, trepidation about attachment, love of honor, longing for love, fear of fear itself, lust for glory, fear of shame, dread of embarrassment, thrill of horror, fear of missing out, hatred of boredom, wanting to be brave, phobophobia, falling in love with love, fear of commitment, disgust at lust, daring to be proud, pride of love, apprehension about guilt and shame, wishing for trust, fear of regret, anxiety about attachment, confidence of love, and fear of disappointment. Montaigne wrote that "He who fears he shall suffer already suffers what he fears." Generalizing to include not only one's own states but also the emotions of others, we get additional examples such as being annoyed at someone else's resentment, being happy at someone else's satisfaction, trusting someone not to let you down, and being fed up with the tensions in an international or romantic relationship.

Nested emotions are a major problem for purely physiological theories of emotion. There are no obvious physiological correlates of specific emotions like fear or humiliation, let alone for the far more complicated situation of suffering from fear of humiliation. Purely cognitive theories are similarly limited in that, even if they could identify the complex appraisal that goes into suffering fear of humiliation, they cannot explain why this goes with the kind of feeling that provides a strong motivation for action. The facts that fear of humiliation feels bad, and that hope for love feels good, demand a physiological component for nested emotions. Fortunately, the semantic pointer theory of emotions can handle both cognitive complexity and physiological input through repeated neural bindings. The human brain's capacity for recursive bindings naturally accommodates nested emotions about emotions.

A key function of emotions is to produce actions. The most important actions leading to wholesale fighting in World War I included the assassination of the Archduke by Serbian nationalists (inspired by patriotism), the delivery of the aggressive ultimatum to Serbia by Austro-Hungarian leaders (inspired by outrage), and the announcement of backing for Serbia by Russia (inspired by pro-Slav feeling and enthusiasm for war). Without emotions, people are not easily motivated to do anything at all, whereas national pride and fear of defeat can generate extreme behaviors in both leaders who declare war and in ordinary people who willingly fight in the trenches. But emotions do not automatically lead to action, for there may be layers of inference that determine how people act.

Inferences

Deductions or inductive generalizations that contributed to the outbreak of war in 1914 are hard to notice, but there were many abductive and emotional inferences. The abductive inferences occur when the leaders of one country try to figure out what the leaders of another country are thinking. Each action and communication generates questions such as: Why did they do that? Why did they say that? Generating answers to such questions is a matter of inference to the best explanation, trying to come up with the most coherent interpretation of what the adversary is doing. For example, when Austria responded to the assassination of the archduke by delivering an ultimatum to Serbia, the Serbs and Russians inferred from the extreme way in which the ultimatum demanded Austrian control over Serbia that Austrians actually wanted war. Attribution of wanting is an act of abductive inference.

The interagent inference required to figure out what an adversary is planning is greatly complicated by the problem that opposing countries are governed by a multitude of agents. It is hard enough to infer what one central figure such as Tsar Alexander was thinking, let alone to infer what whole groups of military and political leaders are also thinking. Moreover, decisions such as declarations of war often result from interactions among various leaders and factions, not to mention public opinion manifested in newspaper reports and editorials. Oscillations in the relative power of different factions can make the overall direction of a government hard to read. Hence the abductive problem of inferring the emotions and intentions of decision makers in opposing countries is daunting.

Anticipating what foreign leaders are likely to do also requires guesses about their multimodal rules that govern their reactions such as trust and mistrust. It is difficult to figure out the conscious representations such as beliefs and emotions that operate in the minds of others, and even harder to discern their rules that are unconscious because they connect a diversity of sensory, motor, and emotional states.

Another problem is that the decision making in a country may result from interactions among subgroups with different interests: diplomats tend to be oriented toward peace, whereas military leaders are more likely to advocate war. Hence interagent inference in international relations is made extraordinarily difficult by the need to consider different factions in opposing countries and by the need to infer multimodal rules that may be hard to express in language.

Emotional inferences also abounded in the run-up to war, both motivated and fear-driven. All leaders were prone to exaggerating the strengths of their own countries and the weaknesses of their opponents. All were clearly overoptimistic about the value of war and its eventual results. For example, Russia ought to have learned from its defeat by Japan in 1905 that its military strength was not proportional to its huge army. Motivated inference inclined people to look for evidence that supported conclusions linked to positive emotions such as national pride, rather than objectively to expect disasters that could result from a drawn-out conflict using new technologies such as machine guns and barbed wire. Just like romantic couples, political ideologues, and stock market speculators, military leaders have a hard time distinguishing actions that really do promote their goals from actions that merely seem to do so. Motivated inference can also make leaders convinced that, even if they want to avoid war, the present is a relatively good time to be involved in war.

It is also easy for military and political leaders to succumb to fear-driven inference, which leads them to believe that a situation is even worse than it is. The spiral of negative emotion, the amplifying feedback loop of fear, suspicion, and mistrust, can contribute to the conviction that war is inevitable. Obsession with honor and fear of humiliation can help people to take actions that they ought to be able to recognize as counter to the best interests of themselves and their country.

It is not at all paradoxical that leaders (and ordinary people) can be prone to both motivated and fear-driven inference, any more than that people are at different times capable of happiness and fear. As in economic crashes described in chapter 7, leaders can undergo an emotional gestalt shift from motivated inference to fear-driven inference, for example transitioning from the pursuit of peace to the execution of war. Such shifts result from adjustments in emotional coherence that result from changing circumstances.

Not all emotional inference is as irrational as motivated and fear-driven inference usually are, because emotions can valuably contribute to judgments about the best way to satisfy one's goals. There have not been many just wars in history, but in a few cases leaders did make emotional decisions that were both prudent and moral. For example, in the Second World War, France, Great Britain, and the United States went to war in response to attacks by Germany and Japan. These decisions were rational even though they were also clearly emotional, driven by well-justified fears of domination. All practical inferences about what to do have an emotional component that takes into account the value for the individual of particular goals. Mathematical cost-benefit analysis is no substitute for caring about things sufficiently to become prone to emotions such as fear and pride.

In sum, military and political decisions about whether and how to wage war result from a combination of abductive, practical, and emotion-driven inferences. Abductive inferences are rational when the conclusion reached is the best explanation that takes into account all the relevant evidence and considers alternative hypotheses. Practical inference is rational when the action chosen is the best plan taking into account all the relevant consequences and considering alternative plans. Rationality is severely undercut, however, when motivation and fear lead people to jump to conclusions about what to believe or what to do without adequate consideration of the full range of evidence and alternatives.

Communication

It is futile to try to reduce the development of war to operations in the minds of individual leaders. How leaders think is dependent on interactions both within countries and across countries. In 1914, the monarchs, political leaders, and generals all had staffs of advisors with whom they regularly communicated. Such interactions produced much transfer of factual information such as troop deployment but also nonverbal communication of emotional information concerning how people were evaluating events. Within each country, leaders shared their hopes and fears as well as their beliefs. Regular meetings ensured that these communications could be face-to-face and therefore not purely verbal.

Emotional communication opened the door for collective motivated inference. Individuals succumb to motivated inference when they use evidence selectively in order to reach conclusions that fit with their goals rather than reality. Communication is also selective, because people can choose what verbal and nonverbal information they want to transfer to which people. Hearers can similarly be biased in what messages they take seriously, guided by goals including the desire to belong and fit in to a group. Hence motivated inference at the group level can be even more distorting than in individuals, providing a major source of groupthink.

Communication brought about the spread of beliefs and emotions within countries that influence overall decisions. For example, the British cabinet and parliament were reluctant to go to war with Germany but were swayed in part by the inspiring oratory of the prime minister. Communication among leaders and the populace can generate emotional waves of support and collective solidarity, both emergent from interactions among individuals.

Direct meetings between heads of state, leaders, and diplomats were rarer in an era without passenger airplanes. Monarchs had occasionally met with each other, but alliances and responses to crises had to be worked out by representatives such as diplomats whose mobility was restricted. Frequent international communication occurred by telegrams, which are restricted to verbal communication and required considerable abductive inference to produce interpretations. One important exception was the trip that the French president made to Russia in July 1914,

which cemented the alliance between Russia and France and firmed up their resolve to take on Germany and Austria-Hungary.

It therefore seems that at the international level there was limited opportunity
for the exchange and elicitation of semantic pointers that relied on more than
verbal information found in sentences. Hence leaders had fewer opportunities to
make good abductive inferences about each other's intentions, so they naturally
fell back on motivated and fear-driven thinking.

MINDS AND GROUPS

As in previous chapters, full understanding of international affairs and the origins
of war cries out for a solution to the person–group problem: pinning down the
relation between individual minds and collectives such as nations and countries.
As chapter 4 noted, this problem arises even for very small groups, because people
use expressions such as "happy couple" or "dysfunctional family." Is the happiness of a couple just the sum or average of the happiness of the two people in it,
or perhaps the happiness of the least happy member of the couple? Alternatively,
perhaps couple happiness is an emergent property of the couple considered as a
whole. Or perhaps, in accord with extreme holism, individuals do not exist because
the couple is only real as a social process.

The person–group problem is even more acute in international affairs, which
requires grasping the complex relationships among minds in individual leaders
and the public, appreciating important collectives such as government cabinets,
military staffs, diplomatic corps, nations, and countries. Historians and international theorists find it natural to talk about the assumptions, desires, and fears of
whole countries, which is puzzling if mental processes are brain processes. How
can it make sense to talk about the fears of Germany or the desires of France, when
a country as a collective of people does not have a brain? Is there an alternative
to the stringent view of methodological individualism that talk of such entities is
bogus and should always be reduced just to talk of individuals, and to the wildly
holistic view that the collective is the fundamental entity so that group mental
states are just social facts?

Social cognitivism helps to solve this empirical and ontological problem by
working out the mental mechanisms operating in individuals, the social mechanisms operating in collectives, and the connections among mechanisms at both
levels. The theory that all mental mechanisms result from construction and transformation of semantic pointers provides an answer at the individual level. The

basis for the interactions between individuals in groups is then semantic pointer communication, including the approximate transfer and elicitation of semantic pointers in one individual by another. These conclusions may sound like methodological individualism, reducing the operations of groups to the operations of brains, but my view is more complicated in several respects, concerning mental representations of groups, interactions governed by groups, and emergent properties of groups.

First, the semantic pointers of the individuals include strong emotional representations of the groups. You cannot have patriotism without a representation of the country that you love, or nationalism without a mental representation of the nation with which you identify. Patriotism and nationalism are not simply abstract ideas but emotionally powerful brain/mind processes connected to action by virtue of the way in which individuals including monarchs, leaders, and the general population view themselves. Patriotism and nationalism assume that there actually are countries and nations about which people have emotions and beliefs.

Second, the existence of groups is needed to explain the nature of the interactions that take place between individuals. If two people form a marriage, or if leaders belong to the same party or club, or even if large groups of people are all citizens of the same country, then such connections affect the frequency and manner with which people interact. These interactions then determine what semantic pointers are communicated between them. For example, two people who are both members of a government cabinet are likely to interact with each other regularly and thereby to communicate cognitive and emotional states in ways differently than would happen with members of the general population.

Third, group interactions have emergent results, allowing the collectives to have properties not found any one individual, such as declarations of war. In autocratic monarchies, the declaration of war by the country is synonymous with the declaration of war by the monarch. But in republics and constitutional monarchies with powerful legislatures, declaration of war has to be performed by a parliamentary decision made through the interactions of the members of parliament and various leaders, partially influenced by the opinion of the populace. Hence properties of the country such as being at war do not reduce to the decisions of individuals.

So social cognitivism avoids the oversimplifications of methodological individualism and collective holism by working out how the parts affect the wholes and how the wholes affect the parts. Resulting changes such as the debacle of the First World War are then best understood as multilevel emergence rather than unidirectional causality. Among other advantages, this approach discourages attributing blame to just one collective such as Germany or to just one individual such as Kaiser Wilhelm. My conclusion is roughly compatible with Christopher Clark's:

> The outbreak of war was the combination of chains of decisions made by political actors with conscious objectives, who were capable of a degree of self-reflection, acknowledged a range of options and formed the best judgments they could on the basis of the best information they had to hand. Nationalism, armaments, alliances and finance were all part of the story, but they can be made to carry real explanatory weight only if they can be seen to have shaped the decisions that—in combination—made war break out.

My main disagreement, however, concerns whether leaders really did form the best judgments they could rather than frequently succumbing, as all people do, to motivated and fear-driven inference.

Historians and specialists in international relations often talk about national interests, but what are they? I take beliefs, concepts, and values to be processes operating in individual brains, but interests in the sense of matters of importance can sometimes also be ascribed to whole countries. Countries can cease to exist or be re-created, as happened with Poland which was eliminated in the eighteenth century but revived in the twentieth. So Poland might be said to have an interest in survival and revival, understood as an aggregate of the desires and needs of the people who constitute the Polish nation and who value having a country. However, this way of talking is figural rather than literal, because interests carefully construed are mental states, which are neural processes.

Groups do not literally have minds or mental states, but speaking of groups as having beliefs and emotions may be figuratively apt when (a) the most powerful individuals in the group have a mental representation, (b) the representation is influenced by the individuals conceptualizing themselves as members of the group, and (c) the representation in each individual results in part from communicative interactions with other members of the group. These conditions are not a definition of group mental states, merely a characterization of when it is communicatively appropriate to mention them in figures of speech. Figural attribution of mental states to groups is even more apt when the groups do literally have emergent nonmental properties such as declaring war that result from the interactions of thinking individuals. In happy romantic couples, the happiness is not a property of the couple, but the interacting happy minds

of the couple may lead the couple to become a marriage, which has emergent
legal properties.

HISTORICAL EXPLANATION

This chapter provides a new account of historical explanations, which are usually just narratives. There is no prospect for converting historical explanations
into deductive ones, because, as with biology, there are few if any mathematical
laws that can be instantiated to apply to rich historical cases. But if social cognitivism is on the right track, then narratives can be deepened by attention to
mental and social mechanisms, all based on semantic pointers. Then narrative
explanation is expanded into mechanistic explanation, producing what might be
called mechanistic-narrative explanation.

Good historians, like good anthropologists, provide thick descriptions of the
details of important events and practices. Social cognitivism offers the prospect of
also generating deep descriptions that tie these details to underlying processes of
inference and communication. Mechanistic-narrative explanation is also valuable
in nonsocial historical fields such as biology (e.g., how humans evolved) and cos-
mology (e.g., how the universe developed).

The writing of history can then benefit from psychology that goes beyond the
scientific limitations of folk psychology and the obsolete ideas of Freud and Jung.
My template for historical explanation is the social cognitive-emotional workup,
applied in previous chapters to prejudice, ideology, economics, and religion. This
kind of investigation depends heavily on the detailed investigations carried out
by historians such as MacMillan and Clark. Only by looking at the rich historical
record found in documents and memoirs can the main concepts, values, beliefs,
and emotions be identified. Historical narratives are invaluable for identifying the
most important groups and interactions that affected historical developments,
such as the outbreak of war. Social cognitivism is not a replacement for history
any more than it is for social psychology, politics, economics, sociology, or anthropology. Rather, theories about mental and social mechanisms enhance any social
science investigation by connecting it to how people think and communicate.

Social cognitivism undercuts a distinction often made between causal explanation and historical understanding, where the latter is supposed to result from
subjective interpretation of the meaning of actions from the actor's point of view.
Such interpretation is supposed to use a kind of ineffable empathy irreducible to
causal relations, as in the verstehen idea discussed in chapter 5 and the reflexivity

approach to economics considered in chapter 7. But I have suggested that empathy is itself a psychological process that operates in three modes: neural mirroring, conscious analogy, and unconscious simulation using multimodal rules. It then becomes possible to evaluate different empathic interpretations based on how well they actually explain the actions of people such as national leaders. Instead of just the subjective feeling that a historian might have about what people were doing, we can combine historical evidence with current understandings of cognition and emotion to construct and evaluate much more detailed accounts of what was plausibly going on in the minds of leaders such as Kaiser Wilhelm.

On this view, historical and social methodology is not radically different from that of the natural sciences, because all of them seek mechanistic explanations using data and models. But there is an important difference in the relevant mechanisms, because people have mental representations, inferences, emotions, and communication not found in atoms, molecules, and most cells. Historians should note these cognitive and emotional factors in their mechanistic narratives.

SOCIAL COGNITIVISM AS A THEORY OF INTERNATIONAL RELATIONS

In addition to providing a new model of historical explanation, social cognitivism offers a new approach to international relations that can absorb some of the insights of current theories but provides much deeper accounts of how countries interact with each other. Like the theory known as realism, social cognitivism acknowledges that nation-states are actors in international politics and that different countries have different interests. But it recognizes that the actions and interests of countries depend on the actions and interests in individual minds, which may be far from rational because of emotional factors such as motivated and fear-driven inference. Social cognitivism improves on realism by (a) tying the actions of states to mental and social processes involving individuals, including leaders and the public, and (b) rejecting implausible assumptions such as rationality and overwhelming self-interest. The First World War illustrates how badly nations can rationally pursue their own self-interest: everybody lost.

The international relations theory called liberalism emphasizes international cooperation based on common goals such as peace and prosperity. It is odd that realism and liberalism have been taken to be competing theories. History makes it clear that sometimes nation-states act in ways that are self-interested applications of power politics but also that sometimes they act in ways that are much more mutually beneficial. Expecting states to be one or the other is like supposing that humans must all be mean or all be nice, or even that one individual must be always mean or always nice. Rather, understanding the complex of beliefs, values, and emotions that operate in individual minds reveals how different leaders operate with different motivations, some benevolent and some malevolent. Social cognitivism goes beyond liberalism by looking at the mental and social mechanisms that can lead countries to act in ways that might be viewed as cooperative as well as power-driven.

In the academic field of international relations, a more recent view called constructivism is seen as a challenge to both liberal and realist theories. Constructivist international relations claims to pay attention to the ideas that define international structures and the identities of states and cultures. However, constructivists fail to connect what are supposed to be cognitive structures operating in individual minds with the theories of mental representation developed in cognitive psychology and neuroscience. Constructivist international relations is just as mind-blind as political theories based on rational choice, despite frequent use of terms such as "idea."

Moreover, constructivists provide no way of understanding the relation between ideas operating in individuals and the social processes that are crucial for the operations of countries. Social cognitivism agrees with constructivism that ideas matter but specifies how they matter by relating them to neural theories of concepts, values, beliefs, and emotions. Moreover, it can explain how ideas have social effects because of the ways in which communication between individuals works through the transfer and elicitation of semantic pointers.

There are other current theories of international relations, but I leave for the reader the task of contrasting social cognitivism with schools such as Marxism, functionalism, and postcolonialism. The approach I recommend, using a social cognitive-emotional workup based on neural theories of thinking and communication, can build on insights from all of these approaches as well as realism, liberalism, and constructivism. But it goes beyond current theories and methods in the study of international relations through an account in which interests and ideas are not just vague stipulations. Instead, they are neural processes occurring in the minds of individuals interacting to form social groups, right up to nations and countries.

As previous chapters showed, social cognitivism is not just a theory of international relations but serves as a general theory of social processes on all scales. After all, people are using the same brains no matter whether they are pursuing romance, practicing a religion, or negotiating treaties. These are all social activities that depend on cognition, emotion, and communication. Hence processes of trust, mistrust, and commitment that are crucial in international relations are not just analogous to what happens in romantic couples but identical.

SUMMARY AND DISCUSSION

Rationality and irrationality concern both what to believe and what to do. In the actions and decisions that preceded the First World War, the leaders of all the main countries were irrational in both ways. They operated with beliefs such as the prospects for a brief and successful war that were not backed by evidence but merely by motivated inferences and biased analogies, all driven by emotion more than evidence. In the performance of important actions such as mobilizing troops and declaring war, they were often myopic in not considering alternative actions that would have provided a better chance of success and sometimes close to panic because of fear-driven inferences.

If we had to pick the most irrational of all the countries, the winner would probably be the leaders of Austria-Hungary, for their decision to respond to the assassination of Archduke Franz Ferdinand by invading Serbia, which cascaded into war against Russia, France, and Great Britain. The eventual consequence of this action was dismemberment of the Austro-Hungarian empire, with Austria and Hungary each reduced to much smaller countries through the loss of chunks that became Poland and Yugoslavia. Austria-Hungary, however, held no monopoly on irrationality, as Germany, Russia, France, and Great Britain also suffered huge losses in people and power through a combination of faulty beliefs and decisions. It is fair to judge leaders in all these countries as irrational because, given their knowledge and goals, they ought to have arrived at more accurate beliefs and more effective actions.

A major contributor to collective irrationality was the impact of concepts such as *nationalism, patriotism, honor,* and *duty.* These emotional values fueled negative anticipations of the potential actions of opponents, generating fear, anxiety, tension, and hostility. With such emotions running riot, it is not surprising that leaders rushed into decisions they later came to regret. Emotions in international relations are not inherently irrational, any more than they are in ordinary life, where emotions ranging from fear to love are sometimes based on appropriate evaluations of a situation. But spirals of emotion operating through social interactions and motivated and fear-driven inference can take human minds far beyond the limits of rationality. Leaders in all countries who instigated the First World War went into it believing that the war would be short, they would win it, and the war would be someone else's fault. They all suffered from failures of empathy resulting from inability to use analogy and multimodal rule simulation to put themselves in the shoes of other leaders.

This chapter has shown how historical explanation and the understanding of international relations can be enhanced by applying detailed psychological, neural, and social mechanisms to real-world events. By applying the method of social cognitive-emotional workups to the origins of the First World War, I have tried to show the relevance of an integrated account of beliefs, concepts, values, rules, analogies, metaphors, emotions, inferences, and communication. The result transcends the limitations of purely narrative explanations in history and provides insight into why the field of international relations has lacked a satisfactory general theory. Explaining social changes in both groups and individuals requires understanding the communicative interactions of cognitive-emotional minds; the result is mechanistic-narrative explanation.

Nations through their leaders can exercise all four kinds of power discussed in chapter 6. The strongest is coercive power via threats of war and economic sanctions, but nations can also wield benefit power through inducements such as trade deals and military aid. Respect power derives from having admired leaders and effective governments, while norm power occasionally operates through social expectations generated by organizations such as the United Nations.

Dealing with complex historical developments such as the outbreak of wars runs headlong into the person–group problem. Social cognitivism offers a solution that takes into account the complexity of both mental mechanisms in individuals and social mechanisms by which individuals interact. Noticing this complexity is superior to trying to reduce the social to the individual or the individual to the social. The person–group problem has the same kind of solution as the mind–body problem addressed in *Brain–Mind*. Just as a rich theory of how the brain works makes plausible suggestions about the emergent properties of mind, so a rich theory of how people interact with each other makes plausible suggestions about the emergent properties of groups. In both cases, explanations highlight multilevel emergence rather than unidirectional causation.

The mind–body problem and the person–group problem turn out to be interdependent. We cannot understand how groups operate via the people in them without appreciating how people work through mental operations in their brains. Correlatively, because social interactions are such an important part of human lives, a full account of brains that can extend to emotions and the self depends on grasping how human minds are dramatically influenced by the minds of other people. What might better be called the brain–mind–group problem has a general solution based on multilevel interacting mechanisms. *Natural Philosophy* (chapter 4) argues that groups are real.

This chapter completes my effort to show that the social sciences benefit from cooperation with the cognitive sciences to explain important kinds of social change. It is fair to ask what has been added by semantic pointer theories of cognition and communication beyond general ideas about minds.

First, semantic pointers explain how thinking can be both embodied and transbodied, tied to human senses and emotions in practices such as military rituals but also transcending them with abstract concepts such as duty and honor. The causes of human action can be factors in the world such as technology and forms of production, as Marx emphasized, but also values and ideas as many other social scientists have emphasized. There is no need to ask misleading questions about what is more fundamental to historical change, the world or ideas; via semantic pointers, minds interact with the world and generate new concepts that can help to change the world.

Second, semantic pointers provide an integrated account of cognition and emotion that covers both effective problem solving and irrational inference. Third, because semantic pointers can incorporate verbal, sensory, motor, and emotional information, they give rise to unconscious multimodal rules that govern actions in ways that are hard to identify verbally. Nevertheless, empathy and neural theory can join forces to try to discern the rules behind human interactions. Fourth, semantic pointer theories of cognition and emotion extend naturally to a theory of interpersonal communication that covers both words and nonverbal messages. Transferring, eliciting, and prompting semantic pointers covers the results of gesturing, drawing, singing, marching, and facial expressions just as well as it covers talking and writing.

Many other kinds of social changes furnish history and international relations with other opportunities to develop social cognitive-emotional workups, for example to answer questions about the rise and fall of nations. Additional branches of social science such as social geography and cultural studies should generate more applications. Instead, my goal now is to apply social cognitivism to professions that depend on the cognitive and social sciences, including medicine, law, education, engineering, and business.

NOTES

On historical explanation, see Mahajan 2011 and Stanford 1998.

Ravenscroft 2016 reviews folk (commonsense) psychology.

For psychohistory, see Freud 1962. Isaac Asimov's psychohistory is a different, statistical enterprise.

Jackson and Sorensen 2010 review theories of international relations. See also Wendt 1999. For new work on emotions in international relations, consult Clément and Sangar 2018. Milkoreit 2017 applies emotion and value maps (cognitive-affective) maps to climate change diplomacy.

Calhoun 2007 discusses nations and nationalism. Mock 2011 examines symbols of defeat that are important for countries like Israel and Croatia. Other countries like the United States and Great Britain revel in symbols of victory.

My account of World War I is primarily based on MacMillan 2013 and Clark 2013 (quote from p. xxix). Wimmer 2014 reviews the sociology of war.

Thagard 1992a analyzes adversarial problem solving based on explanatory coherence. *Natural Philosophy* bases rationality on explanatory and emotional coherence.

On analogical uses of history, see Holyoak and Thagard 1995, Khong 1992, Macmillan 2008, and Neustadt and May 1986.

Nisbett and Cohen 1996 examine cultures of honor.

Natural Philosophy (chapter 6) and Thagard and Finn 2011 consider moral conscience as emotional coherence.

The term "meta-emotion" covers both cognitions and emotions about emotions: https://en.wikipedia.org/wiki/Meta-emotion.

It is not easy to specify the figures of speech used in saying that groups have mental states, because such attributions have aspects of metonymy, metaphor, and synecdoche. For metaphorical uses, the theory of metaphor in *Brain–Mind* (chapter 10) applies.

Currie 2014 discusses the relation between narrative and mechanistic explanations. Mechanistic explanations in theoretical neuroscience are also mathematical.

PROJECT

Do a social cognitive-emotional workup of wars that might have occurred but did not (e.g., the Cuban missile crisis) and draw lessons about how to avoid war. Apply the multilevel mechanism method to other important historical question such as why some societies flourish more than others. Apply the multilevel mechanism method to other important questions in international relations such as how countries resolve disputes. Analyze conceptual change in history and international relations, for example in the decline of colonialism.

PART III
Professions

10

Medicine

MIND, SOCIETY, AND THE PROFESSIONS

What do doctors, lawyers, teachers, engineers, and business leaders have in common? The first part of this book, chapters 1 to 3, describes a set of interacting mental and social mechanisms aimed at explaining all human activities. The second part, chapters 4 to 9, applies these mechanisms to social sciences ranging from social psychology to international relations. The aim of this third part is to show that the same mechanisms account for the successes and failures of major professional activities, including medicine, law, education, engineering, and business.

It is impossible to cover these diverse fields in full generality, so for each of them I address one important topic using the resources already applied to the social sciences. We will see the usefulness of three-analysis, value maps, social cognitive-emotional workups, and explanations via multilevel mechanisms. As in the social sciences, important changes in individuals and groups are explained as resulting from multilevel emergence.

For medicine, I focus on mental illness and the debilitating disorder of depression. The law chapter is concerned with legal responsibility, including how it operates in the minds of individuals and also how it is determined as a social process depending on interactions of juries and judges. Education is similarly treated at both individual and social levels, looking at teaching as a social process dependent on transmission of semantic pointers to learners who undergo substantial conceptual change.

I consider creative design in engineering as both a mental and a social process using the same mechanisms operating in other professions. Notably, emotion mechanisms are just as important as the more familiar cognitive mechanisms of perception and inference. Finally, the chapter on business looks at the key activities of management and marketing, showing how both depend on the same interacting mechanisms.

This chapter begins with general remarks on the nature of medicine and disease, setting the stage for a discussion of mental illness. In particular, I show how depression can be understood from the perspective of social cognitivism.

MEDICINE

Medicine is the scientific practice of the diagnosis, treatment, and prevention of disease. But what is disease? Superficially, a disease is just a set of symptoms; for example influenza is just having fever, body aches, runny nose, cough, and so on. Sets of symptoms can be valuable for diagnosis but alone provide no information about the causes of disease that are highly relevant to finding effective treatments and preventing future occurrences.

Skeptics might say that a disease is just a social construction, the result of human interactions such as power that enable some people to label less powerful ones as sick. Unfortunately, diseases ranging from cancer to heart conditions to schizophrenia are far too destructive to dismiss as mere social constructions, even if many diseases have causes that are in part social.

Biologically, a disease is a physiological malfunction that takes place when bodies stop working how they normally do. This account is far more plausible than the ones based on symptoms and social construction but needs to be spelled out using more specific accounts of bodily functions. Specificity comes by describing what the body does in terms of mechanisms: systems of interconnected parts whose interactions produce regular changes. For example, cell division is an important mechanism that enables the body to grow and renew itself, as when skin cells are replaced monthly. Different forms of cancer result from different kinds of breakdowns in the mechanisms for encouraging and controlling cell division. Genetic diseases such as Huntington's result from damaged parts (gene mutations) that cause malfunctions in mechanisms such as ones controlling movement.

Malfunctions occur because of breakdowns in mechanisms, which happen because of deficiencies in parts, interconnections, and/or interactions. The result of these breakdowns is that the regular changes needed to operate, grow, and maintain the body are blocked, resulting in symptoms. Heart disease, for example, produces symptoms such as shortness of breath because of problems with parts such as blocked veins, interconnections such as valves between the ventricles, and interactions such as oxygen transfer from lungs to heart.

Not all symptoms are equally undesirable, because some may be easily fixed, for example by applying hand cream to dry skin. Other results of biological changes may actually be desirable, for example when a genetic mutation provides Tibetans with the ability to breathe at high altitudes. Hence a purely biological conception of disease is inadequate because of the need to consider normatively whether the effects of mechanism breakdowns are harmful under particular environmental and social conditions. Consideration of harms requires values as well as biological facts.

No concise definition using necessary and sufficient conditions can capture all of the biological and normative aspects of diseases or cover the thousands of diseases described in medical textbooks. But a three-analysis of disease such as the one found in Table 10.1 can characterize it in line with the semantic pointer theory of concepts. There are many familiar exemplars of disease such as influenza and cancer, even if some conditions such as chronic fatigue syndrome are controversial.

Diseases typically have harmful symptoms, even though it may take years for the harmful effects of diseases such as diabetes to become evident. For many diseases, the breakdowns in biological mechanisms that produce symptoms have been identified, for example the disruptions in cell functioning caused by invasion of the influenza virus. But there are also many diseases with harmful symptoms whose biological causes remain to be identified, for example Alzheimer's disease. Hence broken mechanisms should be considered as typical of disease rather than definitional.

Diagnosing someone as having a disease has numerous intellectual and practical benefits. The practical benefits include prognosis to predict the expected course of the disease and treatments to stop its operation. The intellectual benefits are achieving an explanation of why someone has the symptoms of the disease, for

TABLE 10.1

Three-Analysis of *Disease*

Exemplars	Influenza, cancer, scurvy, arthritis, heart failure, diabetes
Typical features	Symptoms, harms with respect to vital needs, broken mechanisms
Explanations	Explains: why people have harmful symptoms
	Explained by: breakdowns in physiological and other mechanisms

example knowing that someone has fever, aches, and pains because of influenza. Diagnosing a disease is rarely a deductive inference through applying a rule that says persons with symptoms X, Y, and Z have the disease. Rather, disease ascription is usually a matter of abductive inference, where the diagnosis provides the best available explanation of all the evidence.

This inference requires considering alternative explanations and the full range of the patient's symptoms, along with other aspects of the patient's background and physiology, such as the results of medical tests. Inferring the best explanation of symptoms requires hypothesizing conditions that cause the disease but often also takes into account possible genetic and environmental causes of those diseases. Hence diagnosis requires a full assessment of explanatory coherence.

Diseases are typically breakdowns in *physiological* mechanisms, but physiology may not be the whole explanation. A fuller story requires attention to what caused the physiological breakdowns, for example how exposure to environmental toxins leads to the kinds of errant cell division that produce some cancers. Lung cancer occurs when cells in the lungs start to divide abnormally and form tumors, but abnormal cell division often results from prolonged exposure to cigarette smoke. Hence the full explanatory story about the origins of lung cancer needs to consider broader environments than merely the physiological breakdowns in the person who gets sick.

Most diseases have cognitive and social influences even if their primary causation is biological. For example, people are more likely to come down with influenza if they are stressed by social situations such as exams, and the placebo effect shows that merely believing that some worthless drug will make you feel better actually can make symptoms such as headache less distressing. But I want to focus on the mental illnesses whose cognitive, emotional, and social aspects are clearest. These are more commonly called disorders rather than diseases because so little is known about their causality, but medical advances should dissolve the differences, and in principle the ideas of illness, disease, and disorder should be equivalent.

MENTAL ILLNESS

Like the concept of disease, *mental illness* is better characterized by three-analysis than definition. Table 10.2 sketches exemplars, typical features, and explanations for mental illness. Standard examples of psychiatric disorders include depression, anxiety, schizophrenia, bipolar disorder, autism, Parkinson's disease, and Alzheimer's. The typical features of illnesses include symptoms such as problems

TABLE 10.2

Three-Analysis of *Mental Illness*

Exemplars	Depression, schizophrenia, bipolar disorder, autism
Typical features	Problems in thinking, emotion, social functioning
Explanations	Explains: cognitive, emotional, and social dysfunctions
	Explained by: breakdowns in molecular, neural, mental, and social mechanisms

in thinking, emotion, and social functioning, with different diseases presenting different symptoms. The intellectual point of saying that people have a particular mental illness is to explain their symptoms, for example using a diagnosis of schizophrenia to explain why someone is having hallucinations.

Mental illnesses typically disrupt such cognitive function as perception, inference, and memory. For example, a patient with schizophrenia may have the perceptual disruption of hallucinations and the inferential disruption of paranoid delusions. A patient with Alzheimer's disease initially has minor problems with memory that develop into major problems with memory and other cognitive and social functions.

Mental illnesses also have disruptions in emotional operations. People with depression have excessive sadness, and people with anxiety have excessive fear. Bipolar disorder produces swings between manic excitement and crushing depression. Schizophrenia can be accompanied by various emotions such as paranoia or complete apathy. Alzheimer's can cause various kinds of distress as memory and inferential abilities fade. A full theory of mental illness has to explain why cognitive and emotional functions are disrupted.

Social functioning is much of what people do, and it is not surprising that cognitive and emotional breakdowns also lead to social disruptions. People who are severely anxious or depressed have difficulty interacting with other people. The difficulties become even more severe with intense stages of debilitating mental illnesses such as schizophrenia and Alzheimer's. For depression and anxiety, the disorder can have social disruptions that feed back to increase depression and anxiety.

Diagnosing a mental illness is intended to explain why people have such symptoms of cognitive, emotional, and social malfunctioning. But how are we to explain mental illnesses? Other branches of medicine have made great progress in figuring out the breakdowns in mechanisms that produce diseases. For 2,000 years before the medical breakthroughs of the mid-nineteenth century, diseases were explained as imbalances in four bodily humors: blood, phlegm, black bile, and yellow bile. Diseases caused by too much blood could simply be treated by opening a vein.

Pasteur's discovery that some diseases are caused by bacteria provided the beginnings of much better explanations of disease, including a broad range of infectious diseases involving viruses, protozoa, and fungi as well as bacteria. But there are also kinds of disease with completely different mechanisms of action, such as nutritional diseases like scurvy, metabolic diseases like diabetes, genetic diseases like Huntington's, and cell division diseases like cancer. In all of these cases, much is known about how cell and organ mechanisms can break down and produce symptoms of disease.

Unfortunately, the study of mental illnesses has not been able to achieve the same mechanistic understanding. Using the example of depression, I fill in the question marks associated with the explanations of mental illness by identifying a complex of molecular, neural, mental, and social causes. I argue that the reason that it has been so hard to specify the causes of mental illness, and thereby fill in the explained-by slot in the three-analysis of mental illness, is that there are interacting causes operating at different levels.

DEPRESSION: SOCIAL COGNITIVE-EMOTIONAL WORKUP

Depression as a mental illness is much more than just occasional feelings of sadness. Rather, it is the prolonged experience of sadness along with other emotional states including feelings of hopelessness, worthlessness, and inability to experience pleasure. More than 10% of people have at least one episode of major depression at some time in their lives, with enormous personal and economic costs because of people's inability to work and maintain social relationships.

My account of depression has four components. First, in place of a definition of depression, I offer a three-analysis that provides exemplars, typical features, and explanations. Second, I provide a comprehensive social cognitive-emotional workup of depression that sketches the mechanisms that cause depression. Third, I develop a full causal explanation of depression by considering how to integrate molecular, neural, mental, and social mechanisms to explain why people experience prolonged sadness and the other serious symptoms of depression. Semantic pointer theories of emotion and communication enable this integration. Fourth, I discuss the implications of this causal account of depression for explaining the efficacy of treatments for depression, including the well-established benefits of combining drug treatments with psychotherapy.

Depression Three-Analysis

Table 10.3 sketches a three-analysis of the concept of depression in line with the best current medical accounts of depression. For exemplars, there are many famous people who are known to have experienced severe depression during their lives, ranging from nineteenth-century figures such as Abraham Lincoln and Kierkegaard to more recent writers such as Ernest Hemingway and Sylvia Plath, both of whom committed suicide.

The typical features of depression include prolonged sadness, inability to experience pleasure, changes in sleep and eating behaviors, and suicidal thoughts. The *Diagnostic and Statistical Manual of Mental Disorders* (DSM) of the American Psychiatric Association recommends diagnosing major depression based on the occurrence of five of nine of the following symptoms over more than two weeks:

1. Depressed mood most of the day characterized by sadness, emptiness, or hopelessness.
2. Markedly diminished interest or pleasure in almost all activities.
3. Significant weight loss or gain.
4. Inability to sleep or oversleeping.
5. Psychomotor agitation or retardation.
6. Fatigue or loss of energy.
7. Feelings of worthlessness or excessive guilt.
8. Diminished ability to concentrate or make decisions.
9. Recurrent thoughts of death.

The five-of-nine requirement is more of an administrative convenience designed to satisfy insurance requirements than a medically justified assessment based on a causal understanding of the disease. The actual diagnosis by medical professionals is a matter of recognizing a strong fit between the thoughts and behaviors of a patient and these typical features of depression, as well as considering the range

TABLE 10.3

Three-Analysis of *Depression*

Exemplars	Lincoln, Kierkegaard, Kafka, Ingmar Bergman, Hemingway, Plath
Typical features	Sadness, reduced interest and pleasure, sleep changes, weight changes, fatigue, worthlessness, hopelessness, suicidal thoughts
Explanations	Explains: sadness, suicide
	Explained by: interacting breakdowns in multilevel mechanisms

of possible causes of the depression. Done this way, psychotherapeutic diagnosis requires explanatory coherence, not just pattern matching.

The concept of depression should not only describe but also explain why peoples' thoughts and behaviors are abnormal. Ordinary sadness results from the losses and setbacks of human life such as failures in work or romantic relationships. Describing people as suffering from depression is supposed to provide a deeper explanation of why they are experiencing prolonged sadness along with other typical features of depression such as hopelessness.

The big gap in contemporary views of depression is lack of specification of the mechanisms that make people depressed. Knowing these mechanisms would make the explanations provided by the concept of depression far more satisfying, because it would go beyond just labeling people as depressed to indicate precisely what mental operations and breakdowns lead to prolonged sadness.

In the history of psychiatry, various explanations of depression have been offered. The ancient Greeks introduced the term "melancholia" to suggest that depression is caused by an excess of black bile, one of the four humors whose balance was thought to be essential for health. Freudians considered depression to be a psychological problem resulting from overreaction to loss. When pharmaceutical treatments for depression became available starting in the 1950s, psychiatry shifted to purely neurochemical explanations of depression, considering it to be a biochemical problem resulting from insufficiencies of neurotransmitters such as serotonin that are boosted by antidepressants such as Prozac and Zoloft. I offer a much more complicated causal story that portrays depression as multilevel emergence from molecular, neural, mental, and social mechanisms.

Concepts and Values

The social cognitive-emotional workup for depression has two different objectives. First, understanding depression benefits from identifying patients' concepts, beliefs, and other mental processes. Second, understanding the thinking of medical professionals (psychiatrists, clinical psychologists, social workers) who are treating people with depression benefits from identifying the concepts that they use to explain and help patients.

To begin, consider the concepts employed by sophisticated writers who have experienced depression, such as William Styron and Andrew Solomon. They describe intense and prolonged feelings that include the following: self-hatred, joylessness, worthlessness, anxiety, agitation, dread, tiredness, despair, desolation, loss, agony, loneliness, and humiliation. It would be easy to put these all into a value map but not illuminating because all of them are emotionally negative. Nobody wants to feel these emotions.

Medical professionals who treat depression have an expanded set of concepts for depression such as *mild, moderate, severe, major depressive disorder, bipolar disorder, dysthymia (chronic depression),* and *seasonal affective disorder*. These characterizations can have serious implications for treatments including small amounts of psychotherapy, various drugs, and electroconvulsive shock treatment and deep brain stimulation used for the most severe cases of depression. For example, in bipolar (manic-depressive) disorder, states of depression alternate with manic episodes that are the opposite of depression in being accompanied by enormous energy and inflated feelings about the self. Bipolar disorder is often treated with lithium, which reduces mania by biological effects on neurotransmitters and other brain mechanisms.

The value maps of medical professionals are much more hopeful than those of the patient suffering depression, because they include concepts suggesting the possibility of treatment and recovery. Figure 10.1 maps some of the values likely to be held by a medical professional who aims to help a depressed patient. Presumably, the professional has an emotionally neutral attitude toward the person at first, even while recognizing that the patient has negative characteristics of depression such as sadness, hopelessness, guilt, and fatigue, likely resulting from loss and/ or stress. However, the professional has the training and experience to think that various forms of treatment might help the patient and lead to recovery. The values of professionals who treat people with depression are best understood as semantic pointers that bind concepts and emotions.

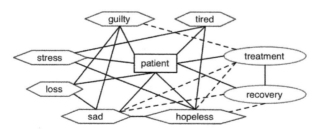

FIGURE 10.1 Value map of medical professional regarding a depressed patient. Ovals are emotionally positive, and hexagons are negative. The rectangle is neutral. Solid lines indicate mutual support, and dotted lines indicate incompatibility.

Images and Embodiment

To describe their conditions, people with depression use abstract concepts such as *hopeless* but also more specific images that can be visual and kinesthetic as well as emotional. The visual images most strongly associated with depression are of darkness and blackness, as in the "darkness visible" of William Styron and the "black dog" of Winston Churchill. Countless songs describe depression as having the blues. Additional visual images are mentioned in the discussion of metaphor.

Kinesthetic images are also part of depression, as when feeling down is accompanied by motor states such as difficulty in moving, for example finding it hard to get out of bed in the morning. The concept *depression* was originally both visual and kinesthetic, signifying a low place in the ground that is hard to climb out of.

Because depression is inherently emotional, emotional imagery is by far the most important kind. When people are depressed they find it hard to generate images of feeling happy and satisfied with their lives. Consistent with mood-congruent memory mentioned in earlier chapters, people suffering from negative moods tend to remember past events that were also sad, so the memories make them even sadder. Moreover, the forward-looking operation of mood-congruent imagination limits people to forming images of future events that are as sad as the current state, without the ability to generate emotional images of future states with feelings such as happiness and pleasure. The problem with depression is not only that the current emotional state is sad, as can easily happen with the setbacks of everyday life, but also that people find it hard to generate images of a better life in the future. They can imagine negative emotional states such as sadness and despair, but happiness and hope are hard to access from the past and project into the future.

Depression is embodied in several ways. The visual and kinesthetic images such as heaviness depend on the body's internal and external senses to generate the perceptions that get turned into images. Similarly, bodily experiences of pain generate imagery that is strongly tied with depression, as when people talk about the agony of heartbreak. In accord with the semantic pointer theory of emotions, all emotions are embodied because bindings include physiological states such as heart rates and facial configurations. Other symptoms of depression such as sleep difficulties, decreased libido, and increased or decreased appetite are also tied into bodily states.

But depression is also transbodied, because it goes beyond perception of internal and external states to include more abstract conceptions such as worthlessness and hopelessness. Both of these require an abstract representation of the self of the sort discussed in *Brain–Mind*, chapter 12. Cognitive therapy encourages people to revalence the self, that is, to attach more positive abstract values such as lovable and successful to the abstract representation of self.

Professionals' representations of patients are obviously transbodied through abstract concepts such as *major depression*, but I do not know whether psychiatrists, clinical psychologists, and social workers use embodied images to represent their patients.

Beliefs and Rules

People with depression are afflicted with a variety of emotionally negative beliefs, some true but others false. Beliefs about loss in love and work can be accurate without implying that the patient's situation will never improve. The job of a cognitive therapist is to identify beliefs that the patient can change as part of the process of improving overall mood. For each of the symptoms of depression, there can be a corresponding belief such as *I am sad* or *I am worthless* or *my situation is hopeless*. The attribution of sadness at a particular time is clearly true, but the ascription of permanent gloom, worthlessness, and hopelessness may be surmountable with treatment.

The medical professionals who treat patients with depression have different beliefs from those of the patients. They can agree that their patients feel sad and tired without sharing the belief that the situation of the patient is hopeless and that the patient will always be joyless. Clinical experience and research literature justify the medical belief that many people can be helped.

Chapter 4 described how people's behavior in romantic relationships are heavily influenced by embodied unconscious rules. What rules govern the thoughts, feelings, and behaviors of depressed people? At the most extreme, the conscious or unconscious rules, concern suicide: *If I kill myself, then I will cease to feel pain*. Other rules express futility, as in *if I try to do anything, then I will only feel worse*. The patient may operate with other rules that support the feeling of hopelessness, such as *nobody likes me*. Part of the contribution of the cognitive therapist is to make a person aware of these rules so that the patients can realize that the rules are both false and harmful.

The reason why these rules may be difficult to make conscious is their nonverbal character. Some of the concepts employed in the rules may be embodied perceptual ones such as *tired* and *heavy*. Many of the concepts in the rules concerned with mood are emotional, such as *sad* and *humiliated*, which are embodied through their incorporation of physiological representations. Hence the rules governing the counterproductive behaviors of people with depression are built out of embodied semantic pointers that are much less accessible to consciousness than

verbal expressions. Communication in romantic relationships can be difficult because unconscious multimodal rules are so hard to identify and share; for the same
reason, recovery from depression can be arduous even with therapy.

Unlike most patients, medical professionals have access to many different rules
about how the lives of depressed people can be improved. For example, if people
have mild to moderate depression, then their conditions can be improved by antidepressant drugs, psychotherapy, or the combination of these. If people have
severe depression resistant to psychotherapy and antidepressants, then their condition may be improved by electroconvulsive shock therapy or deep brain stimulation. If people have bouts of mania as well as depression, then their condition
may be helped by lithium. The job of the medical professional is to select from the
arsenal of treatment rules to help patients overcome their depression. Unlike the
unconscious emotional rules operating in the minds of patients, these rules are
verbally expressible and shareable.

Analogies and Metaphors

Depression involves complexes of emotions and physical feelings that are difficult
to put into words, so patients naturally resort to metaphors to describe their experiences. The discussion of imagery already mentioned some visual metaphors
for depression, such as describing it as the black dog. Pronouncing a person as
depressed was originally metaphorical, introduced in the middle of the nineteenth
century to suggest low points in a person's life. The previously used term "mel-
ancholy," from ancient Greek words for black bile, was used literally rather than
metaphorically because of the medical belief that prolonged sadness is caused by
an excess of black bile.

The following are some metaphors, richly relying on underlying analogies, used
by Andrew Solomon to describe his own experience with depression.

- If one imagines a soul of iron that weathers with grief and rusts with
  mild depression, then major depression is the startling collapse of a
  whole structure. . . . It is not pleasant to experience decay, to find yourself
  exposed to the ravages of an almost daily rain, and to know that you are
  turning into something feeble, that more and more of you will blow off
  with the first strong wind, making you less and less.
- Like childbirth, depression is a pain so severe as to be immemorial.

Depression is not literally structural collapse, decay, childbirth, or pain, but these
comparisons all help to convey the extreme distress that people experience.

Ordinary people also use metaphors, similes, and analogies to describe their depressed mental states. When the website depressionforums.org invited readers to report their metaphors for depression, it received dozens of responses, including the following:

- I am hanging off the edge of a skyscraper. My hands and arms will hold on and will not tire, but the fear, tension, helplessness, and anxiety are all there.
- Waking up every morning of your life with no sunshine, and it being (mentally) only November, a long, cold, desolate winter ahead.
- A weight of lead and treacle plying down on my chest and shoulders.
- I think of it like being in a canoe on the ocean and trying to paddle against the tide.
- It is like quick-sand. You can't get out by using the same methods (thought patterns) that got you into it. The more you struggle, the deeper you sink.
- It feels like being under water. It is hard to move, see, and breathe.
- Like being at the bottom of a dark, wet well, seeing a trickle of light and clawing desperately at the sides with bleeding fingers trying to reach it.

These comparisons to visual, tactile, and kinesthetic experiences enable people to help others understand their dire conditions.

Such metaphors and similes all vivify the physical and emotional depths of feelings of depression, but they actually increase despair because they provide no suggestions about how to recover. How can one get out of the well, or the quicksand, or the treacle? One therapist proposes a set of positive metaphors to help patients see that their situations are in fact improvable.

- Depression is really like a battery that's run out of power. All that firing off of the REM response at night tires out the system, meaning that rather than getting rested from your sleep, it's been tiring you out. As you begin to worry less and relax more during the day, you'll quickly begin to dream less at night. And the extra deep slow wave sleep you'll have as a result will immediately start to "recharge your battery" so that you'll begin to awaken with renewed motivation and energy.
- Imagine a boat going along a river, which has many different streams and smaller rivers running off it. If the way ahead is suddenly blocked, you don't just carry on as if nothing has happened! The boat needs to stop for a while in order to reorientate. It needs to do nothing for a bit. Eventually,

you may decide you can remove the blockage and continue the way you
were going or you might begin to see an alternate route you can take.
- You know, we all go up and down a little bit without becoming depressed,
  and that's fine. When you're travelling in a plane, the plane is constantly
  going up and down a little bit but you don't really notice it. Because, for
  the most part, the plane is traveling forward in the right direction.

Patients are encouraged to think of themselves as not being irrevocably trapped
but instead as analogous to a battery that can be recharged, a boat that is only
temporarily blocked on a river, or an airplane that is traveling in the right direction even though it is also going up and down. Hence metaphors, similes, and analogies can not only help people with depression to describe their mental states but
also to suggest ways in which those states can be changed.

Emotions and Actions

The typical features of depression listed in Table 10.3 indicate some of the emotions strongly associated with it, such as sadness, hopelessness, and worthlessness. Moreover, depression is distinguished by the absence of positive emotions
such as joy, interest, and pleasure. All of these emotional states can be illuminated
by applying the semantic pointer theory of emotions.

There is much more to understanding sadness than simply mentioning syn-
onyms such as "unhappy" and "sorrowful." Rather, the theory of sadness should
explain how bad feelings about loss originate from brain processes that combine
cognitive appraisals and physiological states. So we need to look systematically at
the psychological judgments that contribute to sadness, the physiological states
that correlate with sadness, and the brain operations that perform the integration
of appraisal and physiological perception.

According to appraisal theories of emotion, sadness results from a judgment
that events are inconsistent with the satisfaction of a person goals. People have
various goals such as those derived from biological needs for food, water, and
shelter, as well as those derived from psychological needs for social relationships,
work accomplishments, freedom from control, and having fun. When events such
as a difficult relationship or a work failure signal the inability to accomplish such
goals, then people tend to be sad as a result of the judgment. These appraisal judgments are inferences performed by parallel constraint satisfaction.

What physiological changes occur when people are sad? A review of numerous
studies of nervous system activation in emotion found that sadness is associated with physiological changes such as decreased heart rate, increased heart rate

variability, increased time between contraction of heart ventricles and blood ejection into the aorta, decreased diastolic blood pressure, decreased finger temperature, decreased skin conductance, decreased lung volume, and increase in carbon dioxide pressure. The body has internal sensors for detecting such changes that convey information to the brain. Sadness differs physiologically from other emotions like anger, fear, and happiness, which are accompanied by increases in heart rate and skin conductance rather than decreases.

Other physiological changes are causally correlated with sadness. Sad people have different facial expressions such as frowns, scowls, and crying. The can also have different body language such as slumping, folding arms, and moving laboriously. It is a mistake to ask whether the sadness causes these body changes or whether the body changes cause sadness, because both the emotion and the physiology are part of ongoing interacting mechanisms full of feedback loops.

What happens in brains when people are sad? One study of 26 males with happy and sad states induced by viewing slides of facial expressions reached the following conclusions:

Sad and happy mood in contrast to the control task produced similarly significant activations in the amygdala–hippocampal area extending into the parahippocampal gyrus as well as in the prefrontal and temporal cortex, the anterior cingulate, and the precuneus. Significant valence differences emerged when comparing both tasks directly. More activation has been demonstrated in the ventrolateral prefrontal cortex (VLPFC), the anterior cingulate cortex (ACC), the transverse temporal gyrus, and the superior temporal gyrus during sadness. Happiness, on the other hand, produced stronger activations in the dorsolateral prefrontal cortex (DLPFC), the cingulate gyrus, the inferior temporal gyrus, and the cerebellum.

It is obvious from this and other studies that sadness is not simply activity in a single brain area but rather depends on the interaction of numerous parts of the brain. The brain areas important for sadness as well as other emotions include the amygdala, the ventral lateral prefrontal cortex, and the interior cingulate cortex. However, according to the study quoted there is some neural differentiation among brain areas involved in sadness and happiness, just as there is differentiation in appraisal and physiology.

Sadness is usually the result of loss, which is associated with activity in brain areas already mentioned such as the insula, amygdala, and cingulate cortex but also in additional brain areas such as the habenula. In contrast, gains are neutrally represented with brain areas associated with reward and pleasure, such as the nucleus accumbens and ventral palidium. Cortical areas such as orbitofrontal and ventromedial areas function in considering both gains and losses.

How can we put diverse appraisals, physiological changes, and multiple brain areas into a mechanism that plausibly results in people feeling sad? The semantic pointer theory of emotions provides a suggestion. A semantic pointer occurs in a group of connected neurons that may operate in numerous brain areas because of the many long-distance connections among them. Inputs to the neural group supporting the semantic pointer include: neurons that perform cognitive appraisal by parallel constraint satisfaction; neurons that fire in response to sensors within the body for changes in physiological markers such as heart rate and facial expressions; and neurons that encode the situation that the sadness is about, which could be represented verbally, visually, or using other sensory mortalities.

Figure 10.2 shows a semantic pointer (pattern of neural firing) resulting from a representation of the situation that involves social rejection, appraisal that the rejection is incompatible with the person's social goals, and sensing of physiological changes such as lowered heart rate and facial expression. The semantic pointer may also include motor actions, such as the tendency to withdraw. The neural mechanisms of representation and binding put all this information together into a unified pattern of firing in a broad population of neurons across several brain areas, comprising the semantic pointer for sadness.

How does this pattern of firing result in the feeling of being sad? Answering this question requires the theory of consciousness from *Brain–Mind*, chapter 8, and *Natural Philosophy*, chapter 2. There are countless semantic pointers being formed in the brain all the time but only a few that are sufficiently powerful to

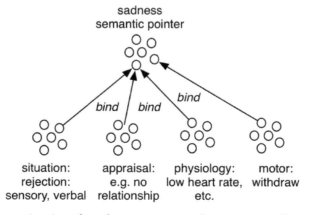

FIGURE 10.2 Semantic pointer for sadness as a pattern of activation in millions of neurons resulting from binding of representations of the situation, cognitive appraisal, physiological changes, and potential action.

outcompete other semantic pointers and cross the threshold into conscious experience. If the situation of social rejection is not important to the individual's goals, then the combined neural representation of appraisal, physiology, and situation will be outcompeted by other semantic pointers and therefore will not achieve the threshold required for the narrow band of conscious experience.

On the other hand, if the appraisal is strongly negative, the physiological changes are large, and the visual or sensory representation of the situation is prominent, then the neurons for the semantic pointer end up with strong patterns of firing. Under those conditions the semantic pointer for sadness will have a sufficiently strong pattern to outcompete other semantic pointers and break through into consciousness. The qualitative nature of the conscious experience that results is an emergent property of the complex neural process of representation, binding, and competition.

Worthlessness is another negative emotion associated with depression, but it is more complicated than sadness because it requires a binding that includes a representation of the self. People with depression often think of themselves as lacking in value and deserving of guilt. As described in *Brain–Mind* (chapter 12), a self-representation is a semantic pointer that combines representations of one's body, memories, and current states. If the current state is emotionally negative, such as the sadness caused by social rejection, then mood-congruent memory may only retrieve previous cases that also involved sadness and rejection. Then the cognitive appraisal of the self will conclude that the self is incapable of accomplishments that would be appreciated by other people, implying that the self is in fact worthless.

Joylessness, also called anhedonia, is the incapacity to find anything interesting or pleasurable. It requires a different kind of explanation than sadness does because it is the absence of emotional states such as joy. Like sadness, joy requires binding of the representations of the situation with the results of cognitive appraisal and physiological change. So explaining the absence of joy in circumstances that would normally bring pleasure to a person requires explanation of why the semantic pointer that normally results from this binding is not formed. Another possibility is that the semantic pointer for joy does get formed but fails to outcompete other semantic pointers for access to consciousness.

Take the example of someone who is so sad as the result of social rejection that there is no joy in usually pleasurable activities such as listening to music. The inability to generate musical pleasure, understood as the inability to form and bring to consciousness a semantic pointer with the appropriate bindings, can result for several reasons. First, neural activity may be insufficient to carry out the parallel constraint satisfaction that produces the inference that the activity of listening to music contributes to the goals of the thinker. Second, there may be insufficient physiological changes or insufficient detections of physiological changes to enable the brain to produce the representation of physiology that needs to be bound into the semantic pointer.

Third, there may be insufficient neural activity to perform the bindings of all the required representations of situation (music), appraisal (good music), and physiology (e.g., faster heart rate). Fourth, even if this semantic pointer is formed, it may be too weak in its firing activity to outcompete other semantic pointers so that the unconscious representation of something pleasurable never breaks through into the experience of pleasure. With sadness dominant, pleasure just cannot compete for the brain capacity for conscious experience. (See *Brain–Mind*, chapter 8, for conjectures about why this capacity is so limited.)

The question naturally arises why neural activity is sometimes not sufficient to carry out all of these functions of representation, binding, and competition. The most plausible answer comes from considering molecular processes involving genetics, epigenetics, and neurochemistry. These mechanisms are crucial for explaining why in some people sadness about loss leads to prolonged sadness and joylessness.

Like joylessness, hopelessness is a chronic absence of emotion subject to the same kind of explanation just given. Whereas joy and pleasure require the representation of a current situation, hope is a feeling about some desirable future state of affairs that requires appraisal and physiological perception on top of representation of something yet to happen. Appraisal results from evaluation of how the future situation might contribute to goals and needs. Because imagination is mood-congruent, people stuck in sadness will find it hard to generate scenarios in which a future situation accomplishes their goals. For the pleasurable feeling of hope, this appraisal needs to be combined with perception of physiological states and changes. People can be incapable of generating hope because of any combination of lack of appraisal, lack of physiological change, lack of binding, and insufficient strength to win in semantic pointer competition.

Psychotherapists can try to help depressed people to overcome sadness, joylessness, and hopelessness in numerous ways. Their major tool is to foster reappraisal by assisting the patient to deal with current losses and stresses in ways that suggest that future joys are possible so that hope is realistic. They can also affect patient's physiological states by suggesting how patients can adopt useful changes such as exercise, better diets, and avoiding substance abuse. Physiology and appraisal can also be influenced by recommended drug treatments.

Mental health professionals also have their own emotional reactions to patients and their progress, including compassion, sympathy, empathy, hope, frustration, annoyance, and despair. Inevitably, these reactions can have impacts on the emotional states of patients, ranging from the benefits of empathy to the harm of intolerance.

As *Brain–Mind* (chapter 9) explained, emotions often result in actions because of a complex of processes that include intentions and motor control. Sadness typically results in withdrawal and inactivity, including problems in forming intentions and acting on them.

Inferences

Feelings of sadness and prolonged depression are influenced by many kinds of inference. Cognitive appraisal requires complex inference about the relevance of the current situation to one's overall goals. If a situation has only one aspect and a person has only one goal, then appraisal can be accomplished by simple rule-based inference that says: *If the situation is X and the goal is Y, then the goal is satisfied or not.* But situations always have various aspects, and people have many goals based on their diverse biological and psychological needs. Appraisal needs to be a process that can comprehensively evaluate the relevance of the situation to multiple goals in order to infer an overall evaluation.

Parallel constraint satisfaction provides this evaluation through emotional coherence. Consider a case where a man's depression results from rejection by a woman he cares about. The initial sadness comes about because of unconscious, parallel evaluation that this event runs contrary to the man's goals that range from the psychological need for belonging to the biological need for sex. If the man's needs for autonomy or sexual variety were greater than his needs for relatedness and intimacy, then the breakup might actually lead to feelings of happiness. The overall appraisal of the rejection requires balancing multiple goals against multiple aspects of the situation, which parallel constraint satisfaction handles well. The overall conclusion resulting from parallel constraint satisfaction is the inference just that things are bad. Depending on other aspects of the situation, the overall appraisal could generate other emotions such as anger and resentment.

Physiological perception could also be described as a kind of parallel constraint satisfaction. Emotions involve changes in many physiological variables concerning the face, body, heart, skin, breathing, and autonomic nervous system activation. There are no simple rules connecting these variables to specific emotions like sadness and anger. Brain areas such as the amygdala and insula receive inputs from internal bodily sensors and attempt to come up with some coherent interpretation of all of these changes. The interpretation is nothing like a verbal description but rather just a pattern of firing in the affected parts of the brain. This pattern of firing is simpler than a semantic pointer for emotion because it does not include bindings for representations of the situation that causes the physiological changes, the appraisal of the situation, or the self that is having the emotions. Nevertheless, physiological perception can be viewed as a kind of inference based on parallel constraint satisfaction, like perception based on the external senses as described in *Brain–Mind*, chapter 2.

Hence both cognitive appraisal and physiological perception are plausibly inferences based on parallel constraint satisfaction. According to the semantic pointer theory of emotion, emotions result when the representations derived from appraisal and physiology are bound with representations of the situation and, often (for humans), with representations of the self. These bindings are not cases of inference or parallel constraint satisfaction, because binding performed by convolution is a much more straightforward operation in which neurons take existing patterns and generate new ones.

Considering mental mechanisms, we can identify several kinds of inference that contribute to feelings of sadness and worthlessness that characterize depression. Deduction might contribute if someone has general insecurity that generates inferences such as the following: I am always a loser, so I lost in the current situation. Inductive generalization can make people infer from current rejection and past reduction that they will always be rejected. More commonly than deduction or inductive generalization, however, abductive inference can support prolonged sadness through inferences such as: I was rejected. My being an inferior, worthless human being would explain why I was rejected. Therefore, I am an inferior, worthless human being.

The mechanisms of mood-congruent memory and imagination can block the accomplishment of more effective abductive inferences that would help a person to recover from sadness. Done properly, abductive inference to the best explanation requires consideration of alternative hypotheses. In the face of rejection, one needs to consider alternative possibilities, such as that a person who rejected you is mistaken or crazy. Then the rejected person can explain the sad situation in ways that do not generate permanent sadness or worthlessness. With better abductive inference, the sadness that inevitably accomplishes a difficult situation need not generate prevailing lack of joy and hope. A major contribution of psychotherapy should be to help people make abductive inferences about their situations and themselves that are both more accurate and more conducive to positive evaluations leading to enjoyable emotions. Then more rigorous inference to the best explanation contributes to better moods.

People suffering from depression may be blocked from making the motivated inferences that would improve their moods. Motivated inference occurs when people do not accurately assess evidence but rather reach conclusions because they help to advance their goals. People rarely have the goal of feeling sad and worthless, so motivated inference is not as available to depressed people. People with depression could actually use some of the positive illusions that make it easier to deal with the difficulties of life. There is even evidence that depressed people have more accurate perceptions of reality than people who succumb to positive illusions.

Why does depression get in the way of motivated inferences? First, as suggested by the discussion of abductive inference, mood may make it difficult for people to generate the hypotheses that they could then illegitimately infer because they fit with their goals rather than with the evidence. Second, even if people are able to consider alternative hypotheses, their positive goals such as feeling good about themselves may not be sufficiently active to be able to support the motivated inference that they really are basically good, despite recent setbacks. Hence people with depression rather than temporary sadness may be unable to perform the motivated inferences that generate the positive illusions that will make them happier in the long run.

Other emotional inferences—fear-driven and rage-driven—can also influence depression. People with depression may be highly susceptible to fear-driven inference that leads them to interpret situations as even worse than they are. Depression is often accompanied by anxiety, another negative mood that involves worries about the future rather than sadness about the past. People with anxiety are highly susceptible to fear-driven inference, because the intensely negative feelings about some future event will lead people to think that it is more likely to be true. As in the Othello syndrome mentioned in chapter 2, where jealous lovers go beyond the evidence to infer that they are being cheated, the anxiety associated with a negative hypothesis makes it more believable because of the intense attention it receives. Hence depressed people who also suffer from anxiety will be inclined to continue their negative view of the world based on fear-driven inferences.

Fear-driven inferences can also fuel rumination, the tendency of some people to obsessively dwell on issues. Rumination is strongly associated with depression, and the mechanisms of fear-driven inference and semantic pointer competition can explain why. For people to overcome depression, they need to replace sad emotional states with more positive ones. But repetitive concern with negative events prevents the formation and adoption of more positive interpretations and expectations. If you always focus on the losses that cause sadness, then you naturally infer that future losses are inevitable, so that alternative views about a better future either never get formed or are too weak to outcompete the sense of loss and sadness. Dwelling on sadness makes it seem inevitable, because the excessive attention produced by fear and rumination provides support for the interpretation that one's situation is irreparably bad.

Similarly, rage-driven inference (see chapters 2 and 6) can encourage prolongation of sadness, joylessness, and hopelessness. If rejection or other kinds of loss are explained by the actions and character of a person or institution, then people become angry in ways that generate harmful actions. For example, someone in a bad romantic relationship may become sufficiently angry to have an affair, which will worsen the relationship and its associated negative emotions.

Mental health professionals are as susceptible to emotional inferences as other people, but their training should help them to overcome them. Motivated inference can lead practitioners to overestimate the extent to which they can help depressed people recover. But this belief may be a valuable positive illusion that encourages renewed efforts to find the best therapies for diverse patients. Fear-driven inference, on the other hand, could lead to premature conclusions about the case being hopeless.

Nevertheless, psychotherapists can help patients to overcome depression by recognizing and altering their inference patterns, concepts, values, rules, metaphors, and emotions. Recovering from depression requires an emotional gestalt shift in the direction of more positive views of life.

In sum, several kinds of inference contribute to depression, starting with the parallel constraint satisfaction that operates in cognitive appraisals and physiological perceptions. More verbal inferences that are deductive, inductive, or abductive can also encourage sadness and lack of hope. Prolonged sadness is maintained in part because of the predominance of fear-driven inference over motivated inference that results from the frequently anxious and ruminative states of people with depression.

Communication

The discussion of depression has so far overconcentrated on the individual minds of people with depression and of professionals who treat them. But it is obvious that depression is also a social process, both in its origins and in its recovery. People's depressions are often triggered by social events such as being rejected by others in love or work. I discuss neurochemical causes of depression, but there are also social causes such as bereavement, divorce, and unemployment. Moreover, there is abundant evidence that recovery from depression can be helped by social support and professional psychotherapy. We therefore need to go beyond the cognitive and neural mechanisms so far discussed to consider social mechanisms of communication.

The semantic pointer theory of communication becomes helpful for understanding how social interactions can be major causes of depression. Communication among people is not simply transferring words from one head to the other but rather instilling complicated neural representations that bind verbal and nonverbal representations of situations with representations of appraisals and physiological states. Hence transfer and modification of semantic pointers is for more complicated than transfer of words.

Consider first the social causes of the generation of the semantic pointer of sadness. Social rejection can be purely verbal as in an email or letter, but in person it is likely to be associated with various kinds of nonverbal communication such as facial scowls and disdainful body language. These nonverbal expressions influence the recipient to undergo the physiological changes and negative cognitive appraisals that combine into sadness.

Once a person is down, sadness can be maintained and reinforced by hanging out with other depressed people. I mentioned the role of rumination in depression, explaining how excessive focusing on negative thoughts can contribute to fear-driven inference. Social rumination occurs when people in conversation focus jointly on negative aspects of events and interpretations, making each other all the more obsessed with what is making them feel bad.

The communication in social rumination is likely to be nonverbal as well as verbal, when people exchange facial expressions such as grimaces, body language such as exasperation, and verbal tones such as groans. Social rumination contributes both to social fear-driven inference and to ongoing negative appraisals of situations. It also contributes to hopelessness because the depressed person is part of a group where nobody can see a way out their joint difficulties. Hence both the onset of sadness and its prolongation can have social causes that result from communication that is much more than transfer of words.

Social rumination leading to depression is not the only kind of collective fear-driven inference relevant to medicine. People who get together to incessantly discuss their physical ailments can suffer from a kind of collective hypochondria, in which social communication encourages fear-driven focusing on undesirable outcomes. The result of collective hypochondria is a group of people who all end up with beliefs that are both false and unpleasant.

Fortunately, social communication can also contribute to recovery from sadness and depression. Friends and family members can use both verbal and nonverbal communication to convey to the sufferer that there are people who care. Through touch, smiles, and body language as well as verbal utterances, people can be encouraged to think that their situations are not entirely bleak. Such support may not be able to overturn initial sadness that results from genuine loss, but it can help to forestall or overcome the feelings of worthlessness and hopelessness that encourage prolonged sadness. If other people really care about you, then you have reason to believe that you are not worthless and to hope that things will get better in the future.

A major component of social support, whether from family, friends, or therapists, is empathy. Earlier chapters described three modes of empathy, by verbal analogy, mirror neurons, and multimodal simulation. All of these modes can help convey to the sufferer that the supporter has some understanding of what the sufferer is experiencing.

Verbal analogy tells the sufferer that the supporter has gone through a similar situation describable in words. Mirror neurons and multimodal simulation produce nonverbal communication through facial expressions and body language that enable the supporter to go through physiological changes that are similar to those experienced by the sufferer. Verbal and nonverbal expressions of empathy provide additional reasons for the sufferer to escape feelings of worthlessness and hopelessness, even if current sadness is unavoidable.

Friendship has been jokingly described as psychotherapy for poor people and can be helpful against depression without any theoretical basis if it combines support and empathy to help overcome negative thoughts. However, folk understandings of depression are often woefully inadequate, when depressed people are told to snap out of it or get their act together. Just as the semantic pointer account of cognition and emotion indicates that thoughts are not simply sentences in the head, the semantic pointer theory of communication explains why it can be so difficult to get people to change their overall mental states. People do not have voluntary control over their mental states, which depend on all the neural operations of representation, binding, and competition that go on below consciousness. Folk psychology has no inkling of the complexity of the processes of appraisal, physiology, binding, and competition that generate sadness and depression.

Compared to ordinary people, psychotherapists are trained with better theories and more systematic means of helping people go beyond preoccupations with negative thoughts. Freudian psychoanalysts thought that the key to overcoming depression was to take many sessions to probe back into the childhood origins of neurotic reactions to loss, but this time-intensive approach is less effective than cognitive-behavioral therapy and interpersonal therapy, which work more efficiently on a scale of months rather than years. However, patients with deep-seated problems resulting from trauma may require more intensive, long-term therapy.

Therapists using effective approaches try to help people achieve a better understanding of their situations concerning love and work. Cognitive changes such as improving abductive inferences about the causes of situations can modify emotional appraisal. Behavioral changes such as increasing exercise and decreasing use of drugs and alcohol can modify physiology. Effective therapists, however, are not simply cognitive-behavioral engineers, because sensitivity and empathy can also assist people with help to overcome sadness and the other emotional afflictions of depression. I provide further discussion of psychotherapy after considering molecular causes and treatments of depression.

DEPRESSION: MULTILEVEL MECHANISMS

The social cognitive-emotional workup of depression dealt with important cognitive, neural, and social mechanisms. But how can these mechanisms be integrated with the molecular mechanisms that are also known to be important for explaining depression? After outlining some of the important molecular mechanisms involving genetics, epigenetics, neurotransmitters, and hormones, I describe how depression results from multilevel emergence in a broad range of mechanisms.

Molecular Mechanisms

There are many reasons for believing that the explanation of depression requires attention to molecular mechanisms. First, depression tends to run in families: it is 2 to 4 times more common in people who have a close relative with a mood disorder. Identical twins are more likely than fraternal twins to share depression, and the same relation holds when the identical twins are adopted by different families. There are numerous genes that seem to be associated with depression, including genes involved in the production, reception, and transportation of serotonin, a neurotransmitter implicated in depression. Other relevant genes include ones that help the brain to modify connections between cells and a gene that affects the neurotransmitters dopamine and norepinephrine. So genetics involving genes, proteins, and various neurochemicals seems highly relevant to understanding depression.

Second, there is recent but mounting evidence that epigenetics is relevant to explaining depression. In identical twins, depression in one is only a partial predictor of depression in the other, so there must be environmental effects as well as genetic ones. Social learning is one kind of environmental effect where people are influenced by their social interactions with others in ways that can prompt depression. But a different kind of environmental effect occurs when the operation of genes is affected by chemical groups that can either enhance or limit their production of proteins that interact to have behavioral effects. Epigenetics is now seen as highly relevant to explaining aspects of personality, mental illness, and possibly even sexual preference. Studies are beginning to reveal that the genes affecting the operation of serotonin are subject to epigenetic modifications.

One of the main influences on chemical attachments to genes is cortisol produced by stress. A plausible chain between the social causes of depression and the molecular causes of depression is that social stress increases cortisol and cortisol changes the chemical modifications of genes, making people more prone to depression. Other epigenetic effects can make organisms more resistant to stress and depression: Baby rats that are licked more by their mothers have decreased DNA methylation of cortisol receptor genes leading to reduced cortisol and less stress.

Third, antidepressant drugs are often useful in treating depression, and their operation depends on molecular modifications such as increasing the functionality of the neurotransmitters serotonin, norepinephrine, and dopamine. The most commonly used antidepressants primarily affect serotonin by increasing reuptake so that neurons can release more serotonin to stimulate the firing of other neurons to which they are connected by synapses. Other antidepressant drugs are known to affect a broader range of neurotransmitters as well as chemicals such as BDNF (brain-derived neurotrophic factor), which is also relevant to neurogenesis.

The success of antidepressant drugs in the 1980s led some psychiatrists to consider depression as essentially a disorder of molecular imbalance to be treated by various medications that restore balance. This chemical explanation cannot be the whole story, however, because antidepressants are often more effective when used in conjunction with psychotherapy, which deals with the social, cognitive, and emotional causes of depression. Nevertheless, the sometimes successful treatments by antidepressants make it clear that neurotransmitters and other brain chemicals are an important part of the explanation as well as of the treatment of depression. The most severe forms of depression are often treated with electroconvulsive therapy, which also affects brain chemistry.

Fourth, depression is affected by hormones, which differ from neurotransmitters in that they are not simply passed from one neuron to another but rather circulate in the blood to affect many cells including neurons. The hormone estrogen, for example, seems to influence depression in the postpartum depression that accompanies the hormonal changes that occur after childbirth. The fact that women are twice as prone to depression as men may in part have a hormonal basis, but there are also many social causes such as stress derived from sexual assault and economic insecurity, as well as cognitive causes such as rumination.

Fifth, depression may be affected by chemical processes affecting neurogenesis, which is the daily addition of thousands of new neurons to the brain. Neurogenesis adds new neurons to the hippocampus, aiding in the formation of new memories. Stress increases the hormone cortisol, which reduces neurogenesis, which increases the occurrence of depression. One possible mechanism for this increase is that having fewer neurons makes it harder for people to interpret new information in ways inconsistent with their existing sad mood. Antidepressants affect not only neurotransmitters such as serotonin but also increase BDNF, which increases neurogenesis and thereby makes brains more flexible to move away from depression.

Therefore, explanation of depression cannot simply be cognitive and social but requires attention to molecular mechanisms concerning genetics, epigenetics, neurotransmitters, hormones, and neurogenesis.

Integration of Mechanisms

The major problem now is to understand the relation between the molecular causes of depression and the cognitive, neural, and social causes discussed previously. The need to integrate a broad range of mechanisms in the explanation of disease is not restricted to mental illness, because other diseases such as heart failure and diabetes can also be multifactorial, for example when a person's heart attack results from a combination of genetics, social stress, lack of physical fitness, and intense worrying. The challenge is to figure out how to integrate these different kinds of causes. The need for such integration is illustrated by postpartum depression, whose biological and psychosocial predictors have been reported extensively in distinct literatures.

The earlier application of the semantic pointer theory of emotions to sadness provides the key to understanding how to integrate social, mental, neural, and molecular mechanisms. I described how sadness can be understood as a neural process resulting from neural firing and binding into semantic pointers, so the mental and neural aspects of depression were merged. The remaining task is to connect social and molecular mechanisms to the semantic pointer ones. I have already done this for social influences on depression by virtue of the semantic pointer theory of communication, where verbal and nonverbal interactions with other people produce mental and neural changes including generation of sadness. But how do genetics, epigenetics, neurotransmitters, hormones, and neurogenesis influence semantic pointers?

The answer is that semantic pointers are patterns of neural firing, and all of the molecular mechanisms influence neural firing. The formation of a semantic

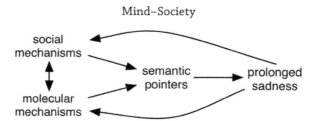

FIGURE 10.3 Approximate interactions among the neurocognitive mechanisms of semantic pointers and social and molecular mechanisms. Arrows indicate causality.

pointer such as sadness and its replacement by emotionally positive ones such as happiness requires many processes: neural representation by patterns of firing, binding of neural representations into more complicated ones that integrate sensory and motor information, and competition among the semantic pointers to reach consciousness. When neurotransmitters are low, as is usually the case in depression, then the firing required to produce new emotions fails to occur. Without adequate amounts of neurotransmitters, neurons cannot be stimulated to fire by the neurons that normally excite them.

Even if unconscious bindings do occur to make a happy interpretation of events possible, lack of neural firing can prevent happiness semantic pointers from outcompeting dominant sadness ones. The emotionally negative semantic pointers usually become established in the first place because of serious loss, for example in social relationships or work. The lack of neural firing in the new semantic pointer for happiness results from failures in mechanisms that require proper operation of genes, epigenetics, neurotransmitters, and hormones.

A simplified representation of this process is shown in Figure 10.3. Prolonged sadness results from neurocognitive processes in which mostly negative semantic pointers are formed and maintained because of social events and limitations in molecular mechanisms. The system shown is full of feedback loops because sadness can affect social interactions by making people withdraw from contact with others, which can increase stress affecting molecular mechanisms such as epigenetics. The causes of depression are not simply cognitive, neural, or molecular but depend on the full system of interactions that has the neural processing of semantic pointers at its core.

Multilevel Emergence

The interactions of social, cognitive, neural, and molecular mechanisms needed to explain depression show that prolonged sadness, worthlessness, joylessness, and hopelessness are the result of multilevel emergence. Depression is not simply the sum of changes in thoughts and neurotransmitters but instead depends on complex interactions among parts that range from the social to the molecular. People communicate semantic pointers with each other while genes are being modified by chemical attachments in ways that affect neurotransmitters and neural firing.

Identifying depression as multilevel emergence puts it in the same camp as numerous other mental/social phenomena discussed in earlier chapters, such as the success or failure of romantic relationships, the spread of ideologies, financial booms and busts, and the outbreak of war. Similarly, recovery from depression requires multilevel emergence through many changes in molecular, neural, mental, and social processes.

The shift to mechanistic accounts of the causes and treatments of mental illness require numerous kinds of conceptual change. This chapter has mentioned many new concepts that need to be introduced into scientific theories to explain mental illness, such as *semantic pointers, neurotransmitters,* and *epigenetics*. These neurobiological theories render obsolete many concepts that have been central to religious, folk-psychological, and Freudian explanations of mental illness, such as *soul, demonic possession, the blues, repression,* and *Oedipus complex*.

Besides introduction and elimination of concepts, adoption of new integrated theories of depression and other mental illnesses requires the two most radical kinds of conceptual change described in chapter 5, reclassification and metaclassification. I have reclassified depression as a process resulting from multilevel emergence rather than as a purely mental or molecular breakdown. My method of classification of mental illnesses is mechanism-based, not just the symptom scheme used in the DSM.

My explanation of depression as multilevel emergence is far richer than vague "biopsychosocial" approaches to medicine. I have specified the biological mechanisms in neural and molecular terms, linked them to the psychology of cognition and emotion via semantic pointers, and shown the relevance of social factors in depression by means of the semantic pointer theory of communication. It is not enough to state that depression has biological, mental, and social causes: these causes need to be spelled out mechanistically in terms of parts and interactions at different levels. Semantic pointer theories of cognition and communication show how to make the required connections.

TREATING DEPRESSION

I argued at the beginning of this chapter that disease occurs when symptoms result from the breakdown of biological mechanisms. Then the treatment of disease consists ideally not just in the alleviation of symptoms but in fixing the biological mechanisms that cause them. For medical conditions such as heart disease and diabetes that result from the interaction of numerous mechanisms, the ideal treatment is a combination of adjustments that fix all of the relevant mechanisms. The same holds for mental illnesses such as depression that emerge from at least four levels of interactions, all of which can helpfully be modified.

The need for repair of multiple mechanisms explains why the most effective treatments for many kinds of depression are combinations of psychotherapy and antidepressant drugs. The antidepressants help to repair the molecular mechanisms that are not functioning normally because of problems with the relevant genes and neurotransmitters. Improving processes of neural firing may make it easier for people to generate and maintain new semantic pointers that carry more positive emotions. Evidence is growing that antidepressants can help to repair epigenetic changes that increase stress and depression.

But people may still need help to generate and evaluate alternative explanations of their current situations and to imagine improved future situations. The verbal and nonverbal communication provided by therapists, including all three modes of empathy using verbal analogies, mirror neurons, and unconscious simulation, can make patients more hopeful about how current difficult situations can be transformed to allow the return of positive emotions such as happiness, hope, and self-confidence.

Psychotherapy can also influence the social causes of depression, because the therapist may help a depressed person to change a stressful social situation that is prolonging sadness. For example, talking with the therapist may help the patient to escape a bad romantic relationship or a toxic work environment. Group therapy helps some patients by providing emotional support and other kinds of verbal and nonverbal communication than include empathic reactions among people with similar afflictions.

Unfortunately, psychotherapy cannot influence the broader socioeconomic causes of depression such as poverty, unemployment, and discrimination. Even without massive social engineering, therapy and other kinds of social support can help individuals with depression to escape prolonged sadness and hopelessness.

SUMMARY AND DISCUSSION

This chapter has provided a multilevel-mechanism approach to disease, particularly the mental illness of depression. Medicine could also be considered much more broadly as a mental and social process involving the minds and inter-actions of many medical personnel, including doctors, nurses, administrators, support staff, psychologists, and so on. It would be fascinating to attempt social cognitive-emotional workups of more aspects of medical practice. My book *How Scientists Explain Disease* examined medicine as a cognitive and social process but neglected neural and molecular processes. Here I have looked at the neural and molecular mechanisms that are relevant to explaining mental illness. It would also be interesting to examine the history of medicine as resulting from multi-level mechanisms.

All mental illnesses involve breakdowns in neural mechanisms for emotions that do not simply reduce to isolated mental, social, or chemical causes. The case of depression shows how illness results from the interaction of many causes that can be social, cognitive, neural, and molecular. Depression emerges from the inter-actions of mechanisms at all of these levels in a way that exemplifies emergence rather than simple reduction.

Accordingly, treatment of depression often benefits from trying to repair mechanisms at multiple levels, most commonly by employing psychotherapy to make changes in mental representations and antidepressants to change neuro-chemistry. Diseases with complex causes require complex treatments to fix the interacting mechanisms responsible for them. Social cognitivism, the approach that integrates social, mental, neural, and molecular mechanisms, provides a new approach to explaining mental illness thanks to semantic pointer theories of cog-nition and communication.

NOTES

On the nature of disease, see Thagard 1999 and Murphy 2015. On medical rea-soning, see Patel, Atocha, and Zhang 2012. Darden, Pal, Kundu, and Moult 2018 discuss strategies for discovering disease mechanisms, which I take to be common ways in which biological mechanisms break down. Solomon 2015 acutely examines how medical knowledge is made.

On mental illness, see Sadock, Sadock, and Ruiz 2017, along with Bentall 2004, Murphy 2006, and Thagard 2008. *Natural Philosophy* (chapters 8, 10) discusses the relevance of mental illness to questions about moral responsibility. Anderson, Cheng, Susser, McKenzie, and Kurdyak 2015 describe the greater incidence of mental illness among immigrants. Thagard and Larocque 2018 model mental health assessment as explanatory coherence.

For overviews of depression, see Andrews 2010, Beck and Bredemeier 2016, Ghaemi 2013, and Solomon 2001. The diagnostic criteria for the DSM are in American Psychiatric Association 2013.

Görgen, Joormann, Hiller, and Witthöft 2015 discuss mental imagery in depression. Metaphors for depression are taken from: Styron 1990, Solomon 2001 (pp. 17, 81), and http://www.depressionforums.org/forums/topic/99359-your-metaphor-for-depression/. Recovery metaphors are at http://www.unk.com/blog/3-depression-metaphors/.

On appraisal dimensions of emotions including sadness, see Oatley 1992 and Sander, Grandjean, and Scherer 2005.

On physiological dimensions of emotions including sadness, see Kreibig 2010 and Niedenthal and Brauer 2012. The brain effects of lithium are reviewed by Malhi, Tanious, Das, Coulston, and Berk 2013.

Human psychological needs are discussed in Deci and Ryan 2002 and Thagard 2010b, which also provides an account of hope as an emotion. *Natural Philosophy* (chapters 6 and 7) shows the relevance of needs to morality and justice.

Neural correlates of emotion are reviewed in Kassam, Markey, Cherkassky, Loewenstein, and Just 2013 and Lindquist, Wager, Kober, Bliss–Moreau, and Barrett 2012. The quote about happy and sad moods in men is from Habel, Klein, Kellerman, Shah, and Schnieder 2005, p. 206. Arnsten 2009 describes how stress alters the function of the prefrontal cortex.

Thagard and Aubie 2008 model cognitive appraisal as parallel constraint satisfaction.

Depressive realism is the view that depressed people are actually more accurate in their judgments: Allan, Siegel, and Hannah 2007.

Berridge and Kringelbach 2015 review research on pleasure in the brain.

Craighead and Dunlop 2014 summarize evidence that the best treatments for depression combine psychotherapy and medication; see also DeRubeis, Siegle, and Hollon 2008.

Lane, Ryan, Nadel, and Greenberg 2014 examine psychotherapies from the perspective of neural mechanisms of memory.

Gotlib and Joormann 2010 discuss cognition and depression. Hong and Cheung 2014 review cognitive vulnerabilities to depression. On rumination, see Lyubomirsky, Layous, Chancellor, and Nelson 2015. Groß, Blank, and Bayen 2017 describe the operation of hindsight bias in depression.

Hames, Hagan, and Joiner 2013 review interpersonal processes in depression. Yim et al. 2015 explain postpartum depression as the interaction of social and biological factors. On stress and depression, see Hammen 2005.

On the genetics of depression, see Flint and Kendler 2014. For studies on epigenetics relevant to depression, see Meaney 2001; McGowan et al. 2009; Sun, Kennedy, and Nestler 2013. Melas et al. 2012 describe epigenetic effects of antidepressant drugs. Sahay and Hen 2007 review the role of hippocampal neurogenesis in depression.

PROJECT

Do a three-analysis of the concept *health*. Apply social cognitivism to other mental illnesses such as schizophrenia. Hints: Hallucinations result from breakdowns in the imagery mechanisms described in *Brain–Mind*, chapter 3; delusions result from breakdowns in mechanisms such as abductive inference, motivated inference, and fear-driven inference. Analyze and model the kinds of conceptual and emotional change experienced by people in effective psychotherapy. Do social cognitive-emotional workups for related professions such as nursing, pharmacy, dentistry, optometry, and veterinary medicine.

11

Law

LEGAL MECHANISMS

Aristotle said that the law is reason free of passion, but we have seen grounds for doubt that human thought is ever passionless. The law is often described as an institution but rarely as a set of mechanisms. Nevertheless, there are many mental and social mechanisms operating in disparate aspects of law, from the interactions between defendants and lawyers to the deliberations of supreme courts. This chapter examines these mechanisms, focusing on criminal investigations; civil law in which people sue each other is amenable to similar analysis. My examples are drawn from the common-law system operating in the United Kingdom, the United States, and Canada, but the pattern of explanation could also be used for different legal systems based on judges rather than juries.

My discussion of law will portray wrongful convictions as breakdowns in legal mechanisms, just as chapter 10 described diseases as breakdowns in biological mechanisms. This chapter also discusses the relevance of neural mechanisms to the fraught question of criminal responsibility: when and how should people be held responsible for their actions?

Recall that a mechanism is a system of connected parts that interact to produce regular changes. In social mechanisms, the parts are people and groups of people, and the interactions are by verbal and nonverbal communication. In murder investigations, for example, the most important people include the defendants, lawyers, prosecutors, witnesses, judges, and jury members, who are connected with each other in various ways. Defendants are connected to their lawyers by contractual agreements when the defendant hires the lawyer or by institutional norms when the lawyer is court-appointed. Prosecuting attorneys and police officers are connected because they are all part of the government legal apparatus. Judges and juries are connected because the judge plays an important role in the selection and ongoing instruction of the jury.

The interactions among parts in the legal mechanisms take place in diverse contexts. There are conversations between suspects and the police, between defendants and their lawyers, between police and prosecutors, and between judges and juries and deliberations among the jurors when they need to come up with a verdict. These conversations involve substantial transfer of verbal information, but they can also be nonverbal when speakers communicate their attitudes by gestures, body language, facial expressions, and tone of voice, and when pictures of physical evidence are presented. Trials are central to television shows, movies, and newspaper reports, but most criminal charges are resolved by plea bargaining, a very different kind of social interaction.

The aim of the criminal legal system is to protect the public by convicting the guilty, which should be accomplished by proper functioning of all of the systems parts and interactions. Sometimes, however, innocent people are convicted, raising the question of what went wrong with the people, communications, and institutions to allow this to happen. In this chapter a social cognitive-emotional workup of an egregious case of wrongful conviction helps us analyze the mechanism breakdowns that lead to legal mistakes.

Deepening the social mechanistic account of law requires looking at the underlying mental mechanisms that operate in the minds of all people participating. We need to consider their cognitions and emotions, all interpretable as neural mechanisms based on semantic pointers—patterns of firing that integrate multimodal information. Proper and improper workings in the legal system, including malfunctions such as wrongful convictions, depend on operations in the minds of defendants, lawyers, police, prosecutors, witnesses, judges, and jurors. Psychologists have identified systematic flaws in how participants in the system think, for example concerning the accuracy of eyewitness testimony. Incorrect legal decisions result from a combination of (a) faulty thinking operating in individuals and (b) faulty communication operating in groups of individuals.

Legal procedures require many kinds of thinking. Accused people have to decide whether to acknowledge guilt, plead innocence and go to trial, or pursue a plea bargain. Defendants presumably know whether or not they are guilty but still face important decisions about whether and how to deal with accusations. Their lawyers also need to make strategic decisions with respect to plea bargaining and trial strategy. Police need to decide which suspects to investigate, and prosecutors have to consider which cases are worth pursuing and what kinds of pleas to consider. These decisions are all practical inferences, aiming to come up with the best action in a given situation.

Other participants in the law are charged with figuring out what actually happened, which goes under the odd name of "fact-finding." Police investigators faced with evidence of a crime are charged with determining who committed it. Prosecutors need to make inferences both about the facts of the crime and about the feasibility of gaining conviction given the available evidence. Jurors and some judges are charged with trying to discern the facts of the crime but also sometimes need to make practical decisions about sentencing.

Probability

Some legal scholars assume that probability theory is the key to understanding inferences about the facts of a case. The task is to calculate the probability that an accused is guilty given all the available evidence, which can be written as $P(G|E)$. According to probability theory, this quantity can be calculated using Bayes theorem, which says that the probability of a hypothesis given evidence is equal to the result of multiplying the prior probability of the hypothesis times the probability of the evidence given the hypothesis, all divided by the probability of the evidence. In the legal case, this becomes $P(G|E) = P(G) \times P(E/G)/P(E)$. Ideally, it should be possible for prosecutors, police, jurors, and judges to plug in the probabilities and compute the probability of guilt given the evidence.

Unfortunately, in real life the needed probabilities are rarely available. Even if we had some wild guess about the prior probability of a person being guilty, taking it into account would conflict with the important legal principle that people should be assumed innocent until proven guilty. Estimating the likelihood of the evidence given the hypothesis of guilt is also problematic. If there were a deductive explanation of the evidence based on the hypothesis of guilt, then $P(E|G)$ would be 1. But the causal chains that might lead from the actions of the accused to the evidence such as fingerprints are looser than deduction requires, so that the probability of the evidence given the hypothesis of guilt will be indeterminate. Similarly, it is hard to attach any reasonable, precise number to the probability of the evidence in the denominator of the theorem. Hence the precision that is supposed to come from the use of Bayes theorem in legal inference is specious.

Explanatory Coherence

Then how are the fact-finders in a criminal case supposed to reason? A plausible answer is provided by the theory of explanatory coherence, which has been used in previous chapters to explain many aspects of human thinking, including inferences about the minds of others and medical causation. Analogously, fact-finding is inference to the best explanation of the evidence, ranging from physical evidence such as fingerprints and DNA samples to eyewitness testimony. The responsibility of police, prosecution, and jurors is to determine whether the hypothesis that the accused is guilty is a better explanation of the evidence than alternative hypotheses. The inference style is the same as that used by physicians and therapists whose responsibility is to determine what condition is the best explanation of a patient's symptoms.

Where do hypotheses about causes of crimes come from? The prosecution and the jury do not have the responsibility to generate new guesses about who might be responsible for the crime, but the police do. The form of inference used in hypothesis generation is abductive, with roughly the following form in legal cases:

Evidence shows that a crime has been committed.
   This evidence might be explained by supposing that person X committed the crime.
   Therefore, X might be the criminal.

This form of inference is obviously shaky, because other people might have been responsible for the crime, and there are cases where apparently criminal activity might have been accidental. To promote abductive generation into inference to the best explanation, it is crucial to consider alternative hypotheses and evaluate them with respect to the full range of evidence. In wrongful convictions, police, prosecutors, and juries often fail in both these requirements by focusing on only one suspect and by neglecting relevant evidence.

For assessing the best explanation, the most obvious requirement is that a hypothesis should explain more of the evidence than alternative hypotheses, but there are three complicating factors. First, the hypothesis should not accomplish its explanations by making a lot of unsubstantiated assumptions, for example with a complicated story about how and why an accused pulled off the murder. We want hypotheses that are simple as well as broadly explanatory.

Second, the question of motive is always important in legal considerations, which requires explaining why the accused committed the crime as well as stating how this supposition explains the evidence. For example, the claim that a suspect murdered a friend becomes more plausible if there is evidence that the suspect was angry at the friend for having an affair with a spouse.

Third, although evidence is important and needs to be explained, there are cases where some pieces of evidence are shoddy and may need to ignored, perhaps because of improper police handling, unreliable eyewitnesses, or corrupt experts. To deal with the complexity of alternative explanations, simplicity, motives, and unreliable evidence, inference to the best explanation has to be more than just counting the number of facts explained.

Hence legal fact-finding requires making judgments about explanatory coherence, about how all of the hypotheses and evidence fit together. This fitting may sound inordinately complex because it goes beyond the usual account of inference as step-by-step verbal reasoning. Fortunately, explanatory coherence can be understood as parallel constraint satisfaction, where the negative constraints connect alternative hypothesis about who was responsible for the crime and the positive constraints connect hypotheses to evidence and to higher level hypotheses such as motives. Efficient neural network algorithms can compute explanatory coherence even in complicated cases, working just as well with distributed neural representations like semantic pointers as they do with less psychologically plausible representations of hypotheses by single neurons.

Figure 11.1 shows the simplified structure of a legal trial. The hypothesis that the accused is guilty of the crime competes with hypotheses that someone else did

FIGURE 11.1 Explanatory coherence in a simplified legal case. Solid lines indicate positive constraints based on explanations, and dotted lines indicate negative constraints based on explanatory incompatibility.

it. They compete to explain the evidence, and confidence that the accused is guilty increases if there is a clear motive that explains why the crime was committed.

Using parallel constraint satisfaction, human brains are well-suited for making judgments of explanatory coherence that evaluate competing stories about criminal actions. But we know from documented wrongful convictions that police, prosecutors, judges, and juries do not always carry out these judgments as responsibly and accurately as they should. A theory of legal inference should be able to explain not only how it works in people's minds when all goes well but also how inference sometimes fails to live up to normative standards.

Emotional Coherence

The theory of emotional coherence fills this gap. Previous chapters documented many cases in which people succumb to motivated and fear-driven inference, for example in romantic relationships and political ideology. Both error patterns result from emotional coherence, in which people's thinking is driven by feelings rather than by cold assessment of hypotheses and evidence. Prosecutors, police, judges, and jurors can all have motivations to find someone guilty that lead them to ignore relevant evidence and fail to consider alternative hypotheses. Social biases such as racism motivate people to assign guilt to people they do not like.

In addition, police have other motivations such as wanting to clear cases rather than to leave them open. Prosecutors are also motivated to secure convictions, especially in the United States where they are sometimes elected rather than appointed. Jurors can be biased by desires to conform to the expectations of other members of the jury or court and also by a desire to get the trial over with. Judges can be biased by motives to support the police and prosecution.

No human brain has a firewall between cognition and emotion, so it is no wonder that people's goals and attitudes sometimes lead them to fall short of the standards of inference to the best explanation based on exploratory coherence. The social cognitive-emotional workup of a notorious case of wrongful conviction will provide a detailed example where motivated inference swamped explanatory coherence in the conviction of an innocent man.

It might seem that intrusions of motivated inference into explanatory coherence are always wrong, with inference to the best explanation to be paramount over emotional coherence. This requirement is usually correct, in law, science, and everyday life, but there are occasional exceptions. Previous chapters described values as emotional brain states, and sometimes they have a legitimate role to play in factual inference based on providing differing thresholds of belief.

In science, it is legitimate to demand more evidence for hypotheses that could have dire impacts on human society, for example concerning potentially dangerous new technologies. One way to deal with this problem would be to demand that potentially dangerous hypotheses have a higher probability before acceptance, but it is hard to make sense of probability here in either of the two standard ways, as a frequency in a population of events or as a subjective degree of belief. The values of science include promoting human welfare as well as achieving truth and explanation, and the value of benevolence can enter into scientific inferences by placing some constraint on how much a hypothesis must be better than alternatives at explaining evidence in order to qualify as acceptable.

In the common law tradition of criminal law, one value that is supposed to operate in criminal trials is that convicting the innocent is worse than acquitting the guilty. From the perspective of probability, this makes no sense, and civil lawsuits do just operate on the preponderance of evidence rather than having to establish guilt beyond a reasonable doubt. Despite their prominence in Anglo-American law, the principles of the presumption of innocence and reasonable doubt are taken as givens rather than as subjects of analysis and justification.

The presumption of innocence is a value that arose historically because of excessive power that enabled officials to judge as guilty anyone they wanted. Requiring convictions to show guilt beyond a reasonable doubt encourages jurors to temper their assessments of evidence by a concern not to convict the innocent, intended as a value rather than as anything like a prior probability. There are no verbal algorithms for incorporating this value into jury deliberations, which rely on brains to unconsciously satisfy constraints that derive from both explanatory coherence and emotional coherence.

Figure 11.2 shows how the value of the presumption of innocence can serve as a constraint on accepting a hypothesis of guilt. Normally, a hypothesis can be

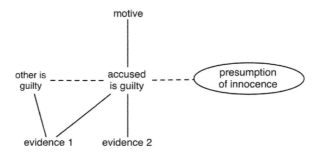

FIGURE 11.2 Legal trial as combining explanatory coherence with the value of presumption of innocence as an additional negative constraint, shown by a dotted line, whereas positive constraints are solid lines.

accepted if it provides a better explanation of the evidence than the alternatives, but the extra constraint makes it harder to conclude guilt unless the evidence is solid and the hypothesis of guilt is substantially better than competing hypotheses. Having the presumption of innocence count against the claim that the accused is guilty should ensure that the claim is not accepted unless it provides a substantially better explanation than alternatives.

Similarly, in science the motivation not to harm people can legitimately enter into considerations of whether to accept theories that have potentially dangerous implications. The value of promoting human welfare serves as a practical constraint on accepting hypotheses unless they are much better than others. In both science and law, however, it would be a mistake to have extraordinarily strict values such as never believing anything dangerous or never convicting the innocent, because there are other truth-dependent practical values that apply, such as keeping criminals off the streets.

The problem in criminal law is to separate the narrowly legitimate motivated inference based on reasonable doubt from all the biased motivations that people inevitably bring to legal and other situations. But the importance of reasonable doubt in law and of social values in science show that mingling explanatory and emotional coherence is not inherently wrong. Chapter 12 argues that the emotional character of values does not prevent them from sometimes being rational, because emotions include a process of cognitive appraisal that can be done rationally in line with human needs.

Besides fact-finding, the legal system also involves practical decisions such as whether to prosecute a suspect and what sentence to give after a conviction. Economists would say that such decisions should be based on calculations that maximize expected utility, but chapters 6, 7 and 9 cast doubt on this account. More plausibly, the legal decisions about what to do are based on emotional coherence that takes into account appropriate goals such as following the law and keeping society safe from criminals. Inevitably, however, inappropriate emotional attitudes can creep into sentencing and other legal decisions, for example when racism and other forms of prejudice lead to biased decisions.

This discussion of legal coherence has concerned individual minds that integrate considerations of evidence, hypotheses, and values. But law, science, and everyday life are social enterprises in which people reach their conclusions in large part through their interactions with others. In legal trials, jurors' inferences depend on information furnished by people such as police, witnesses, and judges. Moreover, motivations can be influenced by emotional communications coming from lawyers and other participants in the legal system. I now turn to a concrete example of how social interactions can influence judgments of coherence in individual minds.

WRONGFUL CONVICTION: SOCIAL COGNITIVE-EMOTIONAL WORKUP

In 1988, Ron Williamson was convicted in Ada, Oklahoma, for the 1982 murder of Debra Sue Carter. He was five days away from execution in 1995 when a district court judge ordered a retrial, and he was finally exonerated by DNA evidence in 1999. My workup of this case is based on the detailed account provided by John Grisham in his nonfiction book *The Innocent Man* and has been informed by the insights about psychological limitations in legal contexts provided by Dan Simon in his comprehensive *In Doubt*.

The participants in the long legal process included Williamson and his co-accused Dennis Fritz, the members of the Ada police department, and the county district attorney Bill Peterson. Witnesses at the trial against Williamson included Glen Gore who was later implicated as the real murderer. Also involved were Williamson's reluctantly appointed defense attorney, the judge and jury at his trial, and eventually a more competent attorney aided by the Innocence Project and the staff and judge of the US District Court.

A full explanation of the wrongful conviction and its overturning requires attention to the mental mechanisms in each of the participants, as well as to the social mechanisms that governed their interactions.

Concepts and Values

There was no direct evidence connecting Williamson with the murder of Carter, so it is puzzling why the police investigated him years after the murder, why the district attorney prosecuted him, and why the jury convicted him. Ada police knew Williamson well as a failed athlete, wild drunk, womanizer, and accused rapist from a charge some years before. As the value map in Figure 11.3 illustrates, most of these concepts have strong negative values, making it easier for the police to assign to him the negatively valued concept of murderer. The guess that Williamson

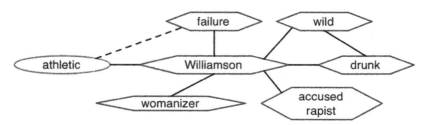

FIGURE 11.3 Value map of police view of Ron Williamson. Ovals are emotionally positive, and hexagons are negative. Solid lines indicate mutual support, and dotted lines indicate incompatibility.

might have raped and killed Carter had no explanatory coherence, but it fit well with the negative emotional values that the police had already assigned to him.

Similarly, the jury could assign negative concepts to Williamson based on witness testimony and his erratic behavior in court stemming from his mounting schizophrenia. The key concepts that the jury needed to be able to apply in this case were *guilty* and *innocent*. My discussion of reasonable doubt suggested that innocent should be given a higher value than guilty, but the behavior of the police, prosecution, and jurors of Ada showed no signs of this preference. They were inclined to assign guilt because it fit with their already negative view of Williamson. Witness testimony introduced other concepts into the deliberation, including *rape, kill, blood, hair sample,* and *jail*.

In other trials, additional concepts can play a role in legal deliberations including racial stereotypes. Many of the convicted prisoners exonerated by the Innocence Project have been Black men convicted by White juries.

Images and Embodiment

Images are important in criminal trials because of the need to report and interpret visual evidence such as fingerprints and blood spatters. Auditory evidence is also relevant, for example when jailhouse snitches report remarks by the accused. Rarely, other kinds of sensory imagery can also be relevant, such as scents associated with the crime.

The mental processes of eyewitness testimony are complex and easily subject to distortion, as shown in the high proportion of cases in the Innocence Project where wrongful convictions resulted in part from inaccurate reports. To identify a subject as present at a crime, the witness has to: see what happened; remember it by storing it as a visual image; retrieve the image from memory days, months, or years later; and finally compare the retrieved image with the perception of the accused presented in a photograph, lineup, or in court.

Because human memories are not stored intact like computer files but instead are subject to decay and distortion by subsequent memories, the process of matching a retrieved image against a perception or other representation of the accused may be highly unreliable. Questions by police and prosecutors, as well as the practice of rehearsing testimony before a trial, can easily lead witnesses to misremember what actually occurred, even when they are motivated to tell the truth. Jurors are heavily inclined to believe eyewitness testimony, lacking knowledge about the extensive psychological research concerning its unreliability. Imagery can be distorted as evidence even more easily when witnesses, police, and prosecutors are motivated to find the accused guilty.

Jurors are also inclined to believe the confessions by suspects that arise during police investigations. It seems obvious that a confession provides strong evidence for the hypothesis that the person confessing is actually guilty. But that presumption is undercut by the findings of the Innocence Project that has used DNA testing to exonerate many convicts who confessed. Police investigations can actually induce sensory memories in people that make them think they might have done the crime. People sometimes confess just to get a break from arduous interrogation. The Ada police had previously used a weird technique of getting people to imagine that they were dreaming that they had committed the crime, and they got a sort of confession out of Williamson as part of a dreaming exercise.

Other parts of the case against Williamson were fabricated using imagery. An eyewitness Glen Gore reported seeing Williamson talking to Carter in the bar the night she was killed. Jurors naturally inferred that this drew a connection between Williamson and Carter and suggested a possible motive for him assaulting her, but the jurors had no awareness that Gore was motivated to make the police happy and to distract them from the suspicion that he was the murderer. Auditory imagery against Williamson was a report by long-time criminal Terri Holland, who had been in jail with Williamson and said that that she had overheard Williams describing his crime. Jurors tend to take such reports as accurate evidence pointing to guilt, but the section on inference discusses the alternative explanation that jailhouse stitches are just trying to work deals with the police and prosecution.

One factor that might have provided visual evidence for Williamson's innocence was a bloody palm print on Carter's wall that was initially judged by experts to be neither Carter's nor Williamson's, suggesting the presence of someone else as the actual murder. The prosecution was highly motivated to remove this interpretation, so they had Carter exhumed after four years and found an expert to say that the palm print might actually have been Carter's. Because Williamson's publicly paid lawyer was blind, he was unable to visually inspect some of the evidence such as the palm prints, and the state refused to pay for any assistance for him.

Because of the importance of visual imagery, auditory imagery, and emotion, it is fair to describe legal proceedings as embodied. Participants from police to jurors all use their sensory-motor representations to capture what might have occurred in the criminal situation. However, embodiment is far from the whole story of legal proceedings, which unavoidably also use abstract concepts such as *guilty, innocent,* and *evidence.*

Beliefs and Rules

Understanding the mental and social mechanisms in legal proceedings requires attention to the many beliefs held by the participants, including defendants, lawyers, police, prosecutors, judges, and juries. Williamson's most important belief was that he was innocent, supported by other beliefs such as that he had never had any contact with Carter. It should not matter whether a defendant's lawyer believes he or she is innocent or not, but perhaps Williamson's lawyer would have done a better job if he had firmly believed in Williamson's innocence.

The police investigators and the prosecuting attorney clearly believed that Williamson was guilty, despite the lack of evidence for this conclusion. The jury's responsibility is to form beliefs about whether the accused is guilty or innocent, without preconceptions, but in a small city like Ada the jurors were likely predisposed to believe that Williamson was guilty, given his dissolute past and the fact that the police had charged him.

The prosecution did give the jury some reasons to believe that Williamson was guilty. Hair analysis said that samples from him were microscopically consistent with some of the hairs found at the murder scene. In an intense interview, the police impelled Williamson to say that he had a dream about killing Carter, including stabbing her, which was not how she died. The jury was not made aware that Williamson was having severe mental problems that were being treated with antipsychotic medication. Glenn Gore, who was in jail on kidnapping and assault charges, testified that Carter had asked Gore to save her because Ron Williamson was pestering her, so the jury acquired the belief that Williamson had opportunity and motive.

Legal proceedings are governed by rules concerning evidence. To be presented in an American trial, evidence must be relevant, making propositions about the facts of the case either more probable or less probable than they would be without the evidence. Relevant evidence must also be material, linked to the legal principles of the case. Even if evidence is relevant, the judge may exclude it for being likely to cause unfair prejudice that outweighs its probative value. Hence legal rules are applied by judges to influence the beliefs acquired by the jury.

Analogies and Metaphors

In Grisham's recounting, analogies and metaphors do not seem to have played much of a role in the Williamson case. The police might have thought that Williamson's alleged behavior with respect to Carter was analogous to his previously dropped charge of sexual assault and to his generally irresponsible actions. Grisham emphasizes a different comparison, between police actions in Williamson's case and their elicitation of a bogus dream confession in an earlier one.

In common law systems, legal precedents are often an important kind of analogical reasoning, when lawyers argue that an issue should be treated in a certain way because it is analogous to a previous one for which legal decisions were made. But such precedents do not seem to have contributed much to legal decisions in Williamson's case.

Emotions and Actions

Emotions are not supposed to contribute to legal fact-finding, as shown by the requirement of excluding evidence that is more prejudicial than probative. Inevitably however, the brains of everyone involved mix cognitions and emotions in ways that can severely distort the proceedings. The discussion of values concerning guilt and innocence showed that these are not purely probabilistic concepts because of associated emotional attitudes. Similarly, the doubt that a jury is supposed to begin with concerning the guilt of an accused has an emotional component, a feeling rather than a probabilistic judgment.

Also emotional is the suspicion that investigating police direct toward possible subjects. To be suspicious of people for committing a crime is not merely to think that there is some probability that they did it but also to have a negative emotion connected to the nasty crime that they might have committed.

Inevitably, presentation of gruesome details in a murder trial evokes negative emotions such as shock, outrage, and disgust in the jury. Previous chapters have argued that trust also has an emotional component, and small-town jurors are much more likely to trust the police and prosecution than a suspect with a dodgy past. Unscrupulous prosecutors can attempt to inspire emotions in jurors by yelling and acting angry about the accused. Although the law is not supposed to work this way, emotions naturally influence the motivated inferences that police, prosecutors, judges, and juries naturally make.

Inferences

I argued that explanatory coherence provides a more plausible account of inference in legal cases than probability theory can provide. I now make the argument more concrete by considering the Williamson case. For wrongful convictions, a full theory of legal inference should be able to explain how four kinds of conclusions come about.

First, we need to understand the inference involved in the decision by police and prosecution that makes someone a suspect. Second, we need an account of what relationships of evidence and hypotheses lead a jury to have confidence that the suspect is guilty. Third, for wrongful convictions, it should be possible to say how a proper consideration of the evidence and the law would have led to acquittal rather than conviction. Fourth, on top of the previous considerations of explanatory coherence, we need a richer psychological theory of how it can be distorted by motivated inference. Purely probabilistic theories of legal inference have no way of explaining why people are so naturally distracted from the evidence to reach biased conclusions. In contrast, because explanatory and emotional coherence are both brain process relying on the same underlying neural mechanisms of parallel constraint satisfaction, it is easy to see how people blend them.

In investigating a crime, police have to generate hypotheses about likely suspects. This hypothesis generation is far from random because it is shaped by the facts of the case and goal-oriented forms of inference such as abduction and analogy. Sometimes the police can generate hypotheses easily, for example, if they can identify the fingerprints on a murder weapon. Then they can consider the following abductive inference:

Murderers sometimes leave their fingerprints on the murder weapon.
　X left fingerprints on the murder weapon.
　Therefore, X might be the murderer.

The police in the Carter case did not have such immediately available evidence for an abductive inference, so they fell back on an even looser kind of analogical inference:

The Carter case included a sexual assault.
　Williamson had been accused in another sexual assault.
　So he may have similarly done the Carter sexual assault and her murder.

This analogy is very weak, although the police were also aware that Williamson occasionally became violent and had been arrested before.

Once a suspect has been identified and the evidence has accumulated, the prosecution has to decide whether the case is strong enough to go to trial. The prosecutor needs to be able to infer that the members of the jury will find the defendant guilty. The inference of the prosecutor and the prosecutor's mental simulation of the prospective jury are both based on considerations of explanatory coherence.

The prosecutor should judge that the hypothesis that the suspect is guilty is the best explanation of the evidence and that the jury will agree.

In the Williamson case, the inference to the best explanation has the following form and content:

1. There is evidence that Carter was murdered and raped, that Williamson reported imagining doing it, that he was heard in the jail by Terri Holland saying that he imagined doing it, that Gore was told by Carter that Williamson was pestering her, and that Williamson's hairs matched ones found at the crime scene.
2. The best explanation of all this evidence is that Williamson murdered Carter.
3. Therefore, Williamson murdered Carter.

Figure 11.4 concisely displays the structure of this inference, showing how a naïve jury member might indeed conclude that Williamson was the murderer because this hypothesis is coherent with the evidence. The claim that Williamson was guilty explains much more than the alternative hypothesis that someone else did the crime and is explained by the motives of lust and anger supported by the report by Gore that Williamson was pursuing Carter in the bar.

More objective reasoners, however, such as the district appeals court and Grisham, can notice that there are alternative explanations that should be considered in a fair judgment of explanatory coherence. Williamson's vague and erroneous confession could be explained by the extreme stress placed on him by police investigators. Dan Simon reports that the standard techniques of interrogation used by American police are unreliable and can easily produce false confessions in

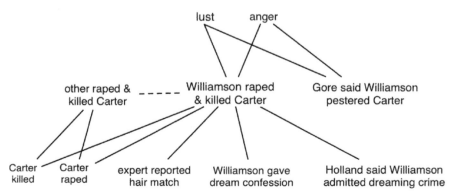

FIGURE 11.4 The explanatory coherence of the prosecution's case against Williamson. Solid lines indicate explanations, and the dotted line indicates incompatibility.

people who are intensely pressured for hours. Williamson did not actually confess to doing the crime but only to imagining doing the crime.

Explanations of why jailhouse snitches say what they do might include that they are telling the truth, but there are strong alternatives such as motives to curry favor with the police and prosecution. Terri Holland was allowed to plea-bargain her way out of legal trouble, and she also had another motive for speaking against Williamson, whom she thought had assaulted her sister.

Glen Gore had various reasons for connecting Carter with Williamson, including trying to please the police who were investigating him for other crimes and also wanting to deflect attention from himself as a possible suspect. An alternative explanation of why a forensic expert reported a match between Williamson's hairs and ones found at the crime scene is that the expert was biased and incompetent. Thus there were alternative explanations for all the pieces of evidence that seem to support Williamson's guilt. Moreover, the jury was never told that another man had (erroneously) confessed killing Carter.

The bloody palm print at the scene could have supported the hypothesis that someone other than Williamson was guilty. But the exhumation of Carter's body led to the conclusion that the print was hers. A plausible explanation of the change in expert opinion about the palm print was that it derived from the prosecution's strong motivation to find Williamson guilty.

If the jury members had been aware of all these alternative explanations and evidence of someone else's confession, then they should have had difficulty finding Williamson guilty beyond a reasonable doubt, especially if they were working with the value of presumption of innocence shown in Figure 11.2. The goal of not convicting the innocent would have had a legitimately motivated, inhibitory effect on the acceptance of the hypothesis of guilt, tipping the balance away from guilt in such close cases.

Unfortunately, the jurors did not do the full assessment of explanatory coherence but instead bought the much simpler prosecution story shown in Figure 11.4. The jurors, like the police and prosecutor, were motivated by negative emotions to find Williamson guilty. Figure 11.5 expands Figure 11.4 to show the motivations that seem to have been operating in this case. People wanted Williamson to be guilty because they did not like him and because they wanted the Carter case to be solved, as shown by the circles on the left. They ought to have been working instead with the value of presumption of innocence shown on the right of the top of Figure 11.5. Moreover, police and prosecutions operate with other motivations such as wanting to enhance their own reputations. Jurors can also be motivated to be liked by other jurors and to be viewed as responsible, law-supporting citizens.

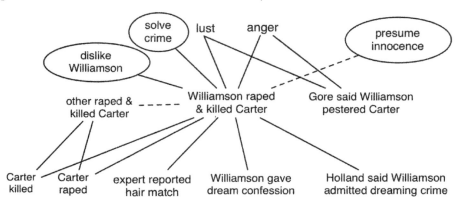

FIGURE 11.5 Motivational contributions to the prosecution's case against Williamson. Solid lines indicate positive constraints, and the dotted lines indicate negative constraints. The circles on the left indicate inappropriate motivations, and the circle on the right indicates the legitimate motive of presuming innocence.

In sum, explanatory coherence provides a rich account of how objective people such as the district appeals judge reasoned in order to doubt Williamson's guilt. But it also shows how a narrower view may conclude that the accusation was coherent with the evidence. Most psychologically interesting, explanatory coherence meshes with emotional coherence to produce motivated inference and a full account of how the conclusion that Williamson was guilty might have been made erroneously.

Communications

So far, the social cognitive-emotional workup of the Williamson case has concentrated on mental mechanisms operating in individuals, neglecting the crucial social mechanisms of communication among the participants. Understanding how the law works undoubtedly requires attention to the psychological processes so far discussed, from concepts and values to explanatory and emotional coherence. But the legal system is also replete with social interactions.

Consider first the communications between defendants and their attorneys. Lawyers need to inform their clients about legal matters, while the clients provide factual information that might be relevant to their defense. Emotional communication is also important, for example when the vehemence of protests of innocence are taken by an attorney as reason to go for an acquittal rather than a plea bargain. In the United States, the vast majority of cases are settled by plea bargains rather than trials, which requires the lawyer to emotionally communicate both factually and emotionally how the accused might be better off taking a deal rather than risking a conviction that would lead to a more substantial punishment.

Even more intensely, the communication that takes place between defendants and police investigators during interrogations involves emotional manipulation. The Reid Technique of interrogation that is widely used in the United States is aimed at extracting confessions, not learning the truth. Police often use intimidation and exhaustion to try to break down the resolve of the accused. They use assertions and emotional displays such as anger to try to convince the accused to confess. Also important are communications between the police and the prosecution, particularly when the police provide the prosecution with facts about relevant suspects and the available evidence.

The most publicly visible communications take place in the trial where the members of the jury are the major targets, listening to witnesses, prosecutors, defense attorneys, and the judge. Verbal communication is enriched by such nonverbal means as facial expressions, gestures, body language, and tone of voice. Lawyers and prosecutors work to influence the cognitions and also the emotions of the jurors, who have the opportunity to evaluate the credibility of the witnesses. There can also be a subtle kind of communication between the defendants and the jury, who watch for the reactions and behavior of the accused as the trial unfolds.

Inside the jury, the members have extensive discussions, ranging from overall votes to specific discussions of the evidence. As in any conversation, the jurors can react to the nonverbal communications from others as well as to their sentences. Peer pressure and the institutional context influence jurors to find a unanimous verdict, which can require cognitive and emotional change as the deliberations proceed. Like humans in any group, jurors form relationships that can be antagonistic because of disagreements or personality differences. Sometimes jurors become friends and the whole jury assumes a group identity as a result of their emotional interactions. The factors that enable jurors to reach consensus on a verdict are social as much as evidential: the perceived reasonableness of other jurors, the dominance of some jurors, the degree of conflict, the strength of social pressure, and the force of judicial instructions.

In all of these contexts, the contributions of perceptual evidence, nonverbal signals, and emotional reactions show that communication in the law is not merely verbal. The semantic pointer theory of communication as the transfer and instillation of multimodal representations captures how legal participants, from defendants to jurors, are affected by social mechanisms that go beyond verbal messaging.

EXPLAINING WRONGFUL CONVICTIONS

In 1999, DNA testing showed that semen from the crime scene excluded Ron Williamson and his co-accused, Dennis Fritz, as did subsequent hair analysis. DNA testing of hair and semen from the crime scene implicated Glenn Gore, who admitted that he testified against Williamson because he had been threatened by the prosecutor.

Wrongful convictions result from interacting breakdowns in mental and social mechanisms. In the Williamson case, the District Court of Appeals that granted him a new trial in 1995 listed many reasons why his first trial was defective. Williamson's lawyer had made serious mistakes, including failure to raise the issue of his client's mental competency, failure to investigate evidence against Glenn Gore, failure to point out that the jailhouse snitch had also testified in other cases, failure to inform the jury that another criminal had confessed to the murder, and failure to undermine the validity of Williamson's dream confession. The police were faulted for concealing evidence, using questionable means to obtain confessions, and sitting on exculpatory evidence. The judge also ruled that the hair evidence was unreliable and that the prosecutors and judge should have inquired into Williamson's mental health.

Such breakdowns in individuals are naturally explained by the emotions and motivated inferences that narrowed the judgments of police, prosecutors, and jurors. These limitations kept them from considering the full range of relevant evidence and alternative hypotheses that would have rendered a different judgment of explanatory coherence. This judgment would have prevented a false conviction, especially when combined with reasonable doubt based on the value of the presumption of innocence. It is also possible that false confessions arise in part from fear-driven inference, when innocent suspects become so terrified by police interrogation that they start to think that they might actually be guilty.

Social mechanisms also broke down in this case. There should have been better communication between Williamson's lawyer and the jury to challenge the evidence and present alternative hypotheses. The interactions between Williamson and the police during interrogations should have been directed at finding out the truth, rather than at extracting a confession by any means. The jurors should have been able to talk among themselves in ways that would have generated more skepticism about the flimsiness of the prosecution's case. Oklahoma state appeal courts should have been able to recognize a faulty trial, without the need to have Williamson saved so close to execution by the federal court.

Overall, wrongful convictions are striking cases of multilevel emergence, in which defective mechanisms at both mental and social levels lead to group actions and decisions that violate legal principles and the truth. The many cases where legal decisions are made correctly also display multilevel emergence because they result from the combination of individual decisions and group interactions, with results that are not simply the aggregate of what goes on in individuals. Communication among individuals such as jury deliberations often produces results beyond those that would result from mental mechanisms alone. Ideally, pooling evidence and hypotheses should result in better inferences to the best explanation, but interactions can also encourage collective motivated inference in which people encourage each other to let emotions dominate facts.

Grisham says wrongful convictions are frequent for a variety of reasons: "bad police work, junk science, faulty eyewitness identifications, bad defense lawyers, lazy prosecutors, arrogant prosecutors". Similarly, the Innocence Project reports that the most common causes of wrongful convictions are eyewitness misidentification, improper forensic science, false confessions, government misconduct, snitches, and bad lawyering. From a more academic and psychological perspective, Simon concludes:

> The investigative process produces evidence that is bound to contain unknown quantities of truth and error, and the adjudicative process is ill-equipped to distinguish between the two. The limited accuracy of criminal investigations, compounded with the limited diagnosticity of critical adjudication, lead to the conclusion that the criminal justice process falls short of delivering the precision that befits its solemn epistemic demands and the certitude it proclaims.

Achieving a higher degree of accuracy and legal justice will require understanding and ameliorating the mental and social mechanisms that I have discussed.

THE BRAIN AND LEGAL RESPONSIBILITY

My social cognitive-emotional workup of wrongful conviction used only the mental and social levels. Previous chapters and *Brain–Mind* substantiate the claim that all mental representations and processes, from concepts to motivated inference, are neural processes that can be specified within Eliasmith's Semantic Pointer Architecture. Moreover, the role of emotions in actions and in motivated inference shows that molecules such as dopamine are also relevant.

Such specifications raise the concern that defendants and other participants in the legal system may not be responsible for their actions. It is conventional to want to blame the actual murderer of Debbie Carter and to blame Williamson's prosecutor for their despicable actions. But how can we blame people if their actions simply resulted from mechanical patterns of neural firing in their brains? Did their neurons and their semantic pointers make them do it? If Williamson's lawyer had the sense to raise the question of his competence based on the mental illness he increasingly displayed in the years after the crime, then the jury would have had to decide whether he was sane enough to be responsible for his alleged actions.

A lively debate now rages concerning the implications of research on how brains work for the operations of the legal system, whose traditions depend on prescientific assumptions about free will and responsibility. Here I lay out two opposing positions and show how a richer account of neural and social mechanisms provides a third perspective on issues about legal responsibility.

For the radical position, consider the argument that rapidly increasing knowledge of the brain is showing that traditional notions of moral and legal responsibility are completely obsolete. Thanks to decades of brain scanning research, more is known about the neural correlates of many kinds of thinking, including decision making. What people naïvely think is free will is actually the result of neural firing in various brain areas. Because all actions result from physical processes, there is no room for free choices that are essential for people to be judged to be responsible for their actions. Neuroscience demands that concepts like free will and responsibility be abandoned along with outmoded ideas about the soul and immortality.

For the conservative position, consider the following alternative argument. Many leading philosophers (and ordinary people in recent surveys) have long thought that free will is actually compatible with physical determinism, including neural processes. On this view, free choice and responsibility are properties of a person, not a brain, and persons can be recognized as having the capacity to act in ways that show they could have done otherwise if they had chosen. When their actions are the result of mental illness such as schizophrenia, or are coerced by other people by vicious threats, then their actions are not free and legal responsibility can be dropped, as it usually is in current legal proceedings. Therefore, the rapid rise of neuroscience is no threat to moral and legal responsibility.

Social cognitivism suggests an intermediate position that is more nuanced, based on a richer understanding of neural and social mechanisms. Inferences about legal responsibility cannot be based merely on the neural correlates found by brain scanning research, because these say little about the causal processes that contribute to people's actions. In contrast, the Semantic Pointer Architecture specifies mechanisms by which perception, cognition, and emotion can lead to action, as described in *Brain–Mind*, chapter 9.

I argue there that the traditional concept of free will does not survive a detailed, mechanistic account of how neural processes lead to action. The beliefs, desires, and intentions that produce human actions are all semantic pointers, and behaviors are caused by interactions among numerous brain areas, including the basal ganglia, amygdala, thalamus, anterior cingulate, prefrontal cortex, and motor cortex. Sometimes these interactions yield conscious will, but whether an action is consciously produced is not under conscious control because it is affected by fatigue, stress, glucose levels, and cognitive load. For example, judges' decisions in Israeli parole hearings are substantially influenced by whether the cases are considered before or after a meal break. Mounting evidence about brain mechanisms for actions make it hard to understand them as free in the traditional sense.

The best that we can retain is a weaker concept I call *freeish* will that applies when the causation of action is not based on any of these factors: random processes such as quantum fluctuations, mental illnesses resulting from the breakdowns of biological mechanisms described in chapter 10, or social coercion resulting from the power mechanisms described in chapters 3 and 6. Whereas traditional free will is a property of a soul immune from causal determination, freeish will belongs to a self that is construed as a multilevel system of mechanisms that are molecular, neural, mental, and social, as described in chapter 12 of *Brain–Mind* and chapter 10 of *Natural Philosophy*.

Freeish will is not compatible with traditional ideas about responsibility based on radical individual freedom, but it is compatible with a more realistic understanding of responsibility operating in social processes. From this perspective, the point of holding people responsible for their actions is not to apply blame and to condemn them to secular or eternal punishment but rather to develop a better society in which people act in ways that enable all people to satisfy their needs.

Holding people responsible for their actions provides them with goals, motivations, and intentions that can accomplish socially desirable actions. As chapter 12 shows, education is difficult but not impossible when it uses communications that are compatible with peoples' mental processes. Educating people to be responsible will not help when people are afflicted with randomness, disease, or coercion, but good societies can aim to treat disease and eliminate coercion. The result should be a society that gives people a sort of freedom that can help them to meet their needs and the needs of others.

In sum, the conclusions to be drawn from social cognitivism are not as extreme as suggested by the radical view based on neural determinism or by the conservative view based on assumptions of compatibility. As other chapters have detailed, advances in neuroscience bring substantial conceptual change, and the traditional view of free will as a property of immortal souls has to be abandoned. Will is rather a complex neural process requiring interactions of semantic pointers for beliefs, goals, emotions, intentions, and motor representations, with consciousness resulting from semantic pointer competition (*Mind–Brain*, chapter 8).

As a replacement for the concept of free will, I propose freeish will that highlights breakdowns in neural and social mechanisms resulting from disease and coercion, while acknowledging that conscious deliberation does sometimes contribute to action through complex neural interactions. Responsibility needs to be reclassified from a property of individuals to a relation that connects selves construed as multilevel mechanisms with other people in layers of social groups. The result is a conception of human action and will that is compatible both with a scientific understanding of mind in society and with important goals about enhancing people's lives and protecting them from harm.

This chapter has shown the benefits of understanding the legal profession as a complex system of mental and social mechanisms. Social cognitivism has yielded new ways of thinking about reasonable doubt, wrongful convictions, and criminal responsibility.

Semantic pointer theories of cognition and emotion explain individual decisions, including defective ones that lead to wrongful convictions. Explanatory coherence shows how people can make judgments of guilt in accord with legal principles and how reasonable doubt based on the value of the presumption of innocence is a legitimate motivated inference. However, illegitimate motivated inferences resulting from emotional coherence with inappropriate values can produce biased and inaccurate verdicts.

Moreover, the social interactions that operate in trials and other legal proceedings can naturally be explained using the semantic pointer theory of communication that mingles verbal and nonverbal modes while accommodating the interactions of cognitions and emotions. Legal outcomes, including both reasonable decisions and appalling ones such as wrongful convictions, are rich cases of multilevel emergence resulting from the interaction of social, mental, neural, and molecular mechanisms.

To show the applicability of social cognitivism to the law, I provided a social cognitive-emotional workup of a dreadful case of wrongful conviction. This workup showed how the mental operations of people from defendants to jurors require concepts, values, beliefs, rules, analogies, and inferences. Explanatory coherence provides a good account of how legal fact-finding worked when done thoroughly and fairly in the Williamson case, but it needs to be supplemented by emotional coherence in order to explain how legal proceedings from police work to jury deliberation are sometimes done badly. Wrongful convictions are not just mental or social but rather the emergent result of interactions between breakdowns in individual thinking and breakdowns in social communication.

This chapter also furnishes a new take on the issue of legal responsibility. Criminals can legitimately be held responsible for their actions but not for the reasons that the law traditionally assumes. The practice of law needs to be based on scientific theories of minds in society rather than on religious metaphysics. Social cognitivism implies the replacement of free will by freeish will and reclassification of responsibility as a social relation rather than a property of individuals. Transforming conceptions of the law to bring about changes that will be both scientifically sound and socially efficacious will require substantial education, conceptual change, and political reform.

This chapter has shown how legal thinking and group decisions depend on the same mental and social processes that operate across communities, from close relationships to international politics. Applying a common set of mechanisms also provides connections with other professions, such as the link between the issue of criminal responsibility and the account of mental illness provided in chapter 10. Other chapters display additional professional connections, for example with the mental and social aspects of education discussed in chapter 12 and the operations of businesses examined in chapters 13 and 14.

NOTES

Aristotle's remark on law is from his *Politics*, III 1287a.32.

My account of legal reasoning as explanatory coherence is in Thagard 1989, which includes mathematical and computational details. Coherence is further analyzed mathematically in Thagard and Verbeurgt 1998; see also Thagard 2000. The role of motivated inference in emotional coherence is discussed in relation to the O. J. Simpson trial in Thagard 2003 (reprinted in Thagard 2006). Compare the combination of explanatory coherence and emotional coherence about climate change in Thagard and Findlay 2011 (reprinted in Thagard 2012b). Thagard and Aubie 2008 show that coherence can be computed by distributed neural representations.

Amaya 2015 provides a thorough account of coherence in law. Empirical studies of coherence relevant to legal inference include Simon 2004 and Simon, Stenstrom, and Read 2015. Byrne 1995 shows that explanatory coherence fleshes out the story model of jury reasoning due to Pennington and Hastie 1992. See also Hastie and Wittenbrink 2006.

For a more thorough critique of the Bayesian approach to legal inference, see Thagard 2004a, 2000 and Amaya 2015. My latest critique of the Bayes craze is in *Natural Philosophy*, chapter 3.

On the psychology of law, see Saks and Spellman 2016, Simon 2012, Spellman and Schauer 2012, and Devine 2012. Haack 2014 examines legal evidence.

My workup of the Williamson case is based on Grisham 2006.

On reasonable doubt, see Thagard 2004b (reprinted in Thagard 2006).

On values in science, see Rudner 1961, Douglas 2009, and Thagard 2012b, chapter 17.

The Innocence Project against wrongful convictions is at http://www.innocenceproject.org.

Graham 1987 reviews American rules of evidence. Thagard 2014c discusses the nature of evidence more generally. See also *Natural Philosophy*, chapter 3.

On abductive inference and analogy, see Thagard 1988, 2012b.

On nonverbal communication in law, see Otu 2015.

The quote of Grisham's summary is from his 2006, p. 356. The quote of Simon's summary is from his 2012, p. 208. The Innocence Project review of causes of wrongful convictions is at https://www.innocenceproject.org/causes-wrongful-conviction./.

On law and neuroscience, see Jones, Marois, Farah, and Greeley 2013 and Buckoltz and Faigman 2014.

Recent books on the implications of neuroscience for criminal responsibility include Freeman 2011, Glannon 2015, Morse and Roskies 2013, Pardo and Patterson 2013, and Vincent 2013. One conservative argument against the relevance of neuroscience to law is that issues about responsibility are conceptual, not empirical, but science changes concepts: Thagard 1992b, 2014a.

Baskin-Sommers 2016 reviews the neural, genetic, and environmental determinants of antisocial behavior.

Danziger, Levav, and Avnaim-Pesso 2011 report the effect of meal times on judges' decisions, although the effect may be confounded by a practice of scheduling easier cases first. Cho, Barnes, and Guanaro 2017 report that judges who are sleep deprived because of Daylight Saving Time give harsher sentences.

PROJECT

Perform three-analyses of legal concepts such as *guilty* and *inflammatory*. Develop an agent-based model of juror deliberation that includes emotional communication. Assess how attributions of legal and moral responsibility are undermined by the four kinds of power described in chapter 6 (coercive, benefit, respect, and norm).

12

Education

LEARNING AND TEACHING

H. G. Wells said that human history is a race between education and catastrophe. Teaching is ubiquitous in human cultures, although formal education has only been around for a few thousand years. In contrast, at most a few nonhuman species of animals teach their young about how to eat and get around in the world. For humans, teaching is a standard activity of parents and other caretakers, but it is also a profession as teachers, professors, managers, and others work to transmit what they know to children and other students.

Because of their practical importance, teaching and education are the subjects of scientific investigation, going back at least to the educational psychology of William James and John Dewey. Since the 1990s, there has been increasing interest in applying insights from neuroscience to deepen understanding of the psychology of education and to suggest better ways of teaching. Current initiatives go under the headings of educational neuroscience, neuroeducation, and studies in mind, brain, and education.

It is not at all obvious, however, how to apply what is known about the brain to improve professional activities in education. Skeptics have worried that the gap between what brains do and teaching is too great for educational neuroscience to be useful. Most brain research uses scanning techniques such as functional magnetic resonance imaging to identify correlations between mental activities and activation in brain areas, but the educational significance of such correlations is hard to extract. Oddly, neuroeducation has had much discussion of learning in individual brains but has largely ignored the social process of teaching.

Various companies that sell products to schools have claimed, with little supporting research, to be "brain-based" in their approaches to learning and teaching. Like the general population, teachers have been susceptible to neuromyths, such as beliefs that individual differences in left/right brain hemispheres generate different learning styles.

Theoretical neuroscience offers a different route to neuroeducation. Instead of relying on disconnected experimental observations and popular myths, educators can benefit from an empirically founded but general theory of how the brain works. In this chapter I use semantic pointer theories of cognition and communication to provide new perspectives on the nature of learning and teaching. Neural mechanisms of representation, binding, competition, and transfer provide a novel understanding of how brains operate when they are learning and teaching.

On this view, learning in individuals is primarily acquisition of semantic pointers—multimodal brain processes that can combine verbal, sensory, motor, and emotion representations. This approach can accommodate some of the most interesting recent approaches to educational theory, including the multiple intelligences of Howard Gardner. Moreover, because semantic pointers integrate cognition and emotion, they can also illuminate current findings about the importance to learning of motivation and emotion.

Educational neuroscience requires much more than a good brain-based theory of individual learning, because teaching is a social activity depending on interactions among one or more learners and one or more teachers. Accordingly, education needs to attend to social mechanisms as well as cognitive and neural ones. Neuroscience usually only studies individual brain processes, but education requires an appreciation of how the knowledge and expertise in the brain of the teacher can be transmitted to the brain of the learner.

The key to bridging from the individual to the social is the expansion of the semantic pointer theory of cognition to a general theory of communication, as previous chapters illustrated. For education, the crucial step is to understand teaching as communication of semantic pointers from the minds of the teachers to the minds of the learners. This transfer is much more than the communication of words and sentences, for it requires the large range of sensory, motor, and emotional representations accommodated by the Semantic Pointer Architecture. Teaching would be a lot easier if it only required getting words from the teachers' heads into the learners' heads. Rather, it requires the transfer or instillation of much more complex representations including visual images, motor patterns, emotional values, and motivating goals.

There are many areas of learning and teaching that could demonstrate the applicability of semantic pointer theories. I illustrate their relevance by considering one important current issue in public education concerning vaccination. In recent years, there has been a serious drop in the rates of vaccination for dangerous diseases such as measles and whooping cough because of misapprehensions about the dangers of vaccines. As a result, some diseases that had virtually been eradicated in wealthy countries such as the United States are making a comeback. Experts in public health and epidemiology are attempting to find ways of educating the public to reestablish full practices of vaccination. To assist this project, I present a social cognitive-emotional workup of vaccination education.

The lessons from this workup transfer naturally to other educational problems such as improving teaching in science and mathematics. In particular, the semantic pointer approach has major implications for understanding conceptual change as acquisition, deletion, reclassification, and revalencing of concepts, construed as semantic pointers. This approach can provide explanations that contribute to the three-analysis of the concept *teach* shown in Table 12.1.

Standard examples of teaching occur in families, schools, and religious and business organizations. Typically, teaching involves one or more teachers, one or more learners, and transfer or implanting of the knowledge (or at least beliefs) of the teacher to the learner, including skills (procedural knowledge) and emotional attitudes crucial for motivation. Teaching explains why beliefs and cultural practices spread through social groups and why learning can operate much more rapidly than if people had to learn everything by themselves. Finally, my explanation of how teaching works is based on semantic pointer communication.

TABLE 12.1

Three-Analysis of *Teach*

Exemplars	Parent-child, schools, universities, religions, management
Typical features	Teacher, learner, transfer of knowledge and skills
Explanations	Explains: spread of culture, why people learn faster than they could alone
	Explained by: transfer or instillation of semantic pointers

VACCINATION: SOCIAL COGNITIVE-EMOTIONAL WORKUP

In the United States, cases of measles have increased dramatically in recent years, from virtually none in 2000 to hundreds in 2014. This reemergence is a result of the refusal by parents to have their children vaccinated, often because they think that there is a link between the measles vaccine commonly given to young children and the incidence of autism. Health agencies such as the US Centers for Disease Control and Prevention have tried to inform skeptical parents about the benefits of vaccines, but these efforts have actually made some skeptics even more opposed to vaccines. More effective means of education should benefit from understanding the mental mechanisms operating in people who resist being educated about the values of vaccines.

Concepts and Values

The debate about vaccination depends on numerous concepts that may operate differently in the minds of ordinary people from how they operate in the minds of scientists. What is the nature of concepts like *vaccination, vaccine, virus, measles,* and *disease*? Chapter 10 provides a three-analysis of a scientific concept of disease that included numerous exemplars, a wide array of typical features, and complex explanations based on mechanisms. Concepts of disease held by ordinary people may be much more limited, with inclusion of only a few exemplars, a limited set of typical features such as a group of symptoms, and little understanding of the mechanisms that cause disease and that connect diseases to symptoms.

As the semantic pointer theory of concepts implies, helping people to acquire a more sophisticated concept of disease is not a matter of just giving them a verbal definition. Rather, concept learning can be better accomplished by expanding and correcting people's understanding of the exemplars, typical features, and explanations associated with the concept. Therefore, to teach people the general nature of disease or particular diseases, it should be helpful to expand their range of exemplars, to incorporate understanding of harms and broken mechanisms, and to impart a grasp of how mechanisms explain normal physiological functioning and how breakdowns in mechanisms explain disease.

Similarly, most people have a limited concept of vaccination compared to medical professionals. Vaccination is not just getting a needle but a complex medical intervention known to be effective for the prevention of many diseases. Table 12.2 gives a three-analysis of the concept of vaccination familiar to public health officials. There are many standard examples ranging from centuries-old inoculations

TABLE 12.2

Three-Analysis of *Vaccination*

Exemplars	Vaccines to prevent smallpox, polio, measles, whooping cough, shingles, pneumonia
Typical features	Vaccine, delivery by injection or other means, autoimmune response, ongoing resistance to disease
Explanations	Explains: why vaccinated people do not get sick
	Explained by: mechanisms of the immune system

against smallpox to modern vaccines against childhood illnesses, influenza, and shingles.

The typical features of vaccination are not the salient experience of a shot but rather the biological contributions of transfer of biological material such as an attenuated virus and an autoimmune reaction that secures degrees of immunity against future infections. Providing vaccinations explains why incidences of diseases like smallpox and measles have been dramatically reduced. The efficacy of vaccinations is well explained by how the body's immune system reacts to exposure to a modified infectious agent by preparing the body for dealing with future infections. Hence education about vaccination requires helping people to achieve a broader concept including some understanding of the underlying mechanisms that play a role in explanations.

Although vaccines are occasionally used against bacteria, as for pneumonia, most of the diseases against which people are vaccinated are caused by viruses. Hence understanding vaccination requires knowledge of the concept of *virus* that is more sophisticated than that held by most people. For example, many people do not know the difference between viruses and bacteria, which leads them to request antibiotics from their doctors that kill bacteria but not viruses.

The historical development of the concept *virus* began with a very general meaning of a poison implicated in a disease. In the nineteenth century, the concept narrowed to concern entities that cause disease even though they could pass through filters that stop bacteria. Twentieth-century advances in theory and instruments led to the modern concept of viruses as infectious agents viewable with an electron microscope and possessing small numbers of genes. Ordinary people have a limited set of exemplars, typical features, and explanations in their conception of viruses. A three-analysis of the much richer medical conception of viruses would indicate the educational target that must be hit for people to acquire an understanding of viruses needed for appreciating vaccines.

This discussion of the concepts *disease, vaccination*, and *virus* may give the misleading impression that such concepts are entirely verbal. But vaccination also has associated sensory representations such as the visual appearance of the needle, the pain of a shot, and the crying of an injected child. Moreover, specific disease concepts may be associated with sensory symptoms, such as the redness of the measles rash, the itchiness of chickenpox, the runny nose of a cold, the fevered heat of influenza, and the hacking sound of whooping cough. Chapter 10 described the immobility and lassitude of depression, which requires a kinesthetic representation. Hence people's mental representations of specific disease concepts such as *measles* have important multimodal aspects accommodated by the semantic pointer theory of concepts through its incorporation of sensory-motor information.

Another advantage of taking concepts to be semantic pointers is their capacity to incorporate emotional information, generating values. Public health debates always concern values as well as facts. I have been arguing that values are not just words, preferences, social constructions, or abstract entities but rather mental representations that combine emotions with cognitive entities such as concepts and sentences. Because emotions incorporate cognitive appraisals as well as physiological perceptions, they can be evaluated as rational or irrational in accord with whether they fit with beliefs based on evidence and the needs of the appraiser. Similarly, saying that values are mental representations does not imply that they cannot be objective if they reflect legitimate needs and beliefs.

The debate about vaccines is as much a conflict about values as about beliefs. The field of public health has a common set of values including those shown in Figure 12.1. Health is not just a personal concern but a human right that people and governments should work collectively to protect and promote, especially for the most vulnerable like children, the poor, and the elderly. Public health institutions

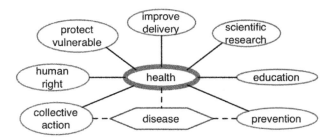

FIGURE 12.1 Core values in public health. Ovals are emotionally positive, and hexagons are negative. Solid lines indicate mutual support, and dotted lines indicate incompatibility.

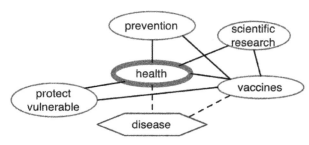

FIGURE 12.2 Value map of pro-vaccine view.

should rely on scientific research to suggest how to improve health care quality
and delivery.

The public health values shown in Figure 12.1 support vaccination policies, as
shown in Figure 12.2. This map ties the concepts of vaccines and vaccination with
views about scientific evidence and the promotion of health. Vaccines are emotionally positive because scientific research shows that they promote health by
reducing disease. Not shown are social and economic benefits that include reduced
overall health expenditures due to less illness and increased productivity due to
less time off work.

In contrast, Figure 12.3 maps the values and attitudes of vaccine skeptics. The
difference with Figure 12.2 is not just that vaccines are considered harmful but
also that *vaccine* is tied to other emotionally powerful concepts such as dangerous
chemicals and greedy pharmaceutical companies. Figure 12.3 shows scientific research as neutral, but some vaccine skeptics are openly mistrustful of it as cor-
rupted by commercial interests. The value map should make it clear that education
about vaccination requires more than adding new concepts and beliefs but also
shifting values and emotional attitudes. Educating people to shift from the view
shown in Figure 12.3 to approximately the view held by public health officials requires substantial transformations.

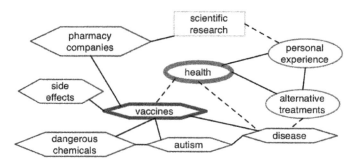

FIGURE 12.3 Value map of anti-vaccine view.

Images and Embodiment

The use of words in Figures 12.2 and 12.3 suggests that the relevant concepts are verbal, but they also involve many kinds of sensory, motor, and emotional imagery. For ordinary people, vaccination is not just an abstract concept of application of a virus to generate an immune response. It also has associated imagery such as a picture of a nurse injecting a vaccine into the arm of a child and the motor motion required for the injection. There can also be auditory associations with vaccination, such as the "ouch" of a flinching adult or the wail of a distressed child.

Emotional imagery can also play a powerful role in parents' decisions not to vaccinate their children. Parents can generate emotional images of how distressing it would be to vaccinate a child who later becomes unresponsive and mentally disabled, and they can also imagine the unhappiness of an autistic child. Reading about vaccine critics such as Jenny McCarthy who had to deal with the problems of their own autistic children makes the negative associations connected with autism and vaccines all the more vivid. Hence public education about vaccines has to deal with sensory, motor, and emotional images as well as verbal claims.

The power of images in public health education is shown by a 2015 study by Zachary Horne and colleagues of effective means of countering anti-vaccination attitudes. Previous studies found that pro-vaccine messages failed to improve people's attitudes toward vaccination and could even backfire when they made vaccine skeptics *more* negative about vaccinations. Informing people by debunking earlier studies claiming an association between vaccines and autism actually led people to associate vaccines with autism more strongly.

In contrast, success in changing people's minds about vaccines came by drawing attention to the consequences of not vaccinating children against measles and other diseases. When parents received warnings of the severity of these diseases in the form of graphic pictures and anecdotes, they became more aware of the risks associated with failures to vaccinate, with resulting improvements in behaviors and attitudes. Abstract arguments that allegations about the risks of vaccine are not scientifically well established pale in comparison to a few stories and pictures about children afflicted with measles.

The importance of imagery in education is highlighted by applications of Howard Gardner's theory of multiple intelligences to pedagogic practices. Gardner argues that there is much more to intelligence than the linguistic, logical, and mathematical talents that have been so prized in the West and measured using standard tests. He identifies other kinds of intelligence: musical, bodily-kinesthetic, spatial, interpersonal, and intrapersonal. All of these are strongly connected with embodied imagery rather than mere words.

Musical intelligence benefits from auditory perception and imagery. Bodily-kinesthetic knowledge is based on motor control and senses of balance and proprioception, which tells you how your body parts are related to each other. Spatial intelligence concerns more broadly where you are located in your environment, which requires visual representations and a sense of movement. Interpersonal intelligence includes the ability to read the intentions and desires of others, which is partly based on emotional imagery as practiced in the three modes of empathy using analogies, mirror neurons, and multimodal rules. Finally, intrapersonal intelligence is knowledge of a person's own internal aspects including the range of emotions. Various educational projects have found value in understanding people's mental capacities as involving all of these kinds of perception and imagery in addition to more conventionally valued linguistic skills.

It is therefore important to understand education as embodied, going beyond words to use images that are sensory, motor, and emotional. However, instruction about vaccines would be deficient if it relied only on embodied images and neglected many more abstract concepts that qualify as transbodied. For example, viruses are naturally imagined as small particles or animals. But they are too small to be seen through a light microscope and can only be detected by electron microscopes that operate differently from the human eye. Viruses consist of a small number of genes, usually fewer than 200, where genes are inadequately visualized as beads on a string. More accurately, genes are strands of DNA, again too small to be adequately visualized.

Understanding how vaccines work also requires grasping how the body's immune system reacts to invaders such as viruses and how antibodies can attack the invaders and prepare the immune system to attack invaders in the future. Although pictures may be of some help in conveying the operation of the immune system stimulated by vaccines, there is no replacement for verbal descriptions of the immune system. As is in concepts in general, representations of how vaccines work needs to be both embodied and transbodied.

Values concerning vaccination are clearly transbodied as is evident in the examples in Figures 12.1 to 12.3. Concepts like *health, protection,* and *human rights* may have embodied aspects, but their exemplars, typical features, and explanations go beyond the senses by introducing abstractions through recursive binding. For example, the concept of *health* depends on other abstractions such as an organism having well-functioning mechanisms and avoiding disease.

Beliefs and Rules

Education requires much more than the acquisition of concepts and values. The magnitude of the problem of educating people about vaccines is evident from considering the intense beliefs held by vaccine skeptics, extolled on various websites. Some of the core beliefs are as follows:

Vaccines are dangerous. Vaccines have not been adequately tested for toxicity especially for their adverse effects when delivered in combination. Vaccines are less effective in providing immunity than when children acquire diseases naturally. Vaccines have dangerous additives such as mercury and aluminum. Vaccines are contaminated by viruses and other such substances. Vaccines are likely responsible for declining health in children as seen in increasing rates of autism, learning disability, and chronic illnesses such as asthma. Vaccines frequently have adverse effects such as seizures and serious diseases. Pharmaceutical companies are fraudulent in conducting biased research and manipulating government officials and journalists into supporting their commercial activities.

Because these beliefs are interconnected, convincing people to get vaccinations for their children and themselves cannot depend on attacking them piecemeal. They form a highly coherent system, often promulgated by proponents of naturopathic medicine who think they have alternative treatments that are more effective than vaccines. The section on inferences will describe how belief revision concerning vaccines needs to be a process that operates in parallel to produce overall coherence, rather than assuming that individual arguments can chip away at the beliefs held by vaccine skeptics.

The generalizations about vaccines in the list of beliefs presented here naturally translates into rules with an *if–then* form. Some action-guiding rules are:

If you are vaccinated, then you are putting yourself in danger.
If children are vaccinated, then they become prone to many diseases such as autism.
If pharmaceutical companies say that a vaccine is safe, then don't trust them.

When such rules are put into words, they are open to conscious scrutiny concerning evidence and overall coherence. But many of these rules are multimodal in that they employ concepts that have important sensory, motor, and emotional aspects. As the discussion of concepts showed, vaccination is not just a verbal concept but also has sensory aspects related to pain and movement. The concept *danger* is embodied because of the physiological aspects of the associated emotions of fear and anxiety. For the vaccine skeptics, vaccination has become an inherently negative concept, akin to barbaric medical practices such as bloodletting and infanticide. Any rule or other belief that includes concepts like *danger, toxic,* and *disease* is inherently emotional, because the concepts have negative valences resulting from past appraisals and ongoing physiological reactions. Hence revising concepts like *vaccine* requires changing emotional attitudes as well as replacing an interconnected set of beliefs.

The discomfort that people feel in planning vaccinations for themselves or their children may be hard to pin down because it is based on general anxiety about medical treatments rather than on specific beliefs that are expressed verbally. Hence public health education may be similar to the problems of romantic couples described in chapter 4 and the problems of psychotherapy for people with depression described in chapter 10. Education then is not simply a matter of identifying false beliefs and challenging them but rather of bringing to light and uprooting unconscious multimodal rules that affect behavior.

Rules can also be a powerful way of expressing mechanisms, and part of the disagreement between public health advocates for vaccination and vaccine skeptics results from emphasizing different mechanisms based on different rules. The main mechanism behind judgments about the values of vaccinations can be stated as rules such as the following:

> *If people are vaccinated, then their immune systems respond by creating antibodies.*
> *If people have antibodies, then they will not be infected and get a serious disease.*

In contrast, vaccine skeptics assume a different mechanism captured by rules like:

> *If people are vaccinated, then their bodies are damaged by toxic substances.*
> *If people's bodies are damaged by toxic substances, then they become susceptible to serious diseases such as autism.*

In biology, mechanisms are often represented by diagrams and movies, not just verbal rules. It would be interesting to see whether videos about the mechanisms of vaccination and their valuable effects could help to change people's minds. To my knowledge, no one has tried to educate vaccine skeptics about the underlying mechanisms. But there is some evidence from research on climate change by Michael Ranney and his colleagues that communication about mechanisms can help to change people's minds by concisely explaining how greenhouse gases increase the world's temperature.

This effective technique teaches people about mechanisms visually, using short videos that combine words with dynamic pictures that show how global warming develops. Such visualization may be a powerful tool for conveying the multimodal rules describing mechanisms to people in a more comprehensible way. In line with the sensory-motor origins of causal thinking proposed in *Brain–Mind* (chapter 3), conveying multimodal rules about mechanisms may gain much from dynamic visual displays, showing the benefit of causal and embodied explanations.

Analogies and Metaphors

Analogies and metaphors are not at the core of the debate about vaccinations but nevertheless contribute. The science of immunology that provides the theoretical basis for vaccination relies heavily on metaphors. Public health advocates attempting to educate people about the value of vaccinations use analogies to try to convince people that vaccines are valuable rather than scary. In response, vaccine skeptics have their own set of metaphors that they use to convey what they see as the emotional threats of vaccination.

Immunology developed by specifying mechanisms for how the body grows antibodies to defend against viruses, bacteria, and other infectious agents. But immunology also employs metaphors as part of the explanation how the body responds to infectious threats and prepares itself to deal more effectively with future threats. Since its origins in the work of Macfarlane Burnet, immunology has relied on a systematic metaphor of the self and non-self, to be distinguished by the immune. There is no literal self and non-self in the biological systems studied by immunology, but the analogy with psychology that studies how people think of themselves and contrast themselves with others has suggested ways of thinking about how immune system operates.

Various other metaphors drawn from the social sphere are used by immunologists: bacteria and viruses are *invaders* that must be *attacked* by antibodies. The immune system can cause problems in autoimmune diseases and organ transplants when it undesirably tells cells to *reject* the transplanted organ. The concepts of invasion, attack, and rejection are metaphorically transferred from the social sphere into the biological one.

Public health advocates sometimes resort to metaphors in order to convince people that vaccines are good practice. The following are some metaphors that have been advocated as useful for teaching people about vaccines:

Vaccination is like a dress rehearsal for your immune system so it is prepared for the "real show."
Getting a vaccine is like putting on bug spray before going out in the woods.
Unvaccinated people are like drivers who are never, ever given instruction on how to drive then made to drive from California to New York. It can be done, but it's risky. Vaccination is like getting taught how to drive, then practicing driving for a while, then driving across the continent.

An experimental study also found that metaphors can be useful for getting people to decide to get vaccinated for influenza, for example by comparing flu to a weed and a flu vaccine to a weed killer. There are obvious problems with this analogy, because the operation of vaccines is more complicated than the operations of antibiotics that can actually kill bacteria like a herbicide kills weeds. Nevertheless, the analogy can help people to see that vaccines can be a useful response to a serious health problem.

Naturally, vaccine skeptics also marshal analogies to defend their position. One says that vaccines are like time bombs, where we do not know when the next one will maim or kill a child. Another compares urging people to vaccinate to urging people to drill for oil despite major oil spills.

Thus the debate about vaccines, like many others, is partly a matter of competing metaphors. Are vaccines like weed killers or like time bombs? Dealing with metaphors is not just accepting some beliefs and rejecting others, because analogies depend on a whole complex of interconnected meanings and emotions. The validity of analogical comparisons depends not just on counting the similarities and differences but also on considering the use the analogies based on their associated goals. The goal of public health educators is to convince people that vaccines are valuable, resulting in positive comparisons to herbicides and bug spray. In contrast, the goal of vaccine skeptics is to stop people from getting vaccinations, resulting in emotionally negative comparisons to bombs and oil spills. The evaluation of these analogies and metaphors needs to be part of a larger process of coherence that involves emotions as well as evidence.

Emotions and Actions

The debate about vaccination concerns actions, not just beliefs. Should people act to arrange vaccinations for themselves and their children? Actions never follow from beliefs alone, because psychologically they also require desires. People get vaccinated if they desire to be healthy and believe that vaccines will help them stay healthy. A much richer account of the causes of actions is available in *Brain–Mind* (chapter 9), which describes how beliefs, intentions, and emotions distributed across multiple brain areas can cause actions triggered in motor areas.

Emotions are a crucial part of producing actions at the neural level, and we have seen many ways in which emotions contribute to people's decisions about whether or not to vaccinate. People who choose to get vaccinations can feel happy that they are doing something to promote their health goals, and they can feel proud that they are looking after their children by getting them vaccinated. At the other extreme, vaccine skeptics experience fear at the thought of getting vaccines that they deem to be dangerous and anger that the mainstream press and government are in cahoots with pharmaceutical companies to spread lies concerning the safety of vaccines. Skeptics can also feel empathic sadness for people whose children have allegedly become autistic or otherwise ill because of vaccines. People who act on their skepticism and resist attempts to make vaccinations mandatory can feel happy that they are managing to escape the ravages of vaccines and proud that they are going against the establishment to resist treatments that they consider harmful.

The last section described the vaccination debate as a battle about metaphors, but it is even more starkly a battle about emotions. Everyone wants to feel happy about their own health and proud that they are looking after their children, but the vaccine debate puts these emotions at odds with each other. As the discussion of depression showed, changing emotions is not simply a matter of changing beliefs but sometimes also requires changing goals and physiological states. Convincing people of the value of vaccines requires overcoming intense emotions of fear and anxiety, a process much more complicated than simply refuting beliefs about bogus studies that purported to show a link between vaccines and autism.

The relevance of emotions to education goes far beyond the vaccine debate. For students to learn effectively in schools, they need to regulate emotion-driven behaviors that impede teaching. Self-discipline is a better predictor of academic achievement than IQ. Acquisition of new conceptual systems benefits from mental executive functions that encourage deliberate planning, impulse control, and goal-directed behavior. Teachers' understanding of students' emotions should help to foster self-regulation that encourages learning by enabling students to focus on tasks at hand.

Inferences

It is often assumed that inference and reasoning are the same, but they are actually very different. Inference is a neural process that is private, parallel, multimodal, emotional, unconscious, fast, and automatic. In contrast, reasoning is usually public, serial, verbal, dispassionate, conscious, slow, and deliberate. So the contributions of reasoning to inference are unclear, and it is legitimate to ask why people including teachers should bother with reasoning at all.

If reasoning and inference were the same, then it should be fairly easy to teach people about the benefits of vaccinations and the deficiency of the arguments against them. Educators could simply mount a set of arguments that provide empirical and theoretical reasons why people should favor vaccinations. In practice, however, the successes of this kind of reasoning are limited, because verbal communication can only begin to influence people to make inferences that actually change their minds about what to believe, feel, and do.

Chapter 2 suggested a different way of thinking about inference as a parallel brain process that reaches conclusions based on parallel constraint satisfaction involving both explanations and emotions. Accordingly, the most that one can hope reasoning will do to change people's minds is to provide them with some of the elements and constraints that can then feed into judgments of explanatory and emotional coherence. Fortunately, there is evidence that sometimes such provision works: experiments found that informing people vividly about the dangers of not vaccinating can lead people to do it, and experiments found that people could change their minds about global warming when informed about the mechanisms that produce it. Ideally, public health education needs to combine evidence and goals, enabling people to see what is true and what ought therefore to be done.

Education would be much easier if people started with empty minds that could simply be filled up by the concepts, beliefs, and values provided by teachers. Such filling rarely works, however, because even six-year-old children starting school already have concepts and beliefs that they have acquired from their parents and personal experience. The section on conceptual change provides a more detailed account of the sorts of changes in concepts and beliefs required for educational success.

Belief change depends on explanatory and emotional coherence, but coherence is not simply a relation among sentences or other purely verbal representations. Because coherence construed as parallel constraint satisfaction can draw on nonverbal representation such as pictures, sounds, tastes, movement, and emotions, inference should be able to employ all the different kinds of intelligence available to people, including spatial, kinesthetic, and interpersonal.

Some people who have to decide whether to get vaccinations for themselves and their children may not have many preconceptions and therefore can be reached by a simple kind of deductive reasoning. Doctors say vaccinate; doctors are always right; so vaccinate. Today, however, many people are skeptical about whether doctors are always right, and they acquire their beliefs about vaccination from nonmedical sources such as friends, websites, Facebook, or naturopathic doctors. In these cases, education requires convincing people to abandon beliefs and emotional attitudes that they have acquired concerning the dangers of vaccines. Giving reasons is only the beginning of a much larger process of explanatory and emotional coherence that can lead eventually to dramatic shifts in beliefs and practices.

What makes this process all the more difficult is that people are prone to use modes of thinking that are much less effective than explanatory and emotional coherence: motivated, fear-driven, and rage-driven inference. Motivated inference impedes learning about vaccines in several ways. First, there are people such as peddlers of alternative treatments who have an interest in exalting their own medical beliefs over those of the medical establishment. Naturopaths and homeopaths are motivated to enlarge the market for their goods and services by convincing people to be treated by them rather than by conventional medical sources.

Second, even for ordinary people, there can be motivations for avoiding vaccines that incline people to fit their beliefs to their goals, rather than their goals to their beliefs as evidence-based thinking requires. People are motivated to secure their own health, and decent parents care deeply about the health of their children. People want to help their children flourish with minimal medical problems, so they may be convinced to trust sources that say vaccines may be dangerous.

Even more powerfully, fear-driven inference can fuel rejection of medical opinion and avoidance of vaccines. Autism and the many other serious conditions that have been attributed to vaccines are genuinely scary. Once you begin to think about the possibility of an association between vaccines and autism, or between influenza shots and autoimmune diseases, it is hard not to keep thinking that the vaccinations and the diseases might go together, just because it is so frightening that they might go together. Negative emotions focus the mind mightily, and such focusing can exclude considerations of relevant evidence. When put into words, the inference that vaccines must be dangerous because you are afraid that they are looks silly, but unconscious mental processes can produce the same result. Websites and videos use testimonials of parents whose children had disastrous occurrences after vaccination to whip up fears and anxieties and to foster fear-driven inference in people who become convinced to avoid vaccines.

For the fanatics who generate anti-vaccine websites, the inference that vaccines are dangerous seems to be in part driven by rage against doctors, scientists, and public health officials who conspire to make money for big pharmaceutical companies. Inevitably, drug companies are prone to motivated inference because they want to increase profits by selling vaccines and therefore risk distorting experimental results in their own favor. There have been enough scandals about unscrupulous commercial practices, for example concerning antidepressant drugs, to warrant some skepticism about the scientific research that supports vaccines. Nevertheless, there are many people outside the pharmaceutical industry, such as scientists, doctors, and public health officials, who are not subject to the same kind of motivated inference and therefore are capable of more evidence-based judgments. Hence rage-driven inference concerning vaccinations is not justified, but it nevertheless can merge with motivated and fear-driven inference to support emotional conclusions about the dangers of vaccines.

In sum, educators concerned with communicating about theory and practice should not naïvely assume that verbal reasoning is a solid route to changing people's minds. Rather, inference at its best is a complex parallel process of considering many constraints concerning evidence, explanations, and emotional goals. This does not mean that reasons should not be given, because sometimes reasoning is the best way to enable people to notice the evidence, constraints, and legitimate goals that should shape their belief revisions and decisions.

Giving reasons is likely to work best when combined with nonverbal communication such as pictures and gestures, along with emotional communication based on tone of voice, facial expressions, and body language. Even after students have acquired a new conceptual system for fields such as mathematics and science, the old system is not simply deleted, so that executive functions such as inhibition are important for focusing attention on superior new concepts and beliefs.

Moreover, educators dealing with controversial issues such as vaccination, climate change, and biological evolution need to be aware that inference is sometimes swamped by motivation, fear, and rage. Then teachers need to identify the goals and emotions of learners to forestall the motivated, fear-driven, and rage-driven inferences that unconsciously fuel misunderstandings. In these common situations, education is like psychotherapy as described in chapter 10.

Emotions are indispensable in human minds and brains for evaluation, attention, and motivation, but their power can sometimes lead people away from more effective considerations of evidence and goal accomplishment. On this view of inference, as a parallel, unconscious, often emotional process distinct from verbal reasoning, education is as much managing emotions as conveying information. An emotional gestalt shift may be required for some people to learn that vaccines are generally valuable and that climate change is substantially caused by human carbon emissions. Managing emotions and conveying information both require communication by teachers.

Communications

The most obvious communication in education is from teacher to student, but this is only part of the system. There also needs to be communication from student to teacher, because teachers need to understand what is going on in the minds of the students if they are going to be effective at modifying their concepts and beliefs. Effective learning also occurs among students who can absorb as much from each other as they do from their teachers. Finally, teachers need to communicate among themselves to ensure a coherent curriculum and to exchange ideas about more effective teaching.

All of these kinds of communication can be fostered by appreciating that they require much more than mere transfer of words. A good teacher has a rich and coherent system of concepts, values, images, beliefs, and metaphors that cannot be conveyed merely by sentences. Images can help even with the more verbal aspects of this cognitive system, for example by presenting diagrams and value maps. Analogies can help students bridge between what they know and what the teacher wants them to know.

Emotions are also crucial to educational communication, because teachers need to convey what is interesting, important, and worth learning. Interest is a mild emotion marked physiologically by dilated pupils, akin to the stronger emotions of curiosity, wonder, and surprise. In keeping with the saying mentioned in chapter 3, education is not filling a pail but lighting a fire. Emotions provide motivation, and without motivation students will not spend time putting in the effort to learn much.

Learning is fostered when students appreciate that taught material is relevant to them, through physiological reactions and goal-based appraisals that add up to positive emotions about what is interesting, intriguing, surprising, gripping, or fascinating. In contrast, irrelevant material generates negative emotions about what is boring, confusing, or annoying.

For teachers to understand the emotions of students, they need empathy. Teachers can use verbal analogies to put themselves in their students' shoes in order to grasp their emotions. More directly, the two more physical modes of empathy can be useful for teachers when they grasp some of what their students are feeling by means of mirror neurons and multimodal rule simulation. Students can contribute to this process by means of reverse empathy, prompting teachers to appreciate the students' emotional feelings about what they are learning. Students collaborating on group projects also need to use empathy and verbal communication in order to work productively with their partners.

The theoretical key to integrating verbal and nonverbal communication is the mechanism of transfer or instillation of semantic pointers, combining verbal, sensory, motor, and emotional information. This perspective makes it easy to see why education is so difficult, much more difficult than one would expect if it were simply a matter of passing words from the head of the teacher into the heads of the students. Unlike the rapid transfer of computer files, education is a laborious, decades-long process of building up in the students' minds the rich set of semantic pointers already possessed by the teacher.

Inevitably, the students will not end up with exactly the same set of neural representations as the teacher, because their learning histories and innate capacities are not the same. Nevertheless, teachers can strive by multiple verbal and nonverbal methods to enable students to acquire some approximation to the teacher's mind. The generation of new educational methods exemplifies the procedural creativity discussed in *Brain–Mind,* chapter 11.

Educational communication can employ all four of the kinds of power outlined in chapter 6. Coercive power derives from threats such as expulsion for not getting vaccinated. Benefit power arises because teachers can give students rewards such as good grades. Instructors who are charismatic or just generally effective can get students to perform by motivating them to respect power. Finally, norm power increases educational effectiveness when institutions such as schools establish social practices that encourage voluntary compliance by students.

This view of educational communication fits well with many of the most effective classroom practices as determined by educational experience and experiments. Tracey Tokuhama-Espinoza lists 50 classroom practices whose effectiveness ought to be explainable by semantic pointer transfer. The following are just a few examples.

Plan activities that grab attention. Attention is limited because of brain capacity for complex bindings, and it is controlled by semantic pointer competition. If the teacher does not communicate in a way that enables new information to surpass the thoughts and emotions operating in the minds of the students, then communication fails and no learning takes place. This limitation justifies my longtime practice of banning use of laptops in my classes, because my best efforts had trouble outcompeting students' interest in Facebook and cat videos.

Use the Socratic method. In Plato's dialogues, Socrates taught by asking questions and then responding to students' answers, a method still commonly used in philosophy classes and law schools. From the perspective of semantic pointer communication, this method has the advantage of enabling teachers to recognize what is going on in the minds of students rather than just assuming that they will absorb whatever is being said in a lecture. Dialog enables communication from the students to the teachers who need to adapt their messages to the audience.

Be passionate. Emotion in education is not an optional addition but an integral part that goes beyond the installation of facts to communicate the values of concepts, beliefs, goals, and methods. Learning requires students to make implicit decisions about how to spend their time and attention, and decisions depend on emotional assessments of value. A passionate teacher communicates enthusiasm and values by gestures, facial expressions, and body language. The semantic pointer theory's integration of cognition and emotion makes it clear why emotional communication is a crucial part of education. I provide some more general advice for improving teaching after discussing conceptual change.

CONCEPTUAL CHANGE

For decades, conceptual change has been an important topic in developmental and educational psychology but always with a meager understanding of the nature of the concepts that are supposed to change. Understanding how teaching can bring about conceptual change requires good theories about concepts and belief revision.

The contention of the semantic pointer theory that concepts are brain processes would not cause problems for most psychologists, who accept that the mind operates by the brain. But several other aspects of the theory are more contentious and therefore more interesting for changing understanding of conceptual change. If concepts are semantic pointers that bind sensory, motor, and emotional information as well as verbal, then there is more to conceptual change than just the changes in sentences that psychologists have usually assumed. Conceptual change can be multimodal.

In the vaccination case, the most dramatic changes are emotional, when education revalences the concept of vaccine from negative to emotionally positive. Accepting vaccination may also require shifts in other values, for example concerning scientific approaches to medicine. Earlier chapters described other important kinds of revalencing, for example in overcoming prejudice.

In other cases of conceptual change, both in the history of science and in science education, there may also need to be changes in visual representations. For example, at the beginning of the twentieth century, there was a dramatic change in the concept *atom,* which since the ancient Greeks had been by definition indivisible. Experiments showed that atoms contain particles within them as well as much empty space. Hence atoms need to be visualized as systems of moving parts like the solar system rather than as solid balls. Therefore, educators who want to bring about conceptual change in their students need to be aware that changing concepts requires changing more than words.

Another strength of the semantic pointer theory of concepts is that it provides unified explanations of many psychological experiments that show that concepts encompass exemplars, typical features, and explanations. Accordingly, accounts of conceptual change ought to look for changes in all three of these aspects. For proponents of vaccination, standard examples include the indisputably successful applications of vaccines to prevent smallpox and polio, along with others in Table 12.2. In contrast, critics focus on a different set of more contentious examples, such as the swine flu scare of 1976, the measles vaccinations that are allegedly associated with autism, and controversial vaccinations for the HPV virus to prevent cervical cancer.

Pro- and anti-vaccination camps also tend to focus on different typical features of vaccines. On the mainstream public health view, vaccines are typically moderate in cost and effective in preventing diseases. In contrast, for vaccine skeptics the typical features of vaccines are low effectiveness and high negative side effects. Changing the concept of vaccine requires both shifting exemplars and dramatically replacing the associated set of typical features, producing a different prototype of vaccines.

In addition, the concept of vaccine plays another explanatory role in the minds of vaccine advocates compared to its role in the minds of vaccine skeptics. For vaccine advocates, vaccination provides a salutary explanation of the virtual eradication of diseases like smallpox and polio, as well as dramatic drops in the number of cases of measles and whooping cough. In contrast, the salient explanations for vaccine skeptics are ones in which vaccine are followed by bad results such as autism in children. Hence changing the concept of vaccine as part of public health education about vaccination is more than simply modifying the definition of the word "vaccination," requiring large shifts in exemplars, typical features, and explanations.

Some instructional problems require conceptual changes more radical than those needed for education about vaccination. Students often have difficulty grasping Darwin's theory of evolution by natural selection. First, it requires acquisition of abstract concepts that are far from the embodied experience of the students, such as random variation in the genes of organisms and selection for desirable genes because of their contribution to survival and reproduction. Second, for many students the theory of evolution runs counter to religious views that species, especially humans, were created by God. Third, the kinds of explanation that evolution gives for species is markedly different from familiar ones based on simple causes. The development of species is a statistical process with emergent properties that are qualitatively different from their predecessors. For example, humans have cognitive abilities not found in our ape ancestors such as the ability to use complex language. Hence to grasp the theory of evolution by natural selection, students need to acquire new concepts, beliefs, and explanatory styles.

The Darwinian revolution also exemplifies extreme kinds of conceptual change that make it difficult to grasp by learners. A major role of systems of concepts is to provide taxonomies that systematically classify things. One rare but important kind of conceptual change requires reclassification, where some things move from one part of the taxonomic tree to another. Darwin's views about the origins of species required one such major reclassification, with a shift from viewing humans as a special part of God's creation to recognizing our species as another kind of animal, like apes, canines, and insects. Some reclassifications have large emotional significance, because of the comfort associated with thinking of people as inherently special and the anxiety provoked in some people by the realization that humans are not special in the universe but merely another evolved animal.

Finally, the Darwinian revolution introduced another major kind of conceptual change that is hard for students to appreciate. Not only does Darwin's theory require reclassification, but it also requires a fundamental change in how classification is done. Before Darwin, species tended to be classified on the basis of their appearance, for example depending on whether they had feathers or fur. Darwin introduced a completely different way of doing classification by historical descent, a kind of conceptual change I call meta-classification.

What matters after Darwin is not just what two species look like but rather how they evolved from earlier species. With twentieth-century discoveries about genes and DNA, genetic information can be used to make inferences about evolutionary history and therefore to provide new classifications of organisms. In the meta-classification kind of conceptual change, the whole way of making classifications changes, which can also lead to reclassifications as well, for example the recognition that birds are related to dinosaurs.

Chapter 10 described the need for a radical transformation of psychiatry based on new ways of classifying diseases. Sadly, medical illnesses are still classified largely on the basis of symptoms, as in the fifth edition of the *Diagnostic and Statistical Manual of Mental Disorders*. It is widely recognized, however, that much deeper understanding and more effective treatment of mental illnesses should be realizable if the whole method of classifying mental disorders changed away from symptoms and toward causal origins. Such transformations have already occurred in classification of species based on evolutionary history and in classifications of diseases based on their origins in infections, nutritional deficiencies, metabolic problems, autoimmune problems, and other mechanism breakdowns. Psychiatry awaits massive conceptual change from meta-classification as well as from the resulting reclassification of diseases, likely introducing new concepts to capture deeper biological understanding of how mechanisms breakdowns cause mental illness.

Even more generally, the brain revolution brings with it major kinds of conceptual change that need to be incorporated into educational practice. Many new concepts for understanding the mind are being introduced, such as neural binding and semantic pointers. Some concepts that are central to folk psychology need to be deleted, such as soul and free will (while introducing freeish will described in chapter 11). Much reclassification is also required, for example recognizing that representations and meanings are processes, not things.

The brain revolution even changes the way in which mental states and events should be classified (meta-classification), because their taxonomy can rely on underlying brain mechanisms rather than on just conscious experience. For example, brain scans identify neural similarities between memory and imagination, which introspection might suggest to be different. The claims that concepts and other mental representations are brain processes is also a revolutionary reclassification. The radical conceptual changes that the brain revolution requires are a major challenge for teachers as well as students.

The difficulties that scientists have had in wrestling with these kinds of conceptual change should make us more sympathetic to the difficulties that young students have in trying to acquire theories and concepts that are very different from their previous experience. The best way to integrate these concerns about reclassification and meta-classification into semantic pointer theory of concepts is to notice that kinds are an important part of the typical features that objects are supposed to have if they fall under a concept. For example, it is a typical feature of atoms that they are a kind of particle. Teachers need to figure out ways of bringing about in their students all the kinds of conceptual change described here, including addition of new concepts, deletion of old beliefs, and modifications in emotional values, exemplars, typical features (including kinds), explanations, and sometimes even the whole method of classification.

TEACHING BETTER

The distinguished social psychologist Kurt Lewin said that nothing is as practical as a good theory. A theory of education based on deep accounts of cognition, learning, and communication should have strong implications for improving teaching. The following are some conjectures teachers should consider to improve their craft.

First, it is important to think of teaching as much more than the transfer of words. Instead, teaching should be viewed as semantic pointer communication, where teachers have to struggle to instill in the minds of learners the complex mental representations that they need to have to understand the subject material. Hence teaching should not be just talking, and lecturing needs to be supplemented by other techniques.

Second, the representations that need to be acquired by learners are multimodal, mixing sensory, motor, and emotional information with words. Depending on the domain, visual, auditory, and other perceptions and images may all need to be acquired by the student. Intelligence, therefore, is much more than linguistic and mathematical ability, because in some domains the sensory-motor aspects are just as important.

Third, for successful teaching, emotional aspects of instruction are just as important as cognitive ones. For students to acquire useful representations, they need to be able to attach emotional significance to specific concepts and beliefs as well as to the overall process of learning. Students need to acquire and change emotional values along with concepts and beliefs. Like overcoming prejudice in chapter 5 and treating depression in chapter 10, teaching often requires changing values.

Fourth, teaching and learning are both embodied and transbodied. They depend in part on the sensory-motor-emotional representations just mentioned, all of which are embodied. But for important domains such as science, engineering, and philosophy, teaching has to take learners beyond their sensory experience to acquire abstract concepts such as *atom, equilibrium*, and *justice*. Body-oriented education is a good start for many concepts such as *force* but is inadequate for abstract learning of concepts such as *gravity*. Teaching techniques should integrate bottom-up, embodied methods such as discovery learning and phonics with top-down, transbodied methods such as whole-word reading and abstract instruction.

Fifth, teaching techniques need to understand the difference between reasoning and inference. A teacher cannot expect that merely providing verbal reasons to students will change their minds. Rather, inference is a parallel process that integrates cognition and emotion, with effects that can be good if students reach conclusions based on explanatory and emotional coherence but bad if they fall back on motivated and fear-driven inference.

Sixth, teachers need to be aware that learning is not simply a matter of accretion of new concepts and beliefs but can require substantial amounts of conceptual change. Students often need to realize that their old concepts and beliefs are defective and need to be replaced by substantially new ones that alter how they classify the world.

Whether teaching can actually be improved by applying these lessons from new theories of cognition and communication is an empirical question. It will be interesting to see whether teachers can modify their teaching styles to make education more effective in ways suggested by semantic pointer theories of cognition, emotion, and communication.

SUMMARY AND DISCUSSION

Educational neuroscience is the attempt to apply rapidly increasing knowledge about the brain to the practical goal of improving learning and teaching. This chapter has proposed a novel approach to neuroeducation based on advances in theoretical understanding of representation, binding, and competition. Semantic pointers provide new insights into learning by specifying what kinds of representations need to be developed in the brains of learners who are acquiring complex information. Some of this information is verbal, but learners need to be able to integrate this verbal information with other modalities such as pictures and sounds.

The importance of multimodal representations is evident in two of the biggest challenges in early education: reading and mathematics. The research of Stanislaus Dehaene and others has shown the need to integrate multiple sources of information in both math and reading. To learn how to read well, children must become proficient at appreciating the connections among mental concepts, spoken words, and written words. Words on paper have a visual form, as do some aspects of concepts that are about visible things. For example, to read the sentence "The bear is on the mountain," a child needs to see the connections among the word "bear," the sound of the spoken word, and the mental representations of bear that could include exemplars stored in memory as pictures of bears.

Similarly, proficiency with numbers requires connecting, for example, the numeral 3, words such as "three," the sound of the word "three," the number sense for identifying small numbers such as three, visual representations of three things, and various procedural operations that can be done with numbers such as addition and subtraction. Multimodal representations are also required for simple concepts such as metal *spring* (visual, tactile, kinesthetic, auditory) and burning *fire* (visual, heat, auditory).

Semantic pointers are well equipped to explain how such an integration takes place in the brain. The child's understanding of the concept *three* must bind together spelling, sounds, and visual information. The ability of semantic pointers to bind together information in various modalities into a package that can be useful for further inference provides a good start at explaining how people children learn to read and do mathematics. It would be a valuable project to work out in rigorous detail how such complex neural representations can contribute to learning how to read and how to do math.

This chapter, however, addressed a different question: How do people learn about the advantages of vaccinations? I provided a social cognitive-emotional workup of the vaccine debate to show how people can learn why vaccines are valuable for public health and the protection of children. Teaching people about vaccines requires communication of many kinds of mental representation: concepts, values, images, beliefs, rules, analogies, and emotions. These representations include those that are embodied, such as mental images of the pain associated with getting a needle, but also those that are transbodied because of the importance of abstract concepts such as *immune system*.

Educating people about vaccines needs to take into account the complexity of the emotions and the inferences required. Convincing people to vaccinate children and themselves requires emotional change that lets people's natural attachment to the welfare of their children overcome fear of vaccination. The concept of vaccine needs to be revalenced to acquire positive emotional associations rather than negative ones. Inference is not a simple chain of verbal argumentation but rather a complex, unconscious, parallel process of satisfying multiple constraints. People need to acquire a set of beliefs and values as a coherent whole, not as isolated beliefs supported by discrete arguments. Such wholesale inferential change can result from systematic education, but it needs to surmount psychological barriers such as the fear-driven inferences that tend to make people leery of vaccination.

Semantic pointer theories of cognition provide a new perspective on learning in individual brains, but they also yield a new view of social aspects of teaching because of the complementary theory of communication. Learning is occasionally a solitary process, but teaching is always social, requiring the interaction among one or more teachers and one or more students. These interactions cannot be construed simply as the transfer of verbal information but instead need to be viewed as the instillation of much more complicated kinds of mental representations that combine sensory, motor, and emotional information with verbal representations.

Teaching, therefore, needs to be interactive, multimodal, embodied, and emotional. The job of teachers is not just to get their words into the minds of students but also a broader range of sensory, motor, information in the form of semantic pointers. A crucial part of this transfer is the transmission of emotional information about the value of particular concepts and beliefs, as well as the value of the whole educational enterprise.

From this perspective, education requires multilevel emergence at all four levels: molecular, neural, psychological, and social. Learning is a molecular and neural process because of the changes that need to take place for the brain to acquire synaptic connections that encode new information and change future behavior. Memory formation depends on changes in synaptic connections prompted by the neurotransmitter glutamate. Molecules such as dopamine and oxytocin are crucial for giving students the appreciation of reward and trust that are needed for learning in social contexts. Educational neuroscience should reach beyond connecting learning and teaching with the results of brain imaging to consider interacting mechanisms that are molecular, psychological, and social as well as neural. Cognitive psychology is indispensable for connecting neuroscience and education.

Patterns of neural firing and stored dispositions to generate such patterns constitute the semantic pointers that provide the means for combining multiple kinds of information. For teaching purposes, these representations are well described by psychological ideas about mental representations such as concepts and beliefs. Learning by imitation and teaching are also social processes in which the interactions that an organism has with another determine what neural and molecular changes take place in brains.

Teaching is a clear case of downward causation from the social to the molecular, because social interactions produce changes in brains right down to neurotransmitters such as glutamate and dopamine. Teaching is a kind of communication that requires transfer, prompting, instillation, replacement, and revalencing of semantic pointers. Learning is far from being a purely individual activity, because education requires people to interact with groups and institutions such as classes, schools, and school districts.

The implications of this view of education go far beyond the profession of teaching. Many organizations besides schools require ongoing education. For example, a major role of managers and businesses is to teach their employees how to perform their jobs better, and ongoing education is also important in medicine, government, and engineering. Hence the view of learning and teaching as the acquisition and transfer of semantic pointers is important for engineering creativity (chapter 13) and business leadership (chapter 14). Psychotherapy (chapter 10) sometimes involves teaching patients about how to improve their lives. To facilitate valuable social changes, people need to be educated about beliefs and values concerning important issues such as vaccination and climate change. Understanding how the brain works can help improve all of these kinds of education.

NOTES

Csibra and Gergely 2011 argue that only humans teach, but Safina 2015 provides nonhuman examples such as meerkats and killer whales. See also Kline 2015.

Some books on educational neuroscience; neuroeducation; and mind, brain and education include: Blakemore and Frith 2005; Della Sala and Anderson 2012; Immordino-Yang 2015; Mareschal, Butterworth, and Tolmie 2013; Posner and Rothbart 2007; Sousa 2011, 2014; and Tokuhana-Espinosa 2014.

On neuromyths about the brain and education, see Howard-Jones 2014; Newton 2015; Satel and Lilienfeld 2013; Tardif, Doudin, and Meyland 2015; and https://www.oecd-ilibrary.org/education/understanding-the-brain-the-birth-of-a-learning-science/dispelling-neuromyths_9789264029132-9-en.

Attempts to understand and overcome skepticism about vaccines include: Downs, de Bruin, and Fischoff 2008; Horne, Powell, Hummel, and Holyoak 2015; Kata 2010; Nyhan, Reifler, Richey, and Freed 2014; and Poland 2011. Goldenberg 2016 argues that vaccine skepticism is partly based on mistrust of science, not just lack of scientific understanding.

On global warming education, see Ranney and Clark 2016 and http://www.howglobalwarmingworks.org.

My map of values in public health is loosely based on the Harvard School of Public Health: https://www.hsph.harvard.edu/orientation/harvard-chan-core-values/

My workup of anti-vaccination views is based on the following websites:

http://educate-yourself.org/vcd/

http://whale.t,

http://www.stopmandatoryvaccination.com/vaccine-dangers/

http://www.ageofautism.com/2010/06/olmsted-on-autism-vaccinate-baby-vaccinate.html

http://www.forbes.com/sites/tarahaelle/2015/02/17/15-myths-about-anti-vaxxers-debunked-part-1/#4e3dd3932655

Gardner 2006 argues for multiple intelligences. Uttal, Miller, and Newcombe 2013 describe how enhancing spatial thinking can improve science education.

Tauber 2015 discusses the history of immunology and self metaphors. For metaphors for improving understanding of vaccination see Scherer, Scherer, and Fagerlin 2015 and http://www.metamia.com/analogize.php?q=vaccination. On the use of analogies in teaching, see Holyoak and Thagard 1995 and Vendetti, Richland, and Bunge 2015.

Angell 2004, 2009 reviews criticisms of drug companies.

On the importance of self-discipline, self-regulation, and executive functions for education, see Duckworth and Seligman 2005, Shtulman and Valcarel 2012, and Vosniadou et al. 2015. For why I banned laptops in my classrooms, see https://www.psychologytoday.com/blog/hot-thought/201007/banning-laptops-in-classrooms.

On conceptual change, see Carey 2009; Nersessian 2008; Thagard 1992b, 2012b, 2014b; Vosniadou 2008; and Vosniadou and Skopeliti 2014. Thagard 1999 recounts the history of the concept *virus*. *Natural Philosophy* (chapter 3), describes conceptual change in the brain revolution.

Thagard and Findlay 2010 discuss cognitive impediments to Darwin's theory of evolution.

The long overdue change in how mental illnesses are classified is illustrated in Clementz et al. 2015.

On brain processes in reading, see Dehaene 2009; Wolf 2007; and Yeatman, Dougherty, Ben-Shachar, and Wandell 2012. On multiple brain representations of number, see Dehaene 2014.

PROJECT

Apply semantic pointer insights to specific kinds of education such as reading, arithmetic, and science. Use the semantic pointer theory of emotion to provide an account of emotions crucial for education, including interest, curiosity, and boredom. Do social cognitive-emotional workups for related professions such as journalism and library and information sciences.

13

Engineering

CREATIVE DESIGN

Apple Inc. became one of the world's most successful companies by engineering products with superior hardware and software. Engineering is the practical application of sciences (such as physics, chemistry, and biology) to design, build, and use machines, structures, and other products, including the computers and iPhones that made Apple's reputation. These applications require various kinds of thinking, especially problem solving, to figure out how to make products that will accomplish goals such as commercial success. Engineering is clearly a cognitive enterprise, because individual engineers need to use their minds to determine how to apply scientific knowledge to solve practical problems. But engineering is also a richly social enterprise, because almost all work in designing and building products from bridges to computers is currently done collaboratively by people working in teams.

This chapter analyzes the mental and social mechanisms relevant to explaining successes and failures in one of the most exciting aspects of engineering, creative design. Construction and use of products are also important kinds of problem solving in engineering, but they depend on the original creation of those products. Design requires devising a system or process to meet the users' needs, and a product is creative if it is new, valuable, and surprising. The most useful technologies such as telephones, televisions, automobiles, airplanes, medical instruments, and computers are all the result of design creativity.

Understanding creative design requires specifying the mechanisms responsible for producing new products in the minds of engineers working in groups. Semantic pointer theories of cognition and emotion provide the relevant mechanisms for individuals, and semantic pointer communication furnishes the relevant mechanisms for group creativity. The key questions are: First, what are the ways in which new semantic pointers are generated in order to accomplish creative designs in the minds of individuals? Second, what are the ways in which group creative design is fostered by semantic pointer communication?

I answer these questions through case studies of technological breakthroughs in the development of Apple products, from their first personal computer to the iPhone. A social, cognitive-emotional workup of the work by Steve Jobs and others provides a thorough account of the relevance of individual and group mechanisms. This workup builds on the account of individual creativity in *Brain–Mind* (chapter 11) to incorporate social factors in the development of ideas that are new, valuable, and surprising. Designing new products requires minds to interact to generate novel concepts, images, and rules, including new procedural methods. To enhance the discussion of group creative design by Apple, I provide additional examples including the invention of the airplane by Wilbur and Orville Wright. Group creativity is an excellent illustration of multilevel emergence.

STEVE JOBS AND APPLE: SOCIAL COGNITIVE-EMOTIONAL WORKUP

By 2018, Apple Inc. was one of the world's largest companies with annual revenue of over $200 billion. But it began in 1976 with virtually no assets as a partnership of two young Californians, Steve Jobs and Steve Wozniak, to develop and sell personal computers. Apple's success depended on a series of engineering triumphs, from the early commercial personal computer, the Apple II, to spectacular consumer products such as the iPod, iPhone, and iPad. A social cognitive-emotional workup provides a systematic means of identifying the mental and social mechanisms that produced these triumphs.

Concepts and Values

Steve Jobs was squeezed out of Apple in 1985 because of disagreements with its CEO and board. When he returned to the desperately failing company in 1997 he said to a meeting of the company's top staff: "Tell me what's wrong with this place. It's the products. The products suck! There's no sex in them anymore." Jobs drastically reorganized the company, simplified its product line, and led the development of enormously successful new products from the iMac to the iPad. These innovations required development of new concepts through combinations of previous ones, all guided by additional concepts whose emotional force marked them as values.

All creativity, including scientific discovery, artistic imagination, social innovation, and technological invention, depends on novel combinations of concepts. The original personal computer developed by Steve Wozniak worked with existing concepts such as *chip, motherboard*, and *program*, but Wozniak put them together with his own ideas about how to connect a basic computer with a keyboard to provide efficient input and with an ordinary television screen to provide convenient output. These concepts are not merely verbal, because keyboards, televisions, and motherboards are also represented using vision, touch, and movement.

The contention that all creativity results from conceptual combination is supported by Table 13.1, which lists Apple's major innovations and indicates the concepts that were combined in novel ways to produce them. When Steve Jobs introduced the iPhone in 2007, he accurately presented it as a revolutionary product that combined a telephone, a music player, and an Internet appliance, all controlled by a novel touchscreen using a new technology that Apple called multi-touch. In contrast to existing smart phones such as the Blackberry, Apple rejected physical buttons as an effective input method despite the fact that they are ubiquitous on regular phones. The result gave people not only a powerful portable telephone but also a device that was effective for playing music and working on the Internet. The iPhone combined beautiful design in an elegant package with powerful technology, including a version of the Macintosh operating system and a flexible touchscreen.

TABLE 13.1

Concepts Contributing to Apple Creative Designs

Product	Year	Contributing Concepts
Apple II	1977	Chip, motherboard, program, keyboard, television
Macintosh	1984	Computer, graphical user interface, mouse, sound
iMac	1998	Computer, translucent shell, egg-shaped
iPod	2001	Music player, small hard drive, iTunes, scroll wheel
iPhone	2007	Telephone, music player, internet appliance, multitouch screen
iPad	2010	Computer, tablet

The accomplishments in Table 13.1 illustrate how Apple generated new products by combining concepts that integrate cutting-edge technology with beautiful design, making attractive products that were easy to use. Apple has always strived toward, and has frequently succeeded in, making systems that integrate powerful hardware and effective software in line with human needs. The concepts in Table 13.1 should not be understood as merely words in the head: their mental representations incorporate sensory modalities that include the visual appearance of an interface, the sound of speakers, the touch of a screen, and the movements of a mouse or scroll wheel.

The concepts behind Apple's success are not merely the technical ones about hardware and software. Steve Jobs and his most important collaborators were also driven by a set of values which are best understood as concepts with emotional attachments. Figure 13.1 presents a map of some of Jobs's most important values as reported by his biographers.

Jobs frequently said that the main driving force behind his work was the desire to make great products, a value shared by his most important collaborators, from Steve Wozniak to Jony Ive. In contrast to many entrepreneurs and executives, the goal of making money was always for them subordinate to the pride that came from producing wonderful machines. What made a device wonderful, however, was not just the engineering feat that it accomplished but also its ease of use by the people who bought it.

A key aspect of successful use of a product is simplicity, providing users with just the features they need rather than all the bells and whistles that some engineers proliferate, as in Microsoft Word. Steve Wozniak valued simplicity in his engineering designs, always trying to get the most results with the fewest number of chips. One key to simplicity is to focus on a small number of products. When Jobs revitalized Apple in 1997, he abandoned a large range of products that the

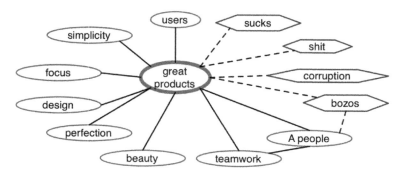

FIGURE 13.1 Value map of Steve Jobs. Ovals are emotionally positive, and hexagons are negative. Solid lines indicate mutual support, and dotted lines indicate incompatibility.

company had been trying to produce such as printers and the Newton personal digital assistant. Instead he insisted that the company focus on four main products: a personal computer for professional users and one for ordinary users, and a laptop for professional users and one for ordinary users.

For Jobs, another key to a positive experience for users is artistic design, not just the provision of powerful technology. Jobs insisted that great products need to combine art and engineering so that devices are beautiful as well as useful. Design should ensure that users feel good about their experiences with the products.

Steve Jobs was notoriously perfectionist, always wanting devices to have just the right appearance and performance. He was sometimes tyrannical in insisting that his coworkers live up to his standards, demanding last-minute changes that created great stress for his employees. But Jobs's perfectionism also often led to components that contributed substantially to the appeal of the products. For example, the iPhone was originally supposed to have a plastic screen, but Jobs insisted that a glass screen would look and wear better, and he managed to convince the president of Corning to produce the desired component.

Jobs realized that he could not produce great products by himself. Almost all the design of the Apple II was done by Steve Wozniak, who was a much more technically proficient engineer than Jobs. Later Apple products required teams of dozens or hundreds of engineers and designers, who had to work closely together to bring about the most effective combinations of hardware and software. Jobs maintained that one of the keys to effective teams was having what he called "A people" rather than "B people," where A people are ones extraordinarily talented in engineering and/or design. He realized from the start that great products depend on having on great team.

Jobs used the term "bozo" for incompetent people, applying this term to engineers, designers, and especially executives who did not pursue the goal of producing great products. In a 1995 video interview, Jobs talks about the "corruption" that set in at Apple during his absence, with managers only concerned about their own power and pay rather than the creative success of the company. For Jobs, the most common way of denigrating products that failed to be great was to say that they "suck" or are "shit." Both of these expressions summarize a set of negative emotions, including disappointment, disgust, and hatred.

The values in Figure 13.1 provided the motivation that drove Jobs and his coworkers to produce the engineering breakthroughs summarized in Table 13.1. The value concepts drove the combinations of technological concepts that produced Apple's revolutionary products.

Images and Embodiment

As already mentioned, the mental representations of computers and electronic devices are not merely verbal. Vision, touch, hearing, and motor control are all important aspects of people's use of machines.

Visual representations are needed for understanding how different components of a device will fit together and also for designing new components and overall systems. The Apple design team, now directed by Jony Ive, usually proceeds by having designers sketch possibilities using pencil and paper, which then can be developed in a more polished form as drawings. Designs can be fleshed out on computers using computer-aided design (CAD). Next, an important step in Apple design has always been the rapid production of physical models, because the look and feel of a constructed prototype can be assessed interactively. When the iPad was being designed, Ive's group produced many different mockups to get a physical feel for which version of the tablet would be best to look at and manipulate. With devices such as the iPod, Jobs wanted not only to see early versions but actually to handle them.

Before the Macintosh computer, people's interactions with computers were largely verbal through commands typed on a single line on the screen. The Macintosh enabled people to work with a visual display, seeing files and folders laid out on a screen. This display also allowed people to deal with different typefaces and layouts, which was one of the reasons why the Macintosh became popular in publishing.

Another major innovation that Apple borrowed from the Xerox Palo Alto Research Center was the mouse, which permitted people to have tactile and kinesthetic control over the screen. The graphical user interface and mouse have become standard in modern computers, but in 1984 they represented an enormous enhancement in controlling a computer by going beyond verbal commands and employing a broader range of sensorimotor representations.

In order to produce these innovations, Apple designers and engineers need to be able to imagine them, going beyond verbal inference to produce and transform images such as what the screen could look like, what the mouse could feel like, and what the speaker could sound like. *Brain–Mind* (chapter 3) shows how visual, spatial, tactile, and motor imagery can be understood as construction and transformation of semantic pointers. Steve Jobs and other people at Apple have been particularly successful in imagining the experiences of eventual customers, including their emotional as well as sensory-motor feelings. For commercial success, creators need to have a mental model of the mental models of their potential customers, so they can simulate how they would react to new products. Mental models are much more than verbal beliefs, because they can include images, analogies, and especially multimodal rules that enable the designer to run a mental simulation of what customers will experience perceptually and emotionally.

One design value shared by Jobs, Ive, and other people at Apple is to make devices a thin as possible, for example the iPhone 6, which is only 7 millimeters thick. In addition to being an aesthetic, emotional value, this preference depends on visual and tactile experience that comes from working with a refined object.

Sensorimotor imagery has been enormously important for the development of consumer products such as the iPod, iPhone, and iPad. Jobs insisted on the efficacy of the finger as an input device, enabling people to control their devices by pointing and moving with all the operations of the multi-touch technology such as swiping using two fingers. In the iPhone, vision, touch, and movement work together to control a powerful computer, which now includes auditory capability thanks to the Siri system for voice recognition. Apple's success, therefore, lies not just in its ability to integrate hardware and software but in its ability to exploit human mental representations that sight, sound, touch, and movement.

Visual and other kinds of imagery are also important for technological invention in other areas. The Wright brothers used sketches and scale models to develop their ideas about human flight. They also used many diagrams to assist visual imagery and concepts like *lift* that have motor associations. In a study of 100 technological inventions, I estimated that 87 had used visual representations to make the invention and 48 had used some additional kind of sensory-motor representation such as touch and hearing. Hence the creative design process for Apple and many other technologies is heavily embodied in the sense that the mental representations used depend intensely on the sensory processes that the body delivers. Another aspect of embodiment is the emotional contribution resulting from physiological changes.

Because engineering produces physical structures with which people can interact, it is much more embodied than nonapplied science with concepts that go beyond sensory imagination. In 100 examples of scientific discovery, I estimated that only 41 used visual representations to make the discovery and only 5 used another kind of sensory representation.

Through its reliance on theoretical entities such as electrons, genes, and viruses and because of its frequent use of abstract mathematics, science is much more transbodied than engineering. Nevertheless, engineering sometimes relies on abstract scientific ideas such as electrical voltage, and science often builds on initially embodied ideas such as force when it builds more abstract transbodied ideas. Hence engineering and science are each both embodied and transbodied but to different degrees.

Beliefs and Rules

Concepts are crucial ingredients of thought, but by themselves they cannot do much. Complex verbal inferences require beliefs, which are mental representations corresponding to sentences. These mental representations result from bindings of concepts into more complex structures that can make assertions about the world. People have tens of thousands of concepts and even more beliefs formed from them.

Steve Jobs left no books, articles, public letters, or emails, so it is not easy to identify his beliefs. His public presentations of Macintosh products are largely available on the Web but are limited to the products of the day and give little idea of his general belief system. Fortunately, in 2005 Jobs gave the graduation address at Stanford University, and its transcript is widely reproduced, including these pronouncements.

> You can't connect the dots looking forward; you can only connect them looking backward. So you have to trust that the dots will somehow connect in your future. You have to trust in something—your gut, destiny, life, karma, whatever. This approach has never let me down, and it has made all the difference in my life. . . .
>
> I'm convinced that the only thing that kept me going was that I loved what I did. You've got to find what you love. And that is as true for your work as it is for your lovers. Your work is going to fill a large part of your life, and the only way to be truly satisfied is to do what you believe is great work. And the only way to do great work is to love what you do. . . .
>
> Your time is limited, so don't waste it living someone else's life. Don't be trapped by dogma—which is living with the results of other people's thinking. Don't let the noise of others' opinions drown out your own inner voice. And most important, have the courage to follow your heart and intuition.

These beliefs about doing great work and loving it fit well with the system of values shown in Figure 13.1.

Steve Jobs's prescriptions about trusting your gut, heart, and intuition may seem obscure and even mystical, but they are consistent with the observations made by many writers on engineering that much of what engineers know is tacit (implicit) knowledge that is hard to put into words. Fortunately, semantic pointers provide a nonmystical way of understanding tacit knowledge, where not everything that people know can be captured by verbal beliefs easily translated into sentences. People's knowledge and expertise does not consist only of propositional knowledge-that but also needs procedural knowledge-how.

Knowledge-how does not reduce to sentences but can be captured by the sensory and motor aspects of semantic pointers. When Jobs looked at a newly designed object or interface and judged it to be ugly or hard to use, his judgment was based on perceptual, motor, and emotional representations that can be interpreted as semantic pointers. The look of a graphical user interface, the feel of a mouse or touchscreen, and the sound of speakers are all sensory-motor representations. The emotional judgment that something is cool or sucks is also a nonverbal neural pattern that combines representations of both physiology and unconscious appraisal into an emotional reaction.

Much of Steve Jobs's mental system is best understood not as verbal beliefs but as unconscious multimodal rules already observed in romantic relationships and other phenomena. Some of the beliefs eloquently stated in his graduation address had underlying multimodal rules better expressed in the notation: *<semantic pointer 1>* → *<semantic pointer 2>*. This notation indicates a nonverbal *if–then* relation between one sensory-motor-emotional representation and another.

For example, the second quote fits with multimodal rules such as the following:

<do great work> → *<be satisfied>*
<love what you do> → *<do great work>*

These rules have large emotional components connected with the concepts of *great, satisfied*, and *love*. Moreover, *work* may have a strong sensory-motor component because of the visual and kinesthetic dimensions of engineering.

Tacitly, Jobs applied multimodal rules when he evaluated existing and proposed products. In its simplest form, these rules could be something like:

<ugly> → *<sucks>*
<hard to use> → *<sucks>*

In these nonverbal rules, *ugly* is both visual and emotional, and *sucks* is clearly emotional. *Hard to use* may also be kinesthetic and motor, if a switch is difficult to reach or a mouse motion is hard to perform.

Hence multimodal rules that encompass sensory, motor, and emotional information were an important part of what enabled Steve Jobs to make effective judgments about the quality of past and future engineering attempts. His collaborators such as Steve Wozniak and Jony Ive were similarly capable of mingling verbal beliefs with sensory-motor-emotional rules.

Steve Jobs's concepts, values, beliefs, and multimodal rules contributed to many products that were creative in the sense of being new, valuable, and surprise.

Brain–Mind (chapter 11) shows that creativity produces especially valuable rules that provide new methods. Did Jobs, Wozniak, or Ive generate new methods in the form of rules that could lead to the production of better products?

One important example of procedural creativity at Apple was the development of the Apple new product process (ANPP), following the 1998 launch of the iMac. The ANPP is a set of rules for bringing new products to market by laying out every stage of product development. The more typical procedure is having a new product developed in the engineering department, then passed on to the design department for cosmetic appearance, then sent to the marketing department to devise a sales strategy. In contrast, ANPP has all of these departments working together at every stage for every product. In order to anticipate and meet the needs of consumers, marketing plays a role in creating products along with engineering and design. ANPP contributes both to speed of development and to the production of more effective products because of collaborative contributions from different departments in the company.

An earlier case of procedural creativity in engineering was the creation by Thomas Edison of the research and development laboratory. The Wright brothers also developed novel methods in their pursuit of the first powered flight, including extensive use of wind tunnels and real-life experiments at Kitty Hawk. Their emphasis on testing and practice helped to make them more successful than previous attempts to fly that were primarily based on theory.

Analogies and Metaphors

Analogies and metaphors have contributed to creativity in many domains of human thinking, including science, technology, and the arts, so it is not surprising that they also contributed to the development of Apple products. The first Apple computer, in retrospect called the Apple I, was inspired by the microcomputer Altair 8800. Steve Wozniak realized that he could put together a superior design, with improved input via a keyboard and improved output via a television screen.

Apple's most important analogical breakthrough was the result of the 1979 visit by Steve Jobs and several Apple engineers to the Xerox Palo Alto Research Center. Jobs was amazed to see the new technologies incorporated in the Xerox Alto computer, including a graphical display that could show pictures on the screen rather than just a single line of words. The Alto also had a mouse to control the cursor on the screen and document processing using what-you-see-is-what-you-get. These features were incompatible with the Apple II computer that was the Apple standard for years but were incorporated into the unsuccessful Lisa computer and eventually into the much cheaper and far more commercial Macintosh computer. Microsoft later borrowed the graphical interface and mouse device for its Windows operating system, by analogy to the Macintosh.

In words, the analogical inference that Jobs made could be understood as: the Xerox Alto has wonderful features, so Apple should build a new computer with similar features. But as the discussion of images and multimodal rules has already indicated, it would be a mistake to try to reduce this analogy to verbal representations. Designing the Lisa and Macintosh to be like the Alto required visual transfer from what the screen on the Xerox computer looked like to what it might look like on an Apple computer.

Similarly, motions for moving the mouse to control the cursor introduce an element of motor control and kinesthetic imagery. The most important multimodal rule required to work with the new interface include representation of how moving the mouse moves the cursor on the visual display: <*move mouse*> → <*move cursor on screen*>. The relevant semantic pointers are tactile, visual, motor, and kinesthetic as well as verbal. Another semantic pointer involved in the analogical transfer from the Alto to the Lisa was emotional, as Jobs transferred his initial excitement over what Xerox had produced into enthusiasm for new Apple products. Hence analogical mapping and transfer are multimodal, not just words.

Part of the analogical transfer that made the Macintosh work was carrying over the metaphors that Xerox had for its graphical interface. The computer screen became a desktop that had various folders containing files. When a file was deleted, it was placed in the metaphorical trash, signified visually by a trashcan. These metaphors were adapted by Microsoft when it produced its Windows interface by analogy to the Macintosh. Ordinary users need know nothing about the inner workings of the computer, because the desktop metaphors allow them to work with familiar ideas such as files and folders.

Another analogy operated when Jony Ive was inspired to come up with a design for the first iMac to use a flat-screen display by a sunflower that he had seen in Steve Jobs's garden. Just as a sunflower has a narrow stalk with a large flower on top, Ive designed the 2002 iMac to have a flat screen on top of a flexible pole that was attached to a base that contained the main parts of the computer. The resulting design does not look like a sunflower, but it carries over a similar relational structure.

Nontechnical analogies can help people to be more effective by adopting successful people as role models. Steve Jobs admired Bob Dylan and Picasso for always risking failures, rather than doing the same thing over and over again. Having such role models encourages creativity over the conventionality that often establishes itself in bureaucracies. Another role model that Steve Jobs applied was Ed Catmull, encountered when Jobs started working with Pixar in 1986. Catmull was an expert in computer graphics who became an effective and imaginative manager of creative people at Pixar, providing Jobs with a model of how a collaboration of highly creative technologists can flourish. Chapter 14 on business discusses Catmull's views on creative leadership.

There are many other cases where analogies contributed to major technological inventions. In developing the airplane, the Wright brothers drew frequently on analogies to the flight of birds, gaining information about fundamental aspects of aerodynamics such as balance and lift. Like the analogical transfer from the Alto to the Lisa, the analogical inferences of the Wright brothers were visual and kinesthetic as well as verbal and mathematical. Observing various kinds of birds such as buzzards, eagles, and hawks enabled them to figure out how flight was possible in general and to develop particular aerodynamic models of how wings provide lift. In current engineering, biomimicry has been used to develop new products such as Velcro by analogy with systems found in nature.

The Gutenberg printing press was partially modeled analogically on available olive presses. The term "press" is metaphorical based on an embodied analogy with how humans press down. Alexander Graham Bell's design for a telephone drew on his knowledge of the workings of the ear, and microscopes are adapted from eyeglasses. Technological analogies are always partly visual, but they can also draw on other senses such as sound, touch, heat, and motor movement. Because of their sensory-motor aspects, engineering analogies are frequently embodied, whereas theoretical analogies in science can be more abstract and transbodied, as when physicists applied the mathematics of non-Euclidean geometry to relativity theory.

Analogies can also provide negative advice about what does not work. Jobs was emphatic in not wanting to repeat the mistakes of the Newton stylus-using personal digital assistant and the clunky operation of early smartphones. Initially, the Wright brothers wanted to model their airplane's propeller on a boat propeller but realized that this was a bad analogy. They also intentionally worked to avoid the mistakes of airplane inventors who did not do sufficient testing. Negative role models are also sometimes a useful kind of analogy, for example, not being like Adolf Hitler.

Emotions and Actions

As my quotes from Steve Jobs's Stanford address show, emotion was a huge part of his success. After Jobs's death in 2011, Ive summarized his attitudes:

Steve loved ideas and loved making stuff, and he treated the process of creativity with a rare and wonderful reverence. He, better than anyone, understood that while ideas ultimately can be so powerful, they begin as fragile, barely formed thoughts, so easily missed, so easily compromised, so easily just squished. His was a victory for beauty, for purity, and as he would say, for giving a damn.

The value map in Figure 13.1 shows Jobs's strong attachment to ideas and products. He cared deeply and enthusiastically about making things that are beautiful, simple, and useful to people.

Another acute description of the large role of emotion in Jobs's thinking was given by Ed Catmull, his long-time collaborator at Pixar:

We tend to think of emotion and logic as two distinct, mutually exclusive domains. Not Steve. From the beginning, when making decisions, passion was a key part of his calculus. At first, he often elicited it in a ham-handed way, by making extreme or outrageous statements and challenging people to respond. But at Pixar, even when we were a long way from being in the black, that aggressiveness was tempered by his acknowledgment that we knew things about graphics and storytelling that he did not. He respected our determination to be the first to make a computer-animated feature film. He didn't tell us how to do our work or come in and impose his will. Even when we were unsure how to reach our goal, our passion was something Steve recognized and valued. That's what Steve, John [Lasseter], and I ultimately bonded over: passion for excellence—a passion so ardent we were willing to argue and struggle and stay together, even when things got extremely uncomfortable.

For Jobs, a passion for excellence provided a much stronger motivation for intense work than any cold cost-benefit calculation ever could.

Steve Jobs's passion for great products and his fervent conviction that they can be produced helped to make him a charismatic leader who could strongly motivate other people to carry out ambitious plans. His energy, enthusiasm, and bravado contributed to this charisma, a kind of leadership inspired by emotional attachments that is discussed further in chapter 14 on leadership. Jobs needed enthusiasm to motivate himself but also to inspire others to work extraordinarily hard at producing new products at great speed. For example, the team that produced the Macintosh wore T-shirts that said: 90 hours a week and loving it. Part of the appeal of being an engineer is finding the work fun—the joy, pride, and other emotions that come from solving challenging problems. Such emotions provide the energy needed to pursue the near-impossible.

Jobs's charisma produced what became known as his "reality distortion field," his ability to convince people to do things that calmer, rational deliberation would rule out, such as producing and shipping new products in a remarkably short period of time. People working with him learned that they could do the impossible, repeatedly. Jobs viewed passion as essential to success: "Unless you have a lot of passion about this, you're not going to survive. You're going to give it up. So you've got to have an idea or a problem or a wrong that you want to right that you're passionate about; otherwise you're not going to have the perseverance to stick it through."

Besides excitement and enthusiasm, other emotions also contribute to high-quality work and creative design. Many technological products originate in frustration, the emotion that results from obstacles blocking goals. Steve Jobs and his coworkers were all frustrated by the cell phones they used, which provided part of the motivation to build something much better in the form of the iPhone.

Pride is also a motivating emotion because engineers can anticipate how proud they would be to carry off the kinds of design that they want. Wozniak and Jobs both wanted to be proud about the computers they produced, not just about the money that they made. Pride is sometimes reviled as the deadliest of sins, but it is often a valuable emotion connected to the fundamental psychological need for competence: people want to feel good about their accomplishments in work, play, and other aspects of life. Other emotions that helped to propel Jobs on his successful path were self-confidence, intensity, focus, and caring deeply about the impact of everything he did.

Unfortunately, strong emotions can also have negative effects, for example when Jobs's drive for perfection made him impatient with other people, sometimes subjecting them to temper tantrums and abrupt dismissals. Partly under the influence of Ed Catmull, however, he became less impulsive and more patient as he grew older.

Interest is an emotion that is milder than excitement but can nevertheless have important long-term effects. While still in their teens, Jobs and Wozniak were sufficiently interested in computers to learn as much about hardware and software that they could, eventually applying that knowledge in developing Apple. Similarly, the Wright brothers developed an interest in flight long before they set out to build an airplane. Orville Wright said: "I got more thrill out of flying before I had ever been in the air at all—while lying in bed thinking about how it would be to fly."

A major part of the commercial success of products such as the iMac and the iPhone was the ability of Steve Jobs and Apple designers to anticipate the emotional responses of consumers. Jobs was always trying to anticipate how purchasers would feel about the products and even about the packaging in which they arrived. Apple does not use focus groups because the aim is to produce products that will provide customers with things that they did not know that they needed. Such innovative product design involves a kind of empathy in which the designers put themselves in the shoes of customers and imagine how they would feel. Such imagining goes beyond the verbal, analogical mode of empathy to employ rule-based simulation, in which the designer imagines customers opening the iPhone box and feeling the beautiful machine in their hands. This kind of empathy is a combination of imagery, multimodal rules, and analogical inference, all of them emotional.

Another aspect of customer satisfaction is trust, which chapter 4 argued has a large emotional basis. People want to be able to trust their computers and other devices, feeling good about them as well as believing that they have a low probability of failure. Macintosh computers were valued by customers compared to competing PCs by virtue of being less likely to crash or be infected by viruses. People grew to trust not only Apple's computers but also the company itself and possibly also its leader, Steve Jobs. Figure 4.3 provides a semantic pointer portrait of trust that binds five components, including representations of the self, what is trusted, the aspect in which it is trusted, and the emotional components of physiology and appraisal. Chapter 14 describes the important contribution of trust to group productivity.

In sum, emotions are important for the motivations and practices of engineers, designers, and marketers, who must also anticipate the emotions and motivations of potential customers. Chapter 14 discusses marketing as emotional, focusing on successful ad campaigns run by Apple.

Inferences

There must have been times when Steve Jobs and other Apple personnel made decisions by conventional deductive, inductive, abductive, and cost-benefit inferences. But it is clear from both Steve Jobs's behavior and his Stanford quote that many of his judgments were intuitive. However, intuition is not a mystical process akin to communication with the gods but rather a process of parallel constraint satisfaction that includes emotional coherence.

What are the sources of Jobs's frequently successful intuitions about successful products? He knew a lot about both design and engineering and also understood how simplicity, elegance, and ease of use matter to customers. All of these provide constraints on product development that are hard to specify as rules but that can contribute to a largely unconscious process of parallel constraint satisfaction. The result comes to consciousness as an emotional reaction such as *wow, cool*, or *sucks*.

Gut feelings do partially come from the gut because nerves from the stomach carry some of the information that goes into the brain's perception of physiological changes. But emotions as semantic pointers also require cognitive appraisal, an assessment of a product or situation with respect to relevant goals. Steve Jobs was equipped to perform competent appraisals because of his extensive knowledge about technology and the world in general. Creative engineers, however, are as susceptible as everyone else to motivated inference and therefore need be cautious that their product evaluations are accurate rather than self-serving.

Communication and Collaboration

My discussion of mental processes based on semantic pointers may give the impression that engineering creativity is a solitary enterprise. But many of the greatest inventions have been produced collaboratively, for example when the Wright brothers worked with each other and their assistants to produce the first airplane. Thomas Edison is famed as a great inventor, but he depended heavily on several teams of workers and co-inventors. Similarly, the great achievements of Apple have all been collaborative, from the first personal computer (Wozniak and Jobs) to the iPhone (Ive, Jobs, and many others). Nearly 100 people contributed directly to the Macintosh, which Jobs viewed as an upper limit for team size. Thousands of people worked on aspects of the iPhone, leading to more than half a billion sales.

What makes successful collaborations work? Answering this question requires merging the mechanisms of individual thinking so far discussed with social mechanisms that enable people to communicate with each other. Social mechanisms of communication must go beyond words because of the importance for technological creativity of multimodal representations that are also sensory, motor, and emotional. The semantic pointer theory of communication can explain the flow of complex representations among collaborators.

Apple Computer started with Steve Jobs and Steve Wozniak, who provided complementary skills. Wozniak was a brilliant computer designer who produced the Apple I and Apple II computers almost entirely on his own, using the kinds of verbal, visual, and kinesthetic planning described earlier. But his designs might only have been local curiosities without the drive of Steve Jobs to turn them into commercial products. Jobs was technologically adept enough to make a few useful suggestions concerning components, but his main contribution was to use his social skills and self-confidence to make valuable connections in marketing as well as in technology. Wozniak much later said about Jobs: "If there was anything that neither of us knew how to do, Steve would do it. He'd just find a way to do it.

He was just gung ho and pressing for this company to be successful." Whereas Wozniak was shy, Jobs was extroverted and even aggressive in dealing with other people, adding valuable social capabilities to Wozniak's introverted technical expertise. Wozniak knew how to build computers, but Jobs knew how to sell them; both skills were crucial for Apple's early success.

For collaborations to be productive, the contributors need to have similar values as well as similar knowledge. Jobs did not know as much about computer design as Wozniak, but he knew enough to appreciate the significance of his breakthroughs. Most importantly, Jobs and Wozniak had similar values about making technological advances and producing great products; Wozniak's writings display many of the values shown in the Jobs's value map in Figure 13.1. However, Wozniak was not interested in dramatically new techniques such as graphical user interfaces that went into the Macintosh, and he contributed little to Apple's progress after the early 1980s. Jobs did not design the hardware or software for the Macintosh, but he heavily influenced its friendliness and use of appealing features such as typefaces and rectangles with curved corners. Jobs eventually had a share of more than 200 patents.

For later developments, from the iMac to the iPad, the most important contributor was Jony Ive, who worked with a large team of designers and engineers including Steve Jobs. After Jobs returned to Apple, he quickly realized that Ive shared his values about producing simple, beautiful, and effective technologies. Jobs frequently visited the design studio where Ive worked, and they had lunch together several times a week. Jobs liked Ive's taste, judgment, and ambition, and their common values frequently gave them the same kinds of emotional intuitions about designs and products. Their shared interest in products and design was intensely emotional, extending to fascination and delight.

Although Ive was sometimes annoyed by Jobs's habit of passing off other people's ideas as his own, Ive acknowledged Jobs's contribution to the creative process. "In so many other companies, ideas and great design get lost in the process. The ideas that come from me and my team would've been completely irrelevant, nowhere if Steve hadn't been here to push us, work with us and drive through all the resistance to turn our ideas into products."

Chapter 3 describes various ways in which emotional communication can be accomplished through facial expressions, body language, and tone of voice that go much beyond the utterance of words. Jobs was particularly uninhibited about conveying his emotional dislike of shoddy work, through yelling, tantrums, and verbal expressions such as "that sucks."

The success of Apple's designs depends on having very creative individuals such as Jony Ive but also on a loose management structure that encourages collaboration and creativity, as the example of ANPP illustrated. Designers work together on various projects with connections to engineering and marketing but also have a high degree of independence. Designers sometimes also work competitively, pursuing different parallel design directions in small groups, and Apple occasionally consults design agencies from outside the company. All proposed designs are documented by photographers.

Jony Ive's biographer summarizes the advantages of the management structure set up by Bob Brunner:

> In hindsight, Brunner's choices—the studio separation from the engineering groups, its loose structure, the collaborative workflow and consultancy mindset—turned out to be fortuitous. One of the reasons Apple's design team has remained so effective is that it retains Brunner's original structure. It's a small, tight, cohesive group of extremely talented designers who all work on design challenges together.

Like the ANPP process, setting up a productive design group in new ways is a kind of procedural creativity, producing new social methods for collaboration.

As the earlier discussion of imagery indicated, much of the communication among collaborating designers is visual, requiring sketches and more detailed drawings. The communication problem here is difficult: how to get the picture that operates in one person's mind for a potential design into the head of another person, at least approximately. Words can only provide a step toward this kind of transfer, because they cannot efficiently convey all of the aspects of appearance and structural organization that go into a picture. It is much more effective for one designer to translate a mental picture into a sketch and then show it to another designer, who can then translate the sketch into a mental picture for future work.

Technological developments have made this kind of complex transfer of visual images much more effective. One was the development in the fifteenth century of linear perspective, enabling drawings to capture the three-dimensional characteristics of a mental picture. A twentieth-century development that fostered visual communication was CAD (computer-aided design), which enabled one designer to use a graphical user interface (thanks to the Macintosh) to produce a three-dimensional image on the screen that other people can immediately translate into their own perceptual experiences.

Despite their psychological power, drawings, and CAD screens are no substitute for complete three-dimensional objects, and Apple moves quickly to the development of physical models in order better to assess the look and feel of potential designs. These models are enormously valuable for communication, because designers can get a better sense of what they all are thinking about what a product should look like. Critically discussing a physical model provides another way of transferring semantic pointers with respect to look and feel, including emotional reactions.

The Wright brothers also learned heavily from physical models, both in wind tunnels and through kites and gliders tested at Kitty Hawk. Their work was also highly collaborative, particularly with each other. They even lived together and so could continue vehement discussions into the evenings.

The importance of collaboration and communication make it clear that Apple's success resulted from much more than the brilliance of individual engineers and designers. It would be a gross mistake to attribute the success of Apple just to the brains of Steve Jobs or Steve Wozniak, because they depended heavily on numerous collaborators with whom they could communicate images and emotions as well as words. Leaders at both Pixar and Apple have devoted much time and expense to creating buildings and workspaces that encourage collaboration.

ENGINEERING CREATIVITY

The phrase "engineering creativity" is valuably ambiguous. It can mean creativity that occurs in engineering through the design and production of products that are new, valuable, and surprising. But the phrase also can mean designing social arrangements to make people and groups more creative. The social cognitive-emotional workup of Apple's success provides some hints about how to make groups more creative. Additional suggestions about group creativity derive from Catmull's account of leadership in chapter 14.

For individual minds, creativity depends on taking representations that were previously unconnected and forming a new representation that can be evaluated for its potential contribution to people's goals. To make individuals more creative, the best advice is to ensure that they have a large stock of representations along with the time and motivation to come up with new combinations.

There are various ways in which a group of people can be more creative than an individual. The simplest is for two individuals in a group to each contribute one of the relevant representations, where one idea from one person gets combined with another idea from the other person. Combination has to take place in the minds of one or both individuals, through a neural mechanism such as the binding of representations into new semantic pointers. But without social interaction between the individuals the combination would never have been made.

The iPhone was the result of this kind of social process with different designers and engineers contributing different ideas. Apple already had the iPod as a successful music player, but various engineers and designers were needed to figure out how to extend the device into a telephone. At the same time, Apple engineers with expertise in operating systems had to discover how to adapt the Macintosh operating system for a small device. The idea of a multi-touch interface was borrowed from another company that Apple bought. Ives and his team figured out how to put the hardware and software together in a graceful design. Steve Jobs made an additional contribution by insisting on an elegant hard glass screen rather than a plastic one. The result of different people contributing different ideas was an astonishingly successful product.

Several modifications are needed to this simple account of group creativity as a mingling of mental representations from different individuals. First, the whole procedure can be iterative, not just the brilliant insightful combination but also the repeated occurrences of new combinations based on new communications. Developing the iPhone was a multiyear process of recurrent creativity as ideas about hardware, software, and design evolved together. Second, sometimes the collaborative contribution looks more like a modification of an existing representation when a collaborator can suggest some useful change. For example, Jobs's addition of a glass screen was a fairly simple modification of the existing design, although it did require the novel combination of *screen* and *glass*.

Third, part of the collaboration is not just the generation of the new representation but also the emotional reaction to it that can be crucial for ongoing pursuit and development. Collaborators share emotions such as enthusiasm and excitement along with the newly created joint concepts, images, beliefs, and rules. Fourth, individual cognition depends on neural and molecular mechanisms as well as mental ones of combining representations, so emphasis on communication and individual thought should not neglect how these depend on lower level mechanisms. For example, the excitement that comes from engineering a great product requires social interactions where neural firing in dopamine-dependent neurons in the nucleus accumbens of one individual leads to similar neurochemical processes in another.

Hence group creativity is an important instance of multilevel emergence. In one individual's mind, creativity is already an emergent process because it results in a new representation such as the concept *iPhone* with properties that are not just the sum of the concepts that went into it. Incorporating social interactions into the process of creativity makes it clear that communicative mechanisms such as the transfer of multimodal representations among individuals are also important for creativity. Whereas the Apple II computer was largely the result of the designs by Steve Wozniak, its commercial success, and later products from the Macintosh to the iPad, resulted from multilevel emergence in interacting mechanisms that include social ones. Moreover, combinations of concepts is best understood as binding of neural representations, and the important contribution of emotions to creativity requires attentions to molecules such as dopamine.

Causality in collaborative engineering and design is therefore not just from lower levels to higher but also in the other direction, for example when social interactions with Steve Jobs made engineers excited. Therefore, creative designs in engineering result from multilevel emergence in systems that are social, mental, neural, and molecular.

What lessons follow for fostering creativity in engineering design and other social enterprises? The following are a few speculative suggestions.

First, find creative individuals. The talents and motivations of people like Steve Wozniak, Steve Jobs, and Jony Ive are rare. For reasons that go beyond IQ, people differ in their abilities to quickly acquire new ideas, to use their working memory capacities to combine concepts into still newer ones, and to have the emotional drive to put the ideas to use. Look for people capable of using mental tactics such as analogy and metaphor to combine existing ideas into novel ones.

Second, make sure that the group of creative individuals contains a diversity of interests and talents. In its early days, Apple needed both the engineering skills of Wozniak and the entrepreneurial skills of Jobs, and later products required a host of engineers and designers. If all the individuals in a group have the same backgrounds, then they will tend to make the same conceptual combinations. But if some members of the group have interests and representations that are unusual, then their ideas may combine with the ideas of someone else to produce something truly novel. For example, Jobs was unusual in having developed an interest in calligraphy during his brief undergraduate education, which carried over into producing attractive typefaces for the Macintosh once graphical user interfaces became feasible.

Third, harmonize cognitive diversity with emotional unity found in shared values and goals. A group will be more effective if people have approximately the same values, such as Apple's commitments to great products, user friendliness, and beautiful design. Chapter 4 described the importance of trust in romantic relationships, with trust viewed as a mental process that is emotional as well as cognitive, and this chapter mentioned the needs of consumers to trust products and companies. Similarly, collaborations work best when the individuals in them proceed on more than self-interest thanks to shared values that enable people to trust each other.

As in my solution to the person–group problem in chapter 9, talk of shared values does not mean that there is some mysterious entity called a group that has another mysterious entity constituting the shared value. Rather, values are shared in the sense that (a) individuals all have similar neural processes and (b) the particular values that people have result in part from their communicative interactions. Values and interactions are influenced by how people represent themselves as members of the relevant group.

Fourth, establish social arrangements that foster communication of all kinds, including verbal, sensory, motor, and emotional transfer. Without such interactions, the development of new ideas by collaborative conceptual combination cannot occur. Encourage people to be socially sensitive and to distribute the conversation equally, providing a psychologically safe environment for constructively critical improvements. Experienced people should be eager to teach their knowledge and skills to newcomers, using all the cognitive-social methods described in chapter 12.

Fifth, encourage social differentiation within the organization, such as the design competition that Apple uses and the ongoing influence of other groups such as outside design teams. Creativity can benefit not only from the interactions of multiple individuals but also from the interactions of multiple teams.

Sixth, encourage cognitive flexibility and exposure to conceptual change in both individuals and groups. Be open to new conceptual combinations, as, for example, when Steve Jobs was able to introduce the iPhone as a combination of phone plus music player plus Internet, three practices that were previously taken to be unconnected. Hence the concept of iPhone introduced a coalescence of previously separate concepts. Be willing to delete concepts that no longer are useful, such as the floppy disks that the iMac controversially discarded and the multiple ports that became unnecessary once USB technology became available. New versions of the iMac do not even have a drive for CDs and DVDs, on the assumption that the Internet has made these largely obsolete. Be willing to reclassify concepts, for example when the Apple II extended *computer* from a corporate machine into a personal item, and when the Wright brothers extended *flight* from an activity of birds to a pursuit of humans.

These are just some of the ways in which creativity in engineering design might be improved by modifying both psychological and social practices. The advice should apply to any organization aimed at creativity, including universities, research organizations, and the businesses discussed in chapter 14.

Can creativity be taught? The six recommendations just given are meant to be transmitted to other people, but the open question is whether any person or group actually becomes more creative as the result of learning them. Design thinking is increasingly being taught in institutions such as Stanford University's d.school (https://dschool.stanford.edu/) and the global design company IDEO (ideou.com), but I know of no study that shows that people who take such courses end up more creative than other people with similar intelligence and industry.

Nevertheless, in the hope of fostering creativity, I offer a set of suggestions based on what contributed to the great success of leading scientific researchers. My sources were a group of psychologists, philosophers, and historians at a conference on scientific thinking, as well as writings by three important scientists: Santiago Ramón y Cajal, Peter Medawar, and James Watson. The following is the resulting list, organized into six categories.

1. **Make new connections**.
   Broaden yourself to more than one field.
   Read widely.
   Use analogies to link things together.
   Work on different projects at the same time.
   Use visual as well as verbal representations.
   Don't work on what everyone else is doing.
   Use multiple methods.
   Seek novel mechanisms.
   Find new ways of making problems soluble (e.g., by new techniques).
2. **Expect the unexpected**.
   Take anomalies seriously.
   Learn from failures.
   Recover from failures.
   Avoid excessive attachment to your own ideas.
   Be willing to recognize and admit mistakes.
3. **Be persistent**.

Focus on key problems.

Be systematic and keep records.

Confirm early, disconfirm late.

Concentrate tenaciously on a subject.

4. **Get excited**.

Pursue projects that are fun.

Play with ideas and things.

Ask interesting questions.

Take risks.

Have a devotion for truth and a passion for reputation.

Have an inclination toward originality and a taste for research.

Have a desire for the gratification of discovery.

Have a strong desire to comprehend.

Never do anything that bores you.

5. **Be sociable**.

Find smart collaborators.

Organize good teams.

Study how others are successful.

Listen to people with experience.

Foster different cognitive styles.

Communicate your work to others.

Marry for psychological compatibility.

Tell close colleagues everything you know.

Communicate research results effectively.

Learn from winners.

Have people to fall back on when you get into trouble.

Avoid boring people.

6. **Use the world**.

Find rich environments.

Build instruments.

Seek inspiration in nature.

Have good laboratory facilities and use them.

Observe and reflect intensely.

Perform experiments that rigorously test hypotheses.

Although this list was derived from reflection on scientific practice, almost all the suggestions are potentially relevant to enhancing creativity in other domains, including technology, the arts, and improving social institutions.

SUMMARY AND DISCUSSION

I have applied social cognitivism to the profession of engineering, concentrating on the development of creative designs. There is nothing mysterious about creativity when it is viewed as the outcome of interacting mental and social mechanisms. In individual designers, thinking is multimodal, depending on sensory, motor, and emotional representations in addition to words. Creativity works in minds that are capable of taking previously unconnected representations and combining them into ones that turn out to be new, valuable, and surprising.

Well-functioning groups such as design teams, scientific laboratories, and artist colonies can be more creative than individuals on their own when the groups foster communication of semantic pointers among individuals. Words and emotions are always an important part of the communication of ideas and attitudes, but in various fields it can be equally important to transfer pictures, sounds, motions, and even tastes. Musicians, for example, need to be able to communicate melodies and rhythms, which they can accomplish more easily by playing an instrument than by writing down musical notes. Chefs working together to produce a new menu can convey their ideas to each other by sharing new concoctions that convey imagined tastes among individuals.

Apple's production of novel and successful products such as the Apple II, Macintosh, iMac, iPod, iPhone, and iPad illustrates the mental and social mechanisms responsible for creative design. Apple's people including Steve Jobs used an interconnected mixture of concepts, values, beliefs, rules, analogies, and metaphors to generate new computers and consumer products. None of these products would have arisen without social processes of communication and collaboration. Collaboration depends not only on the transfer of verbal signals but also on the communication and instilling of sensory-motor information as well as emotional attitudes encapsulated into values.

My social cognitive-emotional workup of the development of Apple technologies suggests lessons for fostering the creativity of other collaborative enterprises, in science, government, and the arts. Assemblies of individually talented individuals can be made even more creative if they possess both unity and diversity. The unity comes from common values and mutual trust, but the diversity comes from having different concepts and methods that can be combined into new ones. Multimodal communication is crucial to ensure that not just the words but also the images and emotions of one person can be transferred into the brain of another. Social arrangements are also required to encourage diversity and flexibility within the groups. These strategies are also useful in other organizations, including businesses, which the next chapter analyzes as cognitive/social enterprises.

NOTES

On creativity in engineering and design, see Chan 2015, Cropley 2015, Dhillon 2006, and Ferguson 1994.

My main sources for the workup of Apple are Dormehl 2012; Isaacson 2011; Lashinsky 2012; Kahney 2009, 2013; Schlender and Tetzell 2015; and Wozniak 2007. The Jobs quote "Tell me what's wrong" is from Kahney 2009, p. 16.

On cognitive processes in creativity, see *Brain–Mind* (chapter 11), Boden 2004, Sawyer 2006, and Thagard 2012b, which includes the analysis of 200 examples of creativity in science and technology. *Natural Philosophy* (chapter 9) discusses creativity in art.

John-Steiner 2000 discusses creative collaboration. Fagerberg, Mowery, and Nelson 2005 review innovation.

Steve Jobs's 1995 interview is at https://vimeo.com/31813340. His remarkable introduction of the iPhone is at https://www.youtube.com/watch?v=x7qPAY9JqE4. His moving Stanford address is at http://news.stanford.edu/news/2005/june15/jobs-061505.html.

On beauty as emotional coherence, see Thagard 2006. *Natural Philosophy* (chapter 9) discusses beauty and other aesthetic emotions.

The achievements of the Wright Brothers are described in McCullough 2015, McFarland 1972, Wright 1953, and Wright and Wright 2002. Johnson-Laird 2005 provides a cognitive explanation of their inventions.

On tacit knowledge in engineering, see Ferguson 1994 and Nightingale 2009.

The contribution of analogy to creativity is discussed by Hofstadter and Sander 2013 and Holyoak and Thagard 1995. On analogies in engineering, see Chan and Schunn 2015.

The Ive quote "Steve loved ideas" is from Schendler and Tetzell p. 411.

Catmull 2014 is an acute analysis of creativity in organizations; see chapter 14. His quote about Jobs is from the Kindle edition.

Silvia 2006 discusses interest as an emotion.

The Jobs quote "Unless you have a lot of passion" is from Kahney 2009, p. 154.

On the importance of emotion for design, see Norman 2003.

The Wright quote "I got more thrill" is from Wright 1953, p. 78.

The Wozniak quote "If there was anything" is from Livingston 2007, p. 48.

The quote "In hindsight, Brunner's choices" is from Kahney 2013, p. 74.

The Ive quote "In so many other companies" is from Kahney 2013, p. 252.

On emotional cognition in urban planning, see Thagard 2016.

On the effectiveness of teams and collective intelligence, see Duhigg 2016; Malone and Bernstein 2015; Muthukrishna and Henrich 2016; and Woolley, Chabris, Pentland, Hashmi, & Malone 2010. In line with the discussion of the person–group problem in chapter 9, talk of collective minds, brains, and intelligence should be viewed as metaphorical, pointing to complex interactions of mental and social mechanisms.

On design thinking, see Cross 2011, Mootee 2013, and Shelley 2017. My advice on how to be a creative scientist originated in Thagard 2005 (reprinted in Thagard 2006).

PROJECT

Do social cognitive-emotional workups of case studies in human-machine interaction, architecture, and urban planning. Develop an agent-based model of group creativity. Do a three-analysis of the concept *style*. Identify and analyze further examples of group procedural creativity, such as Apple's ANPP.

14

Business

VISION

What makes a good leader? Jack Welch, the highly successful chief executive officer of General Electric, said: "Good business leaders create a vision, articulate the vision, passionately own the vision, and relentlessly drive it to completion. Above all else, though, good leaders are open. They go up, down, and around their organization to reach people." This quote raises important questions for social cognitivism as an approach to the professions. What is a vision and how can it be articulated? What passions attach to the vision and drive it forward? How can leaders reach people in their organizations such as businesses?

Business raises many important issues about the operations of minds in groups besides leadership. How can managers and employees make effective decisions? How can managers teach their employees to work more effectively? How can businesses in general, not just the engineering firms discussed in the last chapter, be creative in developing new products and services? Once a business has a product to sell, how can it market the product using advertising and other methods? Answering each of these questions requires an understanding of what goes on in the minds of individuals and also of how they interact with each other. I now focus on questions about leadership and marketing, because the other questions are considered elsewhere: decision making in *Brain–Mind* (chapter 9), teaching in this book (chapter 12), and creativity in *Brain–Mind* (chapter 11) and this book (chapter 13).

Following the procedure already used for many social sciences and professions, I explain business operations as the result of interacting mental and social mechanisms. This chapter provides social cognitive-emotional workups of a very successful leader, Ed Catmull, and of effective marketing campaigns accomplished by Apple. A major theme in both of these workups is the role of emotions, not as distracting elements of irrationality but as crucial components in individual thinking and communication in groups. However, there are also important cognitive elements because thinking and communication are also influenced by concepts, rules, analogies, and inferences.

One of the most prominent strands in current discussions of leadership is emotional intelligence, the ability of people to recognize the emotions of themselves and others and to use emotions to regulate the behaviors of individuals and groups. Because emotional intelligence is important for marketing as well as for leadership, I begin by showing the relevance of semantic pointer theories of cognition, emotion, and communication to understanding how emotional intelligence works. This connection between emotional intelligence and semantic pointer theories provides the basis for the workups of leadership and marketing, as well as for prescriptive advice concerning how businesses and other organizations can operate more effectively.

EMOTIONAL INTELLIGENCE

The concept of emotional intelligence has been frequently applied to the study of organizations, based on the claim that emotional intelligence is far more important than general intelligence and analytic ability for predicting and understanding the success of leaders. Without endorsing this strong claim, I think that emotional intelligence does point to important components of leadership and also can be highly relevant to marketing. My goal in this section is to show how understanding of emotional intelligence can be deepened by considering the mental and social mechanisms based on semantic pointers.

Emotional intelligence is the capacity of people to use understanding of emotions to guide thinking and behavior. According to Daniel Goleman, leaders can enhance the performance of themselves and their organizations by possessing five skills: self-awareness, self-regulation, motivation, empathy, and social skill. Self-awareness and self-regulation largely depend on individual cognitive and emotional mechanisms, whereas empathy and social skill are clearly social, requiring mechanisms of interactive communication. Motivation is both individual and social, because leaders need to strive for excellence themselves but also to inspire other people and organizations to perform well.

Self-awareness is the capacity to recognize your own emotions and their effects, to know your strengths and limits, and to have a strong sense of your own worth and capabilities. Self-regulation is managing your internal states, impulses, and resources to achieve self-control; trustworthiness; conscientiousness; adaptability; and innovation. Motivation consists in the emotional tendencies that lead to the accomplishment of goals such as striving to meet a standard of excellence and to accomplish the objectives of the organization. Empathy is awareness of other people's feelings, needs, and concerns, including understanding coworkers as well as customers. Social skill is the ability to induce desirable responses and others by effective tactics for persuasion, listening, negotiating, inspiring, managing change, nurturing relationships, collaborating, and creating groups that are effective in pursuing collective goals.

Social cognitivism deepens the understanding of emotional intelligence by specifying mechanisms responsible for emotions, intelligent problem solving, the self, motivated action, empathy, and communication. According to the semantic pointer theory of emotion summarized in *Mind–Brain* (chapter 7), emotions are brain processes in which patterns of neural firing bind together several representations: the situation, the self, appraisal of the extent to which the situation fits with the goals of the self, and physiological changes. None of these processes is accessible to consciousness, so recognizing one's own emotions in self-awareness has to rely on attaching to a situation a verbal label drawn from everyday talk about emotions.

For example, people can recognize that they are happy, sad, angry, or afraid by introspecting their feelings and noticing their behavior. Introspection is a crude tool, however, and can be supplemented by monitoring more analytically the nature of the situation, the place of the self in it, the goals that affect the appraisal of the situation, and the physiological changes that contribute to the emotional experience. Wrist computers are available that monitor stress by tracking heart rate, body motion, temperature, and electrical changes across the skin. Other relevant physiological changes are facial expressions, body language, gestures, and internal gut feelings. Reflection on connections between situations and goals can shed light on the basis for unconscious appraisals. Consequently, self-awareness of emotions can draw on all the components in the semantic pointer theory of emotions, not just introspection.

According to chapter 12, intelligence is the ability to solve problems and learn in ways that go beyond verbal, analytic intelligence to include imagery and social abilities. Because many of the most important problems that people face are social, there is a great need for comprehension of emotions that transcends verbal descriptions such as linguistic concepts to encompass nonverbal images, analogies, and multimodal rules. Therefore, thorough analysis of the emotional intelligence of leaders and others needs to consider in detail all of these kinds of mental representations, as illustrated in the social, cognitive-emotional workup of Ed Catmull's leadership advice.

Emotional intelligence emphasizes self-awareness and self-regulation without saying anything about the nature of the self. *Brain–Mind* (chapter 12) presents a theory of the self as a complex system of multilevel mechanisms encompassing the molecular, neural, mental, and social. The self is not just a set of concepts that people apply to themselves but also depends on molecular mechanisms derived from genetics, epigenetics, neurotransmitters, and hormones. Also relevant are neural mechanisms such as patterns of firing, binding, and competition and mental mechanisms such as parallel constraint satisfaction, motivated inference, and fear-driven inference. People are inclined to see themselves more positively than they actually are when using motivated inference, and some people with low self-esteem are prone to see themselves more negatively than they actually are using fear-driven inferences. Social mechanisms are also relevant to understanding the self, because self-awareness can be variable depending on social situations: people, for example, may think of themselves as extraverted when interacting with close friends but introverted when facing a large and hostile audience.

Empathy is highlighted as a major component of emotional intelligence but with little specification of how people recognize the feelings of others. Some inferences about others' emotions are abductive, for example when you infer that the best explanation of people frowning and withdrawing from social contact is that they are sad. Empathy, however, is more than verbal inference, for it involves experiencing something like the emotions of another person, using three modes based on different underlying mechanisms: analogy, mirror neurons, and multimodal rule simulation. Empathic individuals such as effective leaders can employ all these modes of empathy in appropriate circumstances, by imagining themselves in other peoples' shoes, by mirroring their bodies, and by using sensory, motor, and emotional images to simulate their experiences.

Emotional intelligence operates not only in individuals but also in groups. Some teams can be more effective by virtue of possessing collective emotional intelligence. Collective intelligence is an emergent property of a group that results not just from the aggregate of the intelligence of the individuals but also from their interactions that lead the team to get better results than the individuals could on their own. By extension, collective emotional intelligence emerges when the group gets effective results by enhancing the emotional awareness, regulation, motivation, empathy, and social accomplishments of the whole group. The key to such enhancements is communication that transfers words integrated with emotional representations such as values and attitudes. Organizations such as businesses, educational organizations, government agencies, and sports teams can have emergent properties of effectiveness that result from communications that increase emotional intelligence.

An important part of achieving collective emotional intelligence is the establishment of social norms that encourage effective interactions. As chapter 5 argued, social norms are rules that specify what kinds of actions are appropriate in particular kinds of situations, but such rules are often hard to specify verbally. For example, a group could have a social norm that says: *If people are anxious, then support and encourage them.* This rule encourages more effective cooperation than one found in hostile organizations: *If people are anxious, then criticize and embarrass them.*

Such rules may be expressed in this way verbally, but they can also have a large multimodal component that is visual, auditory, kinesthetic, and emotional. You may recognize people as anxious by their visual appearance and body language. The social norm then prompt actions such as kind words, smiles, and other forms of emotional support, prompted by the multimodal rule: <*agitated*> → <*support*>. Group behaviors are then like the interpersonal relationships described in chapter 4, which are heavily driven by unconscious multimodal rules composed of semantic pointers.

Half of the basic qualities for managerial success listed by Henry Mintzberg are emotional: courageous, committed, curious, confident, candid, reflective, open-minded, tolerant, charismatic, passionate, inspiring, visionary, energetic, enthusiastic, upbeat, optimistic, ambitious, tenacious, zealous, engaging, supportive, sympathetic, empathetic, and fair. But his list also includes qualities that are cognitive and physical: insightful, innovative, connected, informed, perceptive, thoughtful, intelligent, wise, pragmatic, decisive, action-oriented, proactive, ambitious, persistent, collaborative, stable, dependable, accountable, ethical, honest, flexible, balanced, integrative, and tall. He concludes that great leaders do not have to be wonderful so much as emotionally healthy and clear-headed.

I have shown how vague ideas about emotional intelligence can be amplified by connecting them with mental and social mechanisms employing semantic pointers. Before looking more specifically at the role of emotional intelligence in leadership and marketing, let us consider the important phenomenon of charisma.

CHARISMA

Charisma is defined as compelling attractiveness or charm that can inspire devotion in others, but this definition does not address the emotional nature of attraction and inspiration. Table 14.1 presents a three-analysis of charisma that provides a richer characterization. The exemplars include Steve Jobs, whose charisma was discussed in chapter 13, and other prominent leaders and celebrities, both good and bad.

The typical features of charismatic people explain the effects they have on others. These are *typical* features, not defining characteristics, so exceptions such as Hitler's lack of empathy do not defeat the three-analysis. Most charismatic people exhibit emotional expressiveness that displays their intensity and confidence, but they are also sensitive to the emotions of others by practicing empathy. Emotional control is important for charisma because sometimes leaders need to disguise their extreme emotions in order to be effective with others.

Social expressiveness is skill in verbal and nonverbal communication that enables charismatic people to be entertaining and effective public speakers. Social sensitivity is the ability to interpret complex social situations by listening to others and becoming intimate with them. Social control is the ability to fit in with all sorts of people and make emotional connections with them by operating with poise and grace.

People who possess these features can influence other people in ways that secure their devotion and contribute to social and business success. Hence charisma has an important explanatory role in assessing leadership. With a leader such as Steve Jobs, who was effective at instilling emotions in the form of values and motivations in other people, a group can be more successful at accomplishing its goals in such fields as politics and business. Charisma can also contribute to marketing

TABLE 14.1

Three-Analysis of *Charisma*

Exemplars	Steve Jobs, Hitler, Lenin, Mao, Ronald Reagan, Justin Trudeau, Oprah Winfrey
Typical features	Charming, visionary, confident, powerful, engaging
	Emotional and social expressiveness, sensitivity, empathy, and control
Explanations	Explains: devotion, political success, business success
	Explained by: mechanisms of emotional communication

when products are endorsed by people who are emotionally attractive and compelling. Chapter 6 describes respect power that leaders have over people who like and admire them, and charisma provides a high degree of this kind of power. Leaders with charisma have less need to resort to coercion or benefit power, and they may subtly be able to establish norm power.

Charismatic leaders usually have a novel but compelling vision, but what is that? Social cognitivism suggests that a vision is an emotionally coherent system of values, goals, beliefs, and plans. Figure 13.1 provides a value map of Steve Jobs' system of values and goals, which constituted an important part of the vision that he used to turn Apple around. Other important elements of his vision included his beliefs about where Apple had gone wrong and his plans to simplify its product line. Charismatic leaders such as Jobs can impart their vision to followers by a combination of verbal and nonverbal communication that instills in coworkers an arrangement of semantic pointers roughly similar to their own. The best way to flesh out a vision is to perform a full social cognitive-emotional workup, which I do next for one of Jobs's most important collaborators.

LEADERSHIP OF ED CATMULL: SOCIAL COGNITIVE-EMOTIONAL WORKUP

Edwin Catmull is an American computer scientist who became president of Pixar Animation Studios and Walt Disney Animation Studios. He contributed to many breakthroughs in computer graphics, including the development at Pixar of the first full-length computer-animated film, *Toy Story*, in 1999. Pixar was founded when Steve Jobs bought the digital division of Lucasfilm, and Catmull worked closely with Jobs for decades. In 2014, Catmull published an insightful book, *Creativity Inc.*, which provides the basis for the following workup.

Concepts and Values

Catmull's book mentions many concepts that he views as important to the success of Pixar and computer animation. His central concept is *creativity*, which requires ways of dealing with uncertainty and instability. He views creativity as a property of organizations, not just individuals, and emphasizes the importance of cooperation, collaboration, and communication. People in creative domains must accept risk and trust the people they work with, engaging with anything that creates fear.

In addition to these social concepts, the success of Pixar has depended on numerous technical concepts drawn from computer graphics and animation, such as 3D rendering. A central concept for figuring out how to make movies that are entertaining as well as technologically impressive is *story*, because people need characters and plot to engage them.

Catmull's concepts were not simply ways of describing the world but also values that guided his emotional reactions and actions. Figure 14.1 maps some of the most important values that Catmull espouses. The creativity required to produce a successful animated movie depends on individual people, how they work as a team, and how together they produce good stories and good animations using new kinds of technologies. The people that Catmull wants to have working with him are individually smart and passionate, but they also work well as part of the large teams that are required for producing animated movies.

Teammates must be capable of collaborating productively with each other, ensuring that improvements can be made to early versions that are rough and flawed. These improvements require communication that brings about constructive criticism accompanied by suggestions about how the product can be improved. The work of the team and its ability to deal with constructive criticism depends on candor, trust, and honesty, all of which combat the fear that Catmull stresses is inimical to creativity. When people are afraid of failure and embarrassment, they become overwhelmed with uncertainty and unduly secretive, which hinders candor and communication. As a leader, Catmull saw his job to establish an atmosphere that encouraged the activation and spread of the desirable values shown in Figure 14.1, while managing and controlling the destructive effects of fear, secrecy, and uncertainty.

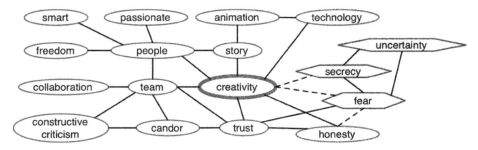

FIGURE 14.1 Map of Catmull's most important leadership values. Ovals are emotionally positive, and hexagons are negative. Solid lines indicate mutual support, and dotted lines indicate incompatibility. For clarity, not all links are shown.

Images and Embodiment

Pixar's business is creating animated movies, so imagery is a central part of its process and products. A story writer needs to be able to imagine what characters are doing, for example two animals talking to each other. Such imagination requires several kinds of representation: visual imagery about what characters look like and how they are spatially organized, sound imagery about their voices and songs, and kinesthetic imagery about how they move their bodies while interacting. If the movie involves food, as in Pixar's *Ratatouille,* then taste and smell imagery can also contribute to a writer's ability to tell a good story. Because emotions are an important part of storytelling, it is also important that writers be able to imagine feelings such as joy, sadness, fear, anger, and disgust, which actually become characters in Pixar's 2015 film *Inside Out.*

Like computer design, story design proceeds in stages from the verbal description to drawings to computer animations produced with the aid of technology. Hence the thinking that goes into producing animated movies is clearly embodied, as evident in the centrality of emotions. Catmull's own thinking is clearly imagistic when he uses metaphors such as balance that are discussed in the section on analogy.

However, even for movies whose primary audience is children, it would be a mistake to suppose that embodiment captures everything. Catmull insists that superb animation requires that each character on the screen be believable as a thinking being, whether it is a toy or a desk lamp. Viewers need to sense not just movement but also intention and emotion for the story to be interesting and credible. These mental states are not directly observable in the shapes, sounds, and motions of the animated characters, but the animation must enable viewers to infer their existence.

Pixar's movies such as *Toy Story* convey not only the immediate intentions and emotions of the characters but also abstract ideas such as friendship, respect, tolerance, teamwork, heroism, and even Buzz Lightyear's "to infinity and beyond." The job of the storytellers and animators is to trigger such inferences in ways discussed in the section on inference. Hence the importance of sensory imagery and embodiment for animated movies is compatible with how even children's entertainment requires a high degree of transbodiment involving inference and abstract concepts.

Beliefs and Rules

Catmull's book contains thousands of sentences that he believes. The most important beliefs relevant to leadership take the form of rules concerning what to do in different circumstances. The following are some paraphrased rules recommended by Catmull that are not always in the *if–then* form but that could easily be reformulated.

When problems arise, finding a solution is often a multistep endeavor.

Organizations should be collaborative and supportive.

People need to be creative not only technically but also in how they work together.

Hire people who are smarter than you are.

Use a flat organizational structure without a lot of hierarchy.

Share your work with the outside world.

Managers need not only to have good ideas but also to gain support for those ideas among the people they manage.

Ignorance plus a driving need to succeed forces rapid learning.

The responsibility for finding and fixing problems should be assigned to every employee.

Every employee should have a voice and be treated with respect.

Self-assessment and constructive criticism should occur at all levels.

Foster a creative culture that continually ask questions.

Build a sustainable credo culture that encourages honesty, excellence, communication, originality, and self-assessment.

Focus on the habits, talents, and values of people.

Find, develop, and support good people.

Creativity is iterative, requiring candid feedback and frequent reworking.

Create an environment where people are open to criticism from others and where everyone has an interest in each other's success.

Seek out people who are willing to be honest with you.

Don't let your actions be governed by fear of failure and mistakes.

The best antidote to fear is trust.

People need to be wrong as fast as they can.

Any time you impose limits or procedures, ask how they will aid people to respond creatively.

People want their leaders to be confident.

Maintain a sense of intensity and playfulness.

A creative company must never stop evolving.

Identify passionate people.

Creativity requires loose controls, acceptance of risk, trust of colleagues, efforts to clear the path for them, and paying attention to what creates fear.

The goal is excellence, not ease.

Imagine making the impossible possible.

Honor the viewpoint of others.

Some of these rules are substantially multimodal, for example that the
 best antidote to fear is trust. Understanding fear and trust as emotional
 experiences, this becomes *prevent <fear>* → *<trust>*. Multimodal rules may
 supply the unwritten rules that provide social norms in an organization.

These rules are general, but Catmull and his colleagues at Pixar also established some more specific rule-like practices that constitute procedural creativity for groups. One practice was the establishment of a "brain trust" to
provide regular evaluations of the progress of all major projects. The brain trust
was a group of top executives who were experienced at giving incisive but constructive and supportive criticism to directors concerning their progress. The
brain trust meets every few months to assess each movie in progress, aiming
to deal with problems and root out mediocrity. Other creative procedures include a job-swapping program that moves people between departments to increase mutual understanding. Another creative procedure includes following
the launch of every new movie with a postmortem session in which people can
evaluate its successes and failures. Technologically, Pixar developed many new
methods for computer animation, such as ways of rendering three-dimensional
images.

Analogies and Metaphors

Analogies and metaphors have also influenced Catmull's leadership practices.
His first creative work environment was the Computer Science Department at
the University of Utah where he completed his PhD. Funded by the Pentagon's
Advanced Research Projects Agency, ARPA (later DARPA), this organization
strongly encouraged excellent work in an atmosphere of freedom and collaboration. Catmull tried to make Pixar work more like a creative academic department
than a traditional, hierarchical, commercial organization.

Another analogy that influenced Catmull's view of leadership was the Toyota
practice of giving employees autonomy in being able to halt an assembly line if
there was a problem that could diminish quality. He instituted analogous practices at Pixar that were aimed at making every employee, regardless of level, feel
responsible for the success of the company.

Catmull frequently resorted to metaphors to describe the difficulties of managing. Sometimes he felt like he was balancing on the backs of a herd of horses,
including thoroughbreds, wild ones, and struggling ponies. Balancing is a rich

metaphor that draws on visual and kinesthetic images to suggest the need to deal with different kinds of people, for example when directors and marketing people are pulling in different directions. Catmull says that the best views of balance are dynamic, coming from sports such as a basketball player spinning around a defender or a running back bursting through the line.

He borrowed some analogies from his colleagues, such as that a firm is like a ship going downriver that had been cut in half or like a train headed West with the most important thing to be moving toward something. Managing is like sailing where you have to embrace the elements rather than trying to control them. It is also like running through a long tunnel where you have to trust that you will eventually come out the other end. Making a movie can be compared to a maze or to an archaeological dig. Writing a screenplay is like climbing a mountain blindfolded. A producer is a chameleon who needs to change colors depending on which constituency is involved. Catmull describes several comparisons concerning the search for an unseen destination.

All of these comparisons, whether in the form of analogy, metaphor, or simile, serve to help a leader deal with the enormously complex problem of managing a creative organization. Metaphors have contributed to the appeal of leaders, according to a study that found that charismatic US presidents use more metaphors than noncharismatic ones, as in Ronald Reagan's influential campaign ad proclaiming that "it's morning again in America." Such positive metaphors can facilitate motivated inference that a leader will make things better, but scary metaphors can facilitate fear-driven inference that there are threats, as in Reagan's "bear in the woods" ad where the bear stands for communism.

Catmull frequently talks about the importance of building and rebuilding mental models, which he seems to understand mostly as a mixture of analogies and metaphors. Such comparisons are an important part of mental models but so are the concepts, images, and rules already discussed.

Emotions and Actions

Catmull never discusses techniques often taken as the pinnacle of management rationality: maximization of expected utility and multiattribute decision making. Instead, he frequently discusses the role of emotions in creative decision making. He frequently stresses the need to manage fear, which interferes with the needs for risk taking and collaboration that are essential to the progress of creative organizations. Another toxic emotion that he warns against is resentment, which interferes with the requirement of a collaborative enterprise that people respect and feel comfortable with each other.

Catmull's major antidotes to fear are the social mechanism of communication, promotion of honesty and candor, and especially the development of trust. As described in chapter 4, trust is an emotional attitude that is crucial for the functioning of social relationships. Trust and mutual respect make it possible for constructive criticism to be effective without generating negative emotions in the person criticized. To prevent fear from arising among employees, leaders must repeatedly demonstrate their trustworthiness. For an organization to be effective, employees should not only trust their leaders but also feel loyalty and respect for their leaders, which are also emotional attitudes. Loyalty is not just a cognitive plan to follow a leader but also a feeling that the leader deserves following. Similarly, respect is a feeling of admiration of someone judged to be good, valuable, and important. Leaders who have earned trust, respect, and loyalty can count on employees to go along with their orders and suggestions. A study of American politicians found that virtuous leaders who manifested wisdom, courage, justice, and temperance were more effective in the long run than leaders who manifested vices such as psychopathy and narcissism.

Trust is normally an attitude toward people, but one of Pixar's core principles is "trust the process." The employees at Pixar view themselves having a different process of making movies than other studios, one better at dealing with the inevitable difficulties and mistakes in any creative endeavor. Through procedures such as constructive criticism and the brain trust, employees of Pixar become confident that difficulties can be overcome. Here the slogan "trust the process" points to a complex of emotional attitudes toward the people involved, the organization, and the procedures developed to work toward creative excellence.

To be effective, leaders must be aware of additional emotions that affect the operation of an organization. Catmull reports that all movies suck at the beginning, and the important goal is to move from "sucks" to "not suck." As it was for Steve Jobs in chapter 13, sucking is an emotional reaction expressing disapproval, disappointment, and even disgust. Not sucking is an understated emotion that suggests that something is at least satisfactory.

Pixar's leaders and personnel aim for much more positive emotions than not sucking, and they sometimes achieve excitement, exhilaration, and pride. Pride builds on the fundamental psychological needs for competency and achievement. The people at Pixar feel pride when they help fix problems in movie developments, respond to crises, hold true to their ideals, make sure that artists and technical people treat each other with respect, generate emotional reactions in audiences and reviewers, invent a new art form while remaining open to new ideas, and run a fine company. A milder positive emotion sometimes experienced is relief, when various crises such as the near failure of the company in its earliest years were dealt with.

Catmull stresses the importance of empathy in people's interactions. He remarks that Steve Jobs in the early years of Pixar exhibited little ability to put himself in others' shoes but eventually acquired the capacity for empathy, caring, patience, and wisdom. Catmull says that the feedback system that is crucial to Pixar's process of developing movies requires empathy to ensure that criticism is viewed as constructive rather than harsh. Empathic feedback built on the idea that people are all in it together operates on a daily basis, as well in the less frequent interventions of the brain trust. Catmull also took steps to foster empathy between departments, so that artistic and technical groups would understand each other's emotions.

Creative people must employ empathy for each other but also for the people intended to buy and use their products. As the later discussion of advertising shows, it is crucial for marketers to anticipate and generate the emotions of consumers. For consumers of movies, this means figuring out how to generate emotions that will make them value the movie, including the emotional journeys of the various characters in the movie.

Finally, it is clear that a passion for excellence drove the actions of Catmull, Jobs, and other leaders at Pixar. Catmull frequently mentions passion as a positive characteristic of leaders and employees. Many actions are required in the execution in the development of a film, under circumstances much too complex for numerical calculations. Instead, emotional judgments aimed at quality and success become the determinants of action. A leader with emotional intelligence can encourage the entire organization to employ these valuable passions.

Inferences

Catmull says that development of a movie such as *Toy Story* requires thousands of decisions made by dozens of people, with frequent inferences about what to do in particular contexts. Sometimes serious problems require a company to pivot and adopt a radically new strategy, which requires inferences that the old strategy was not working and that the new strategy will be better. Catmull does not say much about how decisions are made at Pixar, but he does support the need for insisting on quality and excellence. He also stresses that decision making is better when the company is able to draw on collective knowledge.

Catmull always tries to make decisions to maintain a trusting environment, avoiding finding scapegoats for errors in ways that could establish an atmosphere of fear. Decisions should be shaped in part by the desire to maintain a healthy

creative culture in which people feel free to speak up. It is impossible to understand every facet of a complex environment, so maintaining ways of combining
different viewpoints is crucial for long-term success. Leaders also need to be concerned with the inferences of consumers to develop products and marketing that
provoke decisions to buy.

Communications

From his early days at Pixar and the creation of *Toy Story*, Catmull worried a great
deal about communication. He made a point to be accessible to all employees, including wandering into people's offices. He wanted to make sure that everyone
at Pixar had a voice and was treated with respect. As in the Toyota analogy mentioned earlier, Catmull wanted all employees to be concerned with fixing problems
and to play a role in fixing them by talking to management. Such engagement requires constant flows of two-way communication, with everyone feeling free and
safe to communicate with everyone else.

Collaboration on large projects such as a movie requires communication both
within groups and across groups. In working on Pixar's second film, *A Bug's Life*,
Catmull discovered a serious rift between Pixar's creative and production departments, leading production managers to feel disrespected. The solution he
arrived at was to make the communication structure more flexible than the organizational structure, so that anyone could talk to anyone else without fear
of reprimand. When communication did not have to go through our channels,
there was a much richer exchange of information and people did not become
annoyed. Pixar's headquarters were designed by Steve Jobs and an architect to
promote encounters and unplanned collaborations among animators and computer scientists.

Catmull and other Pixar leaders realized that their goal was not merely to build
a studio that made hit films but also to foster a creative culture that continually
asked questions. A major part of the leader's job is to build a sustainable culture
that is committed to honesty, originality, and self-assessment. Catmull and his
major directors such as John Lassiter were important for maintaining this culture,
particularly when they operated as the brain trust charged with keeping movies on
track. Pixar also aimed to maintain communications with the academic community in order to pick up on research innovations.

What is communicated in organizations such as Pixar is much more than words,
because an animation company depends heavily on the pictures and sounds that
go into its movies. Moreover, Pixar is doubly dependent on the communication of

emotions. Like any organization, its leaders need to be able to communicate emotions such as enthusiasm, respect, and trust in ways that alleviate intrusions from toxic emotions such as fear and resentment.

A movie company has to be centrally concerned with the evocation of emotions in its consumers, so artists and producers need to talk about emotions in order to track their success. Catmull views constructive criticism as crucial to the development of each movie, which requires balancing the negative emotions that come from disapproval with the positive emotions such as pride that support improvements. Communication of emotions and sensory images is naturally understood as the transfer and instillation of semantic pointers that combine sensory embodiment with verbal transbodiment.

MARKETING AND EMOTIONAL COHERENCE

Although the connections between leadership and marketing are rarely noticed, selling products requires the same basic cognitive-emotional skills as managing employees. Marketers need to understand the mental and social mechanisms that direct people to buy things, just as leaders need to understand the mechanisms that direct people to work well.

The book *The Marketing Power of Emotion* by John O'Shaughnessy and Nicholas O'Shaughnessy provides a thorough discussion of the role of emotions in consumer choice. Economists might suppose that consumers buy a product as the result of the rational calculation that the purchase maximizes their expected utility. But evidence suggests that purchases are emotional experiences, so that the aim of marketers should be to figure out how to manipulate the emotions of customers to stimulate purchases. The next section shows how this works concretely in the advertisements and stores that Apple uses to sell its products, but I begin with a more general overview that connects buying with the theory of emotional coherence.

According to O'Shaughnessy and O'Shaughnessy, decisions to buy are based on customers' values that are inherently emotional. Trust in the company and loyalty to a brand can ensure a steady stream of customers. The criteria that govern people's choices are multifaceted, including technical capabilities, price, legal issues, social approval, and appearance. When people make decisions such as what car to buy, they need to balance these criteria against each other, a process naturally understood as parallel constraint satisfaction promoting emotional coherence. The values of people that are tied to consumer buying include lifestyle, environment, meaningful lives, social solidarity, preservation of the past, and preference for staying young rather than looking old.

Marketers need to be aware of consumers' psychological limitations concerning perception, focus, attention, and memory. They need to tap into the consumers' emotions, such as desire for pleasure, pride, and excitement. Sometimes negative emotions can be useful for prompting purchases, for example when fear is used to propel people to buy safety products such as alarm services for old people. Evoking nostalgia can be an effective way of using sadness to encourage people to buy products that revive past glories. Ads for charities and public services may work by inspiring shame or guilt, for example about poverty or starvation.

In industries that sell services, marketers such as salespeople need to avoid arousing negative emotions by being peremptory, condescending, obsequious, or frustrating. Services also need to take into account the need for people to maintain self-esteem and avoid negative emotions such as shame, guilt, and embarrassment. I later discuss how the Apple Store accomplishes these goals.

Advertisers and other marketers can try to elicit relatively simple emotions such as greed and lust by means of vivid images, but they can also try to generate nested emotions. People may be rushed into buying an apparently scarce product through fear of regret. The nested emotion of desire for envy can be generated by ads suggesting that other people will be impressed by a purchased product. A subtle emotion claimed to be important for twenty-first-century purchasers of entertainment is fear of missing out, a kind of anxious anticipation of loss or regret.

If *The Marketing Power of Emotion* is correct about the role of emotion in marketing, then advertising is much more about manipulating emotions than about communicating reasons. The centrality of emotions is evident in marketing campaigns that have led to the success of Apple.

APPLE'S MARKETING: SOCIAL COGNITIVE-EMOTIONAL WORKUP

Apple success in going from close to bankruptcy in the 1990s to one of the world's richest companies resulted not only from its production of superb technology. It also has been highly creative at marketing its products using techniques that include award-winning advertisements, the alluring Apple Stores, and news-making product announcements. Appreciating Apple's marketing achievements depends on grasping both their emotional messages and the mental and social mechanisms on which they depend.

My social cognitive-emotional workup of Apple's marketing examines five advertising campaigns, from the astonishing 1984 ad that introduced the Macintosh computer to the iPhone ads that ran from 2007 to 2014. In between were the television and print ads urging people to "think different" (1997–2002), the iPod silhouette ads (2004–2008), and the humorous "Get-a-Mac" ads (2006–2009). Also relevant are the roles of Apple Stores and product announcements in contributing to Apple's marketing success. As in other workups in this book, I analyze Apple's marketing campaigns by identifying the concepts, values, images, beliefs, rules, analogies, emotions, inferences, and communications that it has employed.

Concepts and Values

All of the Apple marketing attempts provide some information about the products for sale, from computers to iPhones. But Apple is clearly appealing more to people's emotions than to factual inferences, so the technical information is minimal. Rather, the ads serve to convey a set of emotional values designed to appeal to customers who share them. Words and images in an ad serve to activate related concepts and images in the minds of viewers through the mechanism of priming.

The role of values is especially apparent in the famous 1984 ad that Apple ran during the Super Bowl to announce the imminent unveiling of the Macintosh computer. As chapter 13 described, this machine design was enormously creative in introducing graphical user interfaces and the mouse in concert with sophisticated software for word processing and drawing, along with sound, all incorporated in a cute, one-piece box. But the computer is never even shown in the ad, except in a barely visible sketch on the shirt of the heroine who runs with a sledgehammer to explode the screen that shows a bombastic, authoritarian man. The man represents a set of values that Apple wanted to associate with IBM and Microsoft, such as authority, conservatism, and even oppression.

In contrast, the young athletic woman running with a sledgehammer symbolizes values of youth, energy, and novelty. The other characters in the ad include hundreds of passive skinheads who watch the screen and armor-clad security officials chasing after the woman with a sledgehammer. Only at the end of the ad, after the screen explosion, is there the spoken and written announcement that the Macintosh will appear January 24, so that 1984 won't be like "1984."

Figure 14.2 provides a value map of the emotional associations suggested by the ad. The positive, connected set of values associated with the woman contrast strongly with the interconnected negative set of values associated with the authoritarian speaker and passive audience. Value maps provide a succinct representation of the emotional content of advertisements. Subsequent Apple ads

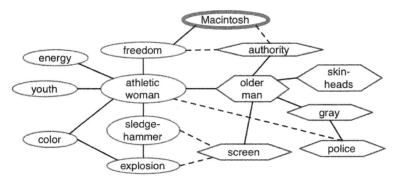

FIGURE 14.2 Map of values in 1984 television ad for Macintosh.

emphasized the ease of use of the Macintosh billed as the "computer for the rest of us."

In 1997, when Steve Jobs returned to Apple, the company embarked on the novel ad campaign under the theme "think different." The initial television advertisement used images of famous twentieth-century figures such as Albert Einstein, Bob Dylan, and Martin Luther King. The ad never even mentioned computers and only showed the Apple logo at the end. Richard Dreyfus's voice espouses a set of values that are not always seen as positive, such as being crazy, but the context associates them together with genius and changing the world. Part of the commercial that Steve Jobs helped to write is as follows:

> Here's to the crazy ones. The misfits. The rebels. The troublemakers. The round pegs in the square holes. The ones who see things differently. They're not fond of rules, and they have no respect for the status quo. You can quote them, disagree with them, glorify or vilify them. About the only thing you can't do is ignore them because they change things. They push the human race forward. And while some may see them as the crazy ones, we see genius. Because the people who are crazy enough to think they can change the world are the ones who do.

Figure 14.3 provides a map of the values associated with the concepts in this text and with the people conveyed in the images. The contrast is between a surprisingly coherent set of concepts such as crazy, genius, and changing the world versus an alternative set of concepts that Apple implicitly associates with IBM, Microsoft, and the status quo.

The Get-a-Mac television ads that aired from 2006 to 2009 also had an antiauthoritarian bent but used humor rather than terror to provide an appealing

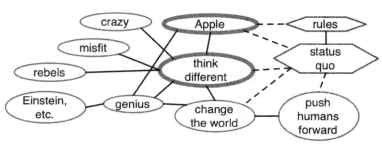

FIGURE 14.3 Map of values in 1997 television ad for Think Different.

value profile for the Macintosh. In these ads, Apple is represented by a young, handsome, and lively actor who routinely makes fun of a stodgy, middle-aged, roundish man who stands for PCs running Windows. These ads convey the values, shown in Figure 14.4, that Macintosh computers are young, cool, stable, secure, and equipped with numerous appealing kinds of software such as iMovie. In contrast, the PC character is associated with negative values such as old, dull, ineffective, unstable because of frequent crashes, and insecure because of viruses.

The Get-a-Mac ads had more technical content than the earlier 1984 and 1997 ads in that they did mention issues of software instability, but the main emphasis was still on the emotional appeal of a coherent set of values. The section on inference indicates how the communication of these values can be expected to invoke in viewers and listeners a response based on emotional coherence. Then customers can be impelled to want to buy Apple computers because they see them as having values that fit well with their own.

With development of the iPod and the iPhone, Apple moved more intensely into the business of entertainment and shifted to convey a different set of values associated with having fun. The silhouette ads for the iPod used in 2004 to 2008

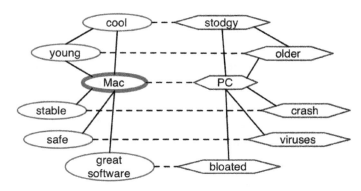

FIGURE 14.4 Map of values in television ad for Get-a-Mac.

did not convey any identifiable person but rather used moving block figures to convey youth, energy, liveliness, and musical enjoyment. Similarly, the iPhone ads beginning in 2007 show enjoyable uses of the new device, from phoning friends to listening to music to accessing Facebook on the Internet. Again, these ads appeal to the customer by suggesting a good match between the values associated with the device and those of the customers, including having fun, social interactions, and entertainment.

Apple product announcements also serve as a kind of marketing, especially when performed by the charismatic Steve Jobs. For example, his 2007 announcement of the iPhone was exciting and inspiring for the journalists and Apple employees in the audience. He starts by announcing three products: a touch screen iPod, a phone, and an Internet device, then builds excitement as people grasp that these products are all the same: the iPhone. Technical concepts mingle with emotional values to generate enthusiasm for the radical new product.

The Apple Stores also convey a set of concepts and values that have enabled them to become a highly profitable retail success. The stores lack conventional store characteristics such as racks, cash registers, and aggressive salespeople and instead have helpful employees and tables displaying cool devices. The stores complement advertisements by portraying Apple as both sophisticated and helpful.

Images and Embodiment

Perceptual images are central to television advertisements that convey their messages using video and sound. Powerful images in the 1984 Macintosh ad include the face and droning voice of the authority figure representing IBM and Microsoft. The portrayal of the running and sledgehammer-throwing female athlete also uses kinesthetic imagery where people can imagine themselves throwing the hammer at the screen, with the satisfying visual and auditory result of the screen exploding. This ad also uses color powerfully, because the skinheads and authority figure are in black and white, whereas the woman and the exploding screen are in color.

The "Think Different campaign was visual in its use of faces of famous people. The Get-a-Mac advertisements provided a strong visual and auditory contrast between the hip, young advocate of the Mac and the whiny proponent of the PC. The iPod silhouette ads were dynamically visual, showing dark figures dancing energetically with their iPods and earphones shown vividly in white. The ads for the iPhone present different images of people using it in diverse ways.

Apple product announcements such as Jobs's 2007 iPhone announcement are also replete with visual and other kinds of imagery. Jobs teased the audience before finally showing them the iPhone and even included a visual joke suggesting that it would look like an iPod with an old-fashioned phone dial on it. The Apple Stores are austerely decorated with only a few images, but the products on display engender ample imagery.

Imagery is a crucial part of advertisements that enable people to identify themselves with characters such as the running woman in the 1984 ad, the geniuses in the Think Different ad, and the exuberant dancers in the iPod ads. Dynamic imagery supports empathy in the sense of multimodal rule simulation, helping people imagine their bodies doing the same things that characters do in the ads, including running, dancing, and pressing icons on their iPhones. Hence Apple marketing is intensely embodied.

Nevertheless, Apple marketing is sometimes transbodied through abstract concepts. Especially in its older computer ads, Apple wanted to challenge authority and invoke abstract ideals such as genius and changing the world. The mode of empathy operating in these ads is verbal analogy rather than multimodal rule simulation, as consumers are encouraged to see themselves as similar to Einstein and other rebels. Even the more entertainment-oriented ads for the iPhone prime abstract concepts such as friendship as enhanced by the Internet connectivity and the telephone capacity of the machine.

Beliefs and Rules

In the Apple advertisements so far discussed, the concepts, values, and images are intended to invoke and generate numerous beliefs. The 1984, Get-a-Mac, and Think Different campaigns all convey the message that Macintosh computers are superior to the available alternatives for reasons ranging from their support of creative genius to their increased reliability. The iPod and iPhone ads were also intended to instill beliefs in customers about the desirable properties of the devices.

Many of the beliefs that Macintosh ads are supposed to inspire are rules such as:

If you buy a Macintosh computer, then you will be more productive.
If you buy an iPod, then you will have fun.
If you buy a PC, then you will be boring and unproductive.

Some of these are multimodal, inspired by the dynamic images and emotions stimulated by the advertisements. For example, the rule about buying an iPod can incorporate the visual and kinesthetic image of picking up the iPod, the auditory and kinesthetic image of dancing while wearing it, and the emotional image of having fun.

Advertisements can change consumer behavior by multimodal rules that go beyond words to connect visual, kinesthetic, and auditory imagery with projected emotional experiences. Ads that are explicitly comparative such as the Get-a-Mac ads, and even those that are implicitly comparative such as the 1984 Macintosh ad, also tend to generate the complex nested emotion of fear of regret using the rule: *If you buy a PC, then you will regret it.*

Analogies and Metaphors

Apple marketing makes rich use of analogies and metaphors to convey its emotional messages. The original Macintosh ad's only text says that after the new computer is released you can learn why 1984 will not be like "1984." The allusion is to George Orwell's dystopian novel *1984*, so the ad is drawing an analogy between the oppressive society that Orwell described and the state of technology dominated by IBM and Microsoft. The sledgehammer hitting the screen serves as a visual metaphor for the Macintosh destroying the dominance of the mainstream computer companies.

The Think Different advertising campaign encouraged consumers to see themselves as analogous to crazy people like Einstein and Bob Dylan by virtue of the fact that they can use new methods to change the world. Such analogies are cases of motivated inference, because they contributed to people's goals of feeling intelligent and successful. In general, endorsement by charismatic figures such as famous actors and musicians provides an emotional analogy that suggests people can be like the stars if they only buy the right products. The Get-a-Mac campaign occasionally used humorous metaphors such as showing the boring PC advocate blown up with air to be bloated, just like Microsoft products.

Apple Stores use metaphors to convey a strikingly different impression from standard retail organizations. Instead of a help center, Apple Stores have a Genius Bar or Grove where people can go for advice. This bar has a long table and stools analogous to bars where alcohol is served, but it does an interesting conceptual shift by suggesting that it is the bar for geniuses or at least a bar staffed by geniuses. Going up to the Genius Bar suggests that people will receive none of the annoying condescension that makes people resent other technology marketing and sales.

Emotions and Actions

The discussion of values already began to show the importance of emotions in Apple's marketing. But there is more to sales than just general emotional coherence, because specific emotions can encourage people to buy a product. The 1984 ad arouses negative emotions about the technological world dominated by a few companies, including resentment and fear of ongoing domination. In contrast, the Macintosh symbolized by the running woman suggests a suite of counter-vailing positive emotions such as joy of victory, pride of overthrowing oppression, and the thrill of running contrasted with the boredom of passively sitting among the skinheads.

Similarly, the Think Different ads accomplished a kind of emotional analogy in which people could transfer over the positive virtues of the geniuses to them-selves, generating enthusiasm, increased self-esteem (i.e., a positive emotion that one has toward oneself), and even pride. Perhaps people could even be encour-aged to feel gratitude toward Apple for providing all of these emotional benefits. These two campaigns and the Get- a-Mac ads also enabled people to feel an emo-tional reaction of superiority over people who are stuck with inferior technology. Emotion concepts that go with such feelings of superiority include *glee, gloating, smugness*, and the German *schadenfreude*, which conveys pleasure at the misfor-tune of others, in this case the misfortune of someone who buys products not made by Apple.

Whereas the 1984 and Think Different ads were deadly serious, the Get-a-Mac ones were often humorous. Humor is a complex emotion that incorporates feel-ings of pleasure, joy, incongruity, superiority, and relief.

The entertainment ads for iPods and iPhones encourage people to feel positive emotions such as exuberance, enjoyment, and the pleasure of having made a smart decision. The silhouette iPod ads especially encouraged a kind of nonverbal emo-tional analogy where the vigorously dancing iPod wearers helped people to see themselves as capable of such exuberant fun.

The point of stimulating emotions using advertising is to generate actions in the form of purchasing Apple products. There is no simple connection, however, between emotion and action because someone can be inspired emotionally by an Apple ad without running out to buy a computer or an iPhone. Ads inspire wants that are meant to be strong enough to inspire intentions, which then get put into action. Wants may not lead to intentions because of competing wants and lack of resources, and intentions may not lead to actions because of competing actions and distractions. Nevertheless, the intended consequences of Apple's intriguing ads is to use emotions to generate people's actions that transfer money to Apple in exchange for the desired products.

Apple Stores are also a marketing technique that works with people's emotions. On the positive side, Apple aims at giving people pleasurable experiences by means of historically appropriate, elegant, and open spaces. An internal video describes

Apple's aim to make a place that people will love. The ads also pull on the negative emotions of feeling intimidated or resentful, which many people feel when dealing with other companies' customer service representatives but avoid when going to an Apple Store.

Inferences

Marketing encourages people to make inferences about what to believe, what to value, and what to do. The Apple advertisements encourage people to believe that Apple products will help them to accomplish their goals in ways that are superior to the alternative available products. The beliefs to be acquired are inseparable from values because they involve judgments about ways in which products are better than others with respect to what the customer cares about. The most important inference that advertisements are meant to generate relates to the decision to purchase the product, thereby making money for the company that produced it. However, not all advertisements are aimed at producing purchases; public service announcements such as vaccination campaigns are aimed at getting people to do things that are actually good for them.

What is the mental nature of all these inferences? Traditional philosophical accounts of belief revision would suggest that people are being encouraged to make various deductive, inductive, and abductive inferences based on the information provided. There may be some such inferences, but what usually goes on when people respond to advertisements is that they make coherence-based inferences that are heavily based on emotion.

The ads in Figures 14.2 to 14.4 indicate configurations of values that the ads are aimed at conveying. These maps should not be just viewed as static depictions of interconnected values but as indicators of the underlying process of emotional coherence that changes people's values and beliefs. Each ad provides a set of positive values that are coherent with each other and collectively opposed to negative values that the customers rejects. The main message to be inferred from the 1984 Macintosh ad is that people should be excited about the imminent announcement of the Macintosh as an escape from authoritarian technology. More concretely, the Get-a-Mac advertisements make Macintosh appealing because of a coherent set of positive values such as coolness and stability that contrasts strongly with a set of negative values associated with the PC. Hence it is much more plausible to see ads as aimed at and sometimes achieving emotional coherence rather than making logical inferences.

Similarly, when people make decisions about what to do, such as buying a Mac rather than a PC, the practical inferences are much better understood in terms of emotional coherence than rational choice theory. Perhaps there are some people who actually do calculations about how to maximize their expected utility when it comes to buying computers, but the ads are not aimed at such maximization. They do not coldly suggest the costs and benefits of buying Apple products but rather serve to inspire emotions such as enthusiasm, excitement, pride, and alleviation of fear of regret. Decisions about how to act operate by parallel constraint satisfaction seeking emotional coherence, just like decisions about what to value and what to believe. Normatively, belief revision should be based on explanatory coherence based on evidence and hypotheses, but the neural interconnections of cognition and emotion make it hard to block the emotional intrusions of motivated and fear-driven inference.

Communications

Marketing is obviously a matter of communication in ways that go far beyond the transfer of verbal messages. The message sender is the company organization that generates advertisements, and the receivers are people who see or hear these advertisements. As the discussion of imagery in Apple advertisement showed, the information transmitted from the ads to people occurs in various modalities: visual, auditory, kinesthetic, and emotional. In other fields such as food advertising, the messages can also invoke images about taste and smell. Touch may also be involved in fashion industries where people are encouraged to imagine the feel of a particular fabric. Purely verbal theories of communication ignore these modalities, but clever marketers do not. The semantic pointer theory of communication can fully accommodate the multimodal nature of advertising as the transfer and instillation of representations that incorporate the full range of sensory and motor representations.

Moreover, the semantic pointer theory of communication also has the advantage of appreciating the large emotional component of social interaction. The words and images that are part of advertising serve not only to transfer verbal and nonverbal information but also to inspire emotions including the values that are crucial to generating people's preferences about what to do. The point of marketing is to communicate in ways that generate inferences based on emotional coherence. Advertising and other forms of marketing are designed to influence people's beliefs, values, and decisions in ways that lead people to act in accord with the goals of the company or organization doing the marketing.

Similarly, the events where Apple announces new products are ways of communicating images and emotions that can influence new sales. As evident in YouTube videos of Steve Jobs's first presentation of the Macintosh and the iPhone, the announcements serve to generate substantial excitement that gets picked up by media outlets such as television and newspapers. Here the communication of verbal facts, images, and emotions goes from the Apple presenter, originally the charismatic Steve Jobs, to the media representatives in the audience, then to a broader population.

The Apple Stores also provide a subtle form of communication. Some are tediously located in shopping malls, but Apple has major flagship stores in cities like New York, London, and Barcelona. These have exciting locations on major shopping streets and elegant buildings that convey beauty and sophistication. The Apple Stores also communicate values such as technological sophistication, ease of use, and helpful staff. Buildings are not usually thought of as communicators, but the Apple Stores help to pass along the sensory and emotional information that encourages people to buy and use Apple products. Friendly and helpful Apple employees in the stores communicate technical and commercial details as well as encouraging transmission of Apple values.

ENHANCING COLLECTIVE EMOTIONAL INTELLIGENCE

Scientific ideas are always open to uses that are evil as well as good. My accounts of leadership and marketing based on cognitive, emotional, and social mechanisms could be used to enhance the worst practices in these fields, such as dictatorships and fraudulent advertising. My assessments of good versus evil, and best versus worst, are based on the ethical principle that social practices should increase rather than decrease the satisfaction of human needs, both biological and psychological. Accordingly, I outline how social cognitivism's understanding of business practices can improve the satisfaction of human needs but also warn against practices that exploit the understanding of mind in society for evil purposes.

First, consider how leaders who genuinely want to act in accord with the needs of their followers can apply lessons concerning the nature of thinking and communication. My discussion of leadership as requiring emotional intelligence, and the case study of Ed Catmull, show that a major part of successful leadership is understanding the emotions of individuals and the nature of emotional communication. It is far from enough for a leader to simply provide good reasons for the members of an organization to act in ways that further the goals of that organization. Rather, the leader needs to inspire relevant emotions such as enthusiasm, excitement, and pride, which serve to motivate effective action while allowing followers a large degree of freedom.

This inspiration requires communication but not simply verbal messages such as emails and dry speeches. Emotionally effective communication is multimodal, employing visual, auditory, and kinesthetic images to transfer not only words but rich semantic pointers. A good leader can employ all the techniques of nonverbal communication, including facial expressions, body language, tone of voice, and gestures, to display and generate the emotions that are crucial for the transfer of values and the generation of motivations that lead people to act in support of an organization.

In addition, an effective leader can strive to establish practices and group norms that improve the interactions among members of the organization. An effective organization is not just one in which the leader communicates well with its members but also one in which the members communicate well with each other. Practices like those that Catmull introduced at Pixar can be used to improve the interactions among employees so that there is an increase in collective emotional intelligence. Such interactions can bring about improved cooperation and collaboration based on better communication of the full range of information—sensory, motor, and emotional as well as verbal. Such communication produces inspiration and hope that lead to action and success.

Recent studies have identified several factors that contribute to collective intelligence, the general ability of a team to perform a wide variety of tasks. Collective intelligence correlates with the average social sensitivity of group members, their ability to understand each other's mental states, the distribution of conversational turn-taking, and the proportion of females in the group. Leaders can work to hire people and shape their interactions in ways that use these factors to help collective intelligence emerge from mental and social mechanisms. Moreover, leaders can foster the kinds of learning and teaching that chapter 12 identified as important for individual and group performance. They can work to bring about constructive conceptual change by introducing new concepts, criticizing defective ones, and revalencing ones that need to be reinterpreted as emotionally positive or negative.

A good leader can also watch out for practices such as excessive criticism that are emotionally destructive. Another valuable role for leaders is to watch out for and limit social feedback interactions that incite collective motivated and fear-driven inference resulting from toxic emotional communications. Chapter 7 on economics describes how irrational exuberance and irrational despair can spread through organizations, and a leader can work to block their effects on collective stupidity.

Appreciation of social and cognitive mechanisms can also be used as antidotes to the efforts by bad leaders to manipulate followers in evil directions. Techniques such as value maps and full social cognitive-emotional workups can be used to identify how charismatic evil leaders manipulate people to act in ways that contravene human needs. Whether the demonic leader is a politician running for office, a business executive, or a religious authority, people can track their communications with an eye to discerning the kinds of emotional manipulation used in support of their malicious goals. Chapter 6 provides such an analysis of the appeal of Hitler and Nazism.

Unfortunately, I have no way of preventing such leaders from using my accounts of cognition, emotion, and communication to try to make their manipulations more effective, but at least the same accounts can be used to provide tools for noticing and countering their attempts. The counters cannot consist merely of logical reasoning, because you cannot fight emotional coherence with reasoning alone. Instead, attacking the apparently persuasive message of evil leaders requires proposing alternative messages that are supported by evidence, theory, and emotionally appealing alternative sets of values. As chapter 6 on ideology suggests, the best way to battle an ideology is with a more appealing set of ideas. The workups of emotional intelligence and marketing provide some guidance about how to mount such a battle.

For organizations acting in support of human needs, and for marketers of genuinely valuable products, my discussion of advertising shows some ways to convey messages effectively in order to influence people's values and beliefs. People can be encouraged to recognize coherence between their values and what the product provides, but ads can also be used to instill values. Advertising can change people's preferences by suggesting new goals and providing information about how these goals can be satisfied. Effective marketing in the pursuit of legitimate ends should include the full range of relevant sensory, motor, and emotional modalities, aiming toward people's judgments and feelings of emotional coherence that lead to changes in beliefs, values, decisions, intentions, and actions.

The best defense against advertisements designed to manipulate people into actions that run contrary to their needs is understanding mental and social mechanisms used by the manipulations. Some products clearly make lives worse, such as unhealthy foods, dangerous cars, and entertainments that waste time and money that people could use to satisfy their needs.

Mental self-defense in response to seductive marketers can use the same set of techniques that I recommended for dealing with evil leaders. For each communication in the form of an advertisement or a sales pitch, you can identify not only the words but also the images and emotions being used to convey the message. Customers should attend to the emotionally coherent packaging of values used to support illegitimate inferences based on motivation and fear rather than evidence.

My value maps and emotional analyses of Apple ads viewed them as relatively benign, because I think that these are good products. But I would like to see the more critical examination of ads for products that are bad for people in order to notice the concepts, values, beliefs, rules, analogies, metaphors, and emotions used to support inferences leading to needless actions.

SUMMARY AND DISCUSSION

Social cognitivism illuminates two of the most important processes in business, leadership and marketing, which turn out to have remarkable similarities. Effectiveness in both endeavors requires understanding cognitive and emotional mechanisms operating in the minds of individuals, and also social mechanisms by which thoughts and emotions are communicated. Both leadership and marketing require elicitation of multimodal semantic pointers that combine verbal, sensory, motor, and emotional information. Leaders and marketers all need to understand the emotional processes of their followers and customers by using theories of emotion (based on semantic pointers, not folk psychology) and modes of empathy ranging from verbal analogy to multimodal rule simulation. For employees and purchasers, emotion is a major contributor to motivations that produce intentions that lead to action.

Emotional intelligence has been claimed as an important component of leadership but without a deep understanding of emotion and intelligence. On my view, intelligence consists of solving problems and accomplishing goals using a full range of mental operations on different kinds of representations, including sensory, motor, emotional, and verbal. Emotional aspects of intelligence require appreciating how semantic pointers amalgamate cognitive appraisals and physiological perceptions in ways that enhance actions. The empathy that emotionally intelligent leaders should practice operates in three modes, based on mirror neurons, analogies, and multimodal rule simulation, all of which depend on the acquisition of semantic pointers.

The values that good leaders are supposed to evoke and convey to their followers are best understood as emotional representations that bind concepts, beliefs, and goals with patterns of neural activation based on appraisals and physiology. The leadership capacity of having a vision is based on mental processes that include values, goals, beliefs, plans, and inferences about the future. Spreading a vision to followers requires instilling these processes in others by verbal and nonverbal communication.

The task of an effective leader is not only to convey values, goals, and beliefs to followers but also to encourage members of an organization to interact in effective ways. Establishing practices by group norms can make accomplishment of the organization's goals greater than the aggregate of individual effectiveness. Organizational achievement is an important kind of multilevel emergence that depends on the interactions of members of the group, where the contribution of the individual members depends on their mental, neural, and molecular mechanisms.

I have neglected the molecular side of organizations, but lessons in earlier chapters about neurotransmitters and hormones apply here also. Positive emotions such as enthusiasm and excitement depend heavily on dopamine functioning, and the emotion of trust so important in leadership and brand loyalty can be influenced by oxytocin. Stressful environments such as harsh criticism increase cortisol to undermine individual health and productivity.

Whereas leadership requires communication between leaders and employees, marketing requires communication between a company and potential customers. But the mental mechanisms in the recipients of the communications are the same: emotional coherence based on multimodal representations. Effective marketing such as the Apple advertising campaigns taps into existing values and sometimes even encourages people to acquire new values, all based on judgments of emotional coherence. Social cognitive-emotional workups are useful for taking into account the full range of mental representations employed in advertising campaigns, analyzing their emotional impact, and preparing countermeasures.

For leadership and marketing alike, analysis based on mental and social mechanisms can be used both for improving desirable practices and for detecting and countering ones that are socially evil. My aim is not to help bad leaders and rapacious marketers to exploit people more effectively but to enable well-intentioned organizations to have better leadership and better public education in ways that supports human needs. Moreover, understanding how irresponsible leaders and marketers manipulate people can help people to defend themselves against their messages. Appreciating how communication is a complex multimodal process that transfers sensory, motor, emotional, and verbal information is an important part of logical self-defense.

Hence social cognitivism can be normative as well as descriptive, as shown in the previous discussions of professions, which all have practical goals accomplished through social and cognitive mechanisms. I have shown how to improve understanding and evaluation of both leadership and marketing by explaining individual thinking through semantic pointers and social communication through the promulgation of semantic pointers.

This examination of business completes my demonstration that social sciences and professions have much to gain from an integrated account of mental and social mechanisms. Integration is accomplished by (a) new theories of cognition and emotion based on Chris Eliasmith's brilliant semantic pointer hypothesis about how brains make minds and (b) a new view of communicative interaction as semantic pointer transfer and instillation. This book has shown how social sciences and professions can be illuminated by social cognitivism using methods such as three-analysis, value maps, and social cognitive-emotional workups.

The workups in this book show the importance of embodied, multimodal representations that take thought and communication beyond words, while attending to transbodied concepts and analogies subject to dramatic changes. Cognition and emotion interact in rational forms of thinking such as decision making based on emotional coherence but also in the irrational forms of motivated and fear-driven inference. Multilevel emergence captures numerous social phenomena, including successful relationships, overcoming prejudice, political revolutions, economic crashes, religious movements, international wars, mental illnesses, wrongful convictions, teaching, creativity, and leadership. Many other important social questions are open to similar investigation.

Like the social sciences, the professions should be engaged not only with explaining changes but also in bringing them about. Medicine is concerned not just with the origins of diseases but also with how to treat and prevent them. Law has methods for dealing with criminals but is also responsible for improving these methods to make them more socially effective. Education depends on theories of learning and teaching but should strive to improve schools to foster human well-being. Engineering can draw on scientific ideas about how technology works to improve the lives of its users. In business, leadership and marketing can be used to control and exploit people, but they can also be used to help people flourish.

These normative questions about the desirability of social change are examined in *Natural Philosophy* in chapters 6 and 7 on morality and justice. Values permeate social thinking, demanding reflection on how to evaluate them. This book has dealt with crucial preliminary questions about how minds and societies work through cognition, emotion, and communication. My proposed solution to the person–group problem, using interacting mental and social mechanisms, provides guidance for understanding social change and also for helping to bring it about. Examination of social sciences and professions can be both effects and causes of social change. Social cognitivism aims to change the world by changing minds and to change minds by changing the world.

I have proposed a unified, mechanistic theory of all social sciences and professions, integrated with the similarly cohesive theory of the cognitive sciences presented in *Brain–Mind*. Marvelously, the humanities join the party in *Natural Philosophy*.

NOTES

The Welch quote is from https://hbr.org/1989/09/speed-simplicity-self-confidence-an-interview-with-jack-welch.

On emotional intelligence, see Salovey and Mayer 1990; Mayer, Salovey, and Caruso 2004; Goleman 1995, 1998; Goleman, Boyatzis and McKee 2013; Harvard Business Review 2015; Riggio and Tan 2014; Harms and Credé 2010. Mintzberg 2009, p. 197, lists management qualities.

On charismatic leadership, see Conger and Kanungo 1994 and Ronald E. Riggio's blog: https://www.psychologytoday.com/blog/cutting-edge-leadership/201504/4-ways-boost-your-charisma. Mio, Riggio, Levin, and Reese 2005 discuss metaphor and charisma. The Reagan TV ads are on YouTube. Willner 1984 examines political charisma.

The study on virtue and vice in American senators is ten Brinke, Liu, Keltner, and Srivastava 2016.

Catmull 2014 discusses leadership and creativity. Support for Catmull's views on the importance of values, communication, and passion comes from interviews with 100 successful CEOs in Yaverbaum 2004.

For emotions in marketing, see O'Shaugnessy and O'Shaugnessy 2002. On the importance of emotion in political campaigning, see Westen 2007. Schröder and Thagard 2013 present a theory of priming tied to semantic pointers.

On Apple marketing, see Dormehl 2012 and Wikipedia articles on each of the advertising campaigns. All of the Macintosh ads mentioned are available on YouTube, including the words from the original Think Different ad. Steve Jobs's 1984 Macintosh announcement and 2007 iPhone announcement are also on YouTube. On the Apple Store, see https://www.youtube.com/watch?v=-AkLOvjl5jo; http://www.marketingapple.com/Apple_Retail_Success.pdf.

Thagard 2010b argues that human needs are the best basis for ethics. Further defense is in *Natural Philosophy*, chapters 6 to 8.

On the correlates of collective intelligence see Woolley et al. 2010 and Engel, Woolley, Jing, Chabris, and Malone 2014. For advice on how to interpret such group properties, see chapter 9 on history.

PROJECT

Do social cognitive-emotional workups of other important aspects of business such as strategy (Gavetti and Menon, 2016) and group decision making. Use value maps to capture both the minds of consumer and the values communicated in advertisements, and see whether successful advertisements provide a good match between the two maps. Do workups for related professions such as accounting, investing, and finance. Do a workup of the contributions to collective leadership and creativity of Apple Park, the spectacular new headquarters opened in 2017.

REFERENCES

Achen, C. H., & Bartels, L. M. (2016). *Democracy for realists: Why elections do not produce responsive government*. Princeton, NJ: Princeton University Press.

Akerlof, G. A., & Kranton, R. E. (2010). *Identity economics*. Princeton, NJ: Princeton University Press.

Akerlof, G. A., & Shiller, R. J. (2009). *Animal spirits: How human psychology drives the economy, and why it matters for global capitalism*. Princeton, NJ: Princeton University Press.

Allan, L. G., Siegel, S., & Hannah, S. (2007). The sad truth about depressive realism. *The Quarterly Journal of Experimental Psychology, 60*(3), 482–495.

Allport, G. W. (1958). *The nature of prejudice*. Garden City, NY: Doubleday.

Amaya, A. (2015). *The tapestry of reason: An inquiry into the nature of coherence and its role in legal argument*. Oxford: Hart.

American Psychiatric Association. (2013). *Diagnostic and statistical manual of mental disorders* (5th ed.). Washington, DC: American Psychiatric Association.

Amodio, D. M. (2014). The neuroscience of prejudice and stereotyping. *Nature Reviews Neuroscience, 15*, 670–682.

Anderson, J. R. (2007). *How can the mind occur in the physical universe?* Oxford: Oxford University Press.

Anderson, K. K., Cheng, J., Susser, E., McKenzie, K. J., & Kurdyak, P. (2015). Incidence of psychotic disorders among first-generation immigrants and refugees in Ontario. *Canadian Medical Association Journal, 187*(9), E279–E286.

Andrews, L. W. (2010). *Encyclopedia of depression*. Santa Barbara, CA: Greenwood.

Angell, M. (2004). *The truth about the drug companies: How they deceive us and what to do about it*. New York: Random House.

Angell, M. (2009). Drug companies & doctors: A story of corruption. *The New York Review of Books, 56*(1), 8–12.

Aristotle. *Politics*. various editions.

Arnsten, A. F. (2009). Stress signalling pathways that impair prefrontal cortex structure and function. *Nature Reviews Neuroscience, 10*(6), 410–422.

Atran, S. (2002). *In gods we trust: The evolutionary landscape of religion*. Oxford: Oxford University Press.

Atran, S. (2016). The devoted actor: Unconditional commitment and intractable conflict across cultures. *Current Anthropology, 57*, S192–S203.

Atran, S., & Henrich, J. (2010). The evolution of religion: How cognitive by-products, adaptive learning heuristics, ritual displays, and group competition generate deep commitments to prosocial religions. *Biological Theory, 5*(1), 18–30.

Back, L., & Solomos, J. (Eds.). (2000). *Theories of race and racism*. London: Routledge.

Banich, M. T., & Compton, R. J. (2011). *Cognitive neuroscience* (3rd ed.). Boston: Houghton Mifflin.

Barrett, L. F., & Russell, J. A. (Eds.). (2015). *The psychological construction of emotion*. New York: Guilford Press.

Barsalou, L. W. (2008). Grounded cognition. *Annual Review of Psychology, 59*, 617–645.

Bartz, J. A. (2016). Oxytocin and the pharmacological dissection of affiliation. *Current Directions in Psychological Science, 25*(2), 104–110.

Baskin-Sommers, A. R. (2016). Dissecting antisocial behavior: The impact of neural, genetic, and environmental factors. *Clinical Psychological Science, 4*(3), 500–510.

Bastardi, A., Uhlmann, E. L., & Ross, L. (2011). Wishful thinking: Belief, desire, and the motivated evaluation of scientific evidence. *Psychological Science, 22*, 731–732.

Batson, C. D. (1991). *The altruism question*. Hillsdale, NJ: Lawrence Erlbaum.

Baumeister, R. F., Ainsworth, S. E., & Vohs, K. D. (2016). Are groups more or less than the sum of their members? The moderating role of individual identification. *Behavioral and Brain Sciences, 39*.

Baumeister, R. F., Bratslavsky, E., Finkenauer, C., & Vohs, K. D. (2001). Bad is stronger than good. *Review of General Psychology, 5*(4), 323–370.

Baumeister, R. F., & Leary, M. R. (1995). The need to belong: Desire for interpersonal attachments as a fundamental human motivation. *Psychological Bulletin, 117*(3), 497–529.

Bechtel, W. (2008). *Mental mechanisms: Philosophical perspectives on cognitive neuroscience*. New York: Routledge.

Beck, A. T., & Bredemeier, K. (2016). A unified model of depression integrating clinical, cognitive, biological, and evolutionary perspectives. *Clinical Psychological Science, 4*, 596–619.

Beinhocker, E. D. (2006). *The origin of wealth: Evolution, complexity, and the radical remaking of economics*. Cambridge, MA: Harvard Business School Press.

Beit-Hallahmi, B. (2015). *Psychological perspectives on religion and religiosity*. Hove, UK: Routledge.

Beller, S., Bender, A., & Medin, D. L. (2012). Should anthropology be part of cognitive science? *Topics in Cognitive Science, 4*(3), 342–353.

Bénabou, R., & Tirole, J. (2016). Mindful economics: The production, consumption, and value of beliefs. *The Journal of Economic Perspectives, 30*(3), 141–164.

Bentall, R. (2004). *Madness explained: Psychosis and human nature*. London: Penguin.

Bering, J. M., & Bjorklund, D. F. (2004). The natural emergence of reasoning about the afterlife as a developmental regularity. *Developmental Psychology, 40*, 217–233.

Berns, G. S., Bell, E., Capra, C. M., Prietula, M. J., Moore, S., Anderson, B., . . . Atran, S. (2012). The price of your soul: Neural evidence for the non-utilitarian representation of sacred values. *Philosophical Transactions of the Royal Society B: Biological Sciences, 367*(1589), 754–762.

Berridge, K. C., & Kringelbach, M. L. (2015). Pleasure systems in the brain. *Neuron, 86*(3), 646–664.

Bicchieri, C. (2005). *The grammar of society: The nature and dynamics of social norms.* Cambridge, UK: Cambridge University Press.

Blakemore, S.-J., & Frith, U. (2005). *The learning brain: Lessons for education.* Malden, MA: Blackwell.

Bloch, M. (2012). *Anthropology and the cognitive challenge.* Cambridge, UK: Cambridge University Press.

Blouw, P., Solodkin, E., Thagard, P., & Eliasmith, C. (2016). Concepts as semantic pointers: A framework and computational model. *Cognitive Science, 40,* 1128–1162.

Boden, M. (2004). *The creative mind: Myths and mechanisms* (2nd ed.). London: Routledge.

Bourdieu, P. (1977). *Outline of a theory of practice.* Cambridge, UK: Cambridge University Press.

Bowie, F. (2000). *The anthropology of religion.* Oxford: Blackwell.

Boyer, P. (2001). *Religion explained.* New York: Basic Books.

Buckholtz, J. W., & Faigman, D. L. (2014). Promises, promises for neuroscience and law. *Current Biology, 24*(18), R861–R867.

Bunge, M. (2003). *Emergence and convergence: Qualitative novelty and the unity of knowledge.* Toronto: University of Toronto Press.

Bunzel, C. (2015). *From paper state to caliphate: The ideology of the Islamic State.* https://www.brookings.edu/research/from-paper-state-to-caliphate-the-ideology-of-the-islamic-state/

Byrne, M. D. (1995). The convergence of explanatory coherence and the story model: A case study in juror decision. In J. D. Moore & J. F. Lehman (Eds.), *Proceedings of the Seventeenth Annual Conference of the Cognitive Science Society* (pp. 539–543). Mahwah, NJ: Lawrence Erlbaum.

Calhoun, C. (2007). *Nations matter: Culture, history, and the cosmopolitan dream.* London: Routledge.

Calhoun, C., Gertheis, J., Moody, J., Pfaff, S., & Virk, I. (Eds.). (2012). *Contemporary sociological theory* (3rd ed.). Chichester, UK: Wiley-Blackwell.

Camerer, C. (2003). *Behavioral game theory.* Princeton, NJ: Princeton University Press.

Carey, S. (2009). *The origin of concepts.* Oxford: Oxford University Press.

Carter, C. S. (2014). Oxytocin pathways and the evolution of human behavior. *Annual Review of Psychology, 65,* 17–39.

Cartwright, E. (2014). *Behavioral economics* (2nd ed.). Abingdon, UK: Routledge.

Cassidy, J. (2009). *How markets fail: The logic of economic calamities.* New York: Penguin.

Catmull, E. (2014). *Creativity, Inc.: Overcoming the unseen forces that stand in the way of true inspiration.* New York: Random House.

Cerulo, K. A. (2010). Mining the intersections of cognitive sociology and neuroscience. *Poetics, 38*(2), 115–132.

Cerulo, K. A. (Ed.). (2002). *Culture in mind: Toward a sociology of culture and cognition.* New York: Routledge.

Chan, C.-S. (2015). *Style and creativity in design.* Berlin: Springer.

Chan, J., & Schunn, C. (2015). The impact of analogies on creative concept generation: Lessons from an in vivo study in engineering design. *Cognitive Science, 39*(1), 126–155.

Cho, K., Barnes, C. M., & Guanara, C. L. (2017). Sleepy punishers are harsh punishers: Daylight saving time and legal sentences. *Psychological Science, 28,* 242–247.

Clark, C. (2013). *The sleepwalkers: How Europe went to war in 1914.* New York: Harper.

Clément, M., & Sangar, E. (2018). Introduction: Methodological challenges and opportunities for the study of emotions. In M. Clément & E. Sangar (Eds.), *Researching emotions in international relations: Methodological perspectives on the emotional turn* (pp. 1–29). New York: Palgrave MacMillan.

Clementz, B. A., Sweeney, J. A., Hamm, J. P., Ivleva, E. I., Ethridge, L. E., Pearlson, G. D., . . . Tamminga, C. A. (2015). Identification of distinct psychosis biotypes using brain-based biomarkers. *American Journal of Psychiatry, 173,* 373–384.

Coates, J. (2012). *The hour between dog and wolf: Risk-taking, gut feelings and the biology of boom and bust.* London: Fourth Estate.

Cole, S. W. (2009). Social regulation of human gene expression. *Current Directions in Psychological Science, 18,* 132–136.

Coleman, J. (1990). *Foundations of social theory.* Cambridge, MA: Harvard University Press.

Collins, R. (2004). *Interaction ritual chains.* Princeton, NJ: Princeton University Press.

Conger, J. A., & Kanungo, R. N. (1994). Charismatic leadership in organizations: Perceived behavioral attributes and their measurement. *Journal of Organizational Behavior, 15*(5), 439–452.

Conte, R., Andrighetto, G., & Campennl, M. (2013). *Minding norms: Mechanisms and dynamics of social order in agent societies.* Oxford: Oxford University Press.

Craighead, W. E., & Dunlop, B. W. (2014). Combination psychotherapy and antidepressant medication treatment for depression: For whom, when, and how. *Annual Review of Psychology, 65,* 267–300.

Craver, C. F., & Darden, L. (2013). *In search of mechanisms: Discoveries across the life sciences.* Chicago: University of Chicago Press.

Cropley, D. H. (2015). *Creativity in engineering.* Amsterdam: Elsevier.

Cross, N. (2011). *Design thinking: Understanding how designers think and work.* Oxford: Berg.

Csibra, G., & Gergely, G. (2011). Natural pedagogy as evolutionary adaptation. *Philosophical Transactions of the Royal Society of London B: Biological Sciences, 366*(1567), 1149–1157.

Currie, A. M. (2014). Narratives, mechanisms and progress in historical science. *Synthese, 191*(6), 1163–1183.

D'Andrade, R. (1995). *The development of cognitive anthropology.* Cambridge, UK: Cambridge University Press.

Danziger, S., Levav, J., & Avnaim-Pesso, L. (2011). Extraneous factors in judicial decisions. *Proceedings of the National Academy of Sciences of the United States of America, 108*(17), 6889–6892.

Darden, L., Pal, L. R., Kundu, K., & Moult, J. (2018). The product guides the process: Discovering disease mechanisms. In E. Ippoliti & D. Danks (Eds.), *Building theories* (pp. 101–117). Berlin: Springer.

Darioly, A., & Mast, M. S. (2014). The role of nonverbal behavior in leadership. In R. E. Riggio & S. J. Tan (Eds.), *Leader interpersonal and influence skills: The soft skills of leadership.* New York: Routledge.

de Beauvoir, S. (2010). *The second sex* (C. Borde & S. Malovany-Chevallier, Trans.). New York: Alfred A. Knopf.

de Groot, J. H., Smeets, M. A., Rowson, M. J., Bulsing, P. J., Blonk, C. G., Wilkinson, J. E., & Semin, G. R. (2015). A sniff of happiness. *Psychological Science, 26*(6), 684–700.

Decety, J., & Cacioppo, J. T. (Eds.). (2011). *The Oxford handbook of social neuroscience.* Oxford: Oxford University Press.

Dechêne, A., Stahl, C., Hansen, J., & Wänke, M. (2010). The truth about the truth: A meta-analytic review of the truth effect. *Personality and Social Psychology Review, 14,* 238–257.

Deci, E. L., & Ryan, R. M. (Eds.). (2002). *Handbook of self-determination research.* Rochester, NY: University of Rochester Press.

Dehaene, S. (2009). *Reading in the brain: The new science of how we read.* New York: Penguin.

Dehaene, S. (2014). The calculating brain. In D. A. Sousa (Ed.), *Mind, brain, & education: Neuroscience implications for the classroom* (pp. 179–200). Solution Tree Press.

Della Sala, S., & Anderson, M. (2012). *Neuroscience in education: The good, the bad, and the ugly.* Oxford: Oxford University Press.

Demeulenaere, P. (Ed.). (2011). *Analytical sociology and sociological mechanisms.* Cambridge, UK: Cambridge University Press.

DeRubeis, R. J., Siegle, G. J., & Hollon, S. D. (2008). Cognitive therapy vs. medications for depression: Treatment outcomes and neural mechanisms. *Nature Reviews Neuroscience, 9*(10), 788.

DeSteno, D. (2014). *The truth about trust.* New York: Hudson Street Press.

Devine, D. J. (2012). *Jury decision making: The state of the science.* New York: New York University Press.

Dhillon, B. S. (2006). *Creativity for engineers.* Singapore: World Scientific.

Dormehl, L. (2012). *The Apple revolution: Steve Jobs, the counter culture and how the crazy ones took over the world.* New York: Random House.

Douglas, H. E. (2009). *Science, policy, and the value-free ideal.* Pittsburgh: University of Pittsburgh Press.

Downs, J. S., de Bruin, W. B., & Fischhoff, B. (2008). Parents' vaccination comprehension and decisions. *Vaccine, 26*(12), 1595–1607.

Driver, J. (2014). The history of utilitarianism. In E. Zalta (Ed.), *Stanford encyclopedia of philosophy.* http://plato.stanford.edu/entries/utilitarianism-history/

Duckworth, A. L., & Seligman, M. E. (2005). Self-discipline outdoes IQ in predicting academic performance of adolescents. *Psychological Science, 16*(12), 939–944.

Duhigg, C. (2016). *Smarter faster better.* New York: Random House.

Durkheim, E. (1995). *The elementary forms of religious life* (K. E. Fields, Trans.). New York: Free Press.

Eichengreen, B. (2015). *Hall of mirrors.* New York: Oxford University Press.

Eliasmith, C. (2013). *How to build a brain: A neural architecture for biological cognition.* Oxford: Oxford University Press.

Eliasmith, C., Stewart, T. C., Choo, X., Bekolay, T., DeWolf, T., Tang, Y., & Rasmussen, D. (2012). A large-scale model of the functioning brain. *Science, 338,* 1202–1205.

Eller, J. D. (2007). *Introducing the anthropology of religion.* New York: Routledge.

Ellis, L., Wahab, E. A., & Ratnasingan, M. (2013). Religiosity and fear of death: A three-nation comparison. *Mental Health, Religion & Culture, 16*(2), 179–199.

Elster, J. (2011). Indeterminacy of emotional mechanisms. In P. Demeulenaere (Ed.), *Analytical sociology and sociological mechanisms* (pp. 50–63). Cambridge, UK: Cambridge University Press.

Elster, J. (2015). *Explaining social behavior: More nuts and bolts for the social sciences* (2nd ed.). Cambridge, UK: Cambridge University Press.

Engel, D., Woolley, A. W., Jing, L. X., Chabris, C. F., & Malone, T. W. (2014). Reading the mind in the eyes or reading between the lines? Theory of mind predicts collective intelligence equally well online and face-to-face. *PLOS One*, 9(12), e115212.

Epstein, R., Robertson, R. E., Smith, R., Vasconcellos, T., & Lao, M. (2016). Which relationship skills count most? A large-scale replication. *Journal of Couple & Relationship Therapy*, 15, 341–356.

Everett, D. (2008). *Don't sleep, there are snakes: Life and language in the Amazonian jungle.* New York: Vintage.

Fagerberg, J., Mowery, D. C., & Nelson, R. R. (2005). *The Oxford handbook of innovation.* Oxford: Oxford University Press.

Ferguson, E. S. (1994). *Engineering and the mind's eye.* Cambridge, MA: MIT Press.

Findlay, S. D., & Thagard, P. (2012). How parts make up wholes. *Frontiers in Physiology*, 3. doi:10.3389/fphys.2012.00455

Findlay, S. D., & Thagard, P. (2014). Emotional change in international negotiation: Analyzing the Camp David accords using cognitive-affective maps. *Group Decision and Negotiation*, 23, 1281–1300.

Finkel, E. J., Cheung, E. O., Emery, L. F., Carswell, K. L., & Larson, G. M. (2015). The suffocation model: Why marriage in America is becoming an all-or-nothing institution. *Current Directions in Psychological Science*, 24, 238–244.

Finkel, E. J., Simpson, J. A., & Eastwick, P. W. (2017). The psychology of close relationships: Fourteen core principles. *Annual Review of Psychology*, 68, 383–411.

Fisher, H. (2004). *Why we love: The nature and chemistry of romantic love.* New York: Henry Holt.

Fiske, S. T., & Taylor, S. E. (2013). *Social cognition: From brains to culture* (2nd ed.). Los Angeles: SAGE.

Fitzsimons, G. M., Finkel, E. J., & vanDellen, M. R. (2015). Transactive goal dynamics. *Psychological Review*, 122, 648–673.

Flannery, K., & Marcus, J. (2012). *The creation of inequality: How our prehistoric ancestors set the stage for monarchy, slavery, and empire.* Cambridge, MA: Harvard University Press.

Flint, J., & Kendler, K. S. (2014). The genetics of major depression. *Neuron*, 81(3), 484–503.

Franks, D. (2010). *Neurosociology: The nexus between neuroscience and social psychology.* Berlin: Springer.

Freeden, M. (2003). *Ideology: A very short introduction.* Oxford: Oxford University Press.

Freeden, M., Sargent, L. T., & Stears, M. (2013). *The Oxford handbook of political ideologies.* Oxford: Oxford University Press.

Freeman, M. (2011). *Law and neuroscience: Current legal issues.* New York: Oxford University Press.

Freud, S. (1962). *Civilization and its discontents.* New York: W. W. Norton.

Galbraith, J. K. (1972). *The great crash 1929.* Boston: Houghton Mifflin.

Galbraith, J. K. (1983). *The anatomy of power.* Boston: Houghton Mifflin.

Gardner, H. (2006). *Multiple intelligences: New horizons.* New York: Basic Books.

Gavetti, G., & Menon, A. (2016). Evolution cum agency: Toward a model of strategic foresight. *Strategy Science*, 1(3), 207–233.

Gentner, D., Holyoak, K. J., & Kokinov, B. K. (Eds.). (2001). *The analogical mind: Perspectives from cognitive science.* Cambridge, MA: MIT Press.

Ghaemi, N. (2013). *On depression: Drugs, diagnosis, and despair in the modern world.* Baltimore, MD: Johns Hopkins University Press.

Giddens, A. (1984). *The constitution of society.* Berkeley: University of California Press.

Giner-Sorolla, R., & Espinosa, P. (2011). Social cuing of guilt by anger and of shame by disgust. *Psychological Science, 22*, 49–53.

Glannon, W. (Ed.). (2015). *Free will and the brain: Neuroscientific, philosophical, and legal perspectives*. Cambridge, UK: Cambridge University Press.

Glimcher, P. W., & Fehr, E. (Eds.). (2013). *Neuroeconomics: Decision making and the brain* (2nd ed.). Amsterdam: Academic Press.

Goffman, E. (1959). *The presentation of self in everyday life*. New York: Anchor Books.

Goldenberg, M. J. (2016). Public misunderstanding of science? Reframing the problem of vaccine hesitancy. *Perspectives on Science, 24*, 552–581.

Goldin-Meadow, S. (2003). *Hearing gesture: How our hands help us think*. Cambridge, MA: Harvard University Press.

Goleman, D. (1995). *Emotional intelligence*. New York: Bantam.

Goleman, D. (1998). *Working with emotional intelligence*. New York: Bantam.

Goleman, D., Boyatzis, R., & McKee, A. (2013). *Primal leadership*. Boston: Harvard Business School Press.

Goodwin, J., Jasper, J. M., & Polletta, F. (2001). *Passionate politics: Emotions and social movements*. Chicago: University of Chicago Press.

Görgen, S. M., Joormann, J., Hiller, W., & Witthöft, M. (2015). The role of mental imagery in depression: Negative mental imagery induces strong implicit and explicit affect in depression. *Frontiers in Psychiatry, 6*. http://www.ncbi.nlm.nih.gov/pubmed/26217240

Gotlib, I. H., & Joormann, J. (2010). Cognition and depression: Current status and future directions. *Annual Review of Clinical Psychology, 6*, 285–312.

Gottman, J. M. (2011). *The science of trust: Attunement for couples*. New York: W. W. Norton.

Gottman, J. M. (2015). *Principia amoris: The new science of love*. New York: Routledge.

Graeber, D. (2009). *Direct action: An ethnography*. Oakland, CA: AK Press.

Graham, M. H. (1987). *Federal rules of evidence in a nutshell*. St. Paul, MN: West Publishing.

Greenspan, A. (2013). *The map and the territory: Risk, human nature, and the future of forecasting*. New York: Penguin.

Grisham, J. (2006). *The innocent man*. New York: Doubleday.

Groß, J., Blank, H., & Bayen, U. J. (2017). Hindsight bias in depression. *Clinical Psychological Science, 5*(5), 771–788.

Gul, F., & Pesendorfer, W. (2008). The case for mindless economics. In A. Caplin & A. Schotter (Eds.), *Handbook of economic methodology, Vol. 1: Perspectives on the future of economics: The foundations of positive and normative economics* (pp. 3–40). Oxford: Oxford University Press.

Haack, S. (2014). *Evidence matters: Science, proof, and truth in the law*. Cambridge, UK: Cambridge University Press.

Habel, U., Klein, M., Kellermann, T., Shah, N. J., & Schneider, F. (2005). Same or different? Neural correlates of happy and sad mood in healthy males. *NeuroImage, 26*(1), 206–214.

Hacking, I. (1999). *The social construction of what?* Cambridge, MA: Harvard University Press.

Haidt, J. (2012). *The righteous mind: Why good people are divided by politics and religion*. New York: Pantheon.

Hames, J. L., Hagan, C. R., & Joiner, T. E. (2013). Interpersonal processes in depression. *Annual Review of Clinical Psychology, 9*, 355–377.

Hammen, C. (2005). Stress and depression. *Annual Review of Clinical Psychology, 1*, 293–319.

Harms, P. D., & Credé, M. (2010). Emotional intelligence and transformational and transactional leadership: A meta-analysis. *Journal of Leadership & Organizational Studies, 17*(1), 5–17.

Harris, S., Sheth, S. A., & Cohen, M. S. (2008). Functional neuroimaging of belief, disbelief, and uncertainty. *Annals of Neurology, 63*, 141–147.

Harvard Business Review. (Ed.). (2015). *HBR's 10 must reads on emotional intelligence.* Boston: Harvard Business Review Press.

Hastie, R., & Wittenbrink, B. (2006). Heuristics for applying laws to facts. In G. Gigerenzer & C. Engel (Eds.), *Heuristics and the law* (pp. 259–280). Cambridge, MA: MIT Press.

Hatfield, E., Cacioppo, J. T., & Rapson, R. L. (1994). *Emotional contagion.* Cambridge, UK: Cambridge University Press.

Hausman, D. M. (2011). *Preference, value, choice, and welfare.* Cambridge, UK: Cambridge University Press.

Hedström, P., & Swedberg, R. (1998). *Social mechanisms: An analytical approach to social theory.* Cambridge, UK: Cambridge University Press.

Hedström, P., & Ylikoski, P. (2010). Causal mechanisms in the social sciences. *Annual Review of Psychology, 36*, 49–67.

Heine, S. J. (2011). *Cultural psychology* (2nd ed.). New York: W. W. Norton.

Henrich, J. (2009). The evolution of costly displays, cooperation and religion: Credibility enhancing displays and their implications for cultural evolution. *Evolution and Human Behavior, 30*(4), 244–260.

Henrich, J. (2016). *The secret of our success.* Princeton, NJ: Princeton University Press.

Henrich, J., Heine, S. J., & Norenzayan, A. (2010). The weirdest people in the world? *Behavioral and Brain Sciences, 33*(2–3), 61–83.

Hitler, A. (1943). *Mein kampf* (R. Manheim, Trans.). London: Pimlico.

Hochschild, A. R. (1983). *The managed heart: Commercialization of human feeling.* Berkeley: University of California Press.

Hoffman, M. L. (2000). *Empathy and moral development: Implications for caring and justice.* Cambridge, UK: Cambridge University Press.

Hofstadter, D., & Sander, E. (2013). *Surfaces and essences: Analogy as the fuel and fire of thinking.* New York: Basic Books.

Holland, J. (2006). *Misogyny: The world's oldest prejudice.* Philadelphia: Running Press.

Holyoak, K. J. (2012). Analogy and relational reasoning. In K. J. Holyoak & R. G. Morrison (Eds.), *The Oxford handbook of thinking and reasoning* (pp. 234–259). Oxford: Oxford University Press.

Holyoak, K. J., & Thagard, P. (1995). *Mental leaps: Analogy in creative thought.* Cambridge, MA: MIT Press/Bradford Books.

Homer-Dixon, T., Leader Maynard, J., Mildenberger, M., Milkoreit, M., Mock, S. J., Quilley, S., . . . Thagard, P. (2013). A complex systems approach to the study of ideology: Cognitive-affective structures and the dynamics of belief systems. *Journal of Social and Political Psychology, 1*, 337–364.

Homer-Dixon, T., Milkoreit, M., Mock, S. J., Schröder, T., & Thagard, P. (2014). The conceptual structure of social disputes: Cognitive-affective maps as a tool for conflict analysis and resolution. *SAGE Open, 4*. doi:10.1177/2158244014526210

Hong, R. Y., & Cheung, M. W. L. (2014). The structure of cognitive vulnerabilities to depression and anxiety: Evidence for a common core etiologic process based on a meta-analytic review. *Clinical Psychological Science, 3*(6), 892–912.

Horne, Z., Powell, D., Hummel, J. E., & Holyoak, K. J. (2015). Countering antivaccination attitudes. *Proceedings of the National Academy of Sciences of the United States of America, 112*(33), 10321–10324.

Howard-Jones, P. A. (2014). Neuroscience and education: Myths and messages. *Nature Reviews Neuroscience, 15*(12), 817–824.

Hrdy, S. B. (2009). *Mothers and others: The evolutionary origins of mutual understanding.* Cambridge, MA: Harvard University Press.

Huebner, B. (2013). *Macrocognition: Distributed minds and collective intentionality.* New York: Oxford University Press.

Hutchins, E. (1995). *Cognition in the wild.* Cambridge, MA: MIT Press.

Immordino-Yang, M. H. (2015). *Emotions, learning, and the brain: Exploring the educational implications of affective neuroscience.* New York: W. W. Norton.

Isaacson, W. (2011). *Steve Jobs.* New York: Simon & Schuster.

Jackson, R., & Sorenson, G. (2010). *Introduction to international relations: Theories and approaches* (4th ed.). Oxford: Oxford University Press.

John-Steiner, V. (2000). *Creative collaboration.* Oxford: Oxford University Press.

Johnson-Laird, P. N. (2005). Flying bicycles: How the Wright brothers invented the airplane. *Mind & Society, 4*(1), 27–48.

Jones, O. D., Marois, R., Farah, M. J., & Greely, H. T. (2013). Law and neuroscience. *Journal of Neuroscience, 33*(45), 17624–17630.

Jost, J. T. (2017). Ideological asymmetries and the essence of political psychology. *Political Psychology, 38*(2), 167–208.

Jost, J. T., Kay, A. C., & Thorisdottir, H. (2009). *Social and psychological bases of ideology and system justification.* New York: Oxford University Press.

Kahneman, D., & Tversky, A. (1979). Prospect theory: An analysis of decision under risk. *Econometrica, 47*, 263–291.

Kahneman, D., & Tversky, A. (Eds.). (2000). *Choices, values, and frames.* Cambridge, UK: Cambridge University Press.

Kahney, L. (2009). *Inside Steve's brain.* New York: Penguin.

Kahney, L. (2013). *Jony Ive: The genius behind Apple's greatest products.* New York: Penguin.

Kajić, I., Schröder, T., Stewart, T. C., & Thagard, P. (forthcoming). The semantic pointer theory of emotions.

Kassam, K. S., Markey, A. R., Cherkassky, V. L., Loewenstein, G., & Just, M. A. (2013). Identifying emotions on the basis of neural activation. *PLOS One, 8*(6), e66032.

Kata, A. (2010). A postmodern Pandora's box: Anti-vaccination misinformation on the Internet. *Vaccine, 28*(7), 1709–1716.

Keltner, D., Oatley, K., & Jenkins, J. M. (2013). *Understanding emotions* (3rd ed.). New York: Wiley.

Keynes, J. M. (1936). *The general theory of employment, interest and money.* London: Macmillan.

Khong, Y. F. (1992). *Analogies at war.* Princeton, NJ: Princeton University Press.

Kille, D. R., Forest, A. L., & Wood, J. V. (2013). Tall, dark, and stable: Embodiment motivates mate selection preferences. *Psychological Science, 24*(1), 112–114.

Kindleberger, C. P., & Aliber, R. (2011). *Manias, panics, and crashes: A history of financial crises* (6th ed.). Houndmills, UK: Palgrave Macmillan.

Kitayama, S., & Uskul, A. K. (2011). Culture, mind, and the brain: Current evidence and future directions. *Annual Review of Psychology, 62*, 419–449.

Kline, M. A. (2015). How to learn about teaching: An evolutionary framework for the study of teaching behavior in humans and other animals. *Behavioral and Brain Sciences, 38*, e31.

Konvalinka, I., Xygalatas, D., Bulbulia, J., Schjødt, U., Jegindø, E.-M., Wallot, S., . . . Roepstorff, A. (2011). Synchronized arousal between performers and related spectators in a fire-walking ritual. *Proceedings of the National Academy of Sciences of the United States of America*, 108(20), 8514–8519.

Kosslyn, S. M., Thompson, W. L., & Ganis, G. (2006). *The case for mental imagery.* New York: Oxford University Press.

Kraus, M. W., Piff, P. K., Mendoza-Denton, R., Rheinschmidt, M. L., & Keltner, D. (2012). Social class, solipsism, and contextualism: How the rich are different from the poor. *Psychological Review*, 119, 546–572.

Kraus, N., & Slater, J. (2016). Beyond words: How humans communicate through sound. *Annual Review of Psychology*, 67, 83–103.

Kreibig, S. D. (2010). Autonomic nervous system activity in emotion: A review. *Biological Psychology*, 84, 394–421.

Kronenfeld, D. B., Bennardo, G., de Munck, V. C., & Fischer, M. D. (2011). *A companion to cognitive anthropology.* New York: Wiley.

Krugman, P. (2009). *The return of depression economics and the crisis of 2008.* New York: Norton.

Kuhn, T. S. (1970). *The structure of scientific revolutions* (2nd ed.). Chicago: University of Chicago Press.

Kunda, Z. (1990). The case for motivated reasoning. *Psychological Bulletin*, 108, 480–498.

Kunda, Z. (1999). *Social cognition: Making sense of people.* Cambridge, MA: MIT Press.

Kunda, Z., & Thagard, P. (1996). Forming impressions from stereotypes, traits, and behaviors: A parallel-constraint-satisfaction theory. *Psychological Review*, 103, 284–308.

Lakatos, I. (1970). Falsification and the methodology of scientific research programs. In I. Lakatos & A. Musgrave (Eds.), *Criticism and the growth of knowledge* (pp. 91–195). Cambridge, UK: Cambridge University Press.

Lane, R. D., Ryan, L., Nadel, L., & Greenberg, L. (2015). Memory reconsolidation, emotional arousal and the process of change in psychotherapy: New insights from brain science. *Behavioral and Brain Sciences, 38*, 1–80.

Lashinsky, A. (2012). *Inside Apple: How America's most admired—and secretive—company really works.* New York: Hachette.

Leader Maynard, J. (2013). A map of the field of political ideologies. *Journal of Political Ideologies*, 18, 299–327.

Leathers, D. G., & Eaves, M. (2017). *Successful nonverbal communication: Principles and applications* (5th ed.). Abingdon, UK: Routledge.

Lerner, J. S., Li, Y., Valdesolo, P., & Kassam, K. S. (2015). Emotion and decision making. *Annual Review of Psychology*, 66, 799–823.

Levinson, S. C. (2012). The original sin of cognitive science. *Topics in Cognitive Science*, 4(3), 396–403.

Lieberman, M. D. (2010). Social cognitive neuroscience. In S. T. Fiske, D. T. Gilbert, & G. Lindzey (Eds.), *Handbook of social psychology* (5th ed., pp. 143–193). New York: McGraw-Hill.

Lindquist, K. A., Wager, T. D., Kober, H., Bliss–Moreau, E., & Barrett, L. F. (2012). The basis of emotion: A meta-analytic review. *Behavioral and Brain Sciences*, 35, 121–143.

Litt, A., Eliasmith, C., & Thagard, P. (2008). Neural affective decision theory: Choices, brains, and emotions. *Cognitive Systems Research*, 9, 252–273.

Livingston, J. (2007). *Founders at work: Stories of startups' early days.* Berkeley, CA: Apress.

Loewenstein, G. F., Weber, E. U., Hsee, C. K., & Welch, N. (2001). Risk as feelings. *Psychological Bulletin*, 127, 267–286.

Lukes, S. (2005). *Power: A radical view* (2nd ed.). Houndmills, UK: Palgrave Macmillan.

Lyubomirsky, S., Layous, K., Chancellor, J., & Nelson, S. K. (2015). Thinking about rumination: The scholarly contributions and intellectual legacy of Susan Nolen-Hoeksema. *Annual Review of Clinical Psychology, 11*, 1–22.

MacMillan, M. (2008). *The uses and abuses of history*. New York: Penguin.

MacMillan, M. (2013). *The war that ended peace: The road to 1914*. New York: Penguin.

Maehr, M. L., & Karabenick, S. A. (Eds.). (2005). *Motivation and religion*. Amsterdam: Elsevier.

Magnani, L. (2009). *Abductive cognition: The epistemological and eco-cognitive dimensions of hypothetical reasoning*. Berlin: Springer.

Mahajan, G. (2011). *Explanation and understanding in the human sciences*. Oxford: Oxford University Press.

Malhi, G. S., Tanious, M., Das, P., Coulston, C. M., & Berk, M. (2013). Potential mechanisms of action of lithium in bipolar disorder. *CNS Drugs, 27*(2), 135–153.

Malone, T. W., & Bernstein, M. S. (Eds.). (2015). *Handbook of collective intelligence*. Cambridge, MA: MIT Press.

Mann, M. (1986). *The sources of social power*. Cambridge, UK: Cambridge University Press.

Mann, M. (2013). *The sources of social power IV: Globalizations, 1945–2011*. Cambridge, UK: Cambridge University Press.

Mareschal, D., Butterworth, B., & Tolmie, A. (2013). *Educational neuroscience*. Hoboken, NJ: Wiley.

Marshall, P. (2010). *Demanding the impossible: A history of anarchism*. Oakland, CA: PM Press.

Matsumoto, D., Frank, M. G., & Hwang, H. C. (2015). The role of intergroup emotions in political violence. *Current Directions in Psychological Science, 24*(5), 369–373.

Mayer, J. D., McCormick, L. J., & Strong, S. E. (1995). Mood-congruent memory and natural mood: New evidence. *Personality and Social Psychology Bulletin, 21*, 736–746.

Mayer, J. D., Salovey, P., & Caruso, D. R. (2004). Emotional intelligence: Theory, findings, and implications. *Psychological Inquiry, 15*(3), 197–215.

McCauley, R. N. (2011). *Why religion is natural and science is not*. Oxford: Oxford University Press.

McCauley, R. N. (2012). The importance of being "Ernest." In E. Slingerland & M. Collard (Eds.), *Creating consilience: Integrating the sciences and the humanities* (pp. 266–281). New York: Oxford University Press.

McCauley, R. N. (2013). Explanatory pluralism and the cognitive science of religion, Or why scholars in religious studies should stop worrying about reductionism. In D. Xygalatas & J. W. W. McCorkle (Eds.), *Mental culture: Classical social theory and the cognitive science of religion* (pp. 11–32). London: Acumen.

McCauley, R. N. (2017). *Philosophical foundations of the cognitive science of religion: A head start*. London: Bloomsbury.

McCauley, R. N., & Lawson, E. T. (2002). *Bringing ritual to mind: Psychological foundations of cultural forms*. Cambridge, UK: Cambridge University Press.

McCullough, D. (2015). *The Wright Brothers: The dramatic story-behind-the-story*. New York: Simon & Schuster.

McCullough, M. E., & Carter, E. C. (2013). Religion, self-control, and self-regulation: How are they related? In K. I. Pargament (Ed.), *APA handbook of psychology, religion, and spirituality* (Vol. 1, pp. 123–138). Washington, DC: American Psychological Association.

McFarland, M. W. (Ed.). (1972). *The papers of Wilbur and Orville Wright* (Vol. 1). New York: Arno Press.

McGowan, P. O., Sasaki, A., D'Alessio, A. C., Dymov, S., Labonte, B., Szyf, M., . . . Meaney, M. J. (2009). Epigenetic regulation of the glucocorticoid receptor in human brain associates with childhood abuse. *Nature Neuroscience, 12*(3), 342–348.

McNamara, P. (2009). *The neuroscience of religious experience.* Cambridge, UK: Cambridge University Press.

McPherson, M., Smith-Lovin, L., & Cook, J. M. (2001). Birds of a feather: Homophily in social networks. *Annual Review of Sociology, 27*(1), 415–444.

Mead, G. H. (1967). *Mind, self & society from the standpoint of a social behaviorist.* Chicago: University of Chicago Press.

Meaney, M. J. (2001). Maternal care, gene expression, and the transmission of individual differences in stress reactivity across generations. *Annual Review of Neuroscience, 24*(1), 1161–1192.

Melas, P. A., Rogdaki, M., Lennartsson, A., Björk, K., Qi, H., Witasp, A., . . . Svenningsson, P. (2012). Antidepressant treatment is associated with epigenetic alterations in the promoter of P11 in a genetic model of depression. *International Journal of Neuropsychopharmacology, 15*(5), 669–679.

Melvern, L. (2004). *Conspiracy to murder: The Rwandan genocide.* London: Verso.

Miles, E., & Crisp, R. J. (2014). A meta-analytic test of the imagined contact hypothesis. *Group Processes & Intergroup Relations, 17*(1), 3–26.

Milkoreit, M. (2017). *Mindmade politics: The cognitive roots of international climate governance.* Cambridge, MA: MIT Press.

Minsky, M. (2006). *The emotion machine: Commonsense thinking, artificial intelligence, and the future of the human mind.* New York: Simon & Schuster.

Mintzberg, H. (2009). *Managing.* Oakland, CA: Berrett-Koehler.

Mio, J. S., Riggio, R. E., Levin, S., & Reese, R. (2005). Presidential leadership and charisma: The effects of metaphor. *The Leadership Quarterly, 16*(2), 287–294.

Mitchell, M. (2011). *Complexity: A guided tour.* Oxford: Oxford University Press.

Mock, S. J. (2011). *Symbols of defeat in the construction of national identity.* New York: Cambridge University Press.

Mootee, I. (2013). *Design thinking for strategic innovation.* Hoboken, NJ: Wiley.

Morgan, G. S., & Wisneski, D. C. (2017). The structure of political ideology varies between and within people: Implications for theories about ideology's causes. *Social Cognition, 35*(4), 395–414.

Morse, S. J., & Roskies, A. L. (Eds.). (2013). *A primer on criminal law and neuroscience.* New York: Oxford University Press.

Murphy, D. (2006). *Psychiatry in the scientific image.* Cambridge, MA: MIT Press.

Murphy, D. (2015). Concepts of disease and health. In E. Zalta (Ed.), *Stanford encyclopedia of philosophy.* http://plato.stanford.edu/entries/health-disease/

Murphy, G. L. (2002). *The big book of concepts.* Cambridge, MA: MIT Press.

Murphy, M. C., & Walton, G. M. (2013). From prejudiced people to prejudiced places: A social-contextual approach to prejudice. In C. Stangor & C. S. Crandall (Eds.), *Stereotyping and prejudice* (pp. 181–203). New York: Psychology Press.

Murray, S. L., & Holmes, J. G. (2011). *Interdependent minds: The dynamics of close relationships.* New York: Guilford Press.

Murray, S. L., & Holmes, J. G. (2017). *Motivated cognition in relationships: The pursuit of belonging.* New York: Guilford Press.

Murray, S. L., Holmes, J. G., Griffin, D. W., & Derrick, J. L. (2015). The equilibrium model of relationship maintenance. *Journal of Personality and Social Psychology, 108,* 93–113.

Muthukrishna, M., & Henrich, J. (2016). Innovation in the collective brain. *Philosophical Transactions of the Royal Society B, 371.* doi:10.1098/rstb.2015.0192

Nave, G., Camerer, C., & McCullough, M. (2015). Does oxytocin increase trust in humans? A critical review of research. *Perspectives on Psychological Science, 10*(6), 772–789.

Nersessian, N. (2008). *Creating scientific concepts.* Cambridge, MA: MIT Press.

Neustadt, R., & May, E. (1986). *Thinking in time: The uses of history for decision makers.* New York: Free Press.

Newton, P. M. (2015). The learning styles myth is thriving in higher education. *Frontiers in Psychology, 6,* 1908.

Niedenthal, P. M., & Brauer, M. (2012). Social functionality of human emotion. *Annual Review of Psychology, 63,* 259–285.

Nightingale, P. (2009). Tacit knowledge and engineering design. In A. Meijers (Ed.), *Philosophy of technology and engineering sciences* (Vol. 9, pp. 351–374). Amsterdam: Elsevier.

Nisbett, R. E. (2003). *The geography of thought: How Asians and Westerners think differently . . . and why.* New York: Free Press.

Nisbett, R. E., & Cohen, D. (1996). *Culture of honor.* Boulder, CO: Westview.

Nisbett, R. E., & Wilson, T. D. (1977). Telling more than we can know: Verbal reports on mental processes. *Psychological Review, 84,* 231–259.

Norenzayan, A. (2013). *Big gods: How religion transformed cooperation and conflict*: Princeton, NJ: Princeton University Press.

Norenzayan, A., Shariff, A. F., Gervais, W. M., Willard, A. K., McNamara, R. A., Slingerland, E., & Henrich, J. (2014). The cultural evolution of prosocial religions. *Behavioral and Brain Sciences, 39,* 1–19.

Norman, D. A. (2003). *Emotional design: Why we love (or hate) everyday things.* New York: Basic Books.

Nye, J. S. (1990). Soft power. *Foreign Policy, 80,* 153–171.

Nyhan, B., Reifler, J., Richey, S., & Freed, G. L. (2014). Effective messages in vaccine promotion: A randomized trial. *Pediatrics, 133*(4), e835–e842.

Oatley, K. (1992). *Best laid schemes: The psychology of emotions.* Cambridge, UK: Cambridge University Press.

O'Shaughnessy, J., & O'Shaughnessy, N. J. (2002). *The marketing power of emotion.* Oxford: Oxford University Press.

Otu, N. (2015). Decoding nonverbal communication in law enforcement. *Salus Journal, 3*(2), 1–16.

Paluck, E. L., & Chwe, M. S.-Y. (2017). Confronting hate collectively. *PS: Political Science & Politics, 50*(4), 990–992.

Pardo, M. S., & Patterson, D. M. (2013). *Minds, brains, and law: The conceptual foundations of law and neuroscience.* New York: Oxford University Press.

Pargament, K. I. (Ed.). (2013). *APA handbook of psychology, religion, and spirituality.* Washington, DC: American Psychological Association.

Parsons, T. (1968). *The structure of social action.* New York: Free Press.

Patel, V. L., Arocha, J. F., & Zhang, J. (2012). Medical reasoning and thinking. In K. J. Holyoak & R. G. Morrison (Eds.), *The Oxford handbook of thinking and reasoning* (pp. 736–754). New York: Oxford University Press.

Pennington, N., & Hastie, R. (1992). Explaining the evidence: Tests of the story model for juror decision making. *Journal of Personality and Social Psychology, 51,* 189–206.

Perry, M., & Schweitzer, F. M. (2002). *Antisemitism: Myth and hate from antiquity to the present.* New York: Palgrave Macmillan.

Pessoa, L. (2013). *The cognitive-emotional brain: From interactions to integration.* Cambridge, MA: MIT Press.

Poland, C. M., & Poland, G. A. (2011). Vaccine education spectrum disorder: The importance of incorporating psychological and cognitive models into vaccine education. *Vaccine, 29*(37), 6145–6148.

Popper, K. (1959). *The logic of scientific discovery.* London: Hutchinson.

Posner, M. I., & Rothbart, M. K. (2007). *Educating the human brain.* Washington, DC: American Psychological Association.

Purzycki, B. G., Apicella, C., Atkinson, Q. D., Cohen, E., McNamara, R. A., Willard, A. K., . . . Henrich, J. (2016). Moralistic gods, supernatural punishment and the expansion of human sociality. *Nature, 530*, 327–330.

Quartz, S. R., & Sejnowski, T. J. (2002). *Liars, lovers, and heroes: What the new brain science reveals about how we become who we are.* New York: William Morrow.

Ranney, M. A., & Clark, D. (2016). Climate change conceptual change: Scientific information can transform attitudes. *Topics in Cognitive Science, 8*(1), 49–75.

Raven, B. H. (2008). The bases of power and the power/interaction model of interpersonal influence. *Analyses of Social Issues and Public Policy, 8*(1), 1–22.

Ravenscroft, I. (2016). Folk psychology as a theory. In E. Zalta (Ed.), *Stanford encyclopedia of philosophy.* http://plato.stanford.edu/entries/folkpsych-theory/

Redlawsk, D. P., Civettini, A. J. W., & Emmerson, K. M. (2010). The affective tipping point: Do motivated reasoners ever "get it"? *Political Psychology, 31*(4), 563–593.

Reinhart, C. M., & Rogoff, K. S. (2009). *This time is different: Eight centuries of financial folly.* Princeton, NJ: Princeton University Press.

Richardson, R. C. (2007). *Evolutionary psychology as maladapted psychology.* Cambridge, MA: MIT Press.

Ridgeway, C. L. (2014). Why status matters for inequality. *American Sociological Review, 79*(1), 1–16.

Riggio, R. E., & Tan, S. J. (2014). *Leader interpersonal and influence skills: The soft skills of leadership.* New York: Routledge.

Rizzolatti, G., & Craighero, L. (2004). The mirror-neuron system. *Annual Review of Neuroscience, 27*, 169–192.

Robinson, D. T., Smith-Lovin, L., & Wisecup, A. K. (2006). *Affect control theory.* Berlin: Springer.

Rudner, R. (1961). Value judgments in the acceptance of theories. In P. G. Frank (Ed.), *The validation of scientific theories* (pp. 31–35). New York: Collier Books.

Ryan, R. M., & Deci, E. L. (2017). *Self-determination theory: Basic psychological needs in motivation, development, and wellness.* New York: Guilford Press.

Sadock, B. J., Sadock, V. A., & Ruiz, P. (2017). *Kaplan and Sadock's comprehensive textbook of psychiatry.* Alphen aan den Rijn, The Netherlands: Wolters Kluwer.

Safina, C. (2015). *Beyond words: What animals think and feel.* London: Macmillan.

Sahay, A., & Hen, R. (2007). Adult hippocampal neurogenesis in depression. *Nature Neuroscience, 10*(9), 1110–1115.

Saks, M. J., & Spellman, B. A. (2016). *The psychological foundations of evidence law.* New York: New York University Press.

Salovey, P., & Mayer, J. D. (1990). Emotional intelligence. *Imagination, Cognition and Personality, 9*(3), 185–211.

Sander, D., Grandjean, D., & Scherer, K. R. (2005). A systems approach to appraisal mechanisms in emotion. *Neural Networks, 18*, 317–352.

Satel, S., & Lilienfeld, S. O. (2013). *Brainwashed: The seductive appeal of mindless neuroscience.* New York: Basic Books.

Sawyer, R. K. (2006). *Explaining creativity: The science of human innovation.* Oxford: Oxford University Press.

Schacter, D. L., Addis, D. R., & Buckner, R. L. (2007). Remembering the past to imagine the future: The prospective brain. *Nature Reviews Neuroscience, 8*(9), 657–661.

Scheffer, M. (2009). *Critical transitions in nature and society.* Princeton, NJ: Princeton University Press.

Scherer, A. M., Scherer, L. D., & Fagerlin, A. (2015). Getting ahead of illness using metaphors to influence medical decision making. *Medical Decision Making, 35*(1), 37–45.

Schjoedt, U., Sørensen, J., Nielbo, K. L., Xygalatas, D., Mitkidis, P., & Bulbulia, J. (2013). Cognitive resource depletion in religious interactions. *Religion, Brain & Behavior, 3*(1), 39–55.

Schlender, B., & Tetzeli, R. (2015). *Becoming Steve Jobs.* New York: Crown.

Schmidt, M. F., Butler, L. P., Heinz, J., & Tomasello, M. (2016). Young children see a single action and infer a social norm: Promiscuous normativity in 3-year-olds. *Psychological Science, 27*(10), 1360–1370.

Schröder, T., & Thagard, P. (2013). The affective meanings of automatic social behaviors: Three mechanisms that explain priming. *Psychological Review, 120,* 255–280.

Schutt, R. K., Keshavan, M., & Seidman, L. J. (2015). *Social neuroscience: Brain, mind, and society.* Cambridge, MA: Harvard University Press.

Schwarz, N. (1990). Feelings as information: Informational and motivational functions of affective states. In E. T. Higgins & R. Sorrentino (Eds.), *Handbook of motivation and cognition: Foundations of social behavior* (pp. 527–561). New York: Guilford Press.

Shelley, C. (2017). *Design and society: Social issues in technological design.* Berlin: Springer.

Shipps, J. (1981). *Mormonism.* Urbana: University of Illinois Press.

Shtulman, A., & Valcarcel, J. (2012). Scientific knowledge suppresses but does not supplant earlier intuitions. *Cognition, 124*(2), 209–215.

Shultz, T. R., & Lepper, M. R. (1996). Cognitive dissonance reduction as constraint satisfaction. *Psychological Review, 103,* 219–240.

Silvia, P. J. (2006). *Exploring the psychology of interest.* Oxford: Oxford University Press.

Simon, D. (2004). A third view of the black box: Cognitive coherence in legal decision making. *University of Chicago Law Review, 71,* 511–586.

Simon, D. (2012). *In doubt: The psychology of the criminal justice process.* Cambridge, MA: Harvard University Press.

Simon, D., Stenstrom, D., & Read, S. J. (2015). The coherence effect: Blending cold and hot cognitions. *Journal of Personality and Social Psychology, 109,* 369–394.

Sinclair, L., & Kunda, Z. (2000). Motivated stereotyping of women: She's fine if she praised me but incompetent if she criticized me. *Personality and Social Psychology Bulletin, 26,* 1329–1342.

Soliman, T. M., Johnson, K. A., & Song, H. (2015). It's not "all in your head": Understanding religion from an embodied cognition perspective. *Perspectives in Psychological Science, 10*(6), 852–864.

Solomon, A. (2001). *The noonday demon: An atlas of depression.* New York: Scribner.

Solomon, M. (2015). *Making medical knowledge.* Oxford: Oxford University Press.

Soros, G. (2008). *The new paradigm for financial markets: The credit crisis of 2008 and what it means.* New York: Public Affairs.

Sosis, R., & Alcorta, C. (2003). Signaling, solidarity, and the sacred: The evolution of religious behavior. *Evolutionary Anthropology: Issues, News, and Reviews, 12*(6), 264–274.

Sousa, D. A. (2011). *How the brain learns.* Thousand Oaks, CA: Corwin Press.

Sousa, D. A. (2014). *Mind, brain, & education: Neuroscience implications for the classroom.* Bloomington, IN: Solution Tree Press.

Spellman, B. A., & Schauer, F. (2012). Legal reasoning. In K. J. Holyoak & R. G. Morrison (Eds.), *The Oxford handbook of thinking and reasoning* (pp. 719–735). New York: Oxford University Press.

Sperber, D. (1996). *Explaining culture.* Oxford: Blackwell.

Stanford, M. (1998). *An introduction to the philosophy of history.* Oxford: Blackwell.

Stangor, C., & Crandall, C. S. (Eds.). (2013). *Stereotyping and prejudice.* New York: Psychology Press.

Stark, R. (2005). *The rise of Mormonism.* New York: Columbia University Press.

Steele, C. M., Spencer, S. J., & Aronson, J. (2002). Contending with group image: The psychology of stereotype and social identity threat. *Advances in Experimental Social Psychology, 34,* 379–440.

Sterelny, K. (2012). *The evolved apprentice.* Cambridge, MA: MIT Press.

Stiglitz, J. E. (2010). *Freefall: America, free markets, and the sinking of the world economy.* New York: Norton.

Styron, W. (1990). *Darkness visible: A memoir of darkness.* New York: Random House.

Sun, H., Kennedy, P. J., & Nestler, E. J. (2013). Epigenetics of the depressed brain: Role of histone acetylation and methylation. *Neuropsychopharmacology, 38*(1), 124–137.

Sun, R. (Ed.). (2012). *Grounding social sciences in cognitive sciences.* Cambridge, MA: MIT Press.

Tappin, B. M., van der Leer, L., & McKay, R. T. (2017). The heart trumps the head: Desirability bias in political belief revision. *Journal of Experimental Psychology: General, 146,* 1143–1149.

Tardif, E., Doudin, P. A., & Meylan, N. (2015). Neuromyths among teachers and student teachers. *Mind, Brain, and Education, 9*(1), 50–59.

Tauber, A. (2015). The biological notion of self and non-self. In E. Zalta (Ed.), *Stanford encyclopedia of philosophy.* http://plato.stanford.edu/archives/sum2015/entries/biology-self

ten Brinke, L., Liu, C. C., Keltner, D., & Srivastava, S. B. (2016). Virtues, vices, and political influence in the US Senate. *Psychological Science, 27,* 85–93.

Thagard, P. (1988). *Computational philosophy of science.* Cambridge, MA: MIT Press.

Thagard, P. (1989). Explanatory coherence. *Behavioral and Brain Sciences, 12,* 435–467.

Thagard, P. (1992a). Adversarial problem solving: Modelling an opponent using explanatory coherence. *Cognitive Science, 16,* 123–149.

Thagard, P. (1992b). *Conceptual revolutions.* Princeton, NJ: Princeton University Press.

Thagard, P. (1999). *How scientists explain disease.* Princeton, NJ: Princeton University Press.

Thagard, P. (2000). *Coherence in thought and action.* Cambridge, MA: MIT Press.

Thagard, P. (2003). Why wasn't O. J. convicted? Emotional coherence in legal inference. *Cognition and Emotion, 17,* 361–383.

Thagard, P. (2004a). Causal inference in legal decision making: Explanatory coherence vs. Bayesian networks. *Applied Artificial Intelligence, 18,* 231–249.

Thagard, P. (2004b). What is doubt and when is it reasonable? In M. Ezcurdia, R. Stainton, & C. Viger (Eds.), *New essays in the philosophy of language and mind (Canadian Journal of Philosophy, Supplementary Vol. 30,* pp. 391–406). Calgary: University of Calgary Press.

Thagard, P. (2005). How to be a successful scientist. In M. E. Gorman, R. D. Tweney, D. C. Gooding, & A. P. Kincannon (Eds.), *Scientific and technological thinking* (pp. 159–171). Mahwah, NJ: Lawrence Erlbaum.

Thagard, P. (2006). *Hot thought: Mechanisms and applications of emotional cognition.* Cambridge, MA: MIT Press.

Thagard, P. (2008). Mental illness from the perspective of theoretical neuroscience. *Perspectives in Biology and Medicine*, 51, 335–352.

Thagard, P. (2010a). Explaining economic crises: Are there collective representations? *Episteme*, 7, 266–283.

Thagard, P. (2010b). *The brain and the meaning of life*. Princeton, NJ: Princeton University Press.

Thagard, P. (2012a). Mapping minds across cultures. In R. Sun (Ed.), *Grounding social sciences in cognitive sciences* (pp. 35–62). Cambridge, MA: MIT Press.

Thagard, P. (2012b). *The cognitive science of science: Explanation, discovery, and conceptual change*. Cambridge, MA: MIT Press.

Thagard, P. (2014a). Economic explanations. In M. Lissack & A. Graber (Eds.), *Modes of explanation* (pp. 161–170). London: Palgrave Macmillan.

Thagard, P. (2014b). Explanatory identities and conceptual change. *Science & Education*, 23, 1531–1548.

Thagard, P. (2014c). Thought experiments considered harmful. *Perspectives on Science*, 22, 288–305.

Thagard, P. (2015a). The cognitive-affective structure of political ideologies. In B. Martinovski (Ed.), *Emotion in group decision and negotiation* (pp. 51–71). Berlin: Springer.

Thagard, P. (2015b). Value maps in applied ethics. *Teaching Ethics*, 15, 115–127.

Thagard, P. (2016). Emotional cognition in urban planning. In J. Portugali & E. Stolk (Eds.), *Complexity, cognition, urban planning and design* (pp. 197–213). Berlin: Springer.

Thagard, P. (2019a). *Brain-mind: From neurons to consciousness and creativity*. Oxford: Oxford University Press.

Thagard, P. (2019b). *Natural philosophy: From social brains to knowledge, reality, morality, and beauty*. Oxford: Oxford University Press.

Thagard, P., & Aubie, B. (2008). Emotional consciousness: A neural model of how cognitive appraisal and somatic perception interact to produce qualitative experience. *Consciousness and Cognition*, 17, 811–834.

Thagard, P., & Findlay, S. (2010). Getting to Darwin: Obstacles to accepting evolution by natural selection. *Science & Education*, 19, 625–636.

Thagard, P., & Findlay, S. D. (2011). Changing minds about climate change: Belief revision, coherence, and emotion. In E. J. Olsson & S. Enqvist (Eds.), *Belief revision meets philosophy of science* (pp. 329–345). Berlin: Springer.

Thagard, P., & Finn, T. (2011). Conscience: What is moral intuition? In C. Bagnoli (Ed.), *Morality and the emotions* (pp. 150–159). Oxford: Oxford University Press.

Thagard, P., & Kroon, F. W. (2006). Emotional consensus in group decision making. *Mind & Society*, 5, 1–20.

Thagard, P., & Larocque, L. (2018). Mental health assessment: Inference, explanation, and coherence. *Journal of Evaluation in Clinical Practice*, 24(3), 649–654.

Thagard, P., & Nussbaum, A. D. (2014). Fear-driven inference: Mechanisms of gut overreaction. In L. Magnani (Ed.), *Model-based reasoning in science and technology* (pp. 43–53). Berlin: Springer.

Thagard, P., & Schröder, T. (2014). Emotions as semantic pointers: Constructive neural mechanisms. In L. F. Barrett & J. A. Russell (Eds.), *The psychological construction of emotions* (pp. 144–167). New York: Guilford Press.

Thagard, P., & Verbeurgt, K. (1998). Coherence as constraint satisfaction. *Cognitive Science*, 22, 1–24.

Thye, S. R., Yoon, J., & Lawler, E. J. (2002). The theory of relational cohesion: Review of a research program research program. In S. R. Thye & E. J. Lawler (Eds.), *Advances in group processes* (pp. 139–166). Bingley, UK: Emerald.

Tokuhama-Espinosa, T. (2014). *Making classrooms better: 50 practical applications of mind, brain, and education science*. New York: W. W. Norton.

Turner, M. (2001). *Cognitive dimensions of social science*. Oxford: Oxford University Press.

Tversky, B. (2011). Visualizing thought. *Topics in Cognitive Science, 3*, 499–535.

Uttal, D. H., Miller, D. I., & Newcombe, N. S. (2013). Exploring and enhancing spatial thinking: Links to achievement in science, technology, engineering, and mathematics? *Current Directions in Psychological Science, 22*(5), 367–373.

Vallacher, R. R., Read, S. J., & Nowak, A. (Eds.). (2017). *Computational social psychology*. Abingdon, UK: Routledge.

van Riel, R., & Van Gulick, R. (2014). Scientific reduction. In E. Zalta (Ed.), *Stanford encyclopedia of philosophy*. http://plato.stanford.edu/entries/scientific-reduction/

VanderWeele, T. J. (2017). Religious communities and human flourishing. *Current Directions in Psychological Science, 26*(5), 476–481.

Varnum, M. E. W., & Grossmann, I. (2017). Cultural change: The how and the why. *Perspectives on Psychological Science*. Advance online publication. doi.org/10.1177/1745691617699971

Velleman, J. D. (2003). Narrative explanation. *Philosophical Review, 112*, 1–25.

Vendetti, M. S., Matlen, B. J., Richland, L. E., & Bunge, S. A. (2015). Analogical reasoning in the classroom: Insights from cognitive science. *Mind, Brain, and Education, 9*(2), 100–106.

Vincent, N. A. (Ed.). (2013). *Neuroscience and legal responsibility*. New York: Oxford University Press.

Vosniadou, S. (Ed.). (2008). *International handbook of research on conceptual change*. London: Routledge.

Vosniadou, S., Pnevmantikos, D., Makris, N., Ikospentaki, K., Lepenioti, D., Chountala, A., & Kyrianakis, G. (2015). Executive functions and conceptual change in science and mathematics learning. In R. Dale (Ed.), *Proceedings of the 37th Annual Meeting of the Cognitive Science Society* (pp. 2529–2535). Pasadena: Cognitive Science Society.

Vosniadou, S., & Skopeliti, I. (2014). Conceptual change from the framework theory side of the fence. *Science & Education, 23*(7), 1427–1445.

Wagamese, R. (2010). One native life. *Canadian Dimension, 44*, 8–9.

Wang, Q. (2016). Why should we all be cultural psychologists? Lessons from the study of social cognition. *Perspectives on Psychological Science, 11*(5), 583–596.

Watson-Jones, R. E., & Legare, C. H. (2016). The social functions of group rituals. *Current Directions in Psychological Science, 25*(1), 42–46.

Weber, M. (2009). *The Protestant ethic and the spirit of capitalism* (T. Parson, Trans.). New York: W. W. Norton.

Weinstein, J. (2010). *Social change* (3rd ed.). Lanham, MD: Rowman & Littlefield.

Weiss, M., & Hassan, H. (2015). *ISIS: Inside the army of terror*. New York: Regan Arts.

Wendt, A. (1999). *Social theory of international politics*. Cambridge, UK: Cambridge University Press.

Westen, D. (2007). *The political brain: The role of emotion in deciding the fate of the nation*. New York: Public Affairs.

Whitehouse, H. (2000). *Arguments and icons: Divergent modes of religiosity*. Oxford: Oxford University Press.

Whitehouse, H., & Laidlaw, J. (Eds.). (2007). *Religion, anthropology, and cognitive science.* Durham, NC: Carolina Academic Press.

Willner, A. R. (1984). *The spellbinders: Charismatic political leadership.* New Haven, CT: Yale University Press.

Wimmer, A. (2014). War. *Annual Review of Sociology, 40,* 173–197.

Wimsatt, W. C. (2007). *Re-engineering philosophy for limited beings.* Cambridge, MA: Harvard University Press.

Winzeler, R. L. (2008). *Anthropology and religion.* Lanham, MD: AltaMira.

Wolf, I., Schröder, T., Neumann, J., & de Haan, G. (2015). Changing minds about electric cars: An empirically grounded agent-based modeling approach. *Technological Forecasting and Social Change, 94,* 269–285.

Wolf, M. (2007). *Proust and the squid: The story and science of the reading brain.* New York: HarperCollins.

Wood, G. (2015). What ISIS really wants. *The Atlantic.* http://www.theatlantic.com/magazine/archive/2015/03/what-isis-really-wants/384980/

Woodward, J. (2014). Scientific explanation. In E. Zalta (Ed.), *Stanford encyclopedia of philosophy.* http://plato.stanford.edu/entries/scientific-explanation/

Wooldridge, M. (2000). *Reasoning about intelligent agents.* Cambridge, MA: MIT Press.

Woolley, A. W., Chabris, C. F., Pentland, A., Hashmi, N., & Malone, T. W. (2010). Evidence for a collective intelligence factor in the performance of human groups. *Science, 330*(6004), 686–688.

Worthy, J. B. (2008). *The Mormon cult.* Tucson: See Sharp Press.

Wozniak, S. (2007). *iWoz: Computer geek to cult icon.* New York: W. W. Norton.

Wright, O., & Kelly, F. C. (1953). *How we invented the airplane.* New York: McKay.

Wright, W., Kelly, F. C., & Wright, O. (2002). *Miracle at Kitty Hawk: The letters of Wilbur and Orville Wright.* Boston: Da Capo Press.

Writers for the 99%. (2011). *Occupying Wall Street: The inside story of an action that changed America.* Chicago: Haymarket Books.

Yamagishi, T., Li, Y., Takagishi, H., Matsumoto, Y., & Kiyonari, T. (2014). In search of homo economicus. *Psychological Science, 25*(9), 1699–1711.

Yaverbaum, E. (2004). *Leadership secrets of the world's most successful CEOs.* Chicago: Dearborn Trade.

Yeatman, J. D., Dougherty, R. F., Ben-Shachar, M., & Wandell, B. A. (2012). Development of white matter and reading skills. *Proceedings of the National Academy of Sciences of the United States of America, 109*(44), E3045–E3053.

Yim, I. S., Tanner Stapleton, L. R., Guardino, C. M., Hahn-Holbrook, J., & Dunkel Schetter, C. (2015). Biological and psychosocial predictors of postpartum depression: Systematic review and call for integration. *Annual Review of Clinical Psychology, 11,* 99–137.

Zaki, J., & Ochsner, K. N. (2012). The neuroscience of empathy: Progress, pitfalls and promise. *Nature Neuroscience, 15*(5), 675–680.

Zalocusky, K. A., Ramakrishnan, C., Lerner, T. N., Davidson, T. J., Knutson, B., & Deisseroth, K. (2016). Nucleus accumbens D2R cells signal prior outcomes and control risky decision-making. *Nature, 531*(7596), 642–663.

Tables and figures are indicated by an italic *t* and *f* following the page number

Tables and figures are indicated by an italic *t* and *f* following the page number.

Jews, prejudice against
  actions in, 120–21
  analogies in, 120
  beliefs in, 119–20
  communication in, 122
  concepts in, 118–19
  embodiment in, 119
  emotions in, 120–21
  images in, 119
  inferences in, 121
  metaphors in, 120
  overview, 117–18
  rules in, 119–20
  social cognitive-emotional workup of, 117–22
  value map of, 118*f*
  values in, 118–19
jihad, 146, 147
joylessness, in depression, 275–76
Judaism, 202–4
judges. *See* law
jury. *See* law
juxtaposition, in imagery, 28

kinesthetic images, 208, 236, 268

language
  communication in of prejudice against
    women, 116–17
  comprehension, 57–58
  overcoming prejudice, 131
  verbal emotion spread, 63
Latter-day Saints (LDS). *See* Church of Jesus
    Christ of Latter-day Saints
law
  actions in, 304
  analogies in, 303–4
  beliefs in, 303
  brain and legal responsibility, 311–14
  communication in, 308–9
  concepts in, 300–1
  embodiment in, 301–2
  emotional coherence, 297–99
  emotions in, 304
  explaining wrongful convictions, 310–11
  explanatory coherence, 295–97
  eyewitness testimony, 301
  images in, 301–2
  inferences in, 304–8
  legal coherence, 294–99

legal mechanisms, 292–95
  metaphors in, 303–4
  probability, 294
  rules in, 303
  social change in, 5–6
  values in, 300–1
  wrongful conviction, social cognitive-
    emotional workup of, 300–9
lawyers. *See* law
LDS. *See* Church of Jesus Christ of
    Latter-day Saints
leaders
  charisma in, 359–60, 379–80
  communication in, 246–47
  emotional intelligence in, 378
  emotions in, 241
  gestalt shifts in, 245
  interagent inference, 244
  metaphors used by, 385
  power, 226
  psychology in historical explanations, 230
  qualities for managerial success, 378
  values of, 235*f*, 234
leadership
  actions in, 385–87
  analogies in, 384–85
  beliefs in, 382–84
  charisma, 379–80
  communication in, 388–89
  concepts in, 380–81
  embodiment in, 382
  emotional intelligence, 378
  emotions in, 385–87
  enhancing collective emotional
    intelligence, 400–2
  images in, 382
  inferences in, 387
  metaphors in, 384–85
  rules in, 382–84
  social cognitive-emotional workup
    of, 380–89
  value map, 381*f*
  values in, 380–81
  vision, 374–78
learning. *See also* education
  attachment-based, 63, 210, 213, 220
  empathetic, 63
  mechanisms, 44–45
  teaching and, 318–20